About the authors

John O'Leary is Education editor of *The Times*. He joined the paper in 1990 as Higher Education Correspondent and assumed responsibility for the whole range of education coverage in 1992. Previously the deputy editor of *The Times Higher Education Supplement*, he has been writing on the subject for more than a decade. He has a degree in politics from Sheffield University.

Andrew Hindmarsh is Planning Officer at the University of Nottingham, where his responsibilities include providing management information and statistical returns to official bodies. Until 1998 he was head of the Undergraduate Admission Office at the University of Sheffield, where for ten years he worked closely with admissions tutors and UCAS. His contributions include the chapters on choosing a university and a course and on applying to university.

Bernard Kingston is now a university consultant, having been Director of the Careers Advisory Service and latterly Director of International Affairs at the University of Sheffield. He is a past president of the Association of Graduate Careers Advisory Services and has advised governments and universities in Africa, Australia and the UK. His contributions include the chapters on student funding and overseas students.

Robert Loynes is Emeritus Professor of Probability and Statistics at the University of Sheffield and is a past chairman of the Committee of Professors of Statistics in the UK. He has been a consultant of UNESCO and the UN and many public and private organizations. He has used his statistical expertise in dealing with the data in the League Table and elsewhere in the book.

THE TIMES
GOOD UNIVERSITY
GUIDE 2001

In association with

Edited by
John O'Leary

with
Andrew Hindmarsh
Bernard Kingston
Robert Loynes

TIMES BOOKS

Published in 2000 by Times Books
HarperCollins Publishers
77-85 Fulham Palace Road
Hammersmith
London W6 8JB

This edition has been produced in association with PricewaterhouseCoopers
To find out more about PricewaterhouseCoopers, please visit their website:
www.pwcglobal.com/uk/graduate_careers/

The HarperCollins website address is www.**fire**and**water**.com
Copies of this book can be ordered through this website.

First published in 1993 by Times Books
Eighth Edition 2000
Copyright © Times Newspapers Ltd 2000

The Times is a registered trademark of Times Newspapers Ltd

ISBN 0-7230-1036-6

British Library Cataloguing in Publication Data
A catalogue record for this book is available from the British Library.

Acknowledgements
We wish to offer our personal thanks to the many individuals who have helped
with this edition of *The Times Good University Guide*. To Gill Rogers and Karen
Davis, of Mayfield University Consultants, for their assiduous research, to Ana
Kingston and Julia Morrison for sharing professional insights, to Jonathan Waller
for this technical advice, to Christopher Riches for his editorial and publishing
expertise, and to Kim Bridges and Sean Mahon of PricewaterhouseCoopers,
our sponsors, for their generous interest and support.

Please see pages 11-12 for a full explanation of the sources of data used in the
League Table. The data providers do not necessarily agree with the data
aggregations or manipulations appearing in this book and are also not
responsible for any inference or conclusions thereby derived.

Printed and bound in Great Britain by
Caledonian International Book Manufacturing Ltd, Glasgow G64

Contents

Introduction

Every year higher education seems to be on the verge of a new challenge, which will transform the lives of students. Lord Dearing's inquiry and the subsequent introduction of tuition fees were the last landmarks, but the advent of a new millennium has done nothing to halt the trend. Applicants for degree courses starting in 2001 will be on the cusp of examination reform, and possibly new fee arrangements, which will bring yet more uncertainty for the consumers of higher education.

This will be a transitional year for schools and universities, as admissions officers prepare for wholesale change 12 months hence and vice-chancellors wait to hear whether they will be allowed to charge their students 'top-up' fees. The first results from the new, one-year AS levels will provide a dry run for the following summer, when the revamped A-level syllabuses will be examined for the first time. Even as they finalise their AS-level options, teenagers have no way of knowing how much weight their grades will carry, any more than their successors know the value that universities will place on a broader package of A levels in 2002. Whether the confusion is the fault of indecisive universities or evasive ministers, all that the examination candidates can do is produce the best possible result and hope for the best. Competition for places at the leading universities is not going to slacken, and every grade may help in the race for selection.

More significant in the long run will be the attitude struck by ministers after a general election to the growing campaign by the top universities to be allowed to set their own fees. The change, favoured in Downing Street if not at the Department for Education and Employment, would put British higher education on a par with American universities and bring hitherto unimaginable charges for the most popular and prestigious courses. Any development along these lines will not affect the cost of starting a degree in 2001, but it could begin to alter the character of individual universities before this year's entrants graduate. Fees of perhaps £5,000 a year, compared with the present £1,025, could produce much-improved facilities in some universities, while others struggle on with a lower level of funding. The impact on the social mix on campus is also unpredictable until the details of a government-approved scheme are known. Ideally, the government would wait to assess the full impact of the current level of fees before sanctioning such sharply-increased charges. Demand for higher education has dropped slightly among school-leavers, after seeming robust immediately after fees were introduced, while mature students have certainly been deterred from applying for courses. But elections do not wait for tidy administrative solutions, and the window of opportunity is about to open for those who see salvation in an American-style system of higher education.

Already it is clear that prospective students are becoming more discriminating about their choice of university and the subjects they intend to take. This book attempts to help applicants make a more informed choice for, unlike other guides, its emphasis is on the quality of courses. The original university rankings, which now have a variety of imitators, are supplemented by 40 separate subject tables providing the detailed comparisons needed to identify the top degree programmes. In addition, experts offer advice for both home and overseas students on how to choose a suitable course, and there are extended profiles of all the universities in our tables.

Despite Cambridge's apparently unassailable lead, the rankings reflect the state of flux which characterises British higher education at the start of the 21st century. Last year, for the first time since *The Times Good University Guide* appeared in 1993, Oxford University slipped out of the top two places. Although Imperial College has retained second place by only a small margin, its success demonstrates the value of specialisation, as well as the enduring strength of the University of London. Further down the table, Oxford Brookes University continues to show that it is possible for the former polytechnics to overhaul some of their older-established counterparts. Other new universities, such as Plymouth and Brighton, are poised to make the same breakthrough.

Mindful of the competition for graduate jobs, applicants are looking as never before for quality and are also gravitating towards the more vocational subjects. The pattern established in Australia, which began charging for higher education more than a decade ago, is being repeated in Britain. Business courses, computing and some branches of engineering are seeing a significant rise in applications, while teacher training and some arts subjects are struggling. The indications are that there will be a place somewhere in higher education for most of those hoping to start a course in 2001, but competition for the top degrees will be as fierce as ever. To give yourself the best possible chance of coming out ahead of the field requires careful consideration of the options, as well as hard academic work.

This book offers a starting point in the increasingly complex search for the right course. No guide can cater for individual tastes, but a wealth of information is available to narrow the possibilities. *The Times Good University Guide* distils some of this information into a more manageable form, with profiles of each institution, rankings and advice on the applications process.

The University Explosion

At first sight, choosing a university appears to have become simpler over the past decade. The distinction between universities and polytechnics was swept away in 1992 and the number of places expanded to the point where far more young (and not so young) people could benefit from higher education. A consensus has grown among politicians and business leaders that, quite apart from the benefits to the individual, a modern economy needs mass higher education. Countries such as the United States and Japan reached the same conclusion long ago but a combination of factors – not all of them planned – has seen Britain making up for lost time at a rate that has prompted concerns about the quality of some courses.

Almost a third of 18-year-olds are now going on to higher education, compared with one in seven in 1980, while at least twice that proportion will take a higher education course at some point in their life. The Labour government has promised to raise that number still further. Yet, paradoxically, by ridding Britain of its elite university system, the last government sowed the seeds of a different form of elitism. The very process of opening up higher education ensured the creation of a new hierarchy of institutions. The old myth that all degrees were equal could not survive in a nation of almost 100 diverse universities and a growing number of degree-providing colleges.

The New Hierarchy

Of course, there always was a pecking order of sorts. Oxford and Cambridge were world leaders long before most British universities were established, and parts of London University have always enjoyed a high status in particular fields. But few could or would discriminate between Aberdeen and Exeter, for example. Employers, careers advisers, even academics, had their own ideas of which were the leading universities, but there was little hard evidence to back their conclusions. Often they were based on outdated, inaccurate impressions of distant institutions.

The expanded higher education system has made such judgements more scientific as well as more necessary. Prospective employers want to know not only what a graduate studied, but where. Those who are committing their money to student sponsorship or funding research are comparing institutions department by department. This has become possible because of a new transparency in what a former higher-education minister described as the 'secret garden of academe'. Official demands for more and more published information may have taxed the patience of university administrators, but they have also given outsiders the opportunity to make more meaningful comparisons.

Many see the beginnings of a British Ivy League in the competitive culture that has ensued. Even before the recent upheavals, the lion's share of research cash went to fewer than 20 traditional universities, enabling them to upgrade their facilities and attract many of the top academics. As student numbers have gone through the roof, however, general higher education budgets have been squeezed and the funding gap has widened. Beneath the veneer of a unified higher education system, three types of university are emerging: the research-based elite; a large group dedicated primarily to teaching; and an indeterminate number of mixed-economy institutions in the middle struggling to maintain a research base.

Whatever the intentions of ministers following the publication in summer 1997 of Lord Dearing's review of higher education, it is hard to imagine that pattern changing in the short or medium term. There is no need for formalised divisions because the market is already taking the university system in the direction that both main political parties probably favour.

Why University?

Doubtless some will be tempted, once the cost of living has been added to the new fees burden and the attractions of university life balanced against loss of potential earnings, to write off higher education. There are plenty of self-made millionaires who still swear by the University of Life as the only training ground for success. Yet even by narrow financial criteria it would be rash to dismiss higher education. The graduate labour market is still recovering from the recession and with so many more competing for jobs, a degree will never again be an automatic passport to a fast-track career. But graduates' financial prospects still compare favourably with school leavers'.

Even for those who cannot or do not wish to afford three or more years of full-time education after leaving school, university remains a possibility. The modular courses adopted by most universities enable students to work through a degree at their own pace, dropping out for a time if necessary, or switching to part-time attendance. Distance learning is another option, and advances in information technology now mean that some nominally full-time courses are delivered mainly via computers.

For many – perhaps most – students, therefore, the university experience is not what it was in their parents' day. There is more assessment, more crowding, more pressure to get the best possible degree while also finding gainful employment for at least part of the year. The proportion of students achieving first-class degrees has risen significantly, while an upper second (rather than the ubiquitous 2:2) has become the norm. Research shows that the classification has a real impact in the labour market: a quarter of those taking a third-class degree in 1992 were unemployed six months later, compared with a mere 4.5 per cent of those with a first.

Toward the Future

There will be no slackening in the pace of change. In the future it is likely that more students will begin their degrees at further education colleges, more will opt initially for two-year courses and the range both of subjects and teaching methods will grow still further. Some predict the rise of the 'virtual university' or the demise of the conventional higher education institution, as companies customise their own courses. However; universities have demonstrated enduring popularity and show every sign of weathering the current turbulence.

The demand for degree places this year will follow a familiar pattern. Especially in traditional universities, arts and social science degrees remain oversubscribed and some science subjects also have high entrance requirements. Places will again be plentiful, however, in engineering, technology and the 'hard' sciences, such as physics, for those with the right qualifications.

1

University Rankings

The Times first published a University League Table in October 1992 as a distinctive way of measuring the quality of British universities. Every year since then the Tables have been the subject of vigorous debate among academics. Subsequently, too, a number of other broadsheet newspapers have got in on the act with not dissimilar university tables and this has inevitably led to a certain amount of confusion. Nonetheless, *The Times* Table retains its position as the respected and authoritative guide to the quality of UK universities and is frequently used and quoted overseas. Indeed, it has been incorporated into recent attempts by some to produce global comparisons among universities across the English-speaking world.

Given that analyses of this type within higher education and elsewhere – in schools, health, etc. – have come to be seen as legitimate aids, it is perhaps surprising that many universities remain implacably opposed to the very notion of comparing one with another, and yet that is what applicants have to do all the time. They claim in defence that each is unique, has a distinct mission and serves a different student community. Be that as it may, universities have been known to quote favourable League Table rankings when these assist their cause. Nor will you find tables of the type reproduced in this book in any material published by UCAS or The British Council and yet we remain convinced that comparisons are valid and helpful to students and their mentors when it comes to choosing a university.

Interestingly, in December 1999, the HEFCE itself published a set of performance indicators for each UK university. We have chosen to use one of them, the so-called Efficiency Measure, in this year's *Times* League Table. This first set of 'official' performance indicators covers access, non-completion rates, teaching and learning outcomes and research output. It is in many ways a commentary on how well each university is doing at delivering Government policy and, as such, has a different purpose to the measures of quality used in *The Times* League Table. The HEFCE promises another set this year, including perhaps a graduate employability measure.

The raw data for the League Table and other tables in later chapters all come from sources in the public domain. The Higher Education Statistics Agency (HESA) provided data for entry standards, student–staff ratios, library and computer spending, firsts and upper seconds, graduate destinations and overseas student enrolments. HESA is the official agency for the collection, analysis and dissemination of quantitative information about the universities. HESA also convenes a Review Group, which meets to consider the definitions and structure of the raw data to be used in *The Times Good University Guide.*

The HEFCE, along with the SHEFC for Scotland and the HEFCW for Wales, are the funding councils whose remit it is to develop policy and allocate public funds to the universities. The 1996 Research Assessment Exercise, conducted by the funding councils, provides the data for the research measure used in the tables. The funding councils also have a statutory responsibility to assess the quality of learning and teaching in the UK universities they fund. They discharge this duty through and with the Quality Assurance Agency for Higher Education (QAA) and we use their rolling programme of Subject Reviews as another measure of quality.

The Office for Standards in Education (Ofsted) assesses the quality of teacher training courses in English universities and the results of this programme complete the Teaching Assessment scores used this year.

In a few cases the source data were not available and were obtained directly from the individual universities.

All universities were provided with complete sets of their own HESA data well in advance of publication. In addition, where anomalous figures were identified in the 1997–98 HESA data, institutions were given a further opportunity to check for and notify any errors. Similarly, we consulted the universities on methodology; in particular in respect of the Subject Tables in Chapter 4. Thus, every effort has been made to ensure accuracy, but no responsibility can be taken for errors or omissions. The data providers do not necessarily agree with data aggregations or manipulations appearing in this book and are also not responsible for any inferences or conclusions thereby derived.

Apart from the efficiency measure, also new this year is a student–staff ratio (SSR) calculated for the first time by HESA itself. This replaces an SSR that was calculated from scratch in earlier versions of *The Times* League Table. Some teething troubles surround the new SSR calculation and three universities (Brunel, North London and London, UCL) declined permission to publish their figures and instead provided their own to us.

Given these various changes and the continuing refinement of the process, it is not possible to compare positions in the League Table from year to year. However, this year's Table lists the same 97 universities and university colleges of Wales and London as previously. The Open University, the privately funded Buckingham University, and universities like Cranfield with mainly postgraduate students are not included.

Two of the nine measures, namely Teaching Assessment and Research Assessment have been weighted 2.5 and 1.5 respectively to reflect the fact that universities are about teaching and research above all else. The maximum score any one university could achieve is 1,100 points and Cambridge once again this year tops the poll.

Apart from noting the overall position of any one university of interest, you can home in on a particular measure of importance to you like entry standards or graduate destinations. But bear in mind that this composite table says nothing about specific subjects at a university and so should be scrutinised in conjunction with the other tables and university profiles in later chapters.

How the Table Works

The table measures nine key aspects of university activity using the most recent data available at the time of going to press. All are designed to reflect in some way the quality of one aspect of the university. For each measure the top score is set at 100 points and the remainder are calculated as a proportion of this based on their actual score relative to the top score. In the case of teaching, research and graduate destinations some additional scaling has been introduced to alter the range of scores in the measure. A measure with a very wide or very narrow range of scores will have a disproportionately large or small effect on the overall ranking. The extent of scaling is a matter of judgement. Given the nature of the readership and the purpose of the table in supporting prospective students and their advisers, the authors considered it appropriate that teaching and graduate destinations should have a greater effect in the table than implied by their un-adjusted scores and research a lesser effect. The details of how the measures were compiled, together with some advice about their interpretation, is given below.

Teaching Assessment

What is it? A measure of the average teaching quality of the university.

Where does it come from? The QAA and the funding councils send teams of assessors to university departments and publish the outcomes.

How does it work? The results of assessments of teaching quality are averaged for each university. Not all subjects in England have been completed and so all the results published so far, ie January 2000, on the QAA website are included. In the early stages of the assessments the outcomes were Excellent, Satisfactory, and (in Scotland) Highly Satisfactory. Now all scores are out of a maximum of 24 and the original categories have been converted to numerical scores on this scale in order to calculate an average. For English universities Ofsted scores for the quality of teacher training courses are also included.

What should you look out for? The very first results (1993–94) are now quite old and a lot may have happened in a department since then. The earlier assess-ments, leading to the Excellent or Satisfactory outcomes, were also undertaken on a rather different methodology to the later ones with numerical outcomes. In particular, the early assessments were an assessment of actual quality while later ones were an assessment of whether the teaching contributed to the depart-ment's objectives. This means that two universities with different objectives and standards could nevertheless achieve the same score – both would be equally good at achieving what they set out to achieve, but they set out to achieve rather different things. The later results are thus more difficult to interpret.

Research Assessment

What is it? A measure of the average quality of the research undertaken in the university.

Where does it come from? The 1996 Research Assessment Exercise undertaken by the funding councils.

How does it work? Each university department entered in the assessment exercise was given a rating of 5* (top), 5, 4, 3a, 3b, 2 or 1 (bottom). These grades were converted to a numerical scale and an average was calculated, weighted according to the number of staff in the department getting each rating.

What should you look out for? A new Research Assessment Exercise will be undertaken in 2001 with the results published in December of that year. Many universities have been investing heavily in their research and so average grades are expected to rise.

Entry Standards

What is it? The average A-level score of new students under the age of 21.

Where does it come from? HESA data for 1997–98.

How does it work? Each student's best three A level or AS grades are converted to a numerical score (A level A=10, B=8 and E=2; AS A=5, B=4 and E=1), added up to give a score out of 30. HESA then calculates an average for all students at the university.

What should you look out for? A-level scores are used for Scottish as well as other UK universities because experience has shown that the usual scoring system for Scottish Highers gives slightly lower results for Scottish universities. There is no widely accepted way of converting scores from other qualifications, eg BTEC awards, GNVQ, International Baccalaureate or Access courses, and so these are not included. This will not matter for some universities, where the majority of the intake has A levels, but for others the score will represent a smaller proportion of the intake. Universities which have a specific policy of accepting students with low grades as part of an access policy will tend to have their average score depressed. Universities with large numbers of medical or law students, or other high demand subjects, will tend to have a higher average score.

Student–Staff Ratio

What is it? A measure of the average staffing level in the university.

Where does it come from? HESA data for 1997–98.

How does it work? HESA has calculated a student–staff ratio, ie the number of students divided by the number of staff, in a way designed to take account of different patterns of staff employment in different universities.

What should you look out for? A low SSR, ie a small number of students for each member of staff, doesn't guarantee good quality of teaching or good access to staff. Universities with a medical school will tend to score better.

Library and Computer Spending

What is it? The expenditure per student on library and computing facilities.

Where does it come from? HESA data for 1995–96, 1996–97 and 1997–98.

How does it work? A university's expenditure on library and computing facilities (books, journals, staff, computer hardware and software, but not buildings) is divided by the number of full-time equivalent students. Expenditure over three years is averaged to allow for uneven expenditure (for example, a major upgrade of a computer network might cause expenditure to rise sharply in one year but fall back the next). Libraries and information technology are becoming increasingly integrated (many universities have a single Department of Information Services encompassing both) and so the two areas of expenditure have been taken together.

What should you look out for? Some universities are the location for major national facilities, such as the Bodleian Library in Oxford and national computing facilities in Bath and Manchester. The local and national expenditure is very difficult to separate and so these universities will tend to score more highly on this measure.

Facilities Spending

What is it? The expenditure per student on student facilities.

Where does it come from? HESA data for 1995–96, 1996–97 and 1997–98.

How does it work? A university's expenditure on student facilities (sports, recreational, health, counselling, etc.) is divided by the number of full-time equivalent students. Expenditure over three years is averaged to allow for uneven expenditure.

What should you look out for? This measure tends to disadvantage Oxford and Cambridge (and possibly some other universities with a form of collegiate structure) as it only includes central university expenditure. In Oxford and Cambridge, a significant amount of facilities expenditure is by the colleges but it has not yet been possible to extract comparable data from the college accounts.

Firsts and Upper Seconds

What is it? The proportion of graduates achieving a first or upper second class degree

Where does it come from? HESA data for 1997–98

How does it work? The number of graduates with first or upper second class degrees is divided by the total number of graduates with classified degrees. Enhanced first degrees, eg an MEng awarded after a four-year engineering course, are treated as equivalent to a first or upper second for this purpose, while Scottish Ordinary degrees (awarded after three years rather than the usual four in Scotland) are excluded altogether.

What should you look out for? Degree classifications are controlled by the universities themselves, though with some moderation by the external examiner system. It can be argued, therefore, that they are not a very objective measure of quality. However, degree class is the primary measure of individual success in British higher education and will have an impact elsewhere, such as employment prospects.

Graduate Destinations

What is it? A measure of the employability of a university's graduates.

Where does it come from? HESA data for 1997–98.

How does it work? The number of graduates who take up employment or further study divided by the total number of graduates with a known destination.

What should you look out for? Universities with large numbers of medical, teaching or engineering graduates will tend to score highly as a high proportion of graduates in these subjects go directly into employment. The outcome is also influenced by how good the university is at collecting the data: a high proportion of 'not knowns' (who are excluded from the calculation) will tend to improve the outcome because the 'not knowns' tend to include a disproportionate number of unemployed graduates.

Efficiency

What is it? A measure of the efficiency of study at the university.

Where does it come from? HEFCE performance indicators, based on data for 1997–98.

How does it work? The HEFCE calculated the length of time students studied at each university compared with the length of time they would be expected to study if they completed the course normally. The main reasons for reduced efficiency are students who fail to complete their course or who repeat a year.

What should you look out for? The efficiency of a university is strongly influenced by the entry qualifications of its students. Thus a university with a high average A-level score will also have high efficiency.

Conclusions

Universities' positions in *The Times* table inevitably reflect more than their performance over a single year. Many of those at the top have built their reputations and developed their expertise over many decades or even centuries, while some of those at the bottom are still carving out a niche in the unified higher education system. Perhaps the least surprising conclusions to be drawn from the table are that Oxbridge and the University of London remain the dominant forces in British higher education and that, on the measures adopted here, the new universities still have ground to make up on the old. The former polytechnics have different priorities from those of any of their more established counterparts, however, and can demonstrate strengths in other areas.

Even on the traditional measures adopted here, the table belies the system's reputation for rigidity. For example, a former polytechnic (Oxford Brookes) continues to outperform several traditional universities. No doubt others will follow before long. The remarkable rise of universities such as Warwick and York, both founded less that 40 years ago, shows what can be achieved in a relatively short space of time.

In an exercise such as this, some distortions are inevitable. Small universities and those specialising in the arts and social sciences tend to be at a disadvantage; those with medical schools the reverse. An institution in an economically deprived area will find it more difficult to raise the private funding which enables its rivals to thrive. The use of a variety of indicators is intended to diminish such facts, but they should be borne in mind when making comparisons.

		Teaching assessment	Research assessment	Entry standards	Student–staff ratios	Library/computing spending	Facilities spending	Firsts and upper seconds	Graduate destinations	Efficiency	TOTAL
	Weighting	2.5	1.5	1	1	1	1	1	1	1	
1	Cambridge	100	100	100	67	88	71	100	95	100	1020
2	London, Imperial	99	87	92	100	79	93	77	95	93	1008
3	Oxford	97	96	98	62	100	65	91	99	99	1001
4	Bristol	90	76	89	62	71	100	84	95	97	937
5	London, UCL	92	86	84	73	78	76	78	93	89	932
6	Edinburgh	89	82	89	53	83	87	87	88	95	927
7	St Andrews	93	76	84	62	73	82	88	96	95	926
8	London, LSE	93	97	93	40	79	67	80	92	94	923
8	Warwick	97	87	87	47	72	76	77	96	96	923
10	York	97	81	83	57	69	76	70	90	97	907
10	Bath	82	81	82	50	84	94	80	93	96	907
12	Nottingham	92	73	87	50	73	75	85	95	97	903
13	Birmingham	89	73	82	57	68	79	78	94	94	884
14	London, SOAS	95	76	73	57	91	69	77	82	83	882
15	London, King's	85	73	79	80	72	68	70	100	87	879
16	Durham	91	76	85	38	69	82	73	90	99	877
17	Newcastle	89	69	77	53	80	83	75	89	91	873
18	Manchester	87	77	81	47	73	72	74	96	93	870
19	Lancaster	90	82	72	42	70	83	72	90	90	867
20	Sheffield	92	74	84	44	66	75	72	95	89	865
21	Loughborough	94	68	70	47	69	84	68	95	93	862
22	Leeds	87	74	79	50	71	74	73	90	93	857
23	Glasgow	90	63	79	53	71	72	83	91	86	855
24	London, Royal Holloway	84	72	71	53	68	85	74	95	87	853
25	London, Queen Mary	89	65	65	67	72	77	64	93	88	847
26	Aberdeen	86	66	72	53	70	78	76	95	86	846

		Teaching assessment	Research assessment	Entry standards	Student–staff ratios	Library/computing spending	Facilities spending	Firsts and upper seconds	Graduate destinations	Efficiency	TOTAL
	Weighting	2.5	1.5	1	1	1	1	1	1	1	
26	Southampton	86	72	75	53	70	74	66	93	91	846
28	UMIST	82	80	76	57	66	76	61	100	85	844
29	Essex	87	80	58	50	70	83	61	91	93	842
30	Cardiff	83	75	77	44	67	77	70	96	89	839
31	Reading	86	72	68	57	68	77	68	82	92	836
32	East Anglia	85	73	72	38	66	76	74	90	94	833
33	Queen's, Belfast	87	59	79	47	67	82	63	95	93	832
34	Aston	87	58	70	42	69	79	74	96	93	829
34	Leicester	84	71	72	50	69	73	65	91	95	829
34	Sussex	79	77	71	50	72	73	67	94	88	829
37	Exeter	83	64	76	47	67	69	76	95	95	827
38	Surrey	83	66	67	57	67	76	62	100	90	825
39	Hull	88	62	66	53	70	63	69	96	90	821
40	Liverpool	84	66	74	53	68	73	60	90	91	820
41	Stirling	87	62	66	44	72	76	72	93	86	819
42	Dundee	83	61	65	62	68	77	67	91	84	814
43	Strathclyde	89	60	68	44	64	74	67	94	87	810
44	Kent	84	62	67	44	70	71	58	94	92	798
45	Swansea	82	59	63	47	65	72	73	88	89	791
46	Keele	80	66	67	44	59	65	74	91	90	789
47	Aberystwyth	81	61	60	38	68	78	66	88	93	783
48	London, Goldsmiths'	73	69	63	50	65	65	67	92	90	779
49	Heriot-Watt	80	59	62	29	76	87	53	93	88	777
50	Bangor	81	53	55	44	72	71	59	90	93	766
51	City	77	47	67	57	67	73	60	91	84	763
52	Oxford Brookes	86	33	51	53	64	82	62	96	88	761

		Teaching assessment	Research assessment	Entry standards	Student–staff ratios	Library/computing spending	Facilities spending	Firsts and upper seconds	Graduate destinations	Efficiency	TOTAL
	Weighting	2.5	1.5	1	1	1	1	1	1	1	
53	Brunel	80	58	60	40	64	66	57	94	85	755
54	Bradford	68	67	58	40	67	84	55	90	89	754
55	Ulster	78	45	64	42	65	64	67	86	90	740
56	Plymouth	80	32	51	53	66	61	59	84	92	716
57	Brighton	82	32	49	40	66	69	59	89	87	714
57	Lampeter	75	59	46	35	67	69	49	85	89	714
59	Robert Gordon	78	26	52	50	66	67	60	97	88	713
59	Salford	77	57	52	35	62	62	51	91	83	713
61	West of England	89	25	56	44	61	65	52	89	85	712
62	Kingston	87	25	46	44	65	69	52	92	87	709
63	Sheffield Hallam	80	27	54	38	66	75	57	88	88	706
64	Northumbria	87	23	55	44	65	56	56	87	87	703
65	Nottingham Trent	78	27	56	40	62	70	56	96	85	701
66	Westminster	78	27	44	44	69	68	60	83	82	685
67	De Montfort	72	33	45	40	62	68	68	85	77	674
68	Abertay Dundee	76	23	30	50	72	62	59	86	90	673
69	Manchester Metropolitan	82	27	47	36	61	58	52	87	86	672
69	Portsmouth	75	32	51	35	61	66	53	84	86	672
71	Glasgow Caledonian	80	25	49	47	58	57	60	89	72	670
71	Hertfordshire	67	25	44	40	69	66	63	94	89	670
73	Anglia	76	20	42	47	61	67	66	86	80	669
73	Napier	75	21	47	44	64	69	65	91	71	669
75	Staffordshire	75	25	45	36	63	67	57	87	87	668
76	Sunderland	76	25	41	42	60	72	56	87	78	664
77	Liverpool John Moores	74	27	49	42	64	62	47	87	85	662
77	Wolverhampton	74	20	43	40	60	77	59	87	82	662

	Weighting	Teaching assessment	Research assessment	Entry standards	Student–staff ratios	Library/computing spending	Facilities spending	Firsts and upper seconds	Graduate destinations	Efficiency	TOTAL
		2.5	1.5	1	1	1	1	1	1	1	
79	Central Lancashire	77	21	49	38	63	63	50	91	83	661
79	Coventry	79	25	45	38	64	68	48	84	80	661
81	Greenwich	75	25	39	38	69	73	47	84	79	653
82	Middlesex	73	29	44	35	66	63	57	78	84	652
83	Luton	81	20	34	44	63	62	43	96	76	650
84	Huddersfield	66	29	45	36	61	64	59	89	84	646
85	Glamorgan	80	20	40	38	65	72	36	83	80	643
86	Leeds Metropolitan	70	22	53	32	60	62	56	88	82	642
87	Teesside	70	21	43	44	63	66	49	84	85	639
88	North London	74	27	29	36	66	70	49	85	70	633
89	Central England	73	23	48	33	58	65	51	82	77	631
90	Bournemouth	63	19	43	50	62	62	52	89	87	629
91	Paisley	77	19	36	42	65	57	54	76	74	626
92	South Bank	73	23	37	44	64	69	44	76	74	625
93	Derby	67	21	43	31	64	67	50	87	83	623
94	East London	69	27	40	40	67	71	52	66	70	619
95	London Guildhall	72	24	41	33	65	62	42	84	72	618
96	Lincs & Humberside	64	21	42	44	66	60	50	70	85	608
97	Thames Valley	69	17	31	26	61	61	43	83	84	587

1. The total is produced by multiplying the scores in the various columns by the corresponding weighting and adding; the maximum score is 1,100.
2. Small differences in the totals, whether visible or not, shouldnot be overinterpreted.

Choosing a University

Choosing a university is a big decision, one which will have an enormous impact on your future life. It will affect the place you live, the friends you make, and quite possibly your future career. It is also a very difficult decision: with a hundred universities to choose from (nearer 200 if you include higher education colleges), all of which have their own distinctive character, it can be difficult to know where to start, let alone which to choose.

For some, the choice of course will narrow the possibilities down to few. If you want to study veterinary science, there are only six places you can go. If you want to study paper science, only one. For many though, particularly if you are interested in one of the major subjects such as English, chemistry, law or mechanical engineering, there may be 20 or more similar courses. Choosing a course will be looked at in more detail in the next chapter, but for now we will assume there are plenty of suitable courses.

So how do you go about choosing a university? There are no easy answers, but it is possible to list a range of factors, which need to be looked at. Different people will attach different levels of importance to each one, but most will need at least to think about them all.

Location

Where do you want to go? Do you really like your parents or do you want to get as far away as possible? Do you want to visit your boyfriend or girlfriend every weekend (or, perhaps, want an excuse not to)? Do you want to find the cheapest way of going to university? One way or another, location is likely to be an important factor. If you want to live at home, the decision might be straightforward, though if you live in London there could easily be half a dozen local universities. If you want to go away from home, then distance or travel time will probably be a factor. Incidentally, if you can go away from home it may be to your longer-term advantage to do so. Some recent research has shown that students who move away from home have better job prospects. This is probably because those who stay at home tend to end up with narrower horizons and have less self-confidence in new situations.

If a particular town or city is acceptable, you will need to look at the location of the university itself in relation to that town or city. Is it in the city-centre or several miles outside? The former will be handy for shops and transport but may be noisy and less than picturesque. The latter may be a beautiful setting, but if you have to live off-campus there could be high travel costs. Another factor might be security: is the university in a well-lit suburban area or in a less desirable and possibly less safe part of town?

The facilities of the town or city may be important for you, too. Whether you like to dance the night away, follow the Premier League or take the theatre seriously, you will want to ensure you can do it. Indeed, your time at university will be a time when you can pursue your interests in a way you may never be able to again. Access to many things, such as sports facilities, will be very cheap and you will have the time to take them seriously. So if you want to do it, make sure you can.

Prospectuses frequently boast about the attractive surrounding countryside, so much so that it seems that *every* university is situated in the most picturesque region of the country. However, unless you have a particular interest that takes you there, such as climbing or fell walking, it is doubtful if you will spend much time taking in the sights.

Then, of course, there is cost. Generally, the south of England and London are more expensive places to live than the rest of the country, so if cost is significant for you, you will want to take this into account.

Type of University

Universities are not all the same, and nor is it easy to put them into simple categories. At one extreme is an ancient collegiate university, a world leader in terms of research, offering traditional academic courses, having most students with AAA at A level, and with large numbers of postgraduates, many from overseas. At the other extreme is a very locally orientated university which does little research, offers more vocational courses to largely local students, many of whom are mature and do not have A levels. Both universities may be very good at what they do, but what they do is very different and they will feel very different to attend as a student.

Generally, older universities (pre-1970) will do more research, recruit a higher proportion of school leavers and offer more traditional academic courses, while newer universities will be more locally and vocationally orientated and recruit more mature and part-time students.

Universities also vary greatly in size, from fewer than 2,000 students to well over 20,000. A small university will be more personal and cosier but have fewer facilities and non-academic activities; a big university will be busier and more impersonal (lectures may be to hundreds at a time) but there will be a lot more going on. Student numbers are a guide to where a university lies on this spectrum, but it is not the whole story. Some large universities are divided into colleges, which helps to create a small university feel within a big university context, while others are on several sites, each of which may be relatively small.

Quality and Reputation

Most people want to go to a good university if they can, and this is where *The*

Times League Table is helpful. By bringing together a variety of measures it tries to give a reasonable basis for deciding how good a university really is. Differences of a few places in the table are insignificant, but a university in the top ten is doing a lot better than one in the bottom ten or even in the middle.

When you look at the subject tables, it is clear that even the best universities vary in quality across subjects. Some universities perform consistently well and

---

Ten Things You Didn't Know About Universities

- The oldest university in the country, Oxford, was probably founded in 1096, but no one knows precisely. It was there in 1187, but must have been founded before that
- There are over 30,000 courses to choose from
- Fancy a degree in Brewing and Distilling? Go to Heriot-Watt
- The total income of universities in 1997-98 was over £11 billion, which is more than that of some countries
- Women outnumbered men among first-year students in 1996-97 for the first time
- In his Will, the philosopher Jeremy Bentham instructed that his skeleton and head be preserved, clothed and mounted in a seated position. He has sat like that in University College London since 1850
- There are about 200,000 overseas students from over 180 countries in the UK
- At some Scottish universities the Rector is elected by the staff and students. This has sometimes resulted in the election of celebrities rather than distinguished academics
- The student population in the UK has increased to 1.8 million from just 200,000 in the 1960s
- 'University' is a legally controlled title in the UK – only institutions with a Royal Charter or some other legal authority can call themselves a university

---

appear in the top 20 of many subject tables, while others come low down in the main table but have one or two very good departments that do well in the subject tables. So it is important to look at the main table alongside the subject tables.

As ever, quality has to be paid for. A Mercedes costs more than a Ford, and Cambridge 'costs' more than other universities, though in this case the currency is A-level grades rather than cash. Look at the entry standards column in the main table and you will see that it follows the main ranking fairly closely. In other words, universities high up the table will, in general, ask for higher grades in whatever qualification you are offering than those lower down the table. You will need to make a judgement about how well you are going to do in your school or college examinations and choose universities where you have a realistic chance of meeting the entry requirements. If you are taking A levels and are going to get AAA, there is no problem, but in many subjects CCC will exclude most of the universities near the top of the table.

Facilities

The facilities offered by universities are fairly similar in general terms. All will have a library, sports halls, a health service, a careers service and so on. But there will be differences and if something is particularly important for you it is worth checking out. Sometimes this will be hard to do – all universities will claim to have a really good careers service, but it is difficult to find out how true those claims are. In other cases, however, it is more straightforward.

Accommodation will be important if you are going away from home. Is there an accommodation guarantee for first years? What about later years? If you are a

Top Ten for Teaching Quality		Top Ten for Average A-Level Score	
1	Cambridge	1	Cambridge	29.6
2	London, Imperial	2	Oxford	28.7
3	York	3	London, LSE	27.3
4	Oxford	4	London, Imperial	27.3
5	Warwick	5	Bristol	26.1
6	London, SOAS	6	Edinburgh	25.9
7	Loughborough	7	Nottingham	25.6
8	St Andrews	8	Warwick	25.1
9	London, LSE	9	Durham	24.8
10	London, UCL	10	London, UCL	24.8

Bottom Ten for Teaching Quality		Bottom Ten for Average A-Level Score	
88	Leeds Metropolitan	88	Sunderland	11.9
89	Teesside	89	East London	11.8
90	Thames Valley	90	Glamorgan	11.8
91	East London	91	Greenwich	11.7
92	Bradford	92	South Bank	11.5
93	Hertfordshire	93	Paisley	11.1
94	Derby	94	Luton	11.0
95	Huddersfield	95	Thames Valley	10.5
96	Lincolnshire & Humberside	96	Abertay Dundee	9.4
97	Bournemouth	97	North London	8.5

computer geek who spends the early hours on the internet, you will want to know if the rooms are wired up. If you are often out late (and how many students are not?) you may want to know where the accommodation is, how you can get back to it late at night and whether you will feel safe doing so. If you can't live in university accommodation for the whole of your course, where is the private accommodation? Is it all in a city five miles down the road (which could be good for access to shops, night-clubs and maybe the beach, but will probably be bad for travel costs), or in the grotty end of town, or in a leafy suburb next to the university?

If you have a particular minority interest you want to follow while at university, then this could be a factor. Most universities will have football pitches and a Liberal Democratic Society, but a climbing wall and a deep-sea fishing group may be harder to find. The students' union will be able to tell you.

In fact students' unions are an increasingly important aspect of student life and have come a long way from the traditional image of providers of cheap beer and student protests. The modern entrepreneurial union will have a wide range of services from food and stationery outlets through to comprehensive advice services. Increasingly they are providers of part-time employment for students and are becoming involved in personal skills development. Inevitably, some are more active and innovative than others, so they are worth looking at.

As the financial position of students has worsened, universities have responded by setting up employment agencies. These are generally based in careers services or students' unions and use their contacts with employers to identify employment

Top Ten for Student Facilities Spending	Top Ten for Library/Computing Spending
1 Bristol	1 Oxford
2 Bath	2 London, SOAS
3 London, Imperial	3 Cambridge
4 Heriot-Watt	4 Bath
5 Edinburgh	5 Edinburgh
6 London, Royal Holloway	6 Newcastle
7 Loughborough	7 London, Imperial
8 Bradford	8 London, LSE
9 Essex	9 London, UCL
10 Lancaster	10 Heriot-Watt

Bottom Ten for Student Facilities Spending	Bottom Ten for Library/Computing Spending
88 Bournemouth	88 Portsmouth
89 Abertay Dundee	89 Anglia
90 London Guildhall	90 Thames Valley
91 Thames Valley	91 Huddersfield
92 Plymouth	92 Leeds Metropolitan
93 Lincolnshire & Humberside	93 Sunderland
94 Manchester Metropolitan	94 Wolverhampton
95 Paisley	95 Keele
96 Glasgow Caledonian	96 Glasgow Caledonian
97 Northumbria	97 Central England

opportunities and their contacts with students to identify suitable employees. The agency will also ensure that rates of pay and hours of work are reasonable. If you think you may be short of cash, a good agency of this type could be vital.

Finally, if you have any particular needs, you will want to know that they can be catered for. Support for students with disabilities has improved greatly in recent years but some universities are particularly good at supporting some kinds of disability, while others have a lot of old buildings that make wheelchair access very difficult.

Making the Decision

For some, location will be critical and this will immediately narrow down the choice. Others may be keen to go to as prestigious a university as possible and then the key question will be whether they can meet the entry requirements. Others may be particularly keen to carry on with an obscure martial art and so will want to go to one of the two or three places where they can do this. But for most, a combination of factors such as these will result in the elimination of most universities so that a manageable list of perhaps five or ten emerges. Then the detailed work begins.

The first source of information will probably be the **undergraduate prospectus**. This is the main recruiting document that universities produce and should include most of what you will need to know, including details of courses, facilities and entry requirements. However, you need to bear in mind that it is not an impartial document, it is a form of advertising designed to make the university

---

Tricks of the Prospectus Trade

The claims made by universities are rarely untrue, but they do need to be read carefully and critically. Here are a few cases where *The Times* League Tables can help you to interpret what the prospectuses and websites are saying.

"Our teaching standards are among the best in the country. The University has scored consistently high ratings in teaching assessments carried out since April 1995 by the Quality Assurance Agency". (Prospectus, 1999-00) *The results this university achieved since 1995 were quite good, but not good enough to get them into the top 40 universities in England for teaching quality scores.*

"Our procedures for ensuring our courses are carefully designed, well taught, relevant to employment, and backed up by research and consultancy work, are nationally recognised as being of the highest quality." (Website, 1999) *Read the sentence carefully: it is the procedures that they claim to be of the highest quality and not the courses themselves. The claim about procedures may well be true, but you are probably more interested to know that this university failed to make the top 50 for teaching quality in the 1999 League Table.*

"More [of our] graduates find permanent employment within six months of getting their degree than graduates from many other British universities." (Website, 1999) *The claim is true, but many universities were also better. This one didn't make the top 40 for graduate destinations in the 1999 League Table.*

"The University prides itself on its impressive research record and we consider the quality of teaching to be central to our mission." (Prospectus, 2000) *The research record is impressive, but in 1999, 33 other universities were more impressive. And while the quality of teaching may well be central to its mission, in 1999, 38 universities scored higher.*

---

seem attractive. Strangely, the sun is always shining in prospectus photographs. They are rarely factually incorrect, but prospectuses can be incomplete or make generalised claims of quality without any supporting evidence (see box, *Tricks of the Prospectus Trade*). In addition to the prospectus, many universities will produce a series of **departmental booklets**, which will give more detail about individual subject areas.

One easy way of obtaining a pile of prospectuses and departmental booklets is to visit **a higher education fair** where most universities will have a stand to give out information. You may also get an opportunity to talk to someone from the university if you have particular questions you want to ask.

Alternatively, universities have always been pioneers in using the internet and many have prospectuses available on their **websites**. Departments will usually have their own sites, too, and you can often access student handbooks aimed at current students for all the detail you will ever need about courses, options, teaching methods and assessment.

If you are still unclear about entry requirements, check them out in the *Big Official UCAS Guide.*

Finally, there is no substitute for a personal visit. All universities will offer some kind of **open day** where you can see for yourself what it would be like to go there as a student. If you can't make the date of the open day, many will make

---

Things To Look Out For

- Most degree courses in Scotland last four years, though many students with good A levels can be exempt from the first year
- Where a university has a split site, check where your course will be based
- Large adverts in the press usually means a university is having difficulty filling its places
- Engineering courses are either MEng or BEng; only the MEng will give maximum credit towards Chartered Engineer status
- Some courses offer the chance of spending a year or part of a year in Europe
- Accommodation might be guaranteed, but check whether it is five miles down the road
- Courses based in two or more departments can feel as if they are based nowhere – check for a 'home' department where you will belong

---

arrangements for you to visit more informally during the summer. A few will offer **residential visits**, which allow for a more extended and comprehensive look at the university.

While trawling through all these sources of information, you will no doubt talk to friends, parents, teachers, careers advisers and anyone else who comes within range. While it is good to talk, be critical of what you hear. A parent or teacher may know what they are talking about, but they may be telling you things based on their experiences of 20 or 30 years ago. Universities have changed a lot since then. Alternatively, your next-door neighbour, whom you rarely see, may just happen to work in a university admissions office and be a real source of good advice.

In the end only you can decide. It won't be easy, but after all the reading, visiting, surfing and talking, you have got to do it. You have to decide which six will go on your UCAS form. Good luck!

3

Choosing a Course

Choosing a university is a difficult business (see previous chapter) and choosing a course is no easier. Once again the decision is made in the face of enormous diversity, or at least it usually is. For a few the decision is easy: they have always wanted to be a brain surgeon or have always had a passion for Tudor England. For most, however, there is a bewildering variety of courses, many of which are not taught in schools or colleges. Somehow you have to narrow down the thousands of courses that are available to just a few. It will help if the decision is broken down into three main components: the *subject*, what it is you want to study; *the type of course*, precisely how you want to study it; and the *quality* of the course.

The Subject

When it comes to choosing a subject there are several things you need to take into account. First, you must make sure you understand the nature of the subject you are considering, especially if it is one you have not studied before. A course in ecology, for example, sounds as if it might deal with conservation and 'green' issues. However, many ecology courses are about the scientific study of the interaction between living organisms and may only deal peripherally with conservation issues. Language courses can vary considerably, from those concerned largely with literature to those which concentrate on translation and contemporary area studies. Psychology is another subject which may not be what is expected. It too can vary depending on whether the course focuses on the social or the neurological end of the subject.

Ten Courses You Didn't Know You Could Choose

BA   Adventure Recreation
BA   Animation
BA   Arabic and Amharic
BA   Byzantine Studies
BSc Equine Science
BA   Packaging Design
BA   Playwork
BSc Science and Football
BA   Valuation and Auctioneering
BA   War Studies

Listed on UCAS website, summer 1999

Having made sure you understand the nature of the subject, you must be interested in it. You will spend a large proportion of three or four years immersed in the subject and that will be pretty dull if you find it boring. More important, you will probably perform better if you are excited by what you are studying. You are also likely to perform better if you have an aptitude for the subject. A course may be really interesting and lead to a guaranteed high-flying career, but if you are no good at it, you may end up performing badly or even failing altogether.

Career opportunities are another important factor. If you know what you want to do after university, your subject must provide a suitable basis for that career. The choice may be wider than you think, as just under half of graduate jobs do not specify any particular subject at all. Conversely, a narrowly vocational course could result in your career options being restricted if you subsequently change your mind about the direction you want to go.

	What do Graduates Do?		
	Employed (%)	Further Study (%)	Unemployed (%)
Design Studies	70.0	10.7	11.1
Media Studies	73.8	9.2	10.9
Environmental Science	64.8	18.0	10.5
Sociology	64.2	20.2	9.5
Biology	54.9	28.5	8.7
Electronic Engineering	76.0	12.2	8.6
Psychology	62.6	22.5	8.1
English	54.6	30.7	7.4
History	55.1	29.7	7.2
Economics	70.8	15.9	7.2
Business and Management	78.9	6.9	7.2
Physics	50.9	38.1	6.4
Computing Science	83.6	7.1	6.4
Mechanical Engineering	76.2	12.7	6.3
Mathematics	60.8	28.3	5.8
Geography	61.5	24.5	5.8
Chemistry	49.4	40.4	5.3
Civil Engineering	76.8	13.0	5.3
French	65.2	24.4	3.5
All Subjects	**67.8**	**19.4**	**6.9**

What do Graduates Do? 1999 AGCAS

Students often refer to employment prospects when they are asked about why they chose their course. However, it is worth looking at the figures. Some courses do, more or less, guarantee a job and the unemployment rates six months after graduation for medicine, veterinary science and education are very low. However, most subjects fall into a narrow range of about 6–9 per cent still seeking employment after six months. In other words, the employability of most subjects is about the same. Interestingly, business studies, a subject that is often considered to be highly employable, comes out almost exactly in the middle at 7.2 per cent, and two highly vocational areas, design studies and media studies, have the highest unemployment rates. Of course there will be some variability within these broad subject groups. Some courses may be tailored towards specific careers and so achieve a very high level of employability, but conversely may be seen as too specialised if you try for an alternative career.

One reason for this similarity in employment prospects is the point mentioned

Top Ten Most Popular Subjects		
1	Business Management	31,334
2	Computer Science	21,777
3	Design Studies	18,065
4	Law	15,811
5	Medicine	10,972
6	Subjects Allied to Medicine	10,940
7	Psychology	10,218
8	English	9,446
9	Drama	8,293
10	Sports Science	8,075

Applications, entry 1999, UCAS

above, that a significant proportion of job vacancies do not specify any subject at all. You can take the most obscure subject in the *UCAS Handbook* and still have nearly 50 per cent of jobs open to you. Another reason is that class of degree is important: students with First Class Honours are very rarely unemployed whatever subject they studied.

You also need to consider entry requirements. Some universities have a General Entrance Requirement, a basic minimum set of qualifications that all students have to have. For most students this is not a problem as they will meet the Requirement easily, but it is worth checking to make sure. Most universities will

Top Ten for Average A-Level Score			Bottom Ten for Average A-Level Score		
1	Veterinary Science	29.1	1	Social Work	13.4
2	Medicine	28.8	2	Institutional Management	13.6
3	Dentistry	27.1	3	Building/Construction	13.8
4	Modern Languages	25.3	4	Computer Systems Engineering	13.9
5	Ophthalmics	24.6	5	Tourism	14.0
6	Physics	23.2	6	Software Engineering	15.0
7=	Mathematics	23.1	7	Land & Property Management	15.1
7=	Pharmacy	23.1	8	Education	15.2
9	Biochemistry	22.1	9	Other Mathematical Subjects	15.4
10	History	22.0	10	Radiography	15.4

Average A-level score of accepted applicants (to subjects with at least 100 acceptances), 1998, UCAS. (Note that Modern Languages here refers to 'Other Modern Languages' involving several languages and not single language courses such as French or German.)

also have various escape clauses to enable them to admit good students with unusual backgrounds even if they don't meet the General Entrance Requirement.

Each course will also have its entry requirements, both in terms of subjects you must already have studied and the examination grades required for entry. Most

Mathematics courses, for example, will require previous study of mathematics. The *Big UCAS Guide* is the easiest way to check this. If you have the right subjects, the grades required will vary between universities (as discussed in the last chapter) and also between subjects. There is little point in applying for Medicine unless you are confident of getting As and Bs at A level (or their equivalent in other qualifications) while Ds and Es will get you into an engineering course at many less popular universities.

Older students, or those with an unorthodox educational background, will generally be treated more flexibly by universities. While you will still be expected to demonstrate your ability and suitability for the course, you will be able to do this through a wide variety of qualifications or an access course or, in some cases, relevant work experience. The GCSEs you flunked as an unhappy adolescent before diving into the first job that became available will be ignored and the emphasis will be on what you can do now.

Bear in mind that entry standards are essentially market-related. Popular courses at popular universities can afford to be very choosy about who they admit and so have the highest entry standards. That doesn't mean the courses are any tougher at those universities (though they could be for other reasons) but it does mean that most of the students on the courses will be very able.

Type of Course

Having decided what you want to study, you will be faced with a variety of ways of studying it. The most basic difference is between the levels of the courses. While most higher education courses lead to a degree, some lead to sub-degree qualifications such as a Higher National Diploma (HND). In general sub-degree courses will be shorter, more vocationally orientated, and have lower entry requirements. Some will be linked to degree courses, giving you the option of progressing to a degree if you perform well enough on the early parts of the course.

Courses can differ markedly in length, varying from two years for most sub-degree courses to six years for a professional course in architecture, and possibly more for some part-time courses. The majority of full-time courses are three years, but most language courses last four years and there is an increasing number of science and engineering courses which lead to a Master's degree (such as MChem or MEng) after four years. In some cases it is possible to add a foundation year to the beginning of a course, making it a further year in length. These foundation courses vary somewhat in nature and entry requirements. Some are essentially a conversion course for students who have the 'wrong' subjects in their examinations and will expect the same or a similar standard for entry as the courses they lead on to (though key subjects for direct entry will not be required). Others are designed to take students who have performed below the normal entry requirements for a course to bring them up to speed. These courses will often have lower entry requirements.

In some cases the length of a course can be misleading if you intend to go on to a profession in the same subject. Five years of medicine or six of architecture will qualify you to start work as a doctor or an architect (though in both cases there are further hurdles before full qualification). However, three years of law does not qualify you to be a lawyer. You must undertake further training (at your own expense) before you can work as a barrister or a solicitor. In the case of engineering, a four-year MEng course will give you maximum credit towards the status of Chartered Engineer, but if you take a BEng course you will have to undertake further study after you have finished.

Some differences between courses relate to aspects of the subject itself. Only the very largest academic departments have expertise in all aspects of a subject and so, especially in the later years, the course will focus on the particular expertise of the department. You will need to decide whether a particular course offers the areas of the subject you want to study. Of course you may not know, or may change your mind as you go through the course. If you think this is likely, then a course in a large department with a wide range of options might be best.

Even for courses with a similar content, there may nonetheless be significant differences. Some of the opportunities you may want to consider are:

- spending a year or part of a year in Europe under an ERASMUS programme
- taking time out on a work placement
- extending the course to four years to obtain a Masters degree (common for engineering and some science courses)
- being taught part of your course by a media personality or a Nobel prize-winner who is a member of staff in the department

Courses also differ in their structure. Some will concentrate on a single subject, some will allow you to combine two subjects in a single course (often called Dual Honours courses), and others will involve several subjects. Some will have a large proportion of the course fixed in advance, while others will allow you to choose options to make up a substantial part of the course. There are even 'pick and mix' courses where you can choose from a wide range of very diverse options (though in making choices on such a course it is worth thinking about a choice that will look coherent to an employer).

Some courses are organised on a modular basis, usually with two semesters rather than three terms per year. Each module will require the same amount of study and will usually be assessed separately. This tends to increase the number of examinations and assessments you will have to do. Modular courses are often advertised as being very flexible, allowing you to choose your options from a very wide range of available modules, and indeed they generally are more flexible than traditionally organised courses. However, they may not be as flexible as they appear as timetable clashes will restrict the real choice that is available to you.

There will be differences in teaching methods and assessment. Some courses will make more use than others of particular teaching methods, such as tutorials (though watch out for groups of 15–20 that are still called tutorials), computer-assisted learning or dissertations. If you seize up in formal examinations, you may want a course with a lot of continuous assessment. Alternatively, if you don't like the continuous pressure that this involves, you may prefer one with an emphasis on final examinations.

Which Subject is Hardest to Get Into?

There is no simple answer to this question. Some courses are very popular – they get a lot of applications – but the standard of those applications may on average be low. For example, primary education makes the top ten most popular subjects but the average A-level score of new entrants is just 15.2, one of the lowest for any subject. Similarly, veterinary science only gets 1,400 applications but has the top A-level score. Generally, the hardest subjects to get into will be those which *both* attract large numbers of applications *and* attract lots of good applicants and so have a high average A-level score. Having said that, an applicant with AAA (or AAAAA in Scotland) in the right subjects will find it easy to get into almost any course he or she want.

Quality

Having narrowed down the course options, you can start to check out their quality, and here *The Times* subject tables can be helpful. These rank universities on the basis of their teaching quality, research quality and the entry standards of their new students. The most important aspect of this is the teaching assessment (technically known as a Subject Review) and this is given the highest weight in the subject tables. **Not all subjects have been assessed yet and so there is only a ranked table for those which have.** Alphabetically organised tables are given for the main subjects where assessments have not been completed.

The results of each Subject Review are available via the websites of the higher education funding councils (HEFCE for England and Northern Ireland, SHEFC for Scotland and HEFCW for Wales). The full reports for England, Northern Ireland and Scotland are also available on the websites, so you can easily find out about the subjects and universities you are interested in (if you haven't got access to the internet you can buy copies). The older reports in England and Wales, which led to an Excellent or Satisfactory rating, were an attempt to judge the absolute level of teaching quality in each university for the subjects covered. The more recent reports, which lead to a score of 1 – 4 on six aspects of teaching (giving a total out of 24), and all reports in Scotland, are an assessment against the universities own objectives in teaching. This is an important distinction. On the old English system you can be reasonably confident that a department with an 'excellent' rating was better at teaching than one with a 'satisfactory' rating (or at least it was back in 1994 or 1995 when the assessment was carried out – a lot could have changed since then). However, on the new English system, all you can say is that a department with a higher score was better at meeting its own objectives than one with a lower score. A department with very high aspirations, trying to offer the best course in the country but not quite succeeding, could end up with a lower score than a much more modest department which aimed to achieve far less but did so completely. So if you read any Subject Reviews, remember to read the section on the department's objectives very carefully.

Every course is different, but every student wants different things, so the chances of finding a perfect match is not that high, despite the huge range of courses. You will almost certainly end up having to decide what is most important to you. Do you want the best course or one, which is quite good but offers the options you really want? Do you want the ideal work placement or the course with least continuous assessment? As with choosing a university, the decision will not be easy and only you can make it. More good luck!

4

The Top Universities by Subject

K nowing where a university stands in the pecking order of higher education is a vital piece of information for any prospective student, but the quality of the course is what matters most. The most modest institution may have a centre of specialist excellence and even famous universities have mediocre departments. This section offers some pointers to the leading universities in those subjects assessed by the higher education funding councils. Expert assessors have produced official ratings for research in every subject, but the judgements on teaching are still not complete. The tables in this chapter come in two parts. Those on pages 38-76 cover subject areas where the teaching assessments in England have been completed. Those on pages 77-98 cover subject areas where the teaching assessments have not been competed. For the first group of tables, a ranking and a commentary is given. For the second group of tables, only raw data is provided, as there is not sufficient data to make any interpretation possible.

Subjects with Completed Teaching Assessments
These tables cover all the areas in which teaching has been assessed in England. Note that only a maximum of 20 universities are given individual scores in the tables. Thereafter, universities are ranked in groups of ten, with the listing within the group being in alphabetical order.

The method used to compare departments takes account of new information on entrance qualifications and to be consistent with the overall university rankings. Three elements are included: average A-level entry scores; the funding councils' ratings for teaching; the funding councils' ratings for research. The three indicators are combined using the same weightings as in the main university League Table: 1 for entrance; 2.5 for teaching; 1.5 for research. To qualify for inclusion in a table, a university had to have data for at least two out of three measures. Where one measure was missing this was taken into account in calculating the overall score. Any university where this occurs is marked with an asterisk in the tables that follow. Differences in the gradings used by the Scottish and Welsh funding councils have been accommodated by calculating an equivalent on the English scale.

The tables confirm the dominance of the traditional universities in most areas of higher education. This is to be expected in research, where decades of differential funding have left the former polytechnics struggling to compete. Less predictably, however, the ratings for teaching have usually told the same story. This is partly because the academics who inspect departments take into account facilities such as library stock, while the traditional universities' generally smaller teaching groups also give them an advantage.

There are exceptions, however. In communications and media studies, for example, Westminster collected maximum ratings for both teaching and research, overtaking numerous universities with higher entrance requirements and placing it fourth. Overall, however, Cambridge is again by far the most successful university, with 14 top placings and bettered in only a handful of the subjects in which it offers undergraduate courses. Oxford has the next highest number of top places with five.

The subject rankings demonstrate that there are 'horses for courses' in higher education. Thus London School of Economics is more than a match for its rivals in social science while Imperial College London confirms its reputation in engineering. In their own fields, table-toppers such as East Anglia (environmental sciences) and Bath (mechanical engineering) are equally well-known.

In the statistics accompanying the tables on the following pages, TQA stands for Teaching Quality Assessment, giving the dates of assessments in England. Research grades date from 1996, while A-level grades and the other statistics relate to 1997–98.

Subjects without Completed Teaching Assessments

For the subjects appearing on pages 77-98, the tables are of a different design. For each subject, the universities are listed in alphabetical order. For each university, where data is available, the following information is provided;

TQA (Teaching Quality Assessment). For some subjects certain universities have been assessed, and all scores published up to January 2000 have been included. The assessment is recorded either with a score (with a maximum of 24) or by a letter – E for Excellent, S for Satisfactory and, in Scotland, an additional category, HS for Highly Satisfactory.

RAE (Research Assessment Exercise). This provides a measure of the average quality of research undertaken in the subject area. The first figure gives a quality rating of 5* (top), 5, 4, 3a, 3b, 2 or 1 (bottom). The letter refers to the proportion of staff included in the numerical assessment, with A including virtually everyone and F hardly anyone. This data is from 1996.

A Level This is the average A-level score for new students under the age of 21, taken from HESA data for 1997–98. Each student's best three A-level or AS grades are converted to a numerical score (A level A=10, B=8, C=6, D=4, E=2; AS A=5, B=4, C=3, D=2, E=1) and added up to give a score out of 30. HESA then calculates an average score for the university.

Agriculture and Forestry	
1 Nottingham	89.7
2 Edinburgh*	87.5
3 Newcastle	82.5
4 Aberdeen*	78.4
5 Reading	74.2
6 London, Wye	74.1
7 Cranfield	72.8
8 Leeds	70.8
9 Queen's, Belfast	67.5
10 Plymouth	58.8
11 Bangor	54.9
12 Aberystwyth*	50.5
13 Lincs & Humberside*	48.2
14 Bournemouth*	47.1
15 Central Lancashire*	46.8
16 De Montfort	37.0

TQA (England) 1996–98

Firsts and 2:1s: 54.4% (forestry 56.7%)

Employment: 72.3% (forestry 73.8%)

Further study: 13.2% (forestry 14.8%)

Unemployment: 7.1% (forestry 4.9%)

Nottingham is a convincing winner, with the best teaching and research assessments, but Edinburgh's high entrance requirements enable it to overtake Newcastle this year. Wye College (now merged with London, Imperial) is included for the first time and breaks straight into the top six. The other new entrant is Central Lancashire.

Plymouth is the top-placed new university, thanks to a teaching assessment which was second only to Nottingham's. Edinburgh aside, entrance requirements are relatively modest. A quarter of those enrolling in agriculture and more than a third in forestry do so without A levels, often coming with relevant work experience. Employment rates are high.

American Studies	
1 Keele*	100.0
2 Nottingham	90.4
3 Sussex*	89.3
4 East Anglia	87.9
5 Hull	82.6
6 Birmingham	79.7
7 Central Lancashire	73.0
8 Middlesex	66.4
9 Kent*	58.1
10 Reading*	58.0
11 Brunel*	55.3
12 Swansea	55.1
13 Wolverhampton*	50.9
14 Aberystwyth*	46.7
15 Thames Valley*	25.3

TQA (England) 1996–98

Firsts and 2:1s: 71%

Employment: 66.7%

Further study: 14.6%

Unemployment: 7.6%

Only 15 universities have been assessed for American Studies, although some others will offer courses in the subject as part of modular degree schemes. Of those listing American Studies separately, Nottingham had the best-qualified entrants, averaging more than an A and two Bs at A level. Although the top six places are filled by traditional universities, two former polytechnics make the top ten. Indeed, Central Lancashire shares with East Anglia and Keele the distinction of the best teaching quality assessment, with 24 points. Keele takes top place because it also ties with Nottingham for the best research grade. Nationally, nine out of ten students taking American Studies have A levels or equivalent qualifications and entrance requirements are high.

Anthropology

1	Cambridge*	100.0
2	Brunel*	95.3
3	Manchester	95.1
4	London, LSE	94.4
5	London, UCL	93.9
6	London, SOAS	91.7
7	Oxford*	90.7
8	Sussex	88.1
9	Durham	87.2
10	Oxford Brookes*	86.0
11	St Andrews*	83.6
12	Kent	82.9
13	Edinburgh*	81.0
14	London, Goldsmiths'	75.5
15	Queen's, Belfast	71.6
16	Hull*	71.5
17	Swansea*	53.7

TQA (England) 1994–95
Firsts and 2:1s: 68%
Employment: 60.3%
Further study: 18.7%
Unemployment: 8.6%

Anthropology offers the best chance of a good degree in the social sciences, but the unemployment rate is also high. Almost one graduate in five goes on to take a higher degree or some form of postgraduate training.

With maximum points for both teaching and research, Cambridge is comfortably ahead of the field in our ranking. It was the only university to achieve a 5-star rating for research. There is little to choose between Brunel, Manchester, London, LSE and London, UCL, however, since all were rated as Excellent for teaching and were graded 5 for research with the maximum number of academics entered for assessment. Brunel benefits from the scoring system for the table because it does not have a single honours degree in anthropology so, like Cambridge, its A-level score is missing from the calculation. The system tends to favour universities with high scores on two measures and a missing third measure.

The teaching scores date from the early rounds of assessment, and the grades were more generous than many subjects: only London, Goldsmiths' and Queen's, Belfast were rated less than excellent.

The subject was not assessed separately for teaching quality in Scotland or Wales, and Hull's assessment was carried out under the current English system, giving a maximum of 24 points.

Architecture		
1	Cambridge	**96.3**
2	Sheffield	**93.8**
3	London, UCL	**93.4**
4	Cardiff	**89.8**
5	Nottingham	**89.3**
6	Newcastle	**87.2**
7	York*	**86.0**
8	Bath	**84.3**
9	Strathclyde	**80.1**
10	Edinburgh	**75.6**
11	Liverpool	**67.9**
12	Greenwich	**66.8**
13	Oxford Brookes	**60.5**
14	Queen's, Belfast	**60.2**
15	Manchester	**57.3**
16	East London	**57.0**
17	Brighton	**55.6**
18	Kingston	**54.9**
18	Robert Gordon	**54.9**
20	Liverpool John Moores	**54.6**

21–35

Central England, De Montfort, Dundee, Huddersfield, Leeds Metropolitan, Lincolnshire & Humberside, Luton, Manchester Metropolitan, North London, Northumbria, Plymouth, Portsmouth, South Bank, West of England, Westminster

TQA (England) 1994
Firsts and 2:1s: 42.1%
Employment:: 33.3%
Further study: 66.7%
Unemployment: 0

Cambridge leads a group of three universities with excellent teaching scores and grade 5 in the last research assessments, profiting from the highest average entry grades. Architecture was among the first subjects to be assessed for teaching qual-ity, and eight universities in England were top rated. The pecking order was clearer in Scotland, where only Strathclyde managed top marks, and in Wales, where Cardiff did the same.

Greenwich is the highest-placed of a number of new universities now running degrees in architecture. Like East London, it was rated as Excellent for teaching quality, although only Oxford Brookes and North London (of the new universities) managed better than the second of seven rungs of the research ladder.

A third of all undergraduates – usually mature students – enter with qualifications other than A level, Highers or the International Baccalaureate. There is a wide spread of entrance requirements for school-leavers, from almost 30 UCAS points at Cambridge to only 10 at Luton and West of England. Unemployment on graduation is low, but the official figure of zero is misleading because two-thirds go on to compete their professional training.

Building

1	Reading	85.2
2	London, UCL*	83.7
3	Loughborough	80.3
4	Ulster	76.4
5	UMIST	74.8
6	Oxford Brookes	70.1
7	Kingston	68.0
8	Salford	67.7
9	Heriot-Watt	64.6
10	Nottingham Trent	63.1
11	Plymouth	62.3
12	Queen's, Belfast*	61.0
13	Liverpool John Moores	60.9
14	Northumbria	60.1
15	Greenwich	58.2
16	Westminster*	57.1
17	Sheffield Hallam	56.4
18	Coventry	56.1
19	Napier	55.9
20	Luton	55.5

21–30
Anglia, Brighton, Central Lancashire, De Montfort, Glamorgan, Leeds Metropolitan, Liverpool, Portsmouth, West of England, Wolverhampton
31–39
Abertay Dundee, Central England, Derby, Glasgow Caledonian, Hertfordshire, Huddersfield, Robert Gordon, South Bank, Staffordshire

TQA (England) 1996–98
Firsts and 2:1s: 48.2%
Employed: 35%
Further study: 60.7%
Unemployed: 3.2%

Building is one of the most open of the tables because there is less correlation than in most subjects between the top performers in teaching and research. Kingston was the only university to be awarded maximum points for teaching quality, but low entry grades and research score restricted it to seventh place in our table. Reading takes top place as one of only two universities rated internationally outstanding for research. Salford was the other, but it suffered from a low teaching score.

Most of the universities offering building are former polytechnics, and this is reflected in the fact that 44 per cent of students are admitted with qualifications other than A level. Those who do take the A-level route tend not to have the highest grades – only Loughborough, Reading and Queen's, Belfast registered an average of more than three Cs, while some are as low as the equivalent of three Es.

Building has been growing in popularity as a degree subject, with almost 10,000 taking full-time courses and 4,000 studying part-time. Although little more than a third of the graduates go straight into jobs, unemployment is low because most graduates go on to professional courses.

Business

1	UMIST	98.5
2	London, LSE	96.3
3	Warwick	95.6
4	Lancaster	94.9
5	Bath	92.0
6	Nottingham	89.7
7	Manchester*	88.1
8	City	86.4
9	Strathclyde	86.1
10	London, Imperial*	83.9
11	Loughborough	83.3
12	Edinburgh	82.4
13	St Andrews	80.8
14	Cranfield*	79.2
15	Reading	75.1
16	Surrey	74.8
17	Cardiff	74.6
18	Southampton	74.5
19	Sheffield	73.4
20	Kingston	72.2

21–30
Birmingham, Bradford, Cambridge, De Montfort, Glasgow, Keele, Leeds, Nottingham Trent, Oxford, Stirling
31–40
Aston, Glamorgan, Heriot-Watt, Hull, Kent, London, King's, London, Royal Holloway, Northumbria, Swansea, West of England
41–50
Aberdeen, Brunel, Durham, Leicester, Manchester Metropolitan, Newcastle, Plymouth, Portsmouth, Robert Gordon, Ulster
51–60
Bangor, Brighton, Glasgow Caledonian, Huddersfield, Leeds Metropolitan, Liverpool John Moores, Oxford Brookes, Salford, Sheffield Hallam, Westminster

61–70
Aberystwyth, Bournemouth, Central England, Central Lancashire, Coventry, Derby, East London, Exeter, Hertfordshire, Staffordshire
71–86
Anglia, Abertay Dundee, East Anglia, Greenwich, Lincolnshire & Humberside, London Guildhall, Luton, Middlesex, Napier, North London, Paisley, South Bank, Sunderland, Teesside, Thames Valley, Wolverhampton

TQA (England) 1994
Firsts and 2:1s: 46.7%
Employment: 24.6%
Further study: 69.9%
Unemployment: 3.3%

Some of the top business schools, such as those at Cambridge, London and Manchester, are absent from the table because they do not offer first degrees. Nevertheless, the universities at the top of the table are acknowledged leaders in the field. The University of Manchester Institute of Science and Technology achieved one of only two 5* research ratings, Lancaster taking the other. Average A-level scores of two As and a B illustrate the high demand for the second-placed London School of Economics.

New universities have the majority of business places, but Kingston is the only one in the top 20. De Montfort, Glamorgan, Northumbria, Nottingham Trent and Nottingham Trent are others with Excellent ratings for teaching. A high proportion of graduates go on to other courses, but the unemployment rate is still low.

Chemical Engineering

1	London, Imperial	**95.5**
2	Cambridge*	**95.3**
3	UMIST	**87.9**
4	Sheffield	**82.6**
5	Loughborough	**82.2**
6	Bath	**79.5**
7	London, UCL	**77.3**
8	Birmingham	**77.2**
9	Queen's, Belfast	**76.4**
10	Newcastle	**74.5**
11	Swansea	**71.8**
12	Nottingham	**69.5**
13	Edinburgh	**67.7**
14	Bradford	**61.0**
15	Leeds	**58.7**
16	Surrey	**58.6**
17	Strathclyde*	**56.9**
18	Heriot-Watt	**56.5**
19	Aston*	**48.2**
20	South Bank	**42.5**
21	Teesside	

TQA (England) 1995–96
Firsts and 2:1s: 55.5%
Employment: 74%
Further study: 13.6%
Unemployment: 7.2%

There is little to separate Imperial College, London, and Cambridge at the top of the chemical engineering table. Imperial is fractionally ahead as the only institution with a five-star rating for research, although Cambridge boasts the best score for teaching quality. Only two new universities offer a subject which requires expensive equipment, both of them at the bottom of the ranking.

With little more than 4,000 full-time undergraduates and tiny numbers taking part-time or sub-degree courses, chemical engineering is one of the smaller branches of engineering. Four out of five students have A levels or equivalent qualifications, and average entry grades are the highest for any engineering subject. This helps produce engineering's largest proportion of firsts and upper seconds but, while almost three-quarters of the students go straight into jobs, the unemployment rate could be lower.

Assessors said the overall standard was high in relation to international competition, with most courses offering industrial placements in the final year and leading to Chartered Engineer status. The size of departments varied widely (from 88 to 336 full-time students) but nowhere was the student–staff ratio more than 16:1. However, the drop-out rate was high in some universities.

Chemistry

1	Cambridge*	100.0
1	Oxford	100.0
3	London, Imperial	95.0
4	Edinburgh	93.1
5	Bristol	92.9
6	Durham	91.3
7	Nottingham	90.9
8	Leeds	89.6
9	Southampton	89.5
10	Strathclyde	88.9
11	St Andrews	87.6
12	Leicester	85.3
13	Manchester	84.2
14	Glasgow	83.4
15	Hull	82.3
16	Cardiff	80.8
17	Sheffield	74.2
18	Birmingham	73.8
19	Bangor	73.3
20	York	73.1

21–30
Aberdeen, Bath, Exeter, Keele, Liverpool, London, UCL, Newcastle, Reading, UMIST, Warwick
31–40
East Anglia, Heriot-Watt, London, King's, Loughborough, Nottingham Trent, Queen's, Belfast, Salford, Surrey, Sussex, Swansea
41–50
Abertay Dundee, De Montfort, Dundee, Essex, Kent, Lancaster, London, Queen Mary, Paisley, Robert Gordon, West of England
51–60
Anglia, Aston, Bradford, Brunel, Derby, Huddersfield, North London, Northumbria, Plymouth, Sunderland
61–73
Central Lancashire, Coventry, Glamorgan, Greenwich, Hertfordshire, Kingston, Liverpool John Moores, Manchester Metropolitan, Portsmouth, Sheffield Hallam, Staffordshire, Teesside, Wolverhampton

TQA (England) 1993–94
Firsts and 2:1s: 49.2%
Employment: 50.5%
Further study: 40.1%
Unemployment: 4.5%

More than 70 universities offer chemistry, but none seriously challenges Oxford and Cambridge, which are locked together at the top of the table. Both were among the 19 institutions rated Excellent for teaching quality and they registered the only 5-star grades for research. Imperial College remains the nearest challenger, as one of the seven universities on the next rung of the research ladder and with the highest entry grades outside Oxbridge.

Chemistry is old university territory, with only Nottingham Trent representing the former polytechnics in the first 40 places. With Robert Gordon, it was the only new university considered excellent at teaching, and only De Montfort did better than the bottom two categories for research.

Chemistry is by far the biggest of the physical sciences, with more than 13,000 full-time degree students. Almost nine out of ten undergraduates have A levels or their equivalent, but entry requirements are not far above the average for all subjects. More than half of the graduates go straight into jobs and the unemployment rate is low.

Civil Engineering

1	Bristol	93.2
2	London, Imperial	90.9
3	Cardiff	89.4
4	Nottingham	88.4
5	Queen's, Belfast	87.1
6	Swansea	86.0
7	Sheffield	81.1
8	Liverpool	80.7
9	UMIST	80.5
10	Edinburgh	80.3
11	Newcastle	79.5
11	Surrey	79.5
13	Loughborough	79.1
14	Dundee	77.6
15	London, UCL	76.9
16	Heriot-Watt	76.3
17	Strathclyde	75.2
18	Southampton	74.1
19	Birmingham	72.9
20	Glasgow	71.1

21–30
Abertay Dundee, Bath, Bradford, Brighton, City, Kingston, Leeds, Manchester, Plymouth, Salford
31–40
Aston, East London, Greenwich, Leeds Metropolitan , Liverpool John Moores, Napier, Oxford Brookes, Paisley, Portsmouth, Westminster
41–51
Coventry, Derby, Glamorgan, Hertfordshire, London, Queen Mary, Nottingham Trent, Sheffield Hallam, South Bank, Teesside, Ulster, Wolverhampton

TQA (England) 1996–98
Firsts and 2:1s: 44.8%
Employmentt:78.1%
Further study: 12.6%
Unemployment: 4.6%

Competition is intense at the head of the civil engineering table. Bristol takes top place despite being only one of eight universities with the best teaching quality score and not being the leader for entry standards or research. Eight English universities managed 22 points out of 24 for teaching, and both Cardiff and Swansea were rated Excellent in earlier assessments in Wales. None of the Scottish universities was rated better than Highly Satisfactory.

Unusually, all three of the universities rated internationally outstanding for research (Newcastle, Swansea and Imperial College, London) entered less than 95 per cent of their academics for assessment and do not receive full credit for their achievement as a result. Imperial also has the highest entry standards, but Bristol's strength across the board is decisive.

More than 50 universities have civil engineering degrees, almost half of them former polytechnics. Nearly four out of ten undergraduates are admitted with A levels or the equivalent, their grades close to the average for all subjects. Civil engineering may have an unglamorous image, but more than 11,000 students take full-time degree courses and the unemployment rate is one of the lowest.

Communcation Studies		
1	Warwick*	100.0
2	East Anglia	95.0
3	Sussex	89.9
4	Birmingham*	87.2
4	Westminster	87.2
6	West of England	86.1
7	Leeds	82.6
8	London, Goldsmiths'*	81.3
9	Leicester	78.5
10	Stirling	78.2
11	Ulster	74.3
12	Nottingham Trent	72.6
13	Liverpool John Moores	69.6
14	Glasgow Caledonian	67.5
15	Sunderland	65.1
16	Central Lancashire*	64.9
17	Bournemouth	63.7
18	Cardiff	63.3
19	Sheffield Hallam	62.5
20	Luton	62.3

21–30
Brunel, City, Coventry, De Montfort, Leeds Metropolitan, Middlesex, Napier, South Bank, Staffordshire, Wolverhampton
31–37
Anglia, East London, Greenwich, Lincolnshire & Humberside, London Guildhall, North London, Thames Valley

TQA (England) 1996–98
Firsts and 2:1s: 56.3%
Employed: 76%
Further study: 9.9%
Unemployment: 7.5%

Much-maligned media studies has been growing in popularity as openings in different types of media have increased. More than 9,000 students are taking full-time degrees either in media studies or communication studies, and three quarters of them find jobs within six months of graduation. The two subjects (which are virtually interchangeable) are mainly the preserve of the new universities, although seven of the top ten places are filled by older institutions. Warwick, East Anglia and Westminster share the best score for teaching quality, but Leeds has the highest entry standards. The grade 5 research ratings were spread more widely, with East London, Stirling and Sussex featuring, as well as the three top teaching universities. Top-placed Warwick was assessed at undergraduate level largely on its BA in film and literature.

Nearly three quarters of the students enter with A levels, but requirements are generally modest, some courses averaging less than three Ds. Only Cardiff, Leeds and Sussex average more than three Bs. Assessors found that courses varied from conventional academic degrees to advanced vocational training, often with new media in mind. Their main concern was a shortage of resources in a fast-changing area of study.

Computer Science

1	Cambridge	100.0
2	Warwick	98.3
3	York	97.7
4	Oxford	96.7
5	London, Imperial	96.3
6	Glasgow	93.2
7	Edinburgh	91.9
8	Manchester	89.7
9	Southampton	89.4
10	Exeter	87.9
11	Swansea	84.6
12	Kent	83.6
13	Bristol	78.4
14	Bath	78.3
15	St Andrews	77.5
16	London, UCL	75.7
17	Heriot-Watt	75.5
18	Lancaster	74.3
19	Nottingham	71.8
20	Dundee	71.6

21–30
Birmingham, Cardiff, Durham, Leeds, Newcastle, Queen's, Belfast, Sheffield, Strathclyde, Sussex, UMIST
31–40
Aberdeen, Aberystwyth, East Anglia, Essex, Liverpool, London, Queen Mary, London, Royal Holloway, Loughborough, Reading, Teesside
41–50
Aston, Bradford, Brunel, City, Hull, Keele, Leicester, London, King's, Stirling, Ulster
51–60
Brighton, Hertfordshire, Huddersfield, Oxford Brookes, Paisley, Plymouth, Robert Gordon, Sunderland, Surrey, West of England
61–70
Glamorgan, Glasgow Caledonian, Kingston, Leeds Metropolitan, Liverpool John Moores, Manchester Metropolitan, Middlesex, Northumbria, Nottingham Trent, Sheffield Hallam
71–80
Bournemouth, Central England, De Montfort, London Guildhall, Napier, Portsmouth, Salford, South Bank, Thames Valley, Westminster
81–93
Abertay Dundee, Anglia, Central Lancashire, Coventry, Derby, East London, Greenwich, Lincolnshire & Humberside, London, Goldsmiths', Luton, North London, Staffordshire, Wolverhampton

TQA (England) 1994
Firsts and 2:1s: 46.6%
Employment: 82.9%
Further study: 7.2%
Unemployment: 6.0%

Computing has seen the biggest increases in enrolment of any subject in recent years and is now second only to business studies in terms of size. The fact that more than four out of five graduates are in work within six months of leaving university helps explain its popularity, although there are plenty of subjects with unemployment rates of less than 6 per cent.

Cambridge tops the table with a perfect score: maximum points in the teaching and research assessments and an average of three As at A level at entry. Both Warwick and York also record top marks for both teaching and research, while Oxford, Glasgow and Imperial College, London, only lag because they entered fewer staff for assessment in research.

Drama, Dance and Cinematics	
1 Warwick	95.7
2 London, Royal Holloway	93.6
3 Hull	90.7
4 Lancaster	89.9
5 Bristol	88.4
6 Reading	87.6
7 Kent	85.9
8 Exeter	82.8
9 Loughborough	81.3
10 Manchester	78.7
11 Birmingham	78.5
12 London, Goldsmiths'	77.0
13 Glasgow*	72.4
14 Surrey	71.4
15 East Anglia	71.2
16 Manchester Metropolitan	70.8
17 Ulster	69.6
18 De Montfort*	69.4
19 Bournemouth*	66.2
20 Brunel*	64.7

21–30
Aberystwyth, Central Lancashire, Glamorgan, Liverpool John Moores, London, Queen Mary, Middlesex, North London, Northumbria, Nottingham Trent, Salford

31–38
Coventry, Derby, East London, Hertfordshire, Huddersfield, Sheffield Hallam, Staffordshire, Wolverhampton

TQA (England) 1996–98
Firsts and 2:1s: 67.1% (drama), 65.8% (cinematics)
Employment: 72.6% (drama), 69.7% (cinematics)
Further study: 13.8% (drama), 10.3% (cinematics)
Unemployment: 7.2% (drama), 11.3% (cinematics)

Only one institution – Royal Holloway, the London University college at Egham, Surrey – was rated internationally outstanding for research in this collection of performing arts, but it just missed out on full marks for teaching quality and, with it, top place in our table. That distinction went to Warwick, as the only one of the five universities with 24 points for teaching which also achieved a grade 5 for research. The other top teaching universities were Hull, Lancaster, Reading and Kent. There were no Excellent ratings in Scotland, but Glamorgan reached the standard in Wales.

The gulf in entry standards between new and old universities is particularly noticeable in this table: entrants to several of the older foundations averaged three Bs at A level, while only Sheffield Hallam, of the former polytechnics, averaged three Cs. Bristol had the highest entry standards.

Dance is not listed separately in the employment statistics, but the 3,000 students taking cinematics seem to have more trouble finding work than the 9,000 studying drama. Freelancing and periods of temporary employment are common throughout the performing arts, but the 11.3 per cent unemployment rate for cinematics is high.

East and South Asian Studies	
1 Cambridge*	100.0
2 Oxford	91.1
3 London, SOAS	89.9
4 Edinburgh*	84.5
5 Leeds	84.1
6 Durham	81.0
7 Hull	80.9
8 Westminster*	78.8
9 Sheffield	78.7
10 Stirling*	70.5

TQA (England) 1996–98

Firsts and 2:1s: 64% (Chinese 62.5%, Japanese 68.7%)

Employment: 63.2% (Chinese 76.1%, Japanese 77.8%)

Further study: 21.1% (Chinese 19.6%, Japanese 11.1%)

Unemployment: 0 (Chinese 2.2%, Japanese 3.7%)

The group of languages which make up South and East Asian studies produced high-scoring teaching quality assessment, in which all eight English universities were awarded 21, 22 or 23 points out of 24. The subjects have not been assessed separately in Scotland. Westminster – the only new university in the ranking – did well to join Cambridge, Leeds and London's School of Oriental and African Studies as top-rated for teaching. Research was more clear-cut, with Oxford the only university rated as internationally outstanding, although a relatively low proportion of the academic staff was entered for assessment.

Fewer than 1,500 students take the languages as their main subject, with Chinese and Japanese vying to be the largest recruiter. Other languages include Korean, Malay, Thai and Mongolian. Four out of five undergraduates enter with above-average A-level scores, so it is no surprise that degree classifications are also high. There is strong demand for graduates, and unemployment is consistently low. Assessors were impressed with the general quality of teaching, awarding top marks to almost half the sessions they observed.

Education

1	Oxford*	95.4
2	East Anglia*	92.7
3	Lancaster*	86.3
4	Birmingham	83.8
5	Sheffield*	81.9
6	Cambridge*	81.6
7	Cardiff	80.7
8	Durham	80.0
9	York	76.5
10	Manchester	76.1
11	Newcastle*	75.3
12	Warwick	75.1
13	Stirling	74.3
14	Bristol	71.5
15	Leeds*	70.0
16	London, King's	68.3
17	Exeter	68.2
18	Brighton	66.8
19	Ulster*	65.2
20	Sussex*	65.0

21–30

Bath, Central England, Keele, Leicester, London, Goldsmiths', Manchester Metropolitan, Nottingham, Paisley, Reading, Strathclyde

31–40

Anglia, Brunel, Hull, Kingston, Loughborough, Middlesex, North London, Oxford Brookes, Southampton, West of England

41–50

Bangor, De Montfort, Hertfordshire, Huddersfield, Liverpool, Nottingham Trent, Plymouth, Sheffield Hallam, Sunderland, Thames Valley

51–58

Central Lancashire, Derby, Greenwich, Leeds Metropolitan, Liverpool John Moores, Northumbria, Portsmouth, Wolverhampton

TQA (England) See below
Firsts and 2:1s: 52.8% (PE 40.8%)
Employment: 92.9% (PE 65.2%)
Further study: 1.0% (PE 21.6%)
Unemployment: 2.9% (PE 6.0%)

Education is unique among the subject tables because English universities are judged on the verdicts of Ofsted inspectors, rather than funding council or quality agency assessors. Only in Scotland and Wales does the normal system operate, and only Cardiff benefits to the extent of registering an excellent verdict for teaching quality.

Oxford's near-perfect teaching score secures top place, with East Anglia close behind. Brighton and Central England have the next-best records for teaching quality, but their research grades prevent them from challenging the leading universities in the table. King's College has the opposite problem, as the only institution rated internationally outstanding for research but relegated to 16th place by Ofsted scores. Entry requirements vary considerably, with Birmingham's average entry grades of three Bs at A level the highest of those universities with separate entry scores for the subject.

Education is the third-biggest subject at degree level. The BEd courses, which train the majority of primary school teachers, also feature among the subjects with the lowest entry grades. Employment levels, however, are predictably high, with only a slight dip in the prospects for the 5,000 physical education students.

Electrical and Electronic Engineering

1	Sheffield	95.0
2	Southampton	94.0
3	London, Imperial	93.8
4	Queen's, Belfast	92.4
5	London, UCL	91.5
6	Bristol	91.0
7	Surrey	88.9
8	Edinburgh	88.3
9	York	86.4
10	Birmingham	83.7
11	Strathclyde*	81.9
12	Essex	78.8
13	Cardiff	78.5
14	Heriot-Watt*	77.7
15	Leeds	77.3
15	UMIST	77.3
17	Hull	76.8
18	Nottingham	76.4
19	Loughborough	74.8
20	London, Queen Mary	73.3

21–30

Aston, Bath, Glasgow, Huddersfield, Liverpool, London, King's, Manchester, Newcastle, Reading, Swansea

31–40

Bangor, Bradford, Brunel, City, Glamorgan, Kent, Northumbria, Portsmouth, Sussex, Westminster

41–50

Brighton, De Montfort, Kingston, Manchester Metropolitan, North London, Nottingham Trent, South Bank, Teesside, West of England, Ulster

51–60

Bournemouth, Derby, Hertfordshire, Middlesex, Napier, Oxford Brookes, Paisley, Plymouth, Robert Gordon, Staffordshire

61–74

Anglia, Central England, Central Lancashire, Coventry, Dundee, East Anglia, East London, Glasgow Caledonian, Greenwich, Leeds Metropolitan, Liverpool John Moores, Salford, Sheffield Hallam, Sunderland

TQA (England) 1996–98

Firsts and 2:1s: 51.3% (electrical), 44.7% (electronic)

Employment: 74.8% (electrical), 76.7% (electronic).

Further study: 14.2% (electrical), 11.6% (electronic)

Unemployment: 7.6% (electrical), 8.3% (electronic)

Sheffield tops the table with a perfect teaching and research assessment record. Although ten English universities achieved maximum points for teaching quality, only Southampton also combined this with a 5* research rating, and it entered fewer academics for assessment than Sheffield. Three Scottish and three Welsh universities were rated Excellent for teaching, but only Edinburgh was considered internationally outstanding for research. Huddersfield was the only new university among those with 24 points for teaching quality, while Glamorgan was rated Excellent.

Now the biggest branch of engineering in terms of size, about half of the students, more in electrical engineering, come with qualifications other than A level. Yet it is electrical engineering which has the higher proportion of firsts and upper seconds, as well as a marginally better unemployment rate. About three-quarters of both sets of graduates go straight into jobs.

English

1	Oxford	99.7
2	London, UCL	99.1
3	Cambridge	97.2
4	Leeds	95.5
5	Birmingham	93.0
6	Nottingham	91.4
7	Sussex	91.3
8	Warwick	91.0
8	York	91.0
10	Bristol	89.9
10	London, Queen Mary	89.9
12	Durham	89.7
13	Liverpool	89.5
14	Sheffield	89.2
15	Leicester	89.1
15	Southampton	89.1
17	Lancaster	86.6
18	Newcastle	85.3
19	Edinburgh	84.4
20	Glasgow	84.2

21–30
Aberdeen, Aberystwyth, Cardiff, Dundee, London, King's, Manchester, Queen's, Belfast, St Andrews, Sheffield Hallam, Stirling

31–40
Anglia, East Anglia, Kent, Kingston, London, Royal Holloway, Northumbria, Oxford Brookes, Reading, Strathclyde, West of England

41–50
Bangor, Essex, Exeter, Hull, Keele, London, Goldsmiths', Loughborough, North London, Nottingham Trent, Swansea

51–60
De Montfort, Hertfordshire, Huddersfield, Lampeter, Liverpool John Moores, Manchester Metropolitan, Middlesex, Plymouth, Staffordshire, Ulster

61–71
Central England, Central Lancashire, Derby, Greenwich, Luton, Salford, Sunderland, Teesside, Thames Valley, Westminster, Wolverhampton

TQA (England) 1994–95
Firsts and 2:1s: 70.1%
Employment: 56.2%
Further study: 31.5%
Unemployment: 6.1%

Cambridge has the highest entry standards for English but misses the top two places in the table on its decision not to enter as many of its staff for research assessment as Oxford and UCL. Students looking for an excellent undergraduate programme have a wide choice, with all but Edinburgh in the top 20 recording the highest possible grading for teaching and research. A further 11 departments received the highest grading for teaching, including the new universities of Sheffield Hallam, Anglia, West of England, Kingston, Northumbria, Oxford Brookes and North London. Edinburgh received the next-best teaching grade of Highly Satisfactory.

The average A-level points score of undergraduates is 25 or above for all but four of the top 20: Queen Mary (23.6), Leicester (24.4), Southampton (24.3) and Lancaster (23.7). The proportion of English students gaining a first or upper second, was among the highest in any subject. Average entrance requirements are high and almost a third of all graduates go onto further study.

Environmental Science

1	East Anglia	95.5
2	Reading	93.6
3	Nottingham	91.6
4	Southampton	88.4
5	Lancaster	88.2
6	London, Imperial*	80.6
7	Plymouth	76.8
8	Stirling	75.3
9	Ulster	73.6
10	Bangor	68.9
11	Hertfordshire	67.5
12	Liverpool*	66.3
13	Newcastle	65.5
14	Aberystwyth*	64.5
15	London, Queen Mary*	62.1
16	Dundee*	61.9
17	Greenwich	61.1
18	Bradford	60.1
19	Manchester Metropolitan	58.0
20	Sheffield*	54.9

21–30
Anglia, Bournemouth, Kent, Liverpool John Moores, Luton, Middlesex, Northumbria, Salford, Sussex, Westminster

31–44
Central Lancashire, Coventry, Derby, East London, Huddersfield, Kingston, Lincolnshire & Humberside, Robert Gordon, Sheffield Hallam, Staffordshire, Sunderland, Teesside, West of England, Wolverhampton

TQA (England) 1994–95
Firsts and 2:1s: 48.2%
Employment: 63.8%
Further study: 20.9%
Unemployment: 7.8%

East Anglia and Reading share the highest teaching and research gradings in environmental science but UEA nudges ahead on the higher average A-level points of its students (23.1 compared to 21 for Reading). Plymouth's position at 7th comes despite the second-lowest A-level average of the top 20 universities of 14.5 and reflects an Excellent rating for its undergraduate programme and the wide-ranging success of its academics in the Research Assessment Exercise. It is one of four new universities to make the top 20, of which Hertfordshire and Greenwich were also graded Excellent for teaching.

Nottingham, Southampton and Lancaster won the next highest ratings for research behind the top two. Nearly half of all environmental science graduates were awarded a first or upper second class degrees in 1997–98. Two-thirds went straight into employment while one in five signed up for further study after graduating.

Assessors in England found a wide variety of courses, reflecting the different types of university offering the subject. Although the reports are now dated, in 1994 many of the interdisciplinary degrees, which amounted to 60 per cent of the total, were found to lack coherence.

Food Science

1	Nottingham	96.3
2	Reading	80.5
3	Surrey	77.8
4	Leeds	74.7
5	Queen's, Belfast	72.5
6	Robert Gordon	68.3
7	Glasgow Caledonian*	56.2
8	Oxford Brookes*	52.1
9	Huddersfield	51.6
10	Lincs & Humberside	50.2
11	Manchester Metropolitan	46.5
12	Bournemouth	44.2
13	South Bank	42.4
14	North London*	41.7
15	Teesside*	37.5
16	Leeds Metropolitan*	34.3

TQA (England) 1996–98
Firsts and 2:1s: 58.3%
Employment: 77.6%
Further study: 8.9%
Unemployment: 5.6%

Nottingham has the most impressive record in the subject by some way with a 5-star rating for research and 23 out of 24 points in the teaching assessment. Reading and Surrey are very close with the same scores in research and Reading just one point ahead in teaching with 22 out of 24. Only Leeds has the same top grading for research as Nottingham but it entered far fewer of its academics for the assessment process.

Students at Surrey pip those at Nottingham for the highest actual A-level points score, with 19.7 compared to 19.5 and followed by Leeds (19) and Reading (17.4). The leading new university, Robert Gordon, claims sixth place on the basis of its Excellent rating for teaching and Glasgow Caledonian is not far behind with a Highly Satisfactory grade.

Nearly four out of five graduates in food science find employment directly after leaving university. Almost a third of entrants to the course arrive with alternative qualifications to A levels. Assessors in England were concerned at the high drop-out rate on more than half of the courses: more than 20 per cent of students failed to progress to the next stage of their degree.

French		
1	Cambridge	95.5
2	Oxford	87.6
3	London, UCL	87.0
4	Durham	86.8
5	Aberdeen*	85.0
6	Glasgow	84.8
7	Leeds	84.6
8	Warwick	84.0
8	Exeter	84.0
10	Sussex	83.8
11	London, Queen Mary	83.7
12	St Andrews	82.3
13	London, King's	80.3
13	Sheffield	80.3
15	London, Royal Holloway	79.6
16	Newcastle	79.2
17	Bristol	78.9
18	Liverpool	78.6
19	Edinburgh	78.5
20	Strathclyde	77.7

21–30

Cardiff, Hull, Keele, Leicester, Manchester, Nottingham, Queen's, Belfast, Reading, Stirling, Westminster

31–40

Aberystwyth, Aston, Birmingham, Heriot-Watt, Lancaster, Oxford Brookes, Portsmouth, Southampton, Swansea, Ulster

41–50

Anglia, Bangor, Central Lancashire, Coventry, East Anglia, Kingston, Lampeter, London Guildhall, Manchester Metropolitan, West of England

51–63

Bradford, Huddersfield, Kent, Liverpool John Moores, London, Goldsmiths', Middlesex, North London, Nottingham Trent, Sunderland, Surrey, Thames Valley, UMIST, Wolverhampton

TQA (England) 1995–96
Firsts and 2:1s: 64.0%
Employment: 64.1%
Further study: 26.1%
Unemployment: 4.4%

Cambridge claims top spot in French with research of international quality, a high score for teaching and the largest A-level points score of its undergraduates. Oxford and UCL also had 5-star research, although Oxford entered fewer staff for assessment than the other two. Nottingham was the only other university to receive a 5-star research assessment but missed the top 20 because of a low score of 16 out of 24 for teaching, although this rating dates to the last review of French in 1995.

Teaching was rated better than Cambridge at Queen Mary, London in 11th place and at the unplaced Westminster and Portsmouth, where low research scores affected their overall position. Both Aberdeen and Glasgow were judged to have Excellent teaching under the Scottish assessment system.

French has one of the lowest unemployment rates of modern language subjects, with fewer than one in 20 of 1998 graduates without a job six months on. It is still by far the most popular language for a first degree, with more than 4,000 full-time undergraduates, nine out of ten of whom enter with A levels or equivalent qualifications.

General Engineering

1	Cambridge	99.9
2	Oxford	99.6
3	Strathclyde*	92.5
4	London, Imperial*	92.3
5	Durham	87.6
6	Warwick	77.9
7	Leicester	74.9
8	Lancaster	73.9
9	Brunel	71.6
10	Ulster	66.3
11	Liverpool John Moores*	63.8
12	Southampton*	63.7
13	Exeter	63.1
14	Bradford	61.9
15	Sussex*	59.7
16	Cranfield*	57.3
17	Aberdeen*	55.7
18	Wolverhampton*	53.1
19	Sheffield Hallam*	51.3
20	Hertfordshire*	49.8

21–34

Bournemouth, Central England, Central Lancashire, Coventry, De Montfort, Greenwich, Leeds Metropolitan, Lincolnshire & Humberside, Liverpool, London, Queen Mary, Luton, Oxford Brookes, Staffordshire, Sunderland

TQA (England) 1996–98
Firsts and 2:1s: 45.7%
Employment: 77.2%
Further study: 11.1%
Unemployment: 7.1%

Cambridge and Oxford are hard to separate at the head of the table with equally impressive records for teaching and research. Cambridge squeaks ahead on the slightly higher A-level score of its undergraduates. Both Imperial and Southampton received the same high grading for teaching as the top two universities with 23 out of 24 and the highest A-level points score (30, equivalent to straight As) came at Strathclyde. Grades of 22 for teaching were awarded to Durham, Lancaster and Brunel, with 21 given to Warwick and Sheffield Hallam. The highest-placed new university, Liverpool John Moores, owes its 11th place to a grading of five for research, placing it on a par for research with Strathclyde, Imperial and Durham. Cambridge and Oxford recorded 5-star ratings.

More than 10,000 undergraduates take general engineering courses, rather than specialising. Employment prospects are close to the norm for all engineering courses, with more than three-quarters going straight into jobs.

Geography

1	Cambridge	100.0
2	Durham	98.7
3	Bristol	98.4
4	London, UCL	96.6
5	Sheffield	94.0
6	Leeds	93.1
7	Oxford	92.0
7	Southampton	92.0
9	Nottingham	90.9
10	East Anglia*	90.7
11	Edinburgh	90.5
12	Birmingham	87.7
13	Manchester	87.6
14	Exeter	87.1
15	Lancaster	86.2
16	Aberystwyth	84.3
17	London, King's	84.2
18	Swansea	84.1
19	Reading	83.1
20	Glasgow	82.6

21–30

Aberdeen, Coventry, London School of Economics, London, Queen Mary, London, Royal Holloway, Newcastle, Plymouth, Portsmouth, St Andrews, Strathclyde

31–40

Dundee, Hull, Lampeter, Leicester, Liverpool, London, SOAS, Loughborough, Oxford Brookes, Queen's, Belfast, Sussex

41–50

Anglia, Brighton, Huddersfield, Kent, Kingston, Liverpool John Moores, Middlesex, Northumbria, Nottingham Trent, Staffordshire

51–64

Brunel, Cardiff, Central Lancashire, Derby, Greenwich, London Guildhall, Luton, Manchester Metropolitan, North London, Salford, Sunderland, Ulster, Westminster, Wolverhampton

TQA (England) 1994–95
Firsts and 2:1s: 61.4%
Employment: 62.3%
Further study: 23.7%
Unemployment: 4.7%

There is little to call between the top four geography departments in the UK. Each has the highest ratings for teaching and research. Their positions reflect differences in the average A-level points of their undergraduates, ranging from 29.4 at Cambridge to 24.5 at UCL in fourth place. The only other department with a 5-star research rating is Edinburgh but its 11th place reflects an assessment of Highly Satisfactory for teaching. All the other universities in the top 20 received an assessment of Excellent for undergraduate programmes, along with eight others: Aberdeen, Coventry (highest-placed new university in 22nd position), Queen Mary, London, Plymouth, Portsmouth, St Andrews, Strathclyde and Oxford Brookes.

Sheffield, Leeds and Southampton all have grade 5 research ratings. Two departments received grades of 5 for research but miss the top 20 because teaching was Satisfactory: Royal Holloway and Newcastle. The second-highest A-level profile of undergraduates is found at Oxford (more than two As and a B each on average). Just 4.7 per cent of geography graduates were unemployed six months on, although the proportion was slightly higher (5.1 per cent) where the subject was studied purely as a physical science.

Geology

1	Cambridge*	100.0
1	Oxford	100.0
3	Newcastle*	98.7
4	Edinburgh	95.4
5	Leeds	95.2
6	Liverpool	90.4
7	Durham	89.3
8	London, UCL	88.1
9	Manchester	87.2
10	London, Royal Holloway	84.3
11	London, Imperial	83.3
12	Southampton	82.8
13	Birmingham	80.8
14	Bristol	80.7
15	Reading	80.3
16	Glasgow	80.1
17	Queen's, Belfast	75.5
18	Cardiff	73.3

19–33

Aberdeen, Anglia, Derby, Exeter, Greenwich, Keele, Kingston, Leicester, Luton, Oxford Brookes, Plymouth, Portsmouth, St Andrews, Staffordshire, Sunderland

TQA (England) 1994–95
Firsts and 2:1s: 52.6%
Employment: 56.5%
Further study: 31.4%
Unemployment: 6.2%

Oxford and Cambridge's equal excellence in teaching and research ensure they share top place in the geology table. They were the only universities considered internationally outstanding in the last research assessment exercise.

Excellent teaching was recorded at all the top 20 departments except Bristol and Cardiff, where it was Satisfactory. Three new universities – Derby, Kingston and Plymouth – also achieved Excellent ratings.

More than nine out of ten geology students enter courses with A levels or their equivalent. However, average entry standards varied from more than two As and a B at Cambridge to little more than the equivalent of three Es at Luton. Over 4,000 students are taking the subject at degree level; numbers have been rising again following the closure of several departments in the 1980s.

The assessment of teaching in England is now dated, but even in 1995 geology departments were complimented on their 'robust' links with industry. Many academic staff had recent industrial experience and were active in research and consultancy. Completion rates were good and the previously low numbers of female students gradually increasing.

German

1	Cambridge	91.7
2	Nottingham	89.5
3	London, UCL	85.2
4	Warwick	84.8
5	Oxford	84.2
6	Exeter	83.5
7	Swansea	81.2
8	St Andrews	79.2
9	London, Queen Mary	78.9
10	London, King's	78.2
11	Durham	77.7
12	Manchester	75.7
13	Leeds	72.6
13	Leicester	72.6
15	Edinburgh*	72.5
16	Glasgow	72.3
17	Bristol	72.1
18	Newcastle	71.5
19	Birmingham	71.1
20	Sheffield	71.0

21–30

Aberdeen, Cardiff, Hull, Lancaster, Liverpool, Queen's, Belfast, Reading, Stirling, Strathclyde, Sussex

31–40

Aberystwyth, Aston, Central Lancashire, Heriot-Watt, Keele, London, Royal Holloway, Manchester Metropolitan, Southampton, Ulster, West of England

41–50

Bangor, Coventry, East Anglia, Kent, Lampeter, Liverpool John Moores, London, Goldsmiths', Middlesex, Portsmouth, Surrey

51–57

Bradford, Huddersfield, Nottingham Trent, Oxford Brookes, Sunderland, UMIST, Wolverhampton

TQA (England) 1995-96
Firsts and 2:1s: 61.7%
Employment: 70.1%
Further study: 19.5%
Unemployment: 4.2%

Exeter was the only university in England to be awarded maximum points for teaching quality, while Swansea was rated as Excellent under the Welsh system. But neither could match the 5-star research performance of Cambridge, Nottingham, Oxford and King's College, London. Cambridge takes top place in our table by virtue of the highest entry grades, its entrants averaging almost three As at A level.

Nearly 60 universities offer German, but the total number of students is now below 2,000, even including certificate and diploma courses. Three quarters of the students are female and nine out of ten enter with A levels or equivalent qualifications. Old universities monopolise the top 30 places, despite good showings in the teaching assessments by Central Lancashire, Coventry, Portsmouth and the West of England, all of which registered 21 points out of 24.

Those who do opt for German enjoy enviable employment prospects, only 4 per cent taking longer than six months to find a job. The teaching assessment extended to Dutch and Scandinavian languages, as related languages, and the assessors were impressed with the general standard of provision.

History

1	Cambridge	100.0
2	Warwick	98.3
3	London, King's	97.9
4	London, UCL	97.3
5	Oxford	96.8
6	London, LSE	95.6
7	Durham	95.4
8	Sheffield	94.9
9	Birmingham	94.1
10	St Andrews	91.3
11	Edinburgh	89.5
12	Hull	89.0
12	Liverpool	89.0
14	London, Royal Holloway	88.9
15	Lancaster	88.4
16	York	88.2
17	Queen's, Belfast	86.1
18	Leicester	85.6
19	Swansea	81.3
20	Bristol	79.7

21–30
Aberdeen, East Anglia, Glasgow, Leeds, London, SOAS, Manchester, Nottingham, Stirling, Strathclyde, Sussex

31–40
Cardiff, Dundee, Exeter, Keele, Kent, London, Queen Mary, London, SEES, Newcastle, Southampton, Ulster

41–50
Aberystwyth, Bangor, Central Lancashire, De Montfort, Essex, London, Goldsmiths', Northumbria, Oxford Brookes, Reading, Sheffield Hallam

51–60
Huddersfield, Kingston, Lampeter, North London, Nottingham Trent, Portsmouth, Teesside, Westminster, West of England, Wolverhampton

61–70
Glamorgan, Hertfordshire, Liverpool John Moores, London Guildhall, Luton, Manchester Metropolitan, Middlesex, Staffordshire, Sunderland, Thames Valley

71–77
Anglia, Brunel, Derby, East London, Greenwich, Leeds Metropolitan, Plymouth

TQA (England) 1993–94
Firsts and 2:1s: 66.7%
Employment: 56.5%
Further study: 29.9%
Unemployment: 6.0%

History was one of the first subjects to be assessed for teaching quality, and there have been big changes in some departments. Almost 20 universities were rated as Excellent, but some of the most popular courses, such as those at Bristol and Nottingham, were only Satisfactory. Four institutions scored maximum points for both teaching and research: King's College, University College, Cambridge and Warwick.

Average entrance qualifications of almost three As at A level tip the balance in favour of Cambridge. No new university features in the top 40 places. None was rated as Excellent for teaching, although Oxford Brookes, Sheffield Hallam and Luton did well in the 1996 research assessments.

History remains one of the most popular subjects, despite the relatively low proportion of graduates going straight into jobs. Almost a third go on to higher degrees or professional courses.

History of Art

1	London, Courtauld	95.3
1	London, UCL	95.3
3	London, SOAS	91.6
4	Cambridge*	89.6
5	Leeds	86.1
6	Nottingham	84.2
7	Reading	82.5
8	Essex	80.4
9	Warwick	80.0
10	East Anglia	79.6
11	Sussex	79.3
12	Edinburgh	77.8
13	Kent	77.0
14	Manchester	76.9
15	Birmingham*	75.6
16	St Andrews	74.9
17	Oxford Brookes	73.1
18	Glasgow	72.3
19	Leicester	70.5
20	Middlesex*	70.2

21–30
Aberdeen, Brighton, Bristol, Central England, De Montfort, Derby, Manchester Metropolitan, Northumbria, Southampton, York

31–37
Aberystwyth, Central Lancashire, Kingston, London, Goldsmiths', Plymouth, Sheffield Hallam, Staffordshire

TQA (England) 1996–98
Firsts and 2:1s: 69.7%
Employment: 61.3%
Further study: 22.8%
Unemployment: 6.7%

Two London University colleges tie for top place in the history of art table, with the Courtauld Institute boasting the better research record and University College rated more highly for teaching. Three institutions are considered internationally outstanding for research (the Courtauld, Cambridge and Sussex) but only UCL and the School of Oriental and African Studies achieved maximum points for teaching quality.

Oxford Brookes, which was only one point off a perfect teaching score and did well in the last research assessments, is the top-placed new university. Middlesex also makes the top 20, squeezing out older rivals such as Bristol, where entry standards are among the highest in Britain.

Fewer than 4,000 undergraduates take degrees in the history of art, although another 1,000 were enrolled on lower-level part-time courses in 1998.

Iberian Languages

1	Cambridge	91.7
2	Hull	85.9
3	London, King's	85.4
4	Aberdeen*	84.9
5	London, Queen Mary	84.5
6	Birmingham	83.7
7	Liverpool	82.5
8	St Andrews	81.5
9	Bristol	81.2
10	Leeds	78.1
11	Sheffield	77.3
12	Glasgow*	75.6
13	Queen's, Belfast	74.8
13	Swansea	74.8
15	Newcastle	73.0
16	Edinburgh	72.5
17	Oxford*	71.7
18	Exeter	70.5
19	Manchester*	69.8
20	Strathclyde*	69.4

21–30

Aberystwyth, Cardiff, Central Lancashire, Coventry, Heriot-Watt, London, UCL, Manchester Metropolitan, Nottingham, Southampton, West of England

31–45

Bradford, Durham, Huddersfield, Liverpool John Moores, London, Goldsmiths', Luton, Middlesex, Nottingham Trent, Portsmouth, Stirling, Sunderland, Surrey, Ulster, Westminster, Wolverhampton

TQA (England) 1995–96
Firsts and 2:1s: 69.6% (Spanish)
Employment: 60.7%
Further study: 25.4%
Unemployment: 6.3%

Hull was the only English university to record maximum points for teaching quality, although Swansea was rated Excellent in Wales. However, Cambridge, with a 5-star rating for research and the highest average entry standards, took top place with something to spare. Queen Mary, London, was the only institution to approach Cambridge's teaching score.

No new university appears in the top 20, but good marks for teaching quality leave the West of England, Central Lancashire, Coventry and Manchester Metropolitan on the fringes of the leading group. Aberdeen is the top-placed Scottish university.

Despite the growing popularity of Spanish as an alternative to French in schools, only 1,400 take the subject at degree level, with another 400 taking Portuguese or Latin American studies. Although six out of ten graduates find jobs within six months of leaving university, employment prospects are not as good as in French or German.

Italian		
1	Cambridge	95.5
2	Oxford	84.3
3	London, UCL	81.2
4	London, Royal Holloway	80.1
5	Birmingham	78.6
6	Exeter	77.7
7	Bristol	76.8
7	Reading	76.8
9	Glasgow*	75.6
10	Strathclyde*	74.9
11	Edinburgh*	74.6
12	Hull	74.0
12	Oxford Brookes*	71.0
14	Lancaster	69.7
15	Leeds	69.0
16	Cardiff	67.8
17	St Andrews*	66.7
18	Warwick	66.2
19	Swansea	66.0
20	Leicester	63.7

21–31

Aberystwyth, Central Lancashire, Coventry, Durham, Kent, Liverpool John Moores, Manchester, Manchester Metropolitan, Queen's, Belfast, Sussex, Westminster

TQA (England) 1995–96
Firsts and 2:1s: 71.2%
Employment: 74.1%
Further study: 12.3%
Unemployment: 8.6%

Only 31 universities offer Italian, with Cambridge well ahead of the rest in our table. Unusually, no institution was awarded more than 22 points out of 24 for teaching quality, although Swansea was rated as Excellent under the Welsh system. Cambridge was one of the eight top scorers for teaching and shared the best research record with University College, London. Leeds also achieved a 5-star research rating, but entered fewer academics for assessment.

Oxford Brookes, one of the other top scorers for teaching, is the only new university in the top 20. Student numbers are small in several of the universities: only 474 were taking the language at degree level in 1998, although many more included Italian in combined degree programmes. Assessors found some cases of overcrowding, but were generally satisfied with learning resources, which generally included satellite television. Most students have no previous knowledge of the language, but there is a high completion rate.

Land and Property Management

1	Reading	**83.7**
2	Cambridge*	**75.6**
2	Liverpool John Moores*	**75.6**
4	Oxford Brookes*	**75.4**
5	De Montfort	**67.5**
6	Kingston*	**64.2**
7	Leeds Metropolitan*	**61.2**
8	West of England*	**61.1**
9	Plymouth*	**58.0**
10	Northumbria	**57.1**
11	Sheffield Hallam	**54.8**
12	City*	**53.4**
13	Greenwich*	**52.6**
14	Salford*	**49.2**
15	Portsmouth*	**48.7**
16	Anglia*	**47.9**
17	South Bank	**47.3**
18	Westminster	**44.8**
19	Central England	**39.4**
20	Staffordshire*	**36.6**

TQA (England) 1996–98
Firsts and 2:1s: 52.7%
Employment: 78.2%
Further study: 7.5%
Unemployment: 8.9%

Even Cambridge cannot match Reading at the head of the land and property management table. Reading's superior research rating and high entry standards prove decisive. Cambridge does not list entry grades for the subject separately so its score is produced from the other two indicators.

Only Kingston scored maximum points for teaching quality, but it did not enter academics in the relevant research category. All but four of the universities in the ranking are former polytechnics. Liverpool John Moores is the top-placed of them, tying with Cambridge. Entry standards are generally modest and research ratings were low in 1996, no university reaching the top two grades. Completion rates are generally higher at the universities with more demanding entrance requirements.

Only about 2,000 students are taking land and property management at degree or diploma level, although the subjects are often included in wider environmental programmes. Recession in the property and construction markets reduced the demand for places during the 1990s. Over three quarters of graduates go straight into jobs, but the proportion still out of work six months after leaving university is the highest of the business subjects.

Law

1	Cambridge	**100.0**
2	Oxford	**99.8**
3	London, King's	**98.3**
4	Manchester	**98.0**
5	London, LSE	**97.9**
5	London, UCL	**97.9**
7	Nottingham	**95.4**
8	Sheffield	**94.6**
9	Warwick	**93.5**
10	Leicester	**91.7**
11	Durham	**91.3**
12	Bristol	**90.7**
13	Liverpool	**88.3**
14	Queen's, Belfast	**87.5**
15	Essex	**86.7**
16	London, SOAS	**85.9**
17	East Anglia	**85.2**
18	Edinburgh	**85.0**
19	Aberdeen	**84.2**
20	Strathclyde	**84.0**

21–30

Birmingham, Brunel, Cardiff, Dundee, Glasgow, Keele, Leeds, London, Queen Mary, Newcastle, Southampton

31–40

Aberystwyth, Exeter, Hull, Kent, Lancaster, Northumbria, Oxford Brookes, Reading, Sussex, West of England

41–50

City, De Montfort, Kingston, Manchester Metropolitan, Nottingham Trent, Plymouth, Sheffield Hallam, Swansea, Ulster, Westminster

51–60

Central Lancashire, Coventry, East London, Glamorgan, Hertfordshire, Huddersfield, Leeds Metropolitan, Liverpool John Moores, London Guildhall, Staffordshire

71–83

Anglia, Bournemouth, Central England, Derby, Greenwich, Lincolnshire & Humberside, Luton, Middlesex, North London, South Bank, Teesside, Thames Valley, Wolverhampton

TQA (England) 1993–94
Firsts and 2:1s: 54%
Employment: 31.4%
Further study: 59.9%
Unemployment: 3.0%

Oxford and Cambridge are the only universities considered internationally outstanding for research, as well as being rated Excellent for teaching, but Cambridge's students are slightly better qualified. A total of 20 universities, including three former polytechnics – West of England, Northumbria and Oxford Brookes – were among the excellent teaching institutions. In Scotland and Wales, however, there were no Excellent ratings, although five Scottish universities were rated Highly Satisfactory, while in Wales, all four institutions were given satisfactory grades.

Entry standards in law are notoriously high, but entrants at some new universities averaged only three Ds and one in five arrives without A levels or their equivalent. With more than 34,000 students taking the subject at degree level, law remains one of the most popular.

Because of the requirement for further professional training for solicitors and barristers, less than a third of undergraduates go straight into jobs. But with six out of ten taking additional courses on graduation, the unemployment rate is still among the lowest in higher education.

Linguistics		
1	London, Queen Mary*	94.7
2	Cambridge*	94.3
3	Lancaster	91.3
4	London, UCL	88.9
5	Edinburgh*	86.9
6	Sheffield*	86.1
7	Newcastle	85.4
8	Oxford*	85.2
9	Manchester	84.2
10	York	84.0
11	Durham*	83.6
12	Sussex	83.1
13	Thames Valley	80.9
14	Essex	77.0
15	London, SOAS	74.5
16	Reading	66.8
17	Hertfordshire*	65.2
18	Bangor	65.0
19	East Anglia	63.3
20	Luton	58.4

21–27

Brighton, East London, Leeds, Southampton, UMIST, Westminster, Wolverhampton

TQA (England) 1995–96
Firsts and 2:1s: 61.4%
Employment: 59.6%
Further study: 26.0%
Unemployment: 6.6%

There is little to choose between Queen Mary, London, and Cambridge at the top of the table for linguistics. Cambridge has the better research record, but Queen Mary's superior teaching quality grade makes the difference since neither has separately listed A-level averages. Unusually, no institution achieved maximum grades for either teaching or research, leaving most of the 27 universities which offer linguistics within three points of each other in the teaching quality assessment.

Thames Valley is the best-placed new university, matching Cambridge for both teaching and research grades, but the subject has been a victim of the cutbacks required as part of the university's survival plan. Hertfordshire and Luton also made the top 20 from the new university sector.

Fewer than 2,000 students take the subject either at degree or diploma level, eight out of ten of them arriving with A levels, although twice that number are on programmes including linguistics. More than a quarter go on to further study, but the unemployment level is relatively high compared with those graduating in particular languages. Assessors found that students were generally satisfied with their courses.

Materials Technology

1	Oxford	**95.8**
2	Cambridge*	**94.8**
3	London, Imperial	**91.2**
4	Sheffield	**85.8**
5	Swansea	**83.9**
6	Manchester	**80.7**
7	Birmingham	**76.4**
7	Liverpool	**76.4**
9	UMIST	**76.0**
10	Loughborough	**73.1**
11	Bath	**72.3**
12	Nottingham	**71.0**
13	London, Queen Mary	**70.8**
14	Surrey	**70.7**
15	Sheffield Hallam	**64.2**
16	Leeds	**63.5**
17	Manchester Metropolitan	**60.8**
18	Brunel	**57.7**
19	Nottingham Trent	**55.4**
20	Exeter*	**51.4**

21–23
De Montfort, London Guildhall, North London

TQA (England) 1996–98
Firsts and 2:1s: 60.5%
Employment: 57.8%
Further study: 31.3%
Unemployment: 4.7%

Few subjects can match the research strength of materials technology, where eight of the 20 universities assessed in 1996 were considered internationally outstanding and all but four finished in the top three categories out of seven. Grades for teaching quality did not reach the same peak, although only two universities scored less than 20 marks out of 24.

Ironically, the only English institution to record top marks for teaching – Imperial College, London – was also the only one of the top nine to miss out on a 5* rating for research. Swansea was rated as Excellent under the different Welsh system. Oxford pips Cambridge to first place in the table with average entry grades close to three As at A level – by far the highest for materials technology. Cambridge does not have separately-listed grades, as the subject forms part of a wider group. Sheffield Hallam is the highest-placed new university, although Manchester Metropolitan and Nottingham Trent also feature in the top 20.

A high proportion of students go on to further study, but fewer than one in 20 is out of work six months after leaving university.

Mechanical, Aeronautical and Manufacturing Engineering

1	Bath*	90.5
2	London, Imperial	88.8
3	Nottingham	87.2
4	UMIST*	83.1
5	Loughborough	82.0
6	Bristol	81.2
7	Queen's, Belfast	80.7
8	Southampton	80.4
9	Cranfield*	76.9
10	Cardiff*	75.2
11	Glasgow*	74.7
12	Liverpool	71.4
13	Bradford*	71.3
14	Manchester	67.5
15	Birmingham	64.3
16	Hull*	63.7
17	Brunel	62.6
18	Kingston	62.3
19	London, Queen Mary*	59.7
20	London, King's*	58.5

21–30

Central England, City, Coventry, De Montfort, Hertfordshire, Salford, Sheffield Hallam, Strathclyde, Sunderland, Swansea

31–45

Anglia, Bournemouth, Derby, East London, Huddersfield, Leeds Metropolitan , Lincolnshire & Humberside, Liverpool John Moores, Middlesex, Northumbria, Nottingham Trent, Plymouth, South Bank, Staffordshire, Teesside

TQA (England) 1996–98

Firsts and 2:1s: 52.9% (aeronautical), 50.9% (production)

Employment: 26.0 % (aeronautical), 22.8% (production)

Further study: 70.0% (aeronautical), 66.7% (production)

Unemployment: 4.0% (aeronautical), 7.0% (production)

The courses assessed under this heading focus mainly on aeronautical or manufacturing engineering, but includes some with a mechanical title. None of the courses covered in the earlier assessment of mechanical engineering were revisited. To add to the confusion, manufacturing degrees often go under the rubric of production engineering. See also *General Engineering*, page 56, and *Mechanical Engineering*, page 69.

There is little separating Bath and Imperial College, London, at the top of the table. Both are rated internationally outstanding for research, as are Queen's, Belfast, and King's College, London. Bath was rated as Excellent for teaching quality under mechanical engineering, whereas Imperial was restricted to 22 points out of 24 in the later assessment.

Grades were widely spread in this group of subjects. Nottingham and Kingston (the sole new university in the top 20) were the only institutions to be awarded maximum points for teaching quality. Nationally, at least two thirds of the graduates go on to further study to meet professional requirements but, particularly for the 3,000 aeronautical engineering students, employment prospects are bright.

Mechanical Engineering

1	Bath	95.6
2	Sheffield	93.4
3	Cardiff	92.4
4	Nottingham	89.6
5	Bristol	88.9
6	Cranfield*	87.3
7	Strathclyde	84.8
8	Manchester	82.7
9	London, Imperial	82.2
10	Leeds	80.5
11	UMIST	77.1
12	Queen's, Belfast	76.3
13	Southampton	75.8
14	London, UCL	75.1
15	Reading	74.9
16	Glasgow	71.4
17	Liverpool	70.8
18	Loughborough	70.6
19	Birmingham	67.8
20	Edinburgh	67.1

21–30

Bradford, Brunel, Coventry, Hull, London, King's, London, Queen Mary, Manchester Metropolitan, Newcastle, Surrey, Swansea

31–40

City, De Montfort, Derby, Greenwich, Heriot-Watt, Lancaster, Plymouth, Portsmouth, Robert Gordon, Salford

40–50

Abertay Dundee, Aston, Brighton, Huddersfield, Liverpool John Moores, Middlesex, Northumbria, Nottingham Trent, Sheffield Hallam, Sussex

51–60

Central England, Central Lancashire, Hertfordshire, Kingston, Napier, Oxford Brookes, South Bank, Staffordshire, Sunderland, Teesside, Ulster, Westminster, West of England

TQA (England) 1993-94
Firsts and 2:1s: 46.7%
Employment: 33.3%
Further study: 57.7%
Unemployment: 5.4%

Bath's all-round strength gives the university first place for mechanical engineering, one of the first subjects in England to be assessed for teaching quality. The only one of the top eight universities to be rated internationally outstanding for research, Bath boasts one of 11 Excellent teaching quality grades, while its entry standards are exceeded only by Bristol and Imperial College, London. Leeds has the best research record, as the only one of the top-scorers to enter all its academics for assessment.

Almost half of the universities offering mechanical engineering are former polytechnics, although only Coventry and Manchester Metropolitan were considered Excellent for teaching. The open-access policies pursued by many of the new universities is reflected in the fact that more than a third of the entrants are admitted without A levels or equivalent qualifications. Several courses have average entry standards of below 10 UCAS points, the equivalent of two Ds and an E at A level.

Only electronic engineering, of the different branches of the discipline, has marginally more students. But the subject still offers better employment prospects than most subjects, with more than half of all graduates going on to other courses.

See also *Electrial and Electronic Engineering*, page 51 and *General Engineering*, page 56.

Middle Eastern and African Studies	
1 Birmingham	**96.2**
2 Cambridge*	**95.3**
3 Oxford	**88.2**
4 Edinburgh*	**85.0**
5 Durham	**84.4**
6 London, SOAS	**79.1**
7 Manchester	**73.9**
8 Leeds	**65.2**
9 Exeter*	**52.2**

TQA (England) 1996–98
Firsts and 2:1s: 68.1% (Mid East), 68.0% (African)
Employment: 61.9% (Mid East), 57.1% (African)
Further study: 28.6% (Mid East), 14.3% (African)
Unemployment: 9.5% (Mid East), 9.5% (Mid East)

Only nine universities offer Middle Eastern or African studies, but there is still a wide range of entry standards. Oxford entrants averaged the equivalent of an A and two Bs at A level in 1998, whereas at Leeds the average was little more than three Ds. Birmingham tops the table as the only university rated internationally outstanding for research and tying with second-placed Cambridge for the best teaching quality grade. No university was awarded less than 20 points out of 24 for teaching quality and only Leeds managed less than a grade 4 in the last research assessment exercise.

Middle Eastern studies is the bigger of two small subjects, in terms of student numbers. Fewer than 100 students were taking African languages, literature or culture at degree level in 1998, compared with just over 500 for Middle Eastern subjects. The vast majority – all in the case of African studies – come with A levels or their equivalent, and a high proportion graduate with first or upper-second class degrees.

Music

1	London, SOAS*	100.0
2	London, King's	98.2
3	Cambridge	96.3
4	Birmingham	94.8
5	Nottingham	94.7
6	Sheffield	93.2
7	Leeds	93.0
8	York	92.7
9	Keele*	90.7
10	Manchester	88.8
11	Surrey	88.0
12	Queen's, Belfast	87.9
13	Southampton	87.6
14	City	84.7
15	London, Goldsmiths'	83.5
15	Sussex	83.5
17	Lancaster	83.4
18	Edinburgh	81.3
19	Oxford	81.2
20	Liverpool	79.5

21–30

Bangor, Bristol, Cardiff, Central England, Durham, Exeter, Glasgow, Huddersfield, London, Royal Holloway, Ulster

31–45

Anglia, Coventry, Derby, East Anglia, Hertfordshire, Hull, Kingston, Middlesex, Napier, Newcastle, Northumbria, Oxford Brookes, Reading, Thames Valley, Wolverhampton

TQA (England) 1994–95
Firsts and 2:1s: 60.8%
Employment: 54.8%
Further study: 37.9%
Unemployment: 3.8%

Two London colleges are practically inseparable at the top of the music table. The School of Oriental and African Studies benefits from not having a separately listed A-level average since maximum points for both teaching and research give it a perfect score overall. King's College, London, matches SOAS for teaching and research, but has marginally lower entry standards than others in the top five. Almost half of the 45 universities offering music were rated excellent at teaching, although the Highly Satisfactory grades at Edinburgh and Glasgow were the best in Scotland.

Selection is as much a matter of musical ability as academic achievement, but nearly nine out of ten students come with A levels. More than half of the sessions observed by assessors in England were rated as Excellent, although there was considerable variation in the character of courses, from the practical and vocational programmes in conservatoires to the more theoretical. Although barely half of the graduates went straight into jobs, the unemployment rate was among the lowest of any subject.

Russian, Slavonic and Eastern European Languages		
1	Sheffield	92.2
2	Cambridge	87.9
3	St Andrews	81.2
4	Bangor*	80.2
5	London, SEES	79.1
6	Nottingham	76.4
7	Birmingham	76.2
8	Oxford	76.0
9	Bristol	75.8
10	Strathclyde*	75.6
11	Glasgow*	73.6
12	London, Queen Mary	73.1
13	Durham	71.0
14	Edinburgh*	70.4
15	Keele*	69.8
16	Leeds	68.7
17	Heriot-Watt*	58.4
18	Wolverhampton*	57.3
19	Exeter	56.8
20	Sussex	51.1

21–27

Coventry, Liverpool John Moores, Manchester, Nottingham Trent, Portsmouth, Surrey, Swansea

TQA (England) 1995-96
Firsts and 2:1s: 64.3%
Employment: 71.4%
Further study: 16.7%
Unemployment: 6.0%

Sheffield tops the table with the maximum points for teaching quality, despite average entry standards three grades below those at second-placed Cambridge. The two 5* research grades which went to Nottingham and London, Queen Mary.

Most of the 27 institutions in the ranking are old universities, but Wolverhampton makes the top 20 with a teaching quality grade bettered by only four universities in England. Bangor achieved maximum points in Wales. Outside the top institutions, entry grades are surprisingly modest: only a dozen universities averaged three Cs at A level in 1998.

Only 700 students take Russian at degree level, and fewer than half of the universities assessed in England offered Russian as a single-honours degree. Most of the students were learning the language *ab initio*, and there was a high drop-out rate from some universities, despite an 'excellent rapport' between staff and students. Employment prospects are relatively good, with more than seven out of ten graduates in work six months after graduation.

Social Policy and Administration	
1 London, LSE	**91.1**
2 Edinburgh	**82.0**
2 York	**82.0**
4 Manchester	**81.2**
5 Bath	**80.5**
6 Brunel*	**80.2**
7 Kent	**80.1**
8 Sheffield	**77.7**
9 Hull	**74.4**
10 Warwick	**74.2**
11 Newcastle	**73.7**
12 Glasgow*	**73.5**
13 Ulster	**72.3**
14 Nottingham	**70.5**
15 Bristol	**69.4**
16 Birmingham	**69.3**
17 London, Royal Holloway	**68.2**
18 Cardiff	**67.5**
19 Sheffield Hallam	**66.1**
20 Loughborough*	**63.5**

21–30

Bangor, Leeds, London Guildhall, London, Goldsmiths', Middlesex, Portsmouth, Queen's, Belfast, Southampton, Sunderland, Sussex

31–42

Brighton, Central Lancashire, East London, Leeds Metropolitan, Lincolnshire & Humberside, Luton, North London, Plymouth, South Bank, Swansea, Teesside, Wolverhampton

TQA (England) 1994–95
Firsts and 2:1s: 49.2%
Employment: 70.4%
Further study: 15.2%
Unemployment: 7.3%

The social policy ranking is complicated by the fact that, even in England, universities were assessed for teaching quality under two different systems. But, with an Excellent grade for teaching and the only 5*rating for research, the London School of Economics is a clear winner. Thirteen universities were considered Excellent at teaching, while Warwick scored the maximum 24 points under the assessment system which was introduced in England in 1995.

Sheffield Hallam is the only new university in the top 20, although London Guildhall did well to capture one of the Excellent teaching grades. Another 16 institutions offering the subject are not included in the table because they chose to to have their teaching assessed under sociology.

Average entry standards are comparatively low. Although two thirds of entrants come with A levels or their equivalent, some courses cater very largely for mature students. The proportion of students getting firsts or upper seconds is also low, but still seven out of ten graduates go straight into employment. Assessors described the subject as an 'eclectic discipline' drawing from psychology, politics, economics and law, as well as sociology.

Social Work

1	East Anglia*	100.0
1	York*	100.0
3	Lancaster	97.4
4	Edinburgh*	94.7
5	Keele*	91.8
5	Sheffield*	91.8
7	Hull*	89.3
7	Southampton*	89.3
9	Bristol	88.9
10	Queen's, Belfast*	87.0
11	Stirling*	85.2
12	Warwick*	81.3
13	Huddersfield	80.4
14	Dundee*	77.7
15	Anglia*	77.5
16	Cardiff*	75.9
16	Leicester*	75.9
18	Bradford	74.7
19	Bath	73.0
20	Swansea	71.7

21–30

Birmingham, Durham, Exeter, Kent, Lincolnshire & Humberside, Liverpool, London, Goldsmiths', Middlesex, Robert Gordon, Ulster

31–40

Central England, Coventry, De Montfort, Derby, Liverpool John Moores, Luton, Manchester Metropolitan, Northumbria, Staffordshire, Strathclyde

41–47

Central Lancashire, Hertfordshire, Leeds Metropolitan , Plymouth, Reading, Sheffield Hallam, Sunderland

TQA (England) 1995
Firsts and 2:1s: 49.2%
Employment: 80.3%
Further study: 9.1%
Unemployment: 5.8%

East Anglia and York tie for first place in applied social work, with maximum points for teaching and research grades which matched the best in England. Like many of the universities in the table, they have no separately listed A-level grades, so the scoring system gives them a better total than Lancaster, which has an identical record for teaching and research but average entry grades of less than a B and two Cs. The only university considered internationally outstanding for research was Stirling, which entered a relatively low proportion of its academics for assessment, and was not among the 13 universities rated Excellent at teaching. Almost half of the 47 universities offering social work are former polytechnics, but only Anglia makes it to the top 20 as the sole representative of the group with an Excellent teaching grade.

Entry standards are low in most of the universities in the ranking. Ulster had the highest average in 1998, with more than two Bs and a C at A level, but only 14 per cent of entrants throughout the UK had grades better than the average for all subjects. Social work is unusual for having more students taking certificate or diploma courses than degrees. Almost two thirds of all students were selected on qualities or qualifications other than A level. The vocational nature of the subject helps produce the highest proportion in all the social sciences of graduates going straight into employment.

Sociology

1	Warwick	93.3
2	Birmingham*	90.7
3	Sussex	88.8
4	Edinburgh	87.9
5	Loughborough	85.9
6	Essex	85.3
7	York	84.5
8	Lancaster	81.2
9	Manchester	80.6
10	Brunel	79.2
11	Sheffield	78.9
12	Aberdeen*	75.6
13	Glasgow	74.9
13	Surrey	74.9
15	London, Goldsmiths'	74.0
16	London, LSE	73.6
17	Southampton	73.4
18	Bristol	72.7
19	Leeds	72.4
20	Durham	70.7

21–30

Exeter, Greenwich, Keele, Kent, London, Royal Holloway, Nottingham, Queen's, Belfast, Reading, Salford, Strathclyde

31–40

Bath, Cardiff, City, Leicester, Liverpool, Oxford Brookes, Plymouth, Portsmouth, Sheffield Hallam, West of England

41–50

Anglia, Coventry, Hull, Kingston, Manchester Metropolitan, North London, Northumbria, Nottingham Trent, Sunderland, Thames Valley

51–60

Bangor, Bradford, Derby, East London, Glasgow Caledonian, Huddersfield, Paisley, Swansea, Teesside, Wolverhampton

61–74

Central England, Central Lancashire, De Montfort, East Anglia, Hertfordshire, Lincolnshire & Humberside, Liverpool John Moores, London Guildhall, Luton, Middlesex, South Bank, Staffordshire, Ulster, Westminster

TQA (England) 1995–96
Firsts and 2:1s: 52%
Employment: 64.9%
Further study: 18.9%
Unemployment: 8.5%

Warwick tops the sociology table as one of the three universities scoring a maximum 24 points for teaching quality, although three others have higher entry standards and two are rated more highly for research. The university's all-round quality edges out Birmingham and Sussex, the other two maximum scorers for teaching.

Essex and Lancaster are the top research universities, while Edinburgh – like Aberdeen, rated Excellent for teaching in Scotland – has the highest entry standards, averaging the equivalent of more than two As and a B at A level. Greenwich is the top-rated new university, narrowly missing a place in the top 20 with one of the best teaching quality assessments.

Still the biggest of the social sciences, sociology has more than 17,500 undergraduates. Other subjects such as criminology, urban studies, women's studies and some communication studies were also covered in the teaching assessment, which included institutions where sociology is taught as part of a combined studies or modular programme.

Town and Country Planning

1	Cardiff	90.0
2	Sheffield	89.5
3	Liverpool	85.1
4	Reading	83.2
5	Nottingham	77.7
6	Oxford Brookes	77.3
7	Newcastle	75.6
8	Queen's, Belfast	73.4
9	Aberdeen	69.6
10	Greenwich*	65.3
11	Kingston*	65.3
12	West of England	63.7
13	Manchester	63.3
14	Sheffield Hallam	61.3
15	South Bank	61.1
16	Leeds Metropolitan	59.7
17	Dundee	59.3
18	Salford*	58.0
19	Strathclyde*	54.6
20	Liverpool John Moores	53.5

21–27
Anglia, Central England, Coventry, De Montfort, Manchester Metropolitan, Northumbria, Westminster

TQA (England) 1996–98
Firsts and 2:1s: 49.4%
Employment: 68.4%
Further study: 21.2%
Unemployment: 5.1%

Cardiff registers Wales's only top place in a subject table, as the only university considered internationally outstanding for research in town and country planning. It was also rated as Excellent for teaching and had higher entry standards than all but Nottingham, Sheffield and Liverpool. In England, the new universities turned the tables on their older-established peers with Oxford Brookes, Greenwich and Kingston recording the the only three perfect scores for teaching quality. All three feature in the top ten.

Only a dozen old universities offer degrees in town and country planning, a subject which was once available only at postgraduate level in most universities. More than 5,000 students now take first degree courses, with almost another 1,000 taking certificate or diploma programmes. The size of departments varies from more than 500 students to less than 150, with about a third of the total postgraduates.

Fewer than half of the students are awarded first-class degrees or upper seconds, but employment prospects are relatively good, with only one graduate in 20 out of work six months after leaving university. The assessors of teaching quality in England reported a 'justifiably high level of satisfaction' among students, employers and external examiners.

Anatomy and Physiology	TQA	RAE Anatomy		RAE Physiology		A-Levels
Aberdeen				3a	A	16.0
Anglia						14.5
Birmingham		5*	D	4	C	
Bristol				5	A	24.5
Cambridge		5	A	5	C	
Cardiff	E					22.0
Dundee		4	B			18.4
Edinburgh		2	B	3a	B	
Glasgow		3a	D	3a	D	21.2
Keele				3a	A	
Leeds				3a	A	21.8
Leeds Metropolitan						15.1
Liverpool	23	5	C	5*	B	19.8
London, King's						20.6
London, UCL		5*	A	4	A	24.0
Loughborough	24					21.4
Luton	22					
Manchester	23					24.4
Middlesex						8.5
Newcastle	24			5	A	24.8
North London						8.4
Nottingham		3b	A			25.8
Oxford		5	A	5	A	29.4
Queen's, Belfast		2	D	3a	C	19.2
Reading						18.9
St Andrews						25.0
Sheffield						23.9
South Bank						8.4
Southampton						22.0
Sunderland	23					9.2
Westminster						9.2
Wolverhampton				2	B	10.0

Archaeology	TQA	RAE		A-Levels
Birmingham		4	A	24.0
Bournemouth		3b	A	12.0
Bradford		5	A	16.1
Bristol		4	A	22.9
Cambridge		5*	A	
Cardiff		4	A	18.8
Durham		5	A	23.6
East London				4.0
Edinburgh		4	A	26.4
Exeter		3a	A	20.8
Glasgow		4	A	30.0
Lampeter		3a	A	14.4
Leicester		5	A	18.5
Liverpool		4	A	18.7
London, UCL		5	A	23.7
Manchester				22.1

Archaeology cont.

Newcastle	3b	B	19.1
Nottingham	3a	A	22.6
Oxford	5*	B	
Queen's, Belfast	5	B	19.2
Reading	5	A	18.1
St Andrews			23.3
Sheffield	5*	A	23.9
Southampton	5	A	18.8
Staffordshire	2	A	
York	4	A	24.3

Art and Design	TQA	RAE		A-Levels
Aberystwyth		3b	A	19.3
Anglia	21	2	B	15.9
Bournemouth		4	F	14.3
Brighton	22	4	B	19.1
Brunel		5*	A	
Central England		3b	D	16.8
Central Lancashire		2	D	12.8
Coventry		4	D	14.7
De Montfort		3b	D	15.9
Derby	20	3b	D	14.4
Dundee	E	5	C	14.0
East London		3a	B	8.0
Edinburgh				28.0
Glamorgan				10.7
Glasgow Caledonian		1	E	
Hertfordshire		3b	E	11.3
Huddersfield		2	D	11.3
Keele		3b	A	
Kingston		3a	D	18.0
Lancaster		3a	A	20.5
Leeds	23			25.0
Leeds Metropolitan	21	3b	D	15.1
Lincs & Humberside		3b	D	13.9
Liverpool John Moores		3b	B	14.4
London Guildhall	23	2	E	13.7
London, Goldsmiths'		5*	C	18.6
London, UCL		5*	A	24.1
Loughborough		3a	B	
Luton				11.0
Manchester Metropolitan		3a	C	16.5
Middlesex		3a	D	14.2
Napier		3b	D	13.3
Newcastle		3b	B	22.2
North London	22			8.5
Northumbria	22	3a	C	15.9
Nottingham Trent		3a	E	19.8
Oxford		5	A	28.0
Oxford Brookes		3b	B	20.6
Plymouth		3a	C	16.2

Art and Design cont.

Portsmouth		3b	E	17.7
Reading		4	A	19.6
Robert Gordon	HS	3a	C	
Salford				12.9
Sheffield Hallam		4	C	18.0
South Bank				11.5
Southampton		4	C	16.4
Staffordshire	22	3a	A	14.2
Sunderland		3a	C	11.6
Teesside		1	F	13.1
Ulster		4	C	16.5
Westminster	21	4	D	16.7
West of England		3a	D	15.1
Wolverhampton		2	D	13.0

Celtic Studies	TQA	RAE	A-Levels
Aberdeen	3a	A	
Aberystwyth	5	A	21.4
Bangor	3a	A	20.8
Cardiff	5	A	19.3
Edinburgh	4	A	
Exeter	3b	E	
Glamorgan	1	C	
Glasgow	4	C	
Lampeter	2	A	10.6
Liverpool			19.0
Oxford	5	A	
Queen's, Belfast	4	A	20.8
Strathclyde	1	A	
Swansea	4	A	15.3
Ulster	4	A	18.6

Classics & Ancient History	TQA	RAE	A-Levels
Birmingham	3b	B	24.1
Bristol	5	A	24.7
Cambridge	5*	A	29.7
Durham	4	B	26.8
Edinburgh	4	B	27.1
Exeter	5	A	22.4
Glasgow	4	C	
Keele	3a	A	
Kent	3b	C	17.7
Lampeter	3b	B	11.7
Leeds	4	B	22.6
Liverpool	4	B	20.2
London, King's	5*	A	25.3
London, Royal Holloway	5	A	19.0
London, UCL	5*	A	24.9

Classics & Ancient History cont.

Manchester	4	C	20.8
Newcastle	4	A	22.1
Nottingham	3a	A	23.8
Oxford	5*	A	
Queen's, Belfast	3a	A	
Reading	5	A	17.7
St Andrews	5	C	25.6
Swansea	4	A	18.3
Warwick	4	A	24.1

Dentistry	TQA	RAE		A-Levels
Birmingham	22	3b	B	26.0
Bristol		4	C	27.9
Dundee	HS	3a	C	22.5
Glasgow	HS	3b	C	27.3
Leeds	23	4	D	26.1
Liverpool	21	3a	C	27.4
London, King's		4	D	25.6
London, Queen Mary		4	B	24.6
London, UCL	23	5	B	
Manchester		5	B	24.3
Newcastle	23	3a	A	26.1
Queen's, Belfast	24	2	C	28.3
Sheffield		3a	C	28.1
Wales College of Medicine	E	3a	C	26.0

Economics	TQA	RAE		A-Levels
Aberdeen		4	A	23.0
Abertay Dundee		1	D	
Aberystwyth		3b	A	14.3
Anglia				11.8
Bangor				14.5
Bath		3a	B	23.9
Birmingham		4	B	25.5
Bradford				12.6
Bristol		5	B	27.2
Brunel				20.9
Cambridge		5	A	29.8
Cardiff				22.1
Central England				12.7
City		3a	B	22.7
Coventry				13.2
De Montfort		3b	B	
Derby				11.0
Dundee		4	B	18.0
Durham				24.9
East Anglia		4	B	19.5

Economics cont.

East London	3a	D	9.2
Edinburgh	4	B	25.4
Essex	5	B	16.4
Exeter	5	C	23.6
Glasgow	4	C	
Greenwich			9.4
Heriot-Watt	3a	C	17.3
Huddersfield			10.3
Hull	3a	A	18.9
Keele	4	B	20.0
Kent	4	A	19.0
Kingston			13.2
Lancaster			23.2
Leeds			25.1
Leeds Metropolitan			14.2
Leicester	3a	A	19.7
Lincs & Humberside			7.8
Liverpool	4	B	21.8
London Guildhall	3b	D	9.6
London, LSE	5*	A	28.2
London, Queen Mary	4	A	20.7
London, Royal Holloway			21.7
London, SOAS	3a	C	
London, UCL	5*	A	27.1
Loughborough	4	A	20.7
Manchester	4	B	25.3
Manchester Metropolitan	3a	D	12.9
Middlesex			12.6
Napier			11.3
Newcastle	5	C	22.4
North London			9.2
Northumbria	2	D	16.0
Nottingham	5	A	28.6
Nottingham Trent	2	F	16.4
Oxford	5*	B	
Plymouth			14.7
Portsmouth	3a	E	14.7
Queen's, Belfast	3a	D	22.3
Reading	4	B	19.9
St Andrews	4	B	22.9
Salford	3a	A	15.5
Sheffield			24.1
Southampton	5	A	23.1
Staffordshire	2	D	10.8
Stirling	4	B	17.1
Strathclyde	4	B	
Sunderland			10.4
Surrey	4	A	20.1
Sussex	4	B	21.6
Swansea	4	B	17.7
Teesside			10.0
Thames Valley			9.0
Ulster			19.1
Warwick	5	A	26.7

Economics cont.

West of England			12.2
Wolverhampton			10.1
York	5	A	23.6

Hospitality	TQA	RAE	A-Levels
Anglia			10.4
Bangor	4	A	
Birmingham	5	A	
Bournemouth			10.5
Brighton	3a	A	12.8
Central England			11.3
Central Lancashire			13.6
Coventry			11.7
De Montfort	2	D	
Derby			14.3
Dundee			13.9
Glamorgan			10.4
Glasgow	4	C	
Greenwich			10.0
Hertfordshire			13.3
Huddersfield			11.1
Leeds	2	A	
Leeds Metropolitan	3b	D	14.4
Lincs & Humberside			11.2
Liverpool	3b	C	
Liverpool John Moores	5	B	11.3
Loughborough	5	C	
Luton			9.0
Manchester Metropolitan	4	E	13.9
Middlesex			10.3
Napier			12.9
North London			9.6
Nottingham Trent			16.9
Oxford Brookes			13.8
Paisley			4.0
Plymouth			11.9
Portsmouth			14.3
Robert Gordon			8.0
Salford			10.6
Sheffield	3a	B	
Sheffield Hallam	3a	E	16.0
South Bank	3b	D	10.4
Southampton	1	E	
Staffordshire	2	C	
Strathclyde	3b	C	13.0
Surrey			20.5
Teesside	1	E	
Thames Valley			8.0
Ulster	2	C	20.3
Westminster			12.3
Wolverhampton	1	D	11.2

Librarianship	TQA	RAE		A-Levels
Aberystwyth		3b	B	14.4
Bath		2	A	
Brighton		3b	C	15.8
Central England		3b	A	18.2
Central Lancashire		2	A	20.0
City		5*	A	
De Montfort		3b	C	
Leeds Metropolitan		2	E	8.5
Liverpool John Moores		2	E	9.9
London, UCL		2	B	22.8
Loughborough		5	C	18.0
Manchester Metropolitan		3b	C	7.8
North London				6.8
Northumbria		3a	C	12.6
Queen's, Belfast		3a	A	21.9
Robert Gordon		3a	B	
Salford		4	A	
Sheffield		5*	A	
Strathclyde		4	A	
Thames Valley		1	E	
West of England		3b	C	

Mathematics	TQA	RAE			A-Levels
		Pure	Applied	Stats	
Aberdeen	HS	3a B		3a A	14.0
Abertay Dundee	HS		2 E	3b D	
Aberystwyth	S	3b A	5 A		17.9
Anglia					16.0
Aston					
Bangor	S	3a C	2 A		21.5
Bath		5 A	5 A	5 B	25.9
Birmingham		4 B	4 C	4 C	25.0
Bournemouth				2 D	
Bradford			2 C		
Brighton	22				10.8
Bristol	23	4 B	5 B	5 A	27.4
Brunel			4 B	4 B	17.9
Cambridge		5 A	5* A	5* A	29.9
Cardiff	S	5 B			21.5
Central Lancashire	19	3a C	1 D		13.1
City			3b A	3b C	20.5
Coventry			3b D	2 E	15.4
De Montfort	20		2 E	3b E	7.3
Derby			2 D		8.0
Dundee	HS		4 C	2 A	16.7
Durham	21	5 C	5 B	3a B	28.9
East Anglia	23	5 A	4 B	3b A	19.9
East London		3b F			10.0
Edinburgh	E	5 B	4 B	4 A	26.4
Essex	20	3a A		3a C	16.0
Exeter	22	3a C	5 C	3b B	22.8

Mathematics cont.

Glamorgan	S		2 C		11.4
Glasgow	HS	4 C	4 A	4 A	26.0
Glasgow Caledonian	HS		3b C		
Greenwich	19			3b C	7.9
Heriot-Watt	HS		5 C	3a C	20.6
Hertfordshire	21				9.7
Hull	22	4 B	3b A		16.0
Keele	22		4 A	3b A	
Kent			3a C	4 C	17.7
Kingston					9.9
Lancaster		4 C		5 B	21.1
Leeds	22	5 B	5 A	3a A	23.4
Leicester		3b C	3a D		20.1
Liverpool		5 B	4 C	3a B	19.3
Liverpool John Moores	21				6.5
London Guildhall			2 D		10.3
London School of Economics		3a B		4 B	28.7
London, Goldsmiths'		3a B	1 A	3b A	9.2
London, Imperial		5* B	5 B	5 B	27.5
London, King's	21	5 B	5 B		21.3
London, Queen Mary	21	5 B	5 C	5 A	15.7
London, Royal Holloway		4 D	3a D		20.8
London, UCL		5 B	5 A	4 B	26.2
Loughborough			4 B		19.5
Manchester	22	5 B	4 B	3a A	24.1
Manchester Metropolitan			2 C		11.4
Middlesex			1 D		6.0
Napier	HS		2 D	3b E	6.0
Newcastle		3a C	4 B	4 B	21.3
North London		3a D		3b C	5.0
Northumbria			3b E	2 F	11.7
Nottingham		4 B	5 B	4 B	28.0
Nottingham Trent	21		3b D	3b E	10.7
Oxford		5* C	5* B	4 B	29.6
Oxford Brookes			3b B	1 E	13.8
Paisley	HS		2 E		
Plymouth	20		2 C	2 D	11.7
Portsmouth			3b D		11.1
Queen's, Belfast		3a E			23.2
Reading		3a C	3a A	3a B	20.3
Robert Gordon	HS		1 C		
St Andrews	E	4 B	5 B	4 A	24.4
Salford				4 A	18.3
Sheffield	21	3a C	4 B	4 B	26.2
Sheffield Hallam	23				10.2
Southampton		3a B	4 B	4 B	20.2
Staffordshire			2 A		
Stirling	HS	3b A			16.7
Strathclyde	HS		4 C	4 C	19.0
Sunderland					11.2
Surrey			3a B	4 A	19.2
Sussex	23	5 C	4 C	3b B	17.3
Swansea	S	4 C		3a C	19.8
Teesside			2 B		10.4

Mathematics cont.

UMIST		5	B	4	B	3a	C	23.4
Warwick		5*	A			5	A	29.2
Westminster								6.5
West of England				2	C	2	E	
Wolverhampton	20							11.5
York	22	4	B	3a	A			24.8

Medicine	TQA	RAE						A-Levels
		Clin Lab Sci	Community	Hospital	Pre-Clinical			
Aberdeen	E	3a A	3a A	3a B				28.2
Birmingham	20	5 C	3b C	4 B				28.3
Bristol		4 D	3a D	3a B				28.8
Cambridge		5 A	5* A	5 A				30.0
Dundee	E	4 B	3b B	3b B				27.4
Edinburgh	HS	4 B	4 A	5 A				29.8
Glasgow	E	4 C	3b C	4 C				
Leeds	18	3a B	3b C	3a B				28.0
Leicester	23	3a B	3a B	3a B	3b D			28.0
Liverpool	24	3a B	3a C	3b B				28.2
London, Imperial		4 B	3a B	4 B	5 B			27.7
London, King's		2 B	3b C	4 B	4 B			
London, Queen Mary		2 C	4 C	3a C	2 C			26.3
London, St George's Hospital		2 B	3b B	3a B	4 A			27.5
London, UCL	21	4 A	5 B	4 A				28.3
Manchester		3b B	4 A	3a B	4 B			28.6
Newcastle	24	3a B	3b C	3a B				29.0
Nottingham		3a B	3b B	3a C				29.0
Oxford		5 B	5* B	5* A				29.7
Queen's, Belfast	22	3b C	3a E	3b C				29.2
St Andrews	HS							27.9
Sheffield	19	2 C	2 C	4 C				28.9
Southampton		4 A	3b A	4 B				27.7
Wales College of Medicine	E	4 B	5 B	4 C				29.2

Molecular Biosciences	TQA	RAE		A-Levels
		Biochem	Biol Sci	
Aberdeen	E		3a A	15.7
Abertay Dundee	HS		2 D	
Aberystwyth	E		2 A	13.3
Anglia				13.5
Aston	23			
Bangor	E		3a C	17.5
Bath			5 C	25.5
Birmingham	23	5 B	4 B	24.2
Bradford				16.3
Brighton				15.2
Bristol		5 A	4 A	26.8

Molecular Biosciences cont.

Brunel			3a	D	15.5
Cambridge		5* B	5*	A	
Cardiff	E		3a	A	23.0
Central Lancashire			3b	D	12.4
Coventry			1	C	13.7
Cranfield			4	A	
De Montfort	21		2	C	
Dundee	E	5* B	3a	B	17.1
Durham			3a	A	26.0
East Anglia	22		5	B	23.2
East London	19		2	E	10.5
Edinburgh	E	3b A	5	A	24.5
Essex			4	B	13.5
Exeter			3a	A	22.4
Glamorgan					10.5
Glasgow	E	5 C	4	C	18.9
Glasgow Caledonian	HS				
Greenwich	20				9.7
Heriot-Watt	HS				12.4
Hertfordshire					9.2
Huddersfield					11.4
Hull			3b	A	18.0
Keele			3a	B	
Kent	24		4	B	15.5
Kingston					13.2
Lancaster	21		4	A	21.1
Leeds		5 A	4	B	22.5
Leicester		5 B	5	A	20.7
Liverpool	19		4	B	21.2
Liverpool John Moores		2 D	3b	C	15.4
London, Imperial	22	5 B	5	A	26.2
London, King's			3a	B	22.0
London, Queen Mary	22		4	B	15.1
London, Royal Holloway			3b	B	18.2
London, UCL	22	5 B	5	B	24.5
London, Wye					13.3
Loughborough					24.5
Luton	22		2	D	
Manchester	23	5 B	4	A	24.8
Manchester Metropolitan			2	C	11.1
Napier	HS				
Newcastle		4 B			22.7
North London	18		1	E	6.0
Northumbria	21				18.6
Nottingham		3a A	5*	A	27.3
Nottingham Trent	24		3b	D	17.2
Oxford		5* A	5	A	29.5
Oxford Brookes			3a	B	
Paisley	HS		2	E	
Plymouth			2	C	16.6
Portsmouth			3a	C	16.0
Queen's, Belfast	21		3a	C	21.1
Reading			3a	B	20.0
Robert Gordon					8.0

Molecular Biosciences cont.

St Andrews	E		4	B	21.0
Salford	24		3b	A	12.7
Sheffield			4	A	23.3
Sheffield Hallam					11.6
South Bank					10.6
Southampton	23		4	B	21.7
Staffordshire			1	D	16.8
Stirling	HS		3a	C	18.0
Strathclyde	HS	2 C			14.0
Sunderland	24		3b	C	11.9
Surrey	21		3a	B	18.3
Sussex			5	B	20.8
Swansea	E		3a	C	17.4
Teesside					13.1
Ulster					17.3
UMIST			5	A	23.8
Warwick	23		5	A	24.5
Westminster	21		2	C	9.6
West of England	24		3b	C	
Wolverhampton			1	E	8.6
York			5	B	23.6

Nursing	TQA	RAE		A-Levels
Abertay Dundee	S			
Anglia		1	F	13.0
Birmingham		2	E	20.4
Bournemouth	22			
Brighton	22	2	F	14.6
Central England		1	F	14.8
Central Lancashire		2	E	13.5
City	20	1	F	15.7
Coventry		1	F	
De Montfort		1	C	15.3
Derby	19			
Edinburgh	HS	3b	A	23.6
Glasgow	HS	2	C	
Glasgow Caledonian	HS	3b	E	16.0
Greenwich				14.2
Hertfordshire		2	F	12.2
Huddersfield				23.0
Hull		3b	D	16.9
Keele	21			
Kingston				10.0
Leeds	20	3a	A	21.0
Leeds Metropolitan	21			16.4
Liverpool		3a	C	22.1
Liverpool John Moores	21	3b	D	13.6
London, King's	21	5	B	20.8
Luton	23			
Manchester		4	A	20.8
Manchester Metropolitan		1	E	

Nursing cont.

Middlesex		1	E	12.7
Northumbria				20.6
Nottingham		3b	C	22.6
Oxford Brookes		2	E	14.9
Portsmouth		2	F	
Robert Gordon		2	E	
Salford				13.7
Sheffield	21	3b	A	
Sheffield Hallam	21			16.1
South Bank				12.3
Southampton		1	E	23.5
Surrey		4	B	18.9
Swansea		2	F	17.5
Thames Valley	20	2	F	
Ulster		3b	D	19.6
Wales College of Medicine	S	1	F	17.6
West of England				16.8
Wolverhampton	21			

Organismal Biosciences	TQA	RAE		A-Levels
Aberdeen	E	3a	A	18.3
Abertay Dundee		2	D	
Aberystwyth	E	2	A	15.1
Anglia				10.6
Aston	23			19.3
Bangor	E	3a	C	18.6
Bath		5	C	22.5
Birmingham		4	B	22.1
Brighton				11.2
Bristol	22	4	A	26.4
Brunel		3a	D	15.3
Cambridge		5*	A	
Cardiff	E	3a	A	22.8
Central Lancashire		3b	D	13.2
Coventry		1	C	9.2
Cranfield		4	A	
De Montfort		2	C	11.6
Derby				12.1
Dundee	E	3a	B	15.3
Durham		3a	A	25.4
East Anglia	22	5	B	20.1
East London	19	2	E	10.0
Edinburgh	E	5	A	25.5
Essex		4	B	10.7
Exeter		3a	A	17.7
Glasgow	E	4	C	20.9
Glasgow Caledonian				12.0
Greenwich	20			8.2
Heriot-Watt				16.8
Huddersfield				11.0
Hull		3b	A	17.9

Organismal Biosciences cont.

Keele		3a	B	
Kent	24	4	B	13.3
Kingston				7.9
Lancaster	21	4	A	18.6
Leeds		4	B	21.9
Leeds Metropolitan				13.2
Leicester		4	A	20.7
Liverpool	19	4	B	20.6
Liverpool John Moores		3b	C	11.1
London, Imperial		5	A	25.5
London, King's		3a	B	20.1
London, Queen Mary	22	4	B	15.6
London, Royal Holloway		3b	B	18.6
London, UCL	24	5	B	24.7
London, Wye				17.8
Luton	22	2	D	
Manchester	23	4	A	23.6
Manchester Metropolitan		2	C	10.9
Napier	HS			11.6
Newcastle	22			19.7
North London	18	1	E	4.6
Northumbria				12.8
Nottingham		4	B	25.5
Nottingham Trent	24	3b	D	13.1
Oxford	24	5	A	29.2
Oxford Brookes		3a	B	12.1
Paisley	HS	2	E	
Plymouth		2	C	16.3
Portsmouth		3a	C	12.0
Queen's, Belfast	21	3a	C	19.3
Reading		3a	B	19.9
St Andrews	E	4	B	23.8
Salford	24	3b	A	15.8
Sheffield		4	A	24.0
South Bank				8.0
Southampton	23	4	B	22.5
Staffordshire		1	D	10.0
Stirling	HS	3a	C	17.7
Sunderland	24	3b	C	8.2
Surrey	21	3a	B	18.2
Sussex	22	5	B	16.9
Swansea	E	3a	C	18.7
Ulster				13.9
UMIST		5	A	
Warwick	23	5	A	24.4
Westminster	21	2	C	6.0
West of England	24	3b	C	
Wolverhampton		1	E	8.4
York		5	B	23.3

Other Subjects Allied to Medicine	TQA	RAE		A-Levels
Aberdeen				22.6
Anglia		1	E	11.4
Aston	23	4	A	26.4
Bangor				17.0
Birmingham				26.0
Bournemouth	20			
Bradford		4	B	22.5
Brighton	22	2	D	17.5
Brunel				22.3
Cardiff		5	A	25.8
Central England		1	F	14.8
Central Lancashire	22	3b	A	14.3
City		3a	B	21.3
Coventry	23	2	F	18.3
Cranfield	21			
De Montfort	20			9.6
Derby		2	F	14.8
Durham				17.1
East Anglia		1	B	24.0
East London		1	D	19.6
Edinburgh				22.0
Essex				13.4
Glamorgan				17.4
Glasgow		4	B	23.2
Glasgow Caledonian	HS	3a	B	16.5
Greenwich	18	4	B	11.4
Hertfordshire		2	E	19.4
Huddersfield		2	C	13.2
Hull				23.1
Keele	20			22.5
Kent	21			
Kingston	23	2	C	11.9
Leeds	24	2	A	13.4
Leeds Metropolitan		2	F	21.7
Lincs & Humberside				9.0
Liverpool				20.4
Liverpool John Moores	24	3a	B	13.9
London, Goldsmiths'		2	C	
London, King's	23	3b	B	23.9
London, Queen Mary				22.7
London, UCL		3b	A	21.8
Loughborough	24	5	A	
Luton	23			
Manchester				23.4
Manchester Metropolitan	22	2	D	15.6
Middlesex				10.3
Napier		4	D	10.5
Newcastle				26.3
North London		3a	C	6.7
Northumbria		2	F	19.1
Nottingham				25.2
Nottingham Trent				14.2
Oxford Brookes		1	D	16.1

Other Subjects Allied to Medicine cont.

Plymouth	20			9.2
Portsmouth		4	C	14.9
Queen's, Belfast				19.8
Reading				26.4
Robert Gordon	S	3b	E	19.1
Salford	22			16.9
Sheffield	21			23.4
Sheffield Hallam		4	D	16.1
South Bank	21			12.9
Southampton		2	E	19.9
Staffordshire				15.2
Strathclyde		5*	B	26.4
Sunderland				7.9
Surrey	21	5	B	
Teesside		2	E	21.5
Thames Valley	20			
Ulster		5*	C	23.0
UMIST		4	A	26.7
Wales College of Medicine				21.3
Westminster				11.1
West of England		3b	F	22.4
Wolverhampton	22	2	C	13.1

Pharmacology	TQA	RAE		A-Levels
		Pharmacology	Pharmacy	
Aberdeen				16.0
Aston	24		3a B	23.0
Bath	23		5 A	24.8
Birmingham		3a A		
Bradford			3a B	21.0
Brighton	23		3b C	20.0
Bristol		5 A		25.2
Cambridge		5 A		
Cardiff	E		5 B	24.8
De Montfort			2 B	19.6
Derby	16			
Dundee		4 A		17.7
East London	19	1 E		10.5
Edinburgh		4 A		
Glasgow				22.7
Greenwich				7.2
Hertfordshire		2 B		
Leeds	23	3a B		21.3
Leicester		5* B		
Liverpool	22	5 B		20.1
Liverpool John Moores			1 D	20.9
London, King's	22		4 B	21.5
London, Queen Mary		4 B		
London, School of Pharmacy		5 B		23.9
London, UCL		5* A		22.6
Luton	22			

Pharmacology cont.

Manchester				5	A	24.3
Middlesex						17.1
North London						5.5
Nottingham	23	4	A	5*	A	27.7
Oxford		5	B			
Portsmouth						18.3
Queen's, Belfast				3b	D	27.5
Robert Gordon	HS			1	C	21.1
Salford						11.3
Sheffield						24.1
Southampton						20.6
Strathclyde	E			4	B	26.0
Sunderland	22			2	C	19.0
West of England	24					

Philosophy	TQA	RAE	A-Levels
Aberdeen	3b	B	
Anglia	2	B	13.3
Birmingham	4	B	23.8
Bradford	4	B	
Brighton	1	A	
Bristol	4	B	27.8
Cambridge	5	A	29.5
Cardiff	3b	C	21.9
Dundee	3b	C	
Durham	4	B	24.2
East Anglia	3a	B	19.6
Edinburgh	3a	B	27.7
Essex	4	B	19.0
Glasgow	3a	D	21.1
Greenwich			9.8
Hertfordshire	2	C	
Hull	4	A	20.0
Keele	3b	A	
Kent	3b	B	21.3
Lampeter	3b	C	12.6
Lancaster	3b	A	18.5
Leeds	4	B	25.0
Liverpool	3a	A	22.8
London, LSE	5	A	28.0
London, King's	5	A	22.0
London, UCL	4	A	24.3
Manchester	2	B	25.1
Manchester Metropolitan	3b	C	
Middlesex	2	D	11.5
North London			10.0
Nottingham	3a	B	26.1
Oxford	5*	B	
Queen's, Belfast	3a	E	23.0
Reading	4	B	20.3
St Andrews	5	A	24.9

Philosophy cont.

Sheffield	5	A	26.0
Southampton	3a	B	20.3
Stirling	4	B	17.7
Sunderland	3b	A	
Sussex	4	B	23.0
Swansea	3b	B	16.2
Ulster			17.0
Warwick	3a	A	25.6
Wolverhampton			12.4
York	3b	A	22.2

Physics and Astronomy	TQA	RAE		A-Levels
Aberystwyth	S	4	B	12.6
Bath	24	4	A	22.7
Birmingham	23	5	B	23.7
Brighton		1	C	
Bristol	23	5	B	26.5
Brunel		2	B	12.4
Cambridge	23	5*	A	
Cardiff	S	4	B	21.6
Central Lancashire	19	3a	D	9.7
Dundee	HS			
Durham	24	5	A	26.8
East Anglia		4	B	
Edinburgh	E	5	B	25.7
Essex		4	B	13.2
Exeter	22	4	B	19.9
Glasgow	E	4	B	
Glasgow Caledonian	HS			14.0
Heriot-Watt	HS	4	B	19.0
Hertfordshire		4	C	
Hull	23			12.4
Keele		3a	B	
Kent		3a	B	16.6
Kingston		1	C	7.8
Lancaster		3a	B	17.8
Leeds		5	B	21.6
Leicester	23	5	B	22.1
Liverpool		5	A	19.9
Liverpool John Moores		4	C	12.5
London, Imperial		5	A	27.6
London, King's	22	4	B	19.0
London, Queen Mary	21	4	A	17.8
London, Royal Holloway	23	4	B	19.8
London, UCL		5	A	25.1
Loughborough	23	3a	B	17.7
Manchester	24	5	B	24.4
Manchester Metropolitan		2	D	
Napier	S			
Newcastle		4	C	17.9
North London		1	C	

Physics and Astronomy cont.

Northumbria	23		10.3
Nottingham		4 A	26.7
Nottingham Trent	24		12.0
Oxford		5* B	29.8
Paisley	S	1 E	
Portsmouth	20		11.5
Queen's, Belfast		5 D	23.7
Reading		4 B	17.5
Robert Gordon	HS		
St Andrews	E	4 B	24.0
Salford		3a C	15.5
Sheffield	22	4 B	24.1
Sheffield Hallam			9.2
Southampton		4 B	20.0
Staffordshire	22	2 D	11.8
Stirling		3b A	
Strathclyde	E	4 B	24.0
Surrey	23	4 A	20.2
Sussex		3a B	14.4
Swansea	E	4 C	16.4
UMIST	21	4 A	23.9
Warwick		4 A	26.9
Westminster			15.5
York		4 B	21.7

Politics	TQA	RAE	A-Levels
Aberdeen		4 B	19.5
Aberystwyth		5 A	18.0
Anglia			16.0
Bath			25.1
Birmingham		3a A	24.5
Bradford		4 A	10.0
Bristol		4 A	27.4
Brunel		3a A	17.0
Cardiff			22.5
Central England			13.3
Central Lancashire			9.9
Coventry		3b D	12.0
De Montfort		3a B	7.3
Dundee		3a B	20.0
Durham		3b B	26.5
East Anglia		3b A	19.9
East London			14.0
Edinburgh		4 B	27.7
Essex		5* B	19.5
Exeter		4 B	24.3
Glamorgan			10.2
Glasgow		5 C	23.2
Glasgow Caledonian		2 C	
Greenwich		2 C	14.8
Huddersfield		3b B	11.6

Politics cont.

Hull	4	A	21.1
Keele	4	A	19.4
Kent	3a	C	20.6
Kingston			13.5
Lancaster	3a	C	19.8
Leeds	3a	A	24.8
Leeds Metropolitan	3b	A	
Leicester	4	A	20.6
Lincs & Humberside			11.6
Liverpool	3a	B	23.0
Liverpool John Moores	2	D	
London Guildhall	3b	B	10.3
London, LSE	5*	B	28.5
London, Goldsmiths'			16.2
London, King's	5*	A	
London, Queen Mary	4	B	24.5
London, SEES	4	A	
London, SOAS	3a	B	
Loughborough			19.7
Luton			14.0
Manchester	4	A	27.2
Manchester Metropolitan	3b	D	14.1
Middlesex	3b	D	13.0
Newcastle	4	B	25.0
North London			8.4
Northumbria	3b	E	15.5
Nottingham	3a	A	25.7
Nottingham Trent	3b	C	16.2
Oxford	5*	B	
Oxford Brookes	3a	C	
Paisley			8.0
Plymouth	3a	B	14.1
Portsmouth			12.2
Queen's, Belfast	4	B	22.0
Reading	3a	B	20.2
Robert Gordon	3b	C	8.8
St Andrews	3a	A	
Sheffield	5	A	25.9
South Bank			9.1
Southampton	4	B	21.3
Staffordshire	3b	B	11.3
Stirling	3a	B	16.0
Strathclyde	5	A	
Sunderland			6.8
Sussex	4	B	21.9
Swansea	4	B	18.2
Teesside	2	B	11.3
Ulster	3b	B	15.0
Warwick	3a	A	26.7
Westminster	3a	B	11.0
West of England			14.6
Wolverhampton	2	A	12.9
York	4	B	25.2

Psychology	TQA	RAE		A-Levels
Aberdeen	HS	4	B	19.7
Abertay Dundee	HS	2	B	
Anglia				13.0
Aston				23.1
Bangor	E	5	A	19.4
Bath				24.6
Birmingham		4	A	27.0
Bournemouth				20.0
Bristol		5	A	25.9
Brunel		3a	B	20.6
Cambridge		5*	A	
Cardiff	E	5	A	26.1
Central Lancashire	24	3b	E	18.1
City	21	4	B	21.5
Coventry		2	E	14.5
De Montfort		2	B	18.0
Derby	20	2	E	19.3
Dundee	E	4	B	17.4
Durham	23	4	B	27.3
East Anglia				22.7
East London	23	2	C	13.1
Edinburgh	HS	3a	B	28.7
Essex	22	4	B	21.6
Exeter		4	B	25.9
Glamorgan				14.6
Glasgow	E	4	C	21.5
Glasgow Caledonian	HS	3b	C	16.5
Greenwich	22	2	B	15.2
Heriot-Watt				19.0
Hertfordshire	23	3a	C	17.2
Huddersfield	20			16.4
Hull	23	3a	B	22.9
Keele		3a	B	
Kent		3a	B	25.2
Lancaster	24	4	B	21.9
Leeds		4	B	26.9
Leeds Metropolitan				12.9
Leicester		3a	A	23.8
Lincs & Humberside		2	D	15.1
Liverpool	22	3a	B	25.3
Liverpool John Moores	19			19.5
London Guildhall		2	D	13.5
London, LSE				28.0
London, Goldsmiths'	22	4	A	21.0
London, Royal Holloway		5	B	22.9
London, UCL	22	5	A	26.1
Loughborough	24	3a	C	23.7
Luton		2	E	9.0
Manchester	22	4	B	27.4
Manchester Metropolitan	22	3b	D	19.4
Middlesex		2	C	11.4
Newcastle		4	D	25.9
North London				8.4
Northumbria	22	2	D	19.0

Psychology cont.

Nottingham	24	4	A	27.2
Nottingham Trent	22	2	C	22.2
Oxford		5*	A	29.1
Oxford Brookes	23	3b	D	
Paisley	HS	2	D	
Plymouth	23	3a	C	20.1
Portsmouth	23	3b	C	18.5
Queen's, Belfast	24	3a	C	24.4
Reading		5	B	22.9
St Andrews	E	5*	A	25.1
Sheffield		5	A	27.5
Sheffield Hallam	24			21.2
South Bank				13.8
Southampton		3a	B	24.1
Staffordshire	23	2	B	15.8
Stirling	E	4	C	22.0
Strathclyde	HS	3a	B	
Sunderland				14.7
Surrey	22	4	A	22.9
Sussex		3a	B	23.4
Swansea	E	4	A	21.2
Teesside		2	D	13.5
Thames Valley		1	E	8.1
Ulster		2	C	17.7
Warwick	21	4	A	26.1
Westminster		3b	C	14.1
West of England				18.3
Wolverhampton		2	D	16.2
York		5*	A	26.5

Theology & Religious Studies	TQA	RAE		A-Levels
Aberdeen		4	A	9.0
Bangor		3a	A	12.7
Birmingham		5	A	22.4
Bristol		4	A	22.6
Cambridge		5	A	28.8
Cardiff		5	A	18.7
De Montfort		3a	A	
Derby		2	C	
Durham		5	A	24.1
Edinburgh		5	A	22.6
Exeter		3a	A	21.9
Glasgow		4	B	18.4
Greenwich				8.7
Hull		4	A	15.6
Kent		3a	B	19.7
Lampeter		4	A	15.3
Lancaster		5*	A	20.0
Leeds		4	B	21.8
London, LSE				25.7

Theology & Religious Studies cont.

London, Goldsmiths'	4	A	
London, King's	5	A	
London, SOAS	5	A	
Manchester	5*	B	19.7
Manchester Metropolitan	2	A	
Middlesex	2	D	14.0
Newcastle	3a	A	20.3
Nottingham	5	C	23.5
Oxford	5	A	28.1
Queen's, Belfast			17.6
St Andrews	5	C	19.4
Sheffield	5*	A	18.1
Southampton			15.7
Stirling	3b	B	
Sunderland	2	A	10.9
Wolverhampton			11.6

Veterinary Medicine	TQA	RAE	A-Levels
Bristol	4	B	29.2
Cambridge	4	A	29.7
Edinburgh	4	B	29.1
Glasgow	4	A	29.5
Liverpool	4	C	28.8
London, Royal Veterinary College	4	B	28.2

Applying to University

Once you have made your decisions about what you want to study and where, you can heave a huge sigh of relief because the really hard part is over. The next stage, making an application, is much easier. However, there are still enough issues and decisions to warrant a closer look at the process and how to go about it.

All applications to UK universities for full-time courses are made through UCAS, the Universities and Colleges Admissions Service. While the *Good University Guide* is only concerned with universities, many colleges of one sort or another also recruit through UCAS and so you will find nearly 300 institutions listed in the *UCAS Handbook*. If you are interested in a part-time course you will need to contact universities individually to find out how to apply.

The Application Form, *Notes for Guidance*, the *UCAS Handbook* (which lists the 30,000 or so courses available) and numerous booklets and leaflets are available from your school, college, local careers service, nearest British Council Office, or direct from UCAS. (The UCAS address is: UCAS, Rosehill, New Barn Lane, Cheltenham, Gloucestershire, GL52 3LZ. Applicants from outside the UK are requested to send a cheque for £5 to cover postage.)

Filling in the UCAS Form

The UCAS Application Form may only be four pages of A4 paper, but it still looks rather daunting. There is no substitute for reading the *Notes for Guidance* and then going slowly and carefully through the form, checking back against the *Notes* as you go. For most applicants, what you (and your referee) put on the form will be all the university uses to make a decision, so it is important to get it right. A good idea is to take a photocopy of the form and fill that in first as a trial run. Don't forget that the form is scanned at UCAS and reproduced half size for universities, so write clearly and neatly.

Provided that you follow the *Notes for Guidance* carefully, most of the form is straightforward, but on the following pages are a few points about some of the more significant sections.

Address

This looks simple, and it is, but don't just fill in your current address and then forget about it. If your address changes, make sure you tell UCAS immediately. UCAS will automatically notify your university choices of the change but there is no harm in contacting them directly as well just to make sure. If you don't keep UCAS informed of your change of address you will find letters (which might be offers or a confirmation of a place) go to the wrong place. It is surprisingly common for applicants at a boarding school to put down their school address on the form but then forget to tell UCAS when they go home for the summer. They then find that the letter confirming a place at university goes to the school instead of to them.

Examination Results

Make sure you get the details of your examinations to be taken exactly right. If you are taking English Language and Literature, put the full title and not just English, even if everyone in your school or college calls it English. This is important because any mistakes could mean that UCAS cannot match your application with your examination results straightaway in the summer, resulting in a delay in universities making their decisions. Listing the full module details of a BTEC award or GNVQ is also important to avoid confusion over precisely what you are studying.

And be honest! Never be tempted to massage your results to make them look a little better. UCAS has some sophisticated fraud-busting techniques and admissions tutors are remarkably good at spotting dodgy applications. If you are found to be giving false information, you will be promptly ejected from UCAS and lose any chance of a place at university that year. Even if you manage to slip through all the detection devices, you will probably be asked by the university to present your certificates. Any sign of tampering, or lame excuses about them having been eaten by the dog, will result in a check with the records of the examining board. When the board points out that the ABB on your form was really DDD, you will politely be shown the door.

Personal Statement

This is your chance to say anything you like, in your own words, to persuade admissions tutors that yours is the brightest and best application ever to have crossed their desk. You can write what you like, but the key things probably include:

- why you want to study your chosen subject
- what particular qualities and experience you can bring to it
- details of any work experience or voluntary activity, especially if it is relevant to your course
- any other evidence of achievement, such as the Duke of Edinburgh award

- details of any sponsorship or placements you have secured or applied for
- your career aspirations
- any wider aspects of life that make you an interesting and well-rounded student

If there is anything about your application that is even slightly unusual, then explain why. If you want to defer your entry to the following year, say why and what you intend to do with your year out. If you have listed more than one subject among your choices this can suggest a lack of commitment, so explain why. If you are a mature student, explain why you want to enter higher education.

As with examinations, be honest. If you say you are interested in philosophy and then get called for interview, you can almost guarantee that some learned professor will ask you about Plato's Theory of Forms or Spinoza's ethics. If you can't talk sensibly about philosophy, you will look rather silly and will be unlikely to get an offer.

There is no ideal way to structure your statement, but it is a good idea to use paragraphs or sub-headings to make the presentation clear and easy for an admissions tutor to read. If you want to say more than there is space available, do not write outside the box or send additional papers to UCAS; they will not automatically be passed on to your chosen universities. If you really can't make it fit, then send any additional material directly to the universities to which you have applied. And, once again, remember that the form will be reduced at UCAS, so write clearly.

Timetable	
May – Sept	Research and make choices about universities and courses
1 Sept – 15 Oct	Apply for Cambridge, Oxford or Medicine in any university
1 Sept – 15 Dec	All other applications (except Art and Design Route B)
1 Jan – 24 March	Art and Design Route B
16 Dec – 30 June	Late applications considered at universities' discretion
1 July onwards	Applications go straight into the Clearing procedure

Choice of Courses

By the time you fill in your form, you should have your choice of courses ready. You are allowed six, but you don't have to use them all. (Indeed if you only use one choice there is a lower application fee.) If you want to apply for Medicine, you are only allowed to use four choices for medical courses, though you can use the other two for different subjects if you wish. Make sure you get the university and course codes exactly right. If they don't match up, your application will be delayed while UCAS sorts out what you ought to have put down.

In all sections of the form, make sure the grammar and punctuation are correct. It is a good idea to show the form to someone else as a final check. When you have finally finished, take a copy and pass the form on to your referee (usually someone from your school or college) with the appropriate fee.

All being well, he or she will fill in the section for the referee and send the form off to UCAS at the appropriate time.

Should I Apply Early?

Universities are required by UCAS rules to treat all applications received by the 15 December deadline on an equal basis. This means that applying early or late should make no difference, as long as the deadline is met, and in practice this is the case for virtually all applicants. Indeed if you are applying for a low-demand subject you will probably get equal treatment even if your application arrives well after the deadline.

It can be a good idea to avoid submitting an application in December as there is a peak in the number of application forms arriving at UCAS then. This will not affect your chances of an offer, but it does create something of a backlog at UCAS and so you may have to wait rather longer before you receive any decisions.

Occasionally, in very high-demand subjects such as Medicine, English or Law, a very popular university may experience a sudden increase in applications which only becomes apparent after it has started making decisions. It will then be faced with a choice of either carrying on making offers in the same way and ending up with an intake way above target, or tightening up its criteria and admitting the right number. Neither of these outcomes is desirable: too many students means large classes and over-worked staff; tightening the criteria means being slightly tougher with some applicants. The university may choose the latter course, in which case a few of the later applicants might be rejected whereas, if they had applied earlier, before the increased number of applications was apparent, they might have received an offer. This situation is very rare, but the conclusion is that applying early never does any harm while applying later to high-demand subjects very occasionally might.

The form can arrive at UCAS any time between 1 September and 15 December (or 15 October if Oxford or Cambridge or any medical course is among your choices – see the *Timetable* box for this and other exceptions). In some circumstances there can be a small advantage in applying early (see box, *Should I Apply Early?*) but generally it will not make any difference. If you apply after the appropriate deadline your form will still be processed by UCAS but universities do not have to consider it. They can, if they wish, reject you on the grounds that they have received enough applications already. However, if you are applying for one of the less competitive courses or are applying from overseas you will probably find your application is treated just like those that arrived on time.

What Happens Next?

The first thing to happen after you have submitted your application to UCAS is the arrival of a confirmation of the courses and universities you have chosen. It is important to check this carefully to make sure there is no mistake. Then there is nothing to do but wait. Universities are increasingly aware that applicants don't like to be kept hanging around so you may find some decisions arriving fairly soon. However, if your form arrived at UCAS in late November or early December it can take several weeks to make its way through UCAS processing and on to your universities. When any offers do arrive, they will be one of the following:

Unconditional Offer (U)	This means you have already met all the entry requirements for the course
Conditional Offer (C)	This means the University will accept you if you meet certain additional requirements, usually specified grades in the examinations you will be taking
Rejection (R)	This means that either you have not got, and will not get, some key requirement for the course, or that you have lost out in competition with other, better applicants

If you receive an offer, you will almost certainly be invited to visit the university concerned. This is a good chance to find out much more about the course and university than you can through reading prospectuses and looking at websites. However, bear in mind that the occasion is designed to encourage you to accept the offer as well as to give you the opportunity to find out more. So, just like reading prospectuses, you have to be critical of what you are told and look for evidence for any claims.

Sometimes you may be invited for an interview before a decision is made. This could be the normal practice for that particular course, or it could be because your application is unusual in some way and the university wants to check that

When is an Interview not an Interview?

Interviews come in two forms. Outwardly both look the same, but in fact they have very different purposes. The first type of interview is the 'real' interview, where a genuine attempt is being made to assess your suitability for the course and your performance in the interview will make a difference to your chances of being made an offer. The second type of interview is the 'psychological' interview. It looks like an interview, feels like an interview, but actually doesn't make any difference. The university has already decided to make you an offer and the interview is merely a psychologically clever way of encouraging you to accept the offer. If you travel half way across the country, answer some tough questions and then get made an offer of a place, it makes you feel good, both about yourself and about the university which made you feel good. Hence you are more likely to accept that offer in favour of one which just arrived in the post. At least that is the idea behind the psychological interview.

The problem for you is that it is hard to tell which type of interview you are facing. Generally speaking, interviews for medical and medically related professions and for education are real (though it is still common for 80 per cent or more of interviewees to be made an offer). Interviews at very competitive universities such as Oxford and Cambridge are also usually real, and interviews for applicants who have an unusual background or lack the usual qualifications are generally genuine attempts to assess suitability. However, interviews for less popular courses, such as chemistry or engineering, at anywhere other than the most competitive universities for these subjects are often the psychological type of interview.

you are really suitable (perhaps you are a mature student without the usual formal qualifications). In some cases interviews are not quite what they seem (see box, *When is an Interview not an Interview?*), but you can never be sure, so it is best to treat any interview as a real interview.

If you do get called for interview, then go – you are unlikely to be made an offer if you don't turn up – and be sure that you arrive on time. Prepare yourself in advance, particularly for the obvious questions such as why you want to study the subject and why you want to go to that university. Re-read the copy of your application form to remind yourself what is in your personal statement. And dress smartly. While it is not necessary to look as if you are going to a wedding, an interview is not the time to make a fashion statement.

All being well, particularly if you have chosen your universities carefully, you will get several offers. You can hold on to any offer you receive until all your chosen universities have made their decisions, but then you have to choose which ones you want to accept.

Replies to Offers

You can accept one offer as your firm acceptance (often called your CF choice) and a second offer as your insurance acceptance (often called your CI choice), but you must decline any others. Most applicants who have more than one offer will accept as CF their first choice university and then a university which has made a lower offer as their CI choice.

You can, in fact, decline all your offers if you wish. Perhaps you have realised that you have made a dreadful mistake in your choice of subject and now wish to look for another subject in the Clearing procedure (see below). However, normally you will want to accept one offer as your firm acceptance.

Once you have done that, you and the university are bound together by the rules of UCAS. If you firmly accept an unconditional offer then you have a definite place at that university. If you firmly accept a conditional offer and then meet all the conditions, the university is obliged to accept you and you are obliged to go there. In making your firm acceptance, assuming you have conditional offers, you will have to balance your desire to attend a particular university against your estimate of whether you can meet the conditions. If you expect to get ABB at A level and the offers are all BCC or below, then it is easy: choose the place you want to go. If, however, you think you will get BCC and your offers are ABB, BBB, BCC and CDD, the decision is more difficult, especially if you really want to go to the university that offered ABB.

This is where the insurance acceptance comes in. If you want to, you can just have a firm acceptance and decline the rest. However, most applicants with more than one offer choose an insurance acceptance as well. If you are accepted by your firm choice then that is it, and the insurance choice becomes irrelevant. However, if your firm choice turns you down because you don't meet their conditions, you might still be accepted by your insurance choice, so you get a second chance before heading for Clearing. Obviously, it makes sense to choose a lower offer for your insurance choice so as to maximise your chances of getting at least one of your two choices. However, make sure it is somewhere you would still like to go because if that is where you are placed, the UCAS rules require you to go there. Remember that in some subjects such as chemistry or electronic engineering, places in Clearing, even at prestigious universities, are easy to obtain, so you could be better off choosing just a firm choice rather than an insurance choice you don't really want. If all this sounds rather complicated, the flowchart *Firm and Insurance Offers on Results Day* may help.

Results Day

If you accepted an unconditional offer, all you have to do is wait for the start of your course and roll up to register. However, most of you will be anxiously waiting for examination results before you find out whether you have been accepted. If you are taking Scottish Highers, an access course or a BTEC qualification, then your results will usually come out before A levels in England. This can be helpful if you don't get accepted as you will then have a chance to find a place somewhere else before the scramble for places after A-level results are published.

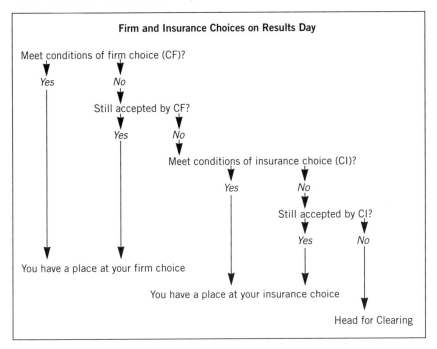

If you find that your results mean you have met all the conditions of your firm choice, congratulations! You have a place at your chosen university and you can relax, at least for now. Do check carefully though, especially if you have an offer expressed in terms of A-level points. Generally a points offer will require you to get a number of points in your best three subjects. So if you are taking four subjects and have an offer of 22 points, BBCE (24 overall, but 22 in the best three) is OK, but BCCD (24 overall, but only 20 in the best three) is not. It is a bit more complicated than this if you are taking a mixture of A levels and AS, but it is all explained in your UCAS offer letter.

If you are sure you have met all the conditions, you don't have to do anything. In a day or two you will receive confirmation of your place from UCAS, with a form to sign to confirm that you still want it, and details of when and where to register from your chosen university will follow a little while later. If you are not sure, or just need reassurance, you can ring the university to check, though bear in mind that several thousand others will be doing the same thing, so it may take a little while to get through. If you do ring, make sure you have your UCAS number handy.

Even if you have not met all the conditions, you may still find your place is confirmed. The university may be short of applicants that year or the other offer-holders had worse results than you (see box, *What if I Just Miss my Grades?*). If you are just one grade down, your chances will often be quite good; more than that and your chances will be much less.

What if I Just Miss My Grades?

Suppose you are offered BBC at A level and get BCC: will you still be accepted? This will depend on two main factors. First, did you drop a grade in a critical subject? If you were asked for a B in, say, chemistry and that was the subject where you got a C, that will reduce the chances of your being accepted. Second, what did everyone else with an offer for the course get? If the university has 50 places and 40 get the grades, the first place they will look for the extra 10 is among those who just missed the offer and you will probably be accepted. However, if 60 get the grades, they will probably reject anyone who didn't meet the offer precisely, and you may well not be accepted. There is nothing you can do about this. Universities are financially penalised for admitting the wrong number of students, so they will always want to admit as near as possible to their target number.

Clearing

If you find that you don't have a place then you will be eligible for the UCAS Clearing scheme, a way of matching universities without students to students without universities. Essentially, it is up to you to find a university that is prepared to accept you. The best way to do this is to ring a university and tell them what you want to do. Usually, if they have vacancies, they will take your details and either give you a decision straightaway or very soon afterwards. Just keep going until somewhere offers you a place. Here are some points to remember if you end up in this position:

- prepare in advance – unless you are very confident you will get the grades, do some contingency planning before results day. Make a list of possible courses and universities where you might be prepared to go in priority order. This will be easy to check against the Clearing vacancy lists when they are published
- be there – don't go on holiday at the critical time
- if you think you may not have a place, check with your firm and insurance choices as soon as possible

- check the Clearing vacancy lists in newspapers or the UCAS website for universities with vacancies in your subject
- think about alternative courses (perhaps a joint course with another subject instead of a single subject course) to maximise the choice available
- start ringing possible universities straight away (places at good universities can be filled very quickly)
- always ring yourself – universities are less impressed by people ringing on your behalf
- if you can't get through, send an e-mail or fax

There will be a few vacancies not listed in the official vacancy lists because the universities know they can fill them with speculative callers and do not need the extra calls generated by the vacancy lists. If there is somewhere you really want to go, it might just be worth ringing even if they are not in the lists. However, such vacancies will be taken within hours, at most within a day of A-level results being published.

Some applicants find that their results are much better than they expected and they are qualified for a much better university than the one where they accepted an offer, or for a high-demand course such as medicine for which they never thought they would be accepted. If you find yourself in this position, you can do one of three things:

1 Carry on with your existing choice, as long as you are sure that is what you want to do now.
2 Find an alternative university which is prepared to accept you and then negotiate with the university where you have been placed to be released into the Clearing scheme. The university is not obliged to do this, and will probably try to persuade you not to, but most will eventually give way if it is clear that you have genuinely thought through what you are doing. Once in the Clearing scheme your alternative university can accept you.
3 Withdraw completely from UCAS and apply again the following year.

If your results are much worse than you expected, the situation can be more difficult. If there were genuine extenuating circumstances (perhaps you were taken ill during your examinations or there was a bereavement in your family) your school should have told the examining board and university about this already. Neither will be impressed by being told about it after your low grades have been published. If the results are just plain surprising, you may wish to seek a re-mark by the examining board. If this brings to light an error, and your grades go up, the university will review its decision, though if you miss the deadline the university may say it can only accept you for the following year.

Trying to get a place in Clearing is not as difficult as it sounds. There is always a lot of talk about 'chaos' and 'scrambling', but in fact universities are getting much better at dealing with large numbers of enquiries very quickly. After all, they have a strong interest in signing up good students as they suffer severe financial penalties if they under-recruit by a large margin. And the range of course available in Clearing is huge. In 1999, for example, there were a number of vacancies on courses in law and English, two very high-demand subjects. They may not have been precisely the right course or in an ideal part of the country, but they were there and anyone with the right grades who acted quickly could have obtained a place. If you wanted chemistry or engineering you could have had a choice of a number of prestigious universities, even with quite low grades in some cases.

Having said that, trying to find a place in Clearing is not much fun for anyone. The best way to avoid it is to be sensible and realistic early on in the application process. If you apply for courses and universities where you have a good chance of being made an offer and accept offers you have a good chance of achieving, then you will probably be able to avoid Clearing altogether. That is much better for both you and the universities.

Do I Apply This Year?

Some students take a year out between finishing at school or college and starting university, often known as a gap year. If you are thinking about doing this it is still best to apply during your final year as a 'deferred applicant'. When you fill in your UCAS form, you cross out the year of entry at the top and write in the next year. This should mean that you get your university place sorted out before starting your job or travels and so don't have to worry about it during your gap year. Indeed, for the more adventurous travellers, trying to fill in a UCAS form on the back of a Mongolian yak or half way across the Australian desert is not recommended. Also, if things go badly wrong in your examinations and you don't get a place, you do get an opportunity to rethink your career options or resit and still start at university when you planned to.

In general, gap years are a good thing. You get a chance to do something useful or interesting, such as work or travel, and maybe save up some money to finance your course. And you will arrive at university a little bit older and wiser. In a few subjects, it may take you a little while to get back into serious study – mathematics is notorious for being a bit harder to take up again after a year away from study – but most students soon catch up again.

In general, universities are happy to consider deferred applicants but, if the prospectus does not make a clear statement about the university's policy, it would be sensible to check.

6

Paying Your Way

The head of one university tells the story of a photographer at Graduation asking the student to place a hand on the parent's shoulder, only to hear the riposte from the parent, "Wouldn't it be more appropriate to have a hand in my pocket!" It is an apocryphal tale but one which will ring true for many parents, given the financial support required of them. Going to university these days can be an expensive family business and student debt has become an accepted fact of life. Indeed, it is not uncommon for students to graduate with a debt of £2,000 or more, over and above their maximum student loan. You will need to muster all the resources you can lay your hands on unless you are one of that small band who has a regular private income. The vast majority of students have to rely on loans, savings, earnings, overdrafts and the generosity of family and friends. But all of that is in the distant future.

Parental Contributions

Parental contribution towards university tuition fees and a student's living cost is means-tested and is based on their so-called Residual Income. This is their gross income from all sources less certain defined allowances. Currently, below a Residual Income of £17,805 no parental contribution is expected. Above this figure, there is a sliding scale of contribution until at £28,505 your parents would be expected to pay the full tuition fee of £1,050. At higher income levels, your parents would also be expected to contribute towards part of your day-to-day living costs.

Mature Students

If, however, you have supported yourself for at least three years prior to becoming a student, your parents will not be expected to contribute to either tuition fees or living costs. Such mature students will be used to managing their finances, but for others reading this we begin with a breakdown of expected expenditure and income.

Expenditure

Tuition fees

Since 1998, full-time undergraduates whose homes are in the UK or in other EU and EEA countries have been liable to pay means-tested fees direct to the university (frequently by instalment), subject to the maximum shown in the table:

Year	£ Sterling	
1998–1999	£1,000	(£500)*
1999–2000	£1,025	(£510)
2000–2001	£1,050	(£520)

*Figures in brackets are fees for students on full year sandwich/industry placements or studying abroad (except for EU exchange programmes such as SOCRATES and ERASMUS students).

However, most students can get a contribution towards these fees, the level of which is dependent on their – and their family's – income. In fact, it is estimated that about a third of students are fully exempt from paying anything and about a third pay the full fee, and any such contribution towards tuition fees is not a loan and does not have to be repaid. UK students must apply through the Local Education Authority (LEA) where they normally live for assessment of any contribution. Scottish students must apply through the Student Awards Agency for Scotland (SAAS) and those in Northern Ireland to the Department of Higher and Further Education, Training and Employment (DHFETE). You should do so as soon as you have received an offer – even a conditional offer – of a university place. Other EU students are sent an application form by the university offering a place.

In a dramatic move (January 2000), the Scottish Parliament has agreed to abolish fees with effect from autumn 2000 for students resident in Scotland and mainland EU full-time students studying in Scotland (but not for other UK students studying in Scotland). However, those students not paying fees will be expected after graduation to pay £2,000 into an endowment fund for less well off students on essentially the same basis as repayment of a student loan (see later). Students resident in Scotland but studying elsewhere in the UK will continue to pay tuition fees to their universities.

Tuition fees for overseas students
Overseas students normally resident in countries outside the EU and EEA pay full-cost tuition fees in all countries of the UK and these are likely to be in the range:

Subject	£ Sterling	$US
Humanities and Social Sciences	£6,000–£7,000	$9,000–$11,200
Sciences and Engineering	£7,000–£9,000	$11,200–$14,400
Clinical Subjects	£16,000–£17,000	$25,600–$27,000

Conversion rate £1.00:$1.60

Whilst many overseas students coming to Britain receive financial support from their home countries, it must be emphasised that UK scholarships and bursaries, whether from the UK government, sponsors or the individual universities themselves are limited. Students from overseas are strongly advised, therefore, to make sure they have sufficient funds for the above full tuition fees and all necessary living costs before leaving home. Indeed, you will almost certainly be asked to guarantee in writing that you have sufficient funds for the complete duration of your course. You should also make sure that you have some ready money or travellers' cheques with you for immediate use on arrival to cover food, travel and other essentials.

Living costs

For all students the biggest expenditure items will be regular living costs: accommodation, food and even, perhaps some clothes! There is evidence to suggest that most university entrants don't know what it costs to be a student and can seriously underestimate these items by as much as 50 per cent. A number stay at home and travel daily to their nearest university and that is probably the cheapest option. However, most first-year students take up a guaranteed place in a university residence. Whilst this is by far the most sensible decision from a social perspective, it can be a relatively expensive and inflexible one. You may perhaps be expected to pay for full-board with all meals even if you choose not to eat in all the time. Of growing interest to many is the possible half-way house of self-catering university accommodation where heating and lighting – no small matters of cost – may still be included but where you can at least control the food bills. You might even be able to engage in a spot of discounted bulk food buying with fellow residents and hence stretch the money further.

Given that these are the biggest items of expenditure – rent alone could account for 60 per cent of weekly income – it is well worth giving the various accommodation options serious thought, making sure that you maintain maximum flexibility within any arrangements. Check what rent you may have to pay in advance and whether or not you have to pay a retainer in the vacations. As a general rule, accommodation costs are highest in London, the southeast England and East Anglia and least expensive in Wales, Scotland and northeast England.

Studying costs

Next come costs associated with course work and the essentials: books, stationery, equipment and perhaps fieldwork or electives, here and overseas. After all, you are at university to get a degree! The recommended reading list might be long and expensive. You would be well advised not to rush out and buy the lot but rather get to know how to use the library at the earliest opportunity. Students' Unions often organise second-hand book sales and access to the internet is easy and free via the university network. Are some textbooks you want available through these sources, at the very least to buy at discount prices? Or is it feasible to share books with a fellow student?

Other costs

But university most definitely shouldn't be all work. Again, the students' union will cater for play in all its guises at a fraction of the cost demanded by commercial providers. In fact, university is a great time – perhaps the only time – to pursue the most common or esoteric of interests at a price you can easily afford. However, expenditure on the social scene, whether it be launderette, cinema or nightclub, drinking or occasional eating out, is still likely to be a significant cost for most students.

Phone bills can be another sizeable item, especially if you ring the old folks at home or that distant loved one for an hour or so every day and they happen to be in Tokyo or San Francisco! Competition for your custom is fierce and the Students' Union may well be able to advise on the best deals amongst a growing army of call providers. The use of mobile phones is increasing rapidly but they remain a relatively expensive option although 'pay as you go' tariffs have been introduced.

Travel costs
Finally, there are travel costs where most students rely on public transport; and this is not just between home and university, perhaps two or three times a year, but also from your accommodation to the university every day. This could be a key factor when choosing where to live, both in terms of time and money. It may well pay you to purchase a Student Card on local or national transport, or better still to opt to live a stone's throw from the university or on frequent bus, train or tram routes to it. Whilst most students manage to live less than three miles from the campus, a recent NUS survey showed that the average distance in East Anglia and Scotland is over four and five miles respectively, and in London about half an hour away.

As a general rule, the cost of living is lower the further north and west you choose to study in the UK.

That, then, is a brief look at what you will need money for. Try looking at your own personal situation to draw up an annual expenditure list and return to it on a regular basis throughout the year to see how you're doing. In other words, begin to estimate an annual budget. This is shown in the chart of income and expenditure at the end of the chapter.

Income

Earning before university
One possible source of earnings to consider prior to coming to university is a gap year – another is sponsorship. Taking a year out is attractive to a growing number of students whether to gain experience, to earn money or both. The reasons for taking a gap year seem to be shifting from solely an opportunity for personal development to more one to boost the bank balance ahead of becoming a student. In other words, a shift away from altruism and towards utilitarianism. This understandable short-term expediency needs to be carefully measured against the somewhat longer-term but less tangible benefits of a placement, here or overseas, of real service to the community, but perhaps with less monetary reward. These days, universities take careful note of extracurricular experience and inter-

ests alongside good exam grades. Employers, too, look more and more to the development of skills and expertise beyond academic performance and class of degree.

Work placements might be structured as, for example, with the 'Year in Industry Scheme' or 'GAP Activity Projects', or casual. Both bring the added bonus of invaluable experience to put on your CV. Sponsorship is available mostly to those wishing to study engineering or business subjects and a good source of information is the *Student Support Sponsorship Funding Directory* published by CRAC/Hobsons.

Student loans

Until 1998, the government operated a system of student grants to help with living costs but these were gradually phased out and finally abolished altogether for the 1999–2000 academic year. Grants in the form of NHS Bursaries do still exist for students on most health-related degree courses. Since October 1999, government support for university students is wholly through a loan. For most UK students going to university now, therefore, a significant source of income will be this student loan from the Student Loan Company. As with an application for contributions towards tuition fees, so with a student loan you must apply without delay in the first instance to your LEA or funding agency, and you should do this even if you feel you do not qualify for a government contribution towards your tuition fees.

You don't have to take out this loan – although about 75 per cent of students do – but if and when you do you will be entering into a legal contract to repay the loan in full **after** leaving university. When and what you repay will depend on your total income and will normally be deducted from your pay. You will repay nothing until your income exceeds £10,000 a year. The interest rate on the loan is linked to the rate of inflation so you will be asked to repay no more, in real terms, than you actually borrowed.

Since the loans-only system was introduced, the maximum annual loan rates have been as shown in the table:

	1999–2000	2000–2001
Living at home:	£2,875	£2,950
Living away from home:		
London	£4,480	£4,590
Elsewhere	£3,635	£3,725

The amount of loan you can obtain depends, amongst other things, on how much you and your family will be expected to contribute to your living costs. However, 75 per cent of the maximum loan is available regardless of family income.

Only UK students can be considered for a student loan or the other support systems outlined below.

Further financial support

There are two further sources of modest government help to students, namely

Hardship Loans and Access Funds, both of which are allocated by the universities themselves to undergraduates in financial difficulties. They decide which students need support and what the level of that support will be. **Hardship Loans** are, as the name implies, another loan, usually in amounts from £100 up to £500, and are added to any existing student loan. **Access Funds** are normally given as a non-repayable grant and may be available as a one-off sum or in the form of a bursary payable every year.

The information in this chapter was correct at the time of writing but the rules and regulations for all of these contributions towards tuition fees, student loans or funds and other **Supplementary Grants** (for disabled students, students with dependants, single parent students and care leavers) are somewhat complicated and you had best consult your own copy of the Department for Education and Employment (DfEE) booklet *Financial Support for Higher Education Students*, *Student Support in Scotland* (SAAS) or *Financial Support for Students in Higher Education* (DHFETE).

If you are ineligible for any of the above financial support, you may still be able to apply for a **Career Development Loan**, available though some high street banks in partnership with the DfEE. Students on a wide range of vocational courses can borrow from £300 to £8,000 and not pay anything back until they finish their studies.

Part-time work

The last few years have seen a significant growth in Student Employment Offices on university campuses, no doubt a response, in part, to the introduction of fees and loans. About a third of all undergraduates now have a part-time job. These offices act as agencies introducing employers with work to students seeking work, perhaps even in the university itself, throughout the academic year. They are also guardians of the student interest, abiding by Codes of Practice which regulate such things as minimum wages, maximum hours worked in term (typically 15 hours a week – so as to avoid adverse effect on studies), non-discrimination, etc. Most universities now have a Student Employment Office run by their Careers Service or the Students' Union and they make a welcome contribution to the local economy. This is hardly surprising given the enormous range of skills and knowledge residing in any student community.

Vacation work

Vacations, too, offer an opportunity to earn cash whilst developing skills for that CV. As with the gap year, such work experience can be casual, formalised in a scheme like the 'Shell Technology Enterprise Programme', or even as part of a sponsorship programme.

Banks

Finally, banks are well disposed to today's university students in the certain knowledge that many will be tomorrow's high-earning professionals. They are sympathetic to the student cause and will generally permit modest overdrafts on your account to ease cash flow problems without pain. It pays – literally – to shop around for the best offers when transferring or opening your account. Check to see if the bank offers a 24-hour service via the internet or telephone and make sure that its cash machines are accessible around the clock. Branches near universities often have dedicated student advisers to tell you about interest-free overdrafts, discount insurance or travel, CD vouchers and other offers to lure you inside.

Your Annual Budget

You can now complete your estimated annual budget by listing all expected income, including any savings you will bring with you to university. See how this compares with expenditure in the hope that the balance sheet almost balances or, better still, that you are left with spare cash in the bank for doing what you've always wanted to do. However, budgeting accurately is never an easy process, and PricewaterhouseCoopers have constructed their simple income and expenditure chart to make monitoring and controlling your finances easier:

Period	1	2	3–11	12	Total
Income					
Student loan	2,765				2,765
Parental contribution	80	80		80	960
Term time/vacation work	50	50		500	1,500
Transfer from savings					
Total Income	2,895	130		580	5,225
Expenses					
Tuition fees	500				500
Rent	200	200		200	2,400
Electricity, gas, water	15	15		15	180
Insurance	30				30
Telephone	10	10		10	120
Travel	30	20		15	200
Food	110	100		105	900
Entertainment	50	50		50	600
Societies, sports	20	10		10	100
Books , stationery	50	35			150
Other (clothing, etc)	75	10		40	250
Vacation				150	250
Total Expenses	1,090	450		595	5,580
Excess (deficit) of income over expenses in period	1,805	(320)		(15)	(355)
Balance brought forward from last period		1,805		(355)	
Balance carried forward	1,540	1,485		(355)	(355)

(In column 3–11: "add figures for each month here")

This format is suitable for recording either budgeted or actual income and expenditure, with the 12 periods shown either representing the months of a year – probably best for budget purposes – or a termly record of actual income and expenses incurred each week. Clearly your patterns of expenditure will differ significantly between term time and vacations. In this example, we have assumed that you are not required to pay full tuition fees, but only £500 instead of £1,050.

It can be difficult to predict accurately some variable expenses such as entertainment. Start by identifying bills which *must* be paid and include in this a small contingency fund. This will leave you with the 'flexible' part of your income to take weekly from the bank. Don't be too optimistic in your first budget, and do be aware of how much you actually spend. Also, do budget for balls at the end of terms, birthdays and parties, or you may find yourself missing out on the best social events of the year. If there is a big gap between budget and actual, perhaps your spending habits need attention rather than your budgeting. Above all, remember to keep a check on your finances so that money worries do not detract from your studying and from enjoying university life.

7

Coming from Overseas

It is difficult enough for individuals living in the UK when faced with the bewildering choice amongst the 100 or so universities. How much more so if you live on the other side of the world where, in addition, you will want to consider the significant costs of living and studying in another country. You will need a great deal of information – considerably more than is available within this chapter – but this, and the previous chapter on funding, will give you a good start and point you in the right direction.

The Country

The British Isles comprise two sovereign and independent states of the European Union, the UK and the Republic of Ireland. Within the UK there are three further countries: England, Scotland and Wales – sometimes collectively called Great Britain – and the province of Northern Ireland. Of the 97 universities covered in *The Times Good University Guide*:

- 76 are in England
- 13 are in Scotland
- 6 are in Wales
- 2 are in Northern Ireland.

In 1999, a Parliament in Scotland and an Assembly in Wales were established, each with devolved powers. These bodies are already having a positive impact on university education in these countries.

The Weather

Most students coming to the UK will find the climate different! Given its position west of the European mainland, Britain tends to have low humidity, warm summers and mild winters. Although there are four distinct climatic seasons, spring, summer, autumn and winter, the weather is unpredictable and liable to change and change again in the course of a day. Rainfall is highest in and close to the hilly regions in the north and west – typically over 1,000 mm a year – whilst daily temperatures range from 5 °C in January to 20 °C in July. Snow falls for a short time most winters. As a general rule, southeast England is relatively dry and sunny and northwest Scotland wet and cloudy.

Entry and Employment Regulations

There are four main receiving countries for university students in the English-speaking world – the USA, the UK, Australia and Canada – and all four have their distinctive characteristics. All four have restrictions on entry and employment for foreign nationals. However, in June 1999 the Prime Minister, Tony Blair, launched a worldwide campaign to encourage overseas students to come to the UK's universities. As part of this initiative, the government is making the passage much easier by streamlining visa and entry procedures. In addition, overseas students can now work for up to 20 hours a week during the academic year and full-time in the vacations without the need for a work permit. Similarly, if they themselves are staying in the UK for a year or more then their spouses and children will be able to take paid employment even if they are here for a shorter period. This is the latest package of new measures on immigration and work experience designed to make the UK a more attractive place to study. The government has promised more.

In addition to a valid passport, some students – called 'visa nationals' – coming to university in Britain will need to obtain a visa from the British Embassy or High Commission before arrival and this could take weeks to arrive. Non-visa nationals do not, as the name implies, require a visa for entry but it might be wise for them to submit their study documents to the British Consulate in their own country just to be on the safe side. Nationals of an EU country, Norway or Iceland are free to travel to the UK without a visa to study or work.

How and When to Apply

Chapter 5 deals with this matter and you should read the information there in conjunction with what follows. If you are applying for a full-time first degree course you will need to fill in a UCAS application form and you can send for one through the UCAS website. You can even complete the form electronically and send it via the internet at some schools and British Council offices.

If you are applying from within an EU country, your application form must be received at UCAS by 15 December otherwise you will be treated as a late applicant. Different, usually earlier, dates apply for Oxford and Cambridge, and medical and art and design courses (see page 101).

If you are applying from a non-EU country, you can send your form to UCAS at any time between 1 September and 30 June preceding the academic year in which you plan to commence your studies. However, most students apply well before 30 June to make sure that places are still available and to allow plenty of time to make immigration, travel and accommodation arrangements.

British Universities

The UK universities have their origins in the ancient seats of learning at Oxford (1096), Cambridge (1209) and St Andrews (1411). They enjoy a worldwide reputation for the quality of their courses, teaching and research which are rigorously assessed by these independent bodies:
- Higher Education Funding Councils
- Quality Assurance Agency for Higher Education

- Office for Standards in Education

The appointment of external examiners at each university also guarantees good standards. These, in turn, are reflected in high entry requirements, short and intensive courses of study, and high completion rates, the latter resulting from an infrastructure which offers strong student support.

This support for overseas students is more comprehensive than in most countries and begins long before students arrive in the UK. Most universities have advisers, even offices, in other countries and they are likely to put students in touch with current students or graduates and answer any queries. Then there may well be pre-departure receptions for students and their families and certainly full written pre-arrival information on all aspects of living and studying in Britain. Arriving in the UK, there are often arrangements made to meet and greet students at the nearest coach or rail station or airport, a guarantee of warm and comfortable university accommodation, an orientation programme – often lasting several days – to meet friends and to help students adjust to their new surroundings, and courses in the English language for those who need them. But it's not all work. Each university has a students' union which organises social, cultural, religious and sporting clubs and events, including many specifically for overseas students, such as short visits to other European countries. Both the university and its students' union are most likely to have full-time staff whose sole purpose is to look after the welfare of overseas students.

And that's not all! Students receive free medical treatment under the National Health Service, full access to a professional counselling service and a university careers service network – with an enviable reputation throughout the world – to help you decide what to do on completion of your studies. The fact that degree courses here are more intensive, and thus shorter, than those in many other countries has an obvious financial advantage, not only in study and living costs, but also in the opportunity to enter, or re-enter, the employment market sooner.

Where overseas students study

Most of what follows in this chapter refers to the tables within it. It must be emphasised that these are based solely on the numbers of overseas students involved and not necessarily on the quality of the university. It is very important, therefore, that you cross refer to the League Table on pages 18-21 and the individual Subject Tables (pages 38-76) which are concerned with quality

The data are based on overseas students enrolling in all years of first degree courses at UK universities in 1997–98 and are the latest figures available. They exclude those students whose complete study programmes were outside the UK but include the majority of students taking part in European Union exchange programmes such as ERASMUS, TEMPUS and LINGUA at UK universities. First degrees are mostly awarded at Bachelor level (BA, BEng, BSc, etc.) and last for three or four years. There are also some so-called 'enhanced' first degrees (MEng, MChem) which take four years to complete. Vocational courses like architecture, dentistry and medicine are one or two years longer. Some universities offer one-year foundation courses, including English language tuition, to act as a bridge for overseas students whose qualifications are insufficient for direct entry to a degree course.

Recent shifts in countries of origin are noteworthy. Whilst Asia remains hugely important as a source of international students (Malaysia, Hong Kong, Singapore, Japan, Brunei and Taiwan), some countries there have been beset with economic problems and this, in turn, has affected demand for study overseas. At the same time, there has been a growth in student numbers from the Americas, particularly Latin America (Argentina, Brazil and Mexico), and from the Indian subcontinent. In many UK universities you could expect to have fellow students from over 100 countries across the world. The British university system is truly a global one and increasingly so with more than one in ten of its student population coming from countries overseas.

Table 1 *Which countries do overseas students come from?*

EU Countries		Non-EU Countries (Top 20)	
Greece	15,983	Malaysia	12,102
Irish Republic	7,889	Singapore	4,175
France	5,244	Hong Kong	3,795
Germany	4,622	Norway	2,072
Spain	2,901	Cyprus	2,028
Italy	1,720	Japan	1,340
Finland	1,358	Kenya*	1,305
Sweden	1,266	United States	1,105
Belgium	1,097	Nigeria*	1,067
Netherlands	963	Israel	980
Portugal	761	Brunei	852
Denmark	705	Taiwan*	773
Austria	405	Mauritius*	620
Gibraltar	395	India*	596
Luxembourg	361	Pakistan*	548
All EU students	45,670	Sri Lanka*	512
		Canada	453
		Switzerland	425
		Oman*	396
		Turkey*	396
		All non-EU students	44,571

* Students from these non-EU countries and the Turkish Republic of North Cyprus, will require a visa to study in the UK.

Tables 1 and 2 give a broad overview of overseas students in Britain. You can see where students come from and what they study here. Greece and Malaysia are prominent as major sending countries, and most students, regardless of where they come from, pursue courses of study which are strongly vocational in that they lead to careers in business, industry and the professions.

Table 2 *What do overseas students study?*

	EU	Non-EU	Total
Engineering and Technology	8,157	10,502	18,659
Business and Administrative Studies	7,711	8,876	16,587
Social and Legal Studies	5,600	6,425	12.025
Mathematics and Informatics	2,573	2,888	5,461
Biological Sciences	3,109	1,348	4,457
Modern and Classical Languages	3,394	920	4,314
Subjects Allied to Medicine	2,048	2,174	4,222
Creative Arts and Design	1,837	1,805	3,642
Architecture, Building and Planning	1,727	1,862	3,589
Physical Sciences	1,990	719	2,709
Medicine and Dentistry	364	1,797	2,161
Humanities	750	413	1,163
Education	380	603	983
Mass Communication and Documentation	597	315	912
Agriculture and Veterinary Science	442	309	751
Combined Subjects	4,991	3,615	8,606
Total	45,670	44,571	90,241

'Subjects allied to medicine' includes nursing; 'business and administrative studies' includes financial management; and 'creative arts and design' includes music and drama.

Table 3 *Where do overseas students study?*

EU Students		Non-EU students	
Ulster	1,885	Middlesex	1,240
Middlesex	1,416	Sheffield	1,082
Coventry	1,227	Portsmouth	1,010
Anglia	1,047	London, UCL	974
Essex	988	Nottingham	968
Portsmouth	985	London, Imperial	962
Glamorgan	875	Hertfordshire	919
Brighton	808	Leeds	915
Queen's, Belfast	787	London, LSE	914
Kingston	783	Manchester	910
Kent	778	UMIST	909
Luton	772	Thames Valley	902
Sunderland	759	Birmingham	823
Wolverhampton	759	East London	801
Manchester Metropolitan	740	Northumbria	791
Sussex	734	Coventry	753
Greenwich	732	Warwick	713
North London	723	Oxford Brookes	691
Westminster	696	Cardiff	685
London Guildhall	688	Cambridge	681
Hertfordshire	684	London, King's	647
South Bank	634	Oxford	644
Lincs & Humberside	627	Salford	633
Plymouth	597	Luton	627
West of England	576	Kent	612
All EU Students	45,670	*All Non-EU Students*	44,571

Table 3 lists those universities with large numbers of overseas students. Ulster owes much of its popularity to its close proximity to the Republic of Ireland whilst big numbers at Middlesex, particularly in business and administrative studies, include students on large exchange programmes. EU students are well represented in the new universities whereas students from other countries gravitate to all parts of the sector. This pattern of distribution largely reflects chosen fields of study and the universities where these subjects are available. As emphasised earlier, you must satisfy yourself about quality by going back to Chapters 1 and 4.

Probably the most useful information is to be found in Table 4 which lists the universities by numbers of overseas students in the 20 most popular subjects, each of which has at least a thousand overseas students. Again, use this information in conjunction with the tables that measure quality in the earlier chapters. The subjects are listed in the order of popularity.

Table 4 *The most popular subjects and universities*

Business Studies	EU	Non-EU	Total
Middlesex	376	218	594
Lincs & Humberside	341	117	458
Northumbria	125	301	426
Coventry	202	197	399
Wolverhampton	281	103	384
South Bank	275	88	363
Brighton	231	83	314
Westminster	150	143	293
Glamorgan	185	107	292
Thames Valley	63	185	248
All overseas students	5,599	3,945	9,544

Law	EU	Non-EU	Total
Thames Valley	104	198	302
London, King's	104	153	257
Wolverhampton	13	212	225
Kent	99	114	213
Essex	104	105	209
Cardiff	9	190	199
Sheffield	4	183	187
Bristol	7	156	163
East London	29	106	135
Staffordshire	33	102	135
All overseas students	1,487	3,723	5,210

Electrical & Electronic Engineering	EU	Non-EU	Total
Hertfordshire	71	178	249
Sussex	109	78	187
Leeds	29	156	185
Coventry	74	94	168
Kent	102	58	160
Sheffield	23	134	157
Glamorgan	98	40	138
Northumbria	40	90	130
Essex	75	55	130

Nottingham Trent	12	107	119
All overseas students	2078	2571	4649

Computer Science	EU	Non-EU	Total
Staffordshire	54	141	195
Portsmouth	57	118	175
Oxford Brookes	25	149	174
UMIST	57	103	160
Coventry	74	83	157
Hertfordshire	49	106	155
Ulster	132	0	132
Westminster	58	64	122
East London	11	103	114
Teesside	79	29	108
All overseas students	1,931	2,324	4,255

Economics	EU	Non-EU	Total
London, LSE	108	283	391
Anglia	347	23	370
Essex	114	42	156
Leicester	3	127	130
London, UCL	38	90	128
Cambridge	26	100	126
Warwick	35	80	115
Middlesex	77	33	110
Portsmouth	92	18	110
London, Queen Mary	50	47	97
All overseas students	2,157	1,637	3,794

Mechanical Engineering	EU	Non-EU	Total
Portsmouth	88	164	252
UMIST	20	134	154
London, Imperial	23	121	144
Sheffield	10	130	140
Glasgow	35	105	140
Sussex	79	50	129
Coventry	51	73	124
Liverpool	42	80	122
Leeds	25	85	110
Birmingham	7	84	91
All overseas students	1,513	2,054	3,567

Civil Engineering	EU	Non-EU	Total
Hertfordshire	65	125	190
East London	104	84	188
Leeds	49	121	170
Portsmouth	85	78	163
London, UCL	31	88	119
Coventry	79	37	116
Brighton	90	20	110
London, Imperial	38	70	108
Birmingham	30	77	107
Liverpool	55	41	96
All overseas students	1,781	1,570	3,351

Accountancy	EU	Non-EU	Total
Lincs & Humberside	1	243	244
London, LSE	20	159	179
Thames Valley	14	150	164
Middlesex	12	143	155
Lancaster	7	142	149
Portsmouth	30	96	126
South Bank	6	113	119
Leeds Metropolitan	13	85	98
Sheffield	0	96	96
Glamorgan	27	68	95
All overseas students	370	2,541	2,911

Design Studies	EU	Non-EU	Total
Middlesex	54	134	188
Surrey Institute	77	97	174
Central England	28	107	135
Westminster	71	63	134
De Montfort	49	37	86
Wolverhampton	30	51	81
Nottingham Trent	19	59	78
Kingston	28	40	68
Manchester Metropolitan	21	37	58
Newport	39	18	57
All overseas students	927	1,036	1,963

Architecture	EU	Non-EU	Total
Greenwich	100	41	141
Portsmouth	60	53	113
Westminster	82	28	110
Oxford Brookes	70	39	109
East London	51	39	90
Manchester Metropolitan	24	58	82
South Bank	52	26	78
Nottingham	11	64	75
North London	55	12	67
Robert Gordon	35	30	65
All overseas students	1,112	799	1,911

Catering & Institutional Mgt	EU	Non-EU	Total
Surrey	91	124	215
Thames Valley	43	74	117
Oxford Brookes	46	69	115
Glasgow Caledonian	11	91	102
Brighton	48	40	88
Luton	33	39	72
Middlesex	16	51	67
Portsmouth	26	37	63
Manchester Metropolitan	42	20	62
South Bank	32	27	59
All overseas students	782	858	1,640

Psychology	EU	Non-EU	Total
Middlesex	95	18	113
Ulster	107	2	109
Queen's, Belfast	95	0	95

Thames Valley	36	29	65
Kent	38	25	63
London, UCL	17	45	62
Essex	50	8	58
Sussex	38	19	57
London, Royal Holloway	37	15	52
London, Goldsmiths'	37	15	52
All overseas students	1,152	477	1,629

General Engineering	EU	Non-EU	Total
Coventry	187	13	200
Cambridge	24	120	144
Aberdeen	17	109	126
Oxford	29	93	122
De Montfort	61	38	99
Portsmouth	50	35	85
Warwick	11	53	64
Brunel	16	44	60
Lincs & Humberside	13	22	35
Glasgow Caledonian	25	9	34
All overseas students	695	756	1,451

Building	EU	Non-EU	Total
Greenwich	4	144	148
Northumbria	40	107	147
South Bank	6	103	109
Glamorgan	82	21	103
Ulster	92	8	100
Nottingham Trent	6	62	68
Heriot-Watt	10	49	59
UMIST	4	49	53
Central England	16	35	51
Napier	41	9	50
All overseas students	454	913	1,367

Chemical Engineering	EU	Non-EU	Total
London, Imperial	22	112	134
UMIST	17	95	112
Birmingham	8	98	106
Sheffield	13	66	79
Leeds	18	49	67
Surrey	27	36	63
London, UCL	8	53	61
Bradford	19	33	52
Teesside	33	17	50
Bath	17	28	45
All overseas students	313	753	1,066

English	EU	Non-EU	Total
Luton	118	12	130
Salford	27	33	60
Anglia	52	5	57
Oxford	7	29	36
Lampeter	33	1	34
Cambridge	11	22	33
Sunderland	27	4	31

Aberdeen	29	2	31
Kent	23	7	30
Stirling	11	19	30
All overseas students	689	371	1,060

Pharmacy	EU	Non-EU	Total
Strathclyde	14	156	170
Sunderland	108	33	141
Brighton	87	43	130
Liverpool John Moores	25	96	121
Robert Gordon	68	30	98
Nottingham	0	80	80
Portsmouth	37	24	61
Bradford	23	27	50
London, King's	22	26	48
Cardiff	4	40	44
All overseas students	411	636	1,047

Medicine	EU	Non-EU	Total
Sheffield	14	122	136
Queen's, Belfast	19	68	87
Liverpool	7	73	80
Cambridge	16	47	63
Nottingham	5	51	56
Edinburgh	11	34	45
Leeds	4	40	44
Glasgow	7	37	44
Manchester	3	40	43
Leicester	2	39	41
All overseas students	154	852	1,006

Politics	EU	Non-EU	Total
Sussex	93	34	127
London, LSE	46	52	98
Kent	49	30	79
Aberystwyth	37	17	54
Keele	20	19	39
Warwick	14	23	37
Birmingham	20	11	31
Reading	17	13	30
Staffordshire	18	10	28
Plymouth	22	2	24
All overseas students	654	352	1,006

Mathematics	EU	Non-EU	Total
Essex	156	3	159
London, Imperial	37	42	79
Cambridge	26	43	69
Middlesex	54	3	57
Heriot-Watt	27	24	51
London, Queen Mary	19	31	50
Oxford	18	29	47
London, UCL	12	33	45
Sussex	20	8	28
Warwick	3	21	24
All overseas students	549	451	1,000

Further information

Advice and information on the UK universities are available through the British Council and its Educational Counselling Service. The Council maintains a comprehensive network of information centres in cities throughout the world and organises more than 50 university exhibitions in some 25 key countries every year. Its 'Virtual Campus' is a good guide to studying and living in Britain. It is worth visiting at: http://www.educationuk.org

The individual universities have their own profiles in the 'Virtual Campus' where you can find further details of their support services for overseas students. There is also information on course fees, living costs and English language requirements. Website addresses are also given in each of the university profiles in this book. UKCOSA, the Council for International Education, is another useful source of advice and information to overseas students. Its web site can be viewed at: http://www.ukcosa.org.uk

8

Oxbridge

Oxbridge is another world when it comes to university admissions. Although part of the UCAS network, the two universities have different deadlines from the rest of the system, and applications are made direct to colleges. There is little to choose between them in terms of entrance requirements, but a formidable number of successful applicants have the maximum possible A-level score.

However, that does not mean the talented student should be shy about applying: both Oxford and Cambridge have fewer applicants per place than many less prestigious universities, and admission tutors are always looking to extend the range of schools and colleges from which they can recruit. For those with a realistic chance of success, there is little to lose except the possibility of a wasted space on the UCAS form. While a few universities are said to look askance at candidates who consider them second best to any other institution, most are likely to see an Oxbridge application as a welcome sign of ambition and self-confidence.

Overall, there are about three applicants to every place at Oxford and Cambridge, but there are big differences between subjects and colleges. As the tables in this chapter show, competition is particularly fierce in subjects such as medicine and English, but those qualified to read metallurgy or classics have a high chance of success. The pattern is similar to that in other universities, although the high degree of selection (and self-selection) that precedes an Oxbridge application means that even in the less popular subjects the field of candidates is likely to be strong.

These two universities' power to intimidate prospective applicants is based partly on myth. Both have done their best to live down the *Brideshead Revisited* image, but many sixth-formers still fear that they would be out of their depth there, academically and socially. In fact, the state sector produces about half the entrants to Oxford and Cambridge, and the drop-out rate is lower than at many other universities. The 'champagne set' is still present and its activities are well publicised, but most students are hard-working high achievers with the same concerns as their counterparts on other campuses. A joint poll by the two universities' student newspapers showed that undergraduates were spending much of their time in the library or worrying about their employment prospects, and relatively little time on the river or in the college bar.

State School Applicants

Student organisations at both universities have put in a great deal of effort trying to encourage applications from state schools, and some colleges have launched their own campaigns. Such has been the determination to convince state school pupils that they will get a fair crack of the whip that a new concern has grown up of possible bias against independent school pupils. In reality, however, the dispersed nature of Oxbridge admissions discounts any conspiracy. Some colleges set relatively low-standard offers to encourage applicants from the state sector, who may reveal their potential at interview. Some admissions tutors may give the edge to candidates from comprehensive schools over those from highly academic independent schools because they consider theirs the greater achievement in the circumstances. Others stick with tried and trusted sources of good students. The independent sector still enjoys a degree of success out of proportion to its share of the school population.

Choosing the Right College

Thorough research to find the right college is therefore very important. Even within colleges, different admissions tutors may have different approaches, so personal contact is essential. The college is likely to be the centre of your social life, as well as your home and study centre for at least a year, so you need to be sure not only that you have a chance of a place, but that you want one at that college. Famously sporty colleges, for example, can be trying for those in search of peace and quiet.

The tables in this chapter give an idea of the relative academic strengths of the colleges, as well as the varying levels of competition for a place in different subjects. But only individual research will suggest which is the right place for you. For example, women may favour one of the few remaining single-sex colleges (St Hilda's at Oxford; New Hall, Newnham and Lucy Cavendish at Cambridge). Men have no such option.

Neither the Norrington Table, for Oxford, nor the Tompkins Table, for Cambridge, is published by the university concerned. Indeed, Oxford tried without success to make compilation impossible. However, both tables give an indication of where the academic power-houses lie – information which can be as useful to those trying to avoid them as those seeking the ultimate challenge. Although there can be a great deal of movement year by year, both tables tend to be dominated by the rich, old foundations.

In both universities, teaching for most students is based in the colleges. In practice, however, this arrangement holds good in the sciences only for the first year. One-to-one tutorials, which are Oxbridge's traditional strength for undergraduates, are by no means universal. However, teaching groups remain much smaller than in most universities, and the tutor remains an inspiration for many students.

Both Oxford and Cambridge give applicants the option of leaving the choice of college to the university. For those with no ready source of advice on the colleges, this would seem an attractive solution to an intractable problem, b ut it is also a risky one: a lower proportion gets in this way than by applying to a particular college and, inevitably, you may end up somewhere that you hate.

The Applications Procedure

Both universities have set a deadline of 15 October 2000 for entry in 2001. The UCAS form and a Preliminary Application Form (PAF) should be submitted simultaneously to your chosen university and to UCAS. You may apply to only one of Oxford or Cambridge in the same admissions year, unless you are seeking an Organ award at both universities. Interviews take place in September for those who have left school or applied early, but in December for the majority. By the end of October, the first group can expect an offer, a rejection or deferral of a decision until January. The main group of applicants to Oxford will receive either a conditional offer or a rejection by Christmas, while in Cambridge the news arrives early in the new year.

There are other differences between the two universities, however. Some Cambridge colleges take into account S levels, as well as A levels or their equivalent, or ask candidates to sit the university's Sixth Term Examination Papers.

Oxford abolished its entrance examination because of claims that it favoured candidates from independent schools. Applicants are now given conditional offers in the normal way, although they may be asked to sit tests when they are called for interview. Oxford is more likely than Cambridge to make an offer as low as two E grades if it is sure that it wants the applicant, but the practice is no longer common.

For general information about Oxford and Cambridge universities, including student numbers and main undergraduate subject areas, *see* pages 298 and 192 respectively.

The College League Tables

Both tables are compiled from the degree results of final-year undergraduates. A first is worth five points, a 2:1 four, a 2:2 three, a third one point. The total is divided by the number of candidates to produce each college's average.

OXFORD The NorringtonTable 1999

99	98		99	98	
1	2	St John's	16	10	Worcester
2	3	Wadham	17	8	St Edmund Hall
3	6	University	18	18	Exeter
4	24	Corpus Christi	19	22	St Anne's
5	2	Merton	20	13	Lady Margaret Hall
6	9	Keble	21	19	Brasenose
7	5	Balliol	22	27	St Hugh's
8	25	Trinity	23	16	Oriel
9	23	Hertford	24	29	Somerville
10	1	Jesus	25	21	Pembroke
11	11	Magdalen	26	26	St Hilda's
12	12	Christ Church	27	28	St Catherine's
13	7	Queen's	28	15	Mansfield
14	14	New College	29	20	St Peter's
15	17	Lincoln	30	30	Harris Manchester

CAMBRIDGE TheTompkinsTable 1999

99	98		99	98	
1	3	Christ's	13	10	King's
2	1	Trinity	14	9	Pembroke
3	2	Queens'	15	6	Clare
4	17	Sidney Sussex	16	11	Downing
5	5	Emmanuel	17	23	Peterhouse
6	4	Gonville and Caius	18	7	Trinity Hall
7	15	Selwyn	19	12	Fitzwilliam
8	18	Corpus Christi	20	13	Churchill
9	19	Robinson	21	21	Girton
10	14	St Catharine's	22	24	New Hall
11	16	Jesus	23	22	Magdalene
12	8	St John's	24	20	Newnham

Applications and Acceptances by Faculty: Oxford

ARTS	Applications		Acceptances		%places to applications	
	1998	1997	1998	1997	1998	1997
Ancient and Modern History	61	60	16	25	26.2	41.7
Archaeology and Anthropology	62	56	24	23	38.2	41.1
Classics	183	172	130	130	71.0	75.6
Classics and English	26	26	11	15	42.3	57.7
Classics and Modern Languages	15	17	11	9	73.3	52.9
Economics and Management	485	444	77	80	15.9	18.0
English	938	879	269	262	28.7	29.8
English and Modern Languages	113	131	26	34	23.0	25.9
European and Middle Eastern Languages	11	4	4	2	36.4	50.0
Fine Art	113	126	19	21	16.8	16.7
Geography	245	223	97	102	39.6	45.7
Law	811	838	239	239	29.5	28.7
Law with Law Studies in Europe	261	247	24	24	9.2	9.7
Mathematics and Philosophy	43	46	20	22	46.5	47.8
Modern History	722	695	271	279	37.5	40.1
Modern History and Economics	48	56	15	10	31.3	17.9
Modern History and English	72	68	7	15	9.7	22.1
Modern History and Modern Languages	85	72	18	22	21.2	30.6
Modern History and Politics	146	n/a	30	n/a	20.5	n/a
Modern Languages	337	381	201	204	59.6	53.5
Music	101	77	63	52	62.4	67.4
Oriental Studies	79	110	29	37	36.7	67.5
Philosophy and Modern Languages	59	60	29	24	49.2	40.0
Philosophy and Theology	51	56	26	22	51.0	39.3
Physics and Philosophy	42	41	12	15	28.6	36.6
PPE	952	990	283	295	29.8	29.8
Theology	78	70	42	43	53.8	61.4
TOTAL ARTS	6,139	5,924	1,993	2,013	36.6	34.0

SCIENCE	1998	1997	1998	1997	1998	1997
Biochemistry	140	160	87	83	62.1	51.6
Biological Sciences	262	237	99	109	37.8	46.0
Chemistry	299	315	177	183	59.2	58.1
Computation	83	64	21	16	25.3	25.0

Earth Sciences (Geology)	**54**	56	**27**	33	**50.0**	58.9
Engineering Science	**278**	327	**119**	135	**42.8**	41.3
Engineering and Computer Science	**57**	58	**14**	19	**24.1**	32.8
Engineering Economics and Management	**90**	77	**21**	22	**23.3**	28.6
Engineering and Materials	**8**	9	**6**	5	**75.0**	55.6
Experimental Psychology	**199**	155	**48**	38	**24.1**	24.5
Human Sciences	**91**	91	**40**	46	**44.0**	50.5
Mathematics	**432**	423	**194**	185	**44.9**	43.7
Mathematics and Computation	**63**	77	**27**	36	**42.9**	46.8
Medicine	**536**	654	**112**	109	**20.9**	16.7
Metallurgy and MEM	**29**	38	**19**	23	**65.5**	60.5
Physics	**415**	438	**170**	184	**41.0**	42.0
Physiological Sciences	**41**	44	**15**	21	**36.6**	47.7
PPP	**189**	192	**50**	48	**26.5**	25.0
TOTAL SCIENCES	**3,166**	**3,416**	**1,246**	**1,295**	**41.4**	**37.9**

TOTAL	**9,305**	**9,535**	**3,239**	**3,219**	**39.0**	**33.8**

Applications and Acceptances by Faculty: Cambridge

	Applications		Acceptances		%places to applications	
ARTS	**1998**	**1997**	**1998**	**1997**	**1998**	**1997**
Anglo-Saxon	**26**	41	**11**	17	**65.4**	41.5
Archaeology and Anthropology	**118**	172	**57**	61	**48.3**	35.5
Architecture	**219**	227	**39**	33	**17.8**	14.5
Classics	**126**	152	**71**	79	**56.3**	52.0
English	**814**	994	**205**	212	**25.2**	21.3
Geography	**277**	279	**97**	88	**35.0**	31.5
History	**530**	617	**207**	197	**39.1**	31.9
History of Art	**75**	n/a	**21**	n/a	**28.0**	n/a
Modern and Medieval Languages	**513**	594	**168**	201	**32.7**	33.8
Music	**163**	188	**59**	67	**36.2**	35.6
Oriental Studies	**70**	76	**28**	28	**40.0**	36.8
Philosophy	**169**	160	**46**	54	**27.2**	33.8
Theology and Religious Studies	**70**	81	**33**	35	**47.1**	43.2
TOTAL ARTS	**3,170**	**3,581**	**1,042**	**107**	**32.9**	**29.9**
SOCIAL SCIENCE	**1998**	**1997**	**1998**	**1997**	**1998**	**1997**
Economics	**671**	745	**167**	161	**24.9**	21.6
Land Economy'	**92**	76	**36**	23	**39.1**	30.3
Law	**875**	813	**201**	198	**30.0**	24.4
Social and Political Sciences	**403**	425	**95**	101	**23.6**	23.8
TOTAL SOCIAL SCIENCES	**2,041**	**2,059**	**499**	**483**	**24.4**	**23.5**
SCIENCE AND TECHNOLOGY	**1998**	**1997**	**1998**	**1997**	**1998**	**1997**
Computer Science	**418**	295	**86**	79	**20.6**	26.8
Mathematics	**859**	748	**251**	276	**29.2**	36.9
Natural Sciences	**1,713**	**1,904**	**579**	607	**33.8**	31.9
Engineering	**1,061**	**1,069**	**293**	306	**27.6**	28.6
Medical Sciences	**1,189**	**1,273**	**268**	243	**22.5**	19.1
Veterinary Medicine	**672**	508	**66**	58	**9.8**	11.4
TOTAL SCIENCE AND TECHNOLOGY	**5,936**	**5,797**	**1,543**	**1,569**	**26.0**	**27.1**

TOTAL	**11,147**	**11,437**	**3,084**	**3,214**	**27.7**	**27.3**

Mathematics includes those applying for Mathematics, Mathematics with Computer Science, and Mathematics with Physics.

The tripos courses at Cambridge in Chemical Engineering and Information Sciences, History of Art, Management Studies, and Manufacturing Engineering can only be taken after a part of another tripos. The entries for these courses are recorded under the first-year subjects taken by the students involved.

OXFORD COLLEGE PROFILES

BALLIOL

Balliol College, Oxford OX1 3BJ (tel. 01865-277777)
Students: 380 **Male/female ratio:** 64/36

Famous as the alma mater of many prominent post-war politicians, including Harold Macmillan, Denis Healey and Roy Jenkins, the university's current Chancellor, Balliol has maintained a strong presence in university life and is usually well represented in the Union. Academic standards are formidably high, as might be expected in the college of Wycliffe and Adam Smith, notably in the classics and social sciences. A dive down the Norrington Table in 1996 was as surprising as it was temporary. PPE in particular is notoriously oversubscribed. Library facilities are good and include a 24-hour law library. Balliol began admitting overseas students in the 19th century and has cultivated an attractively cosmopolitan atmosphere, of which the lively JCR (Junior Common Room) is a natural focus. Most undergraduates are offered accommodation in college for three years, while the 147 graduate students are usually lodged in the Graduate Centre at Holywell Manor. Centrally located with a JCR pantry that is open all day, Balliol is convenient as well as prestigious.

BRASENOSE

Brasenose College, Oxford OX1 4AJ (tel. 01865-277830)
Students: 347 **Male/female ratio:** 66/34

Brasenose may not be the most famous Oxford college but it makes up for its discreet image with a consistently healthy academic performance, an advantageous position in the centre of town, and lesser known attractions such as Gertie's Tea Bar. Brasenose was one of the first colleges to become co-educational in the 1970s, although men still take two thirds of the places. In its defence, the college prospectus points out that the major undergraduate office, President of the JCR, has been filled as often by a woman as a man. But BNC, as the college is often known, still has the image of a rugby haven. Named after the door knocker on the 13th-century Brasenose Hall, the college has a pleasant, intimate ambience which most find conductive to study. Law, PPE and modern history are traditional strengths and competition for places in these subjects is intense. Sporting standards are as high as at many much larger colleges and the college's rowing club is one of the oldest in the university. The college has recently restructured accommodation charges for its students. A new annex, the

St Cross Building, means all undergraduates can live in. Most third years live in the Brasenose annex at Frewin Court, just a few minutes' walk away.

CHRIST CHURCH
Christ Church, Oxford OX1 1DP (tel. 01865-276150)
Students: 420 **Male/female ratio:** 50/50

The college founded by Cardinal Wolsey in 1525 and affectionately known as The House has come a long way since Evelyn Waugh mythologised its aristocratic excesses in *Brideshead Revisited*. The social mix at Christ Church is much more varied than most applicants suspect and the college has gone out of its way recently to become something of a champion of political correctness. The male/female ratio has been improving steadily and a code of practice on sexual harassment has been implemented. Academic pressure at Christ Church is reasonably relaxed, although natural high-achievers prosper and the college's history and law teaching is highly regarded. The magnificent 18th-century library, housing 100,000 books, is one of the best in Oxford. It is supplemented by a separate law library. Christ Church has its own art gallery, which holds over 2,000 works of mainly Italian Renaissance art. Sport, especially rugby, is an important part of college life. The playing fields are a few minutes' walk away through the Meadows. The river is also close at hand for the aspiring oarsman, and the college has good squash courts. Accommodation is rated by Christ Church students as excellent and includes flats off Iffley Road as well as a number of beautifully panelled shared sets (double rooms) in college. The modern bar adds to the lustre of a college justly famous for its imposing architecture and cathedral, the smallest in England.

CORPUS CHRISTI
Corpus Christi College, Oxford OX1 4JF (tel. 01865-276700)
Students: 225 **Male/female ratio:** 60/40

Corpus, until recently Oxford's smallest college, is naturally overshadowed by its Goliath-like neighbour, Christ Church, but makes the most of its intimacy, friendly atmosphere and exquisite beauty. Like The House it has an exceptional view across the Meadows. Although the college has only 310 students including postgraduates (with men and women in equal number), it has an admirable library open 24 hours a day. Academic expectations are high and English, PPE and medicine are especially well established. Despite this, the undergraduate prospectus asserts that it is 'considered much more important to be sociable than to get good results' The college is beginning to make the most of ties with its namesake at Cambridge, establishing a joint lectureship in history in 1999. Corpus is able to offer accommodation to all its undergraduates, one of its many attractions to those seeking a smaller community in Oxford.

EXETER

Exeter College, Oxford OX1 3DP (tel. 01865-279600)

Students: 307 **Male/female ratio:** 70/30

Exeter is the fourth oldest college in the university and was founded in 1314 by Walter de Stapeldon, Bishop of Exeter. Nestling halfway between the High Street and Broad Street, site of most of the city's bookshops, it could hardly be more central. The college boasts handsome buildings, the exceptional Fellows' garden and attractive accommodation for most undergraduates for all three years of their university careers. Exeter's academic record is strong and the college is a consistent high performer in the Norrington Tables. It is, however, often accused of being rather dull. Given its glittering roll-call of alumni, which includes Martin Amis, J.R.R. Tolkien, Alan Bennett, Richard Burton, Imogen Stubbs and Tariq Ali, this seems an accusation that on the face of it at least is hard to sustain. College food is not rated highly by students although the bar is popular with students from other colleges. The social scene is livelier than the male/female ratio might suggest.

HARRIS-MANCHESTER

Harris-Manchester College, Oxford OX1 3TF (tel. 01865-270999)

Students: 300 **Male/female ratio:** 45/55

Founded in Manchester in 1786 to provide education for non-Anglican students, Harris-Manchester finally settled in Oxford in 1889 after spells in both York and London. A full university college since 1996, its central location with fine buildings and grounds in Hollywell Street is very convenient for the Bodleian, although the college itself does have an excellent library. Harris-Manchester admits only mature students of mostly 25 years and above to read for both undergraduate and graduate degrees, predominantly in the arts. There are also groups of visiting students from American universities and some men and women training for the ministry. Most of its members live in and all meals are provided, indeed the college encourages its members to dine regularly in hall. The college has few sporting facilities but its students do still manage to represent Harris-Manchester in football, cricket, swimming and chess as well as playing on other college or university teams. Other outlets include the college Drama Society and also the chapel, a focal point to many there.

HERTFORD

Hertford College, Oxford OX1 3BW (tel. 01865-279400)

Students: 360 **Male/female ratio:** 67/33

Though tracing its roots to the 12th century, Hertford is determinedly modern. It was one of the first colleges to admit women (in 1976) though they still account for only a third of the places. Hertford also helped set the trend towards offers of places conditional on A levels, which paved the way for the abolition of the entrance examination. It is still popular with state school applicants. The college lacks the grandeur of Magdalen, of which it was once an annex, but has its own architectural trademark in the Bridge of Sighs. It is also close to the History Faculty library (Hertford's neighbour), the Bodleian and the King's Arms, perhaps Oxford's most popular pub. Academic pressure at Hertford is not high but the quality of teaching, especially in English, is generally thought admirable. Accommodation is improving, thanks in part to the new Abingdon House complex, and the college can now lodge almost all its undergraduates at any one time. Like most congenial colleges, Hertford is often accused of being claustrophobic and inward-looking – a charge most Hertfordians would ascribe simply to jealousy.

JESUS

Jesus College, Oxford OX1 3DW (tel. 01865-279700)
Students: 305 **Male/female ratio:** 67/33

Jesus, the only Oxford college to be founded in the reign of Elizabeth I, suffers from something of an unfair reputation for insularity. Its students, whose predecessors include T.E. Lawrence and Harold Wilson, describe it as 'friendly but gossipy' and shrug off the legend that all its undergraduates are Welsh. Close to most of Oxford's main facilities, Jesus has three compact quads, the second of which is especially enticing in the summer. Academic standards are high and most subjects are taught in college. Physics, chemistry and engineering are especially strong. Rugby and rowing also tend to be taken seriously. Accommodation is almost universally regarded as excellent and relatively inexpensive. Self-catering flats in north and east Oxford have enabled every graduate to live in throughout his or her Oxford career. The range of accommodation available to undergraduates is similarly good. The college's Cowley Road development is described by the student union as 'some of the plushest student housing in Oxford'.

KEBLE

Keble College, Oxford OX1 3PG (tel. 01865-272727)
Students: 440 **Male/female ratio:** 65/35

Keble, named after the leader of the Oxford Movement, was founded in 1870 with the intention of making Oxford education more accessible and the college remains proud of 'the legacy of a social conscience'. That said, little more than a third of undergraduates are women, so the college is still rather male-dominated. With 400 undergraduates, Keble is one of the biggest colleges in Oxford, while its uncompromising Victorian Gothic architecture also makes it one of the most distinctive. Once famous for the special privileges it extended to rowers, the college is now academically strong, particularly in the sciences where it benefits from easy access to the Science Area, the Radcliffe Science Library and the Mathematical Institute. At the same time, the college's sporting record remains exemplary, providing a large number of rugby Blues in recent years. Undergraduates are guaranteed accommodation in their first two years (or two out of three years), although rent increases in recent years have been the cause of some friction between undergraduates and the college authorities. Students who live in must eat in Hall 30 times a year. The Starship Enterprise bar is a particular attraction.

LADY MARGARET HALL
Lady Margaret Hall, Oxford OX2 6QA (tel. 01865-274300)
Students: 407 **Male/female ratio:** 50/50

Lady Margaret Hall, Oxford's first college for women, has been co-educational since 1978 and is now equally balanced. For many students, LMH's comparative isolation – the college is three quarters of a mile north of the city centre – is a real advantage, ensuring a clear distinction between college life and university activities, and a refuge from tourists. Although the neo-Georgian architecture is not to everyone's taste, the college's beautiful gardens back onto the river, which allows LMH to have its own punt house. The students union describes academic life at the college as 'fairly lax' while commending its record in English, history and law. Accommodation should soon be available to all undergraduates. The college's two tower-blocks have the remarkable attraction of private bathrooms in all their rooms. LMH shares most of its sports facilities with Trinity College though it has squash and tennis courts on site. Recently, it has become one of Oxford's dramatic centres.

LINCOLN
Lincoln College, Oxford OXI 3DR (tel. 01865-279800)
Students: 270 **Male/female ratio:** 50/50

Small, central Lincoln cultivates a lower profile than many other colleges with comparable assets. The college's 15th-century buildings and beautiful library – a converted Queen Anne church – combine to produce a delightful environment in which to spend three years. Academic standards are high, particularly in arts subjects, although the college's relaxed atmosphere is justly celebrated. Accommodation, rated 'excellent' by the student union, is provided by the college for all undergraduates throughout their careers and includes rooms above The Mitre Hotel, a medieval inn. Students parade around Oxford in *sub fusc* (formal wear) on Ascension Day while choristers beat the bounds. Graduate students have their own centre a few minutes' walk away in Bear Lane. Lincoln's small size and self-sufficiency have led to the college's being accused of insularity. Lincoln's food is outstanding, among the best in the university. Sporting achievement is impressive for a college of this size, in part a reflection of its good facilities.

MAGDALEN
Magdalen College, Oxford OX1 4AU (tel. 01865-276000)
Students: 375 **Male/female ratio:** 50/50

Perhaps the most beautiful college in Oxford or Cambridge, Magdalen is known around the world for its tower, its deer park and its May morning celebrations when students throw themselves off Magdalen Bridge. The college has shaken off its public school image to become a truly cosmopolitan place, with a large intake from overseas and an increasing proportion of state school pupils. Magdalen's record in English, history and law is second to none, while its new science park at Sandford is bound to bolster its reputation in the sciences. Library facilities are excellent, especially in history and law. First-year students are accommodated in the Waynflete Building and allocated rooms in subsequent years by ballot. Undergraduates can be housed for all three years, since the opening of the first phase of the Grove Quad in 1996. Sets in cloisters and in the palatial New Buildings are particularly sought after. Magdalen is also conveniently placed for the wealth of rented accommodation in east Oxford. The college bar is one of the best in Oxford and the college is a pluralistic place, proud of its drama society and choir. Enthusiasm on the river and sports field makes up for a traditional lack of athletic prowess.

MANSFIELD
Mansfield College, Oxford OX1 3TF (tel 01865 27099)
Students: 300 **Male/female ratio:** 56/44

Mansfield's graduation to full Oxford college status marked the culmination of a long history of development since 1886. Its spacious, attractive site is fairly central, close to the libraries, the shops, the University Parks and the River Cherwell. With only 195 undergraduates, the community is close-knit, although this can verge on the claustrophobic. The male to female ratio is slightly better than for the university as a whole. Women may prefer the less intimidating atmosphere of Mansfield, perhaps helped by its strong representation of state school students at 50 per cent. First and third years live in college accommodation. Mansfield students share Merton's excellent sports ground and have numerous college teams although it is in drama that its students truly excel. Despite its former theological background, students are not admitted on the basis of religion and can read a wide variety of subjects. Mansfield is home to the Oxford Centre for the Environment, Ethics and Society (OCEES) and also the American Studies Institute, evidence of the strong links between Mansfield and the United States, which is reflected by some 70 visiting students annually.

MERTON
Merton College, Oxford OX1 4JD (tel. 01865-276310)
Students: 347 **Male/female ratio:** 66/34

Founded in 1264 by Walter de Merton, Bishop of Rochester and Chancellor of England, Merton is one of Oxford's oldest colleges and one of its most prestigious. Quiet and beautiful, with the oldest quad in the university, Merton has high academic expectations of its undergraduates, often reflected in a position at the top of the Norrington Table. History, law, English, physics and chemistry all enjoy a formidable track record. The medieval library is the envy of many other colleges. Accommodation is cheap, of a good standard and offered to students for all three years. Merton's food is among the best in the university; formal Hall is served six times a week. No kitchens are provided for students who live in college, however. Merton's many diversions include the Merton Floats, its dramatic society, an excellent Christmas Ball and the peculiar Time Ceremony, which celebrates the return of GMT. Sports facilities are excellent, although participation tends to be more important than the final score.

NEW COLLEGE
New College, Oxford OX1 3BN (tel. 01865-279555)
Students: 420 **Male/female ratio:** 60/40

New College is large, old (founded in 1379 by William of Wykeham) and much more relaxed than most expect when first confronting its daunting facade. It is a bustling place, as proud of its excellent music and its bar as of its strength in law, history and PPE. The college has been making particular efforts to increase the proportion of state school students, inviting applications from schools that have never sent candidates to Oxford. The Target Schools Scheme, designed to increase applications from state schools, is well established. Accommodation is good and guaranteed for the first two years, after which most live out. The college's library facilities are impressive, especially in law, classics and PPE. The sports ground is nearby and includes good tennis courts. Women's sport is particularly strong. A new sports complex, named after Brian Johnston, opened in 1997, at St Cross Road. The sheer beauty of New College remains one of its principal assets and the college gardens are a memorable sight in the summer. In spite of these traditional charms, the college has strong claims to be considered admirably innovative. Music is a feature of college life and the Commemoration Ball, held every three years, is a highlight of Oxford's social calendar.

ORIEL
Oriel College, Oxford OX1 4EW (tel 01865-276555)
Students: 280 **Male/female ratio:** 60/40

In spite of its reputation as a bastion of muscular privilege, Oriel is a friendly college with a strong sense of identity and has adjusted rapidly to co-educational admissions (women were not admitted until 1985). The students' union describes the college as having 'a strong crew spirit' reflecting its traditions on the river. Academic standards are better than legend suggests and the college's well-stocked library is open 24 hours a day. But Oriel's sporting reputation is certainly deserved and its rowing eight is rarely far from the head of the river. Other sports are well catered for, even if their facilities are considerably farther away than the boathouse, which is only a short jog away. Accommodation is of variable quality but Oriel can usually provide rooms for all three years for those students who require them. Scholars and Exhibitioners chasing firsts in their final year are given priority in the ballot for college rooms. Extensive new accommodation is being rolled out one mile away at Nazareth House and at the Island Site on Oriel Street. Oriel also offers a lively drama society, a Shakespearian production taking place each summer in the front quad.

PEMBROKE

Pembroke College, Oxford OX1 1DW (tel. 01865-276444)
Students: 390 **Male/female ratio:** 60/40

Although its alumni include such extrovert characters as Dr Johnson and Michael Heseltine, Pembroke is one of Oxford's least dynamic colleges. Academic results are solid, and the college has Fellows and lecturers in almost all the major university subjects. But severe financial problems have led to confrontation with the students over rents. Pembroke promises accommodation to 'a fair proportion' of undergraduates throughout their courses. The nine-year-old Sir Geoffrey Arthur building on the river, ten minutes' walk from the college, offers excellent facilities. College food is reasonable, though some find formal Hall every evening rather too rich a diet. Rugby and rowing are strong, with Pembroke second only to Oriel on the river, and squash and tennis courts are available at the nearby sports ground.

QUEEN'S

Queen's College, Oxford OX1 4AW (tel. 01865-279120)
Students: 465 **Male/female ratio:** 50/50

One of the most striking sights of the High Street, Queen's has now shed its exclusive 'northern' image to become one of Oxford's liveliest and most attractive colleges. The college's academic record is good. According to the students' union, 'the general attitude to work is fairly relaxed and seems to bring good results'. Modern languages, chemistry and mathematics are reckoned among the strongest subjects. Queen's does not normally admit undergraduates for the honour school of English language and literature or geography. The library, open till 10 pm, is as beautiful as it is well stocked. All students are offered accommodation, first years being housed in modernist annexes in east Oxford. The college's beer cellar is one of the most popular in the university and the JCR's facilities are also better than average. An annual dinner commemorates a student who is said to have fended off a bear by thrusting a volume of Aristotle into its mouth.

ST ANNE'S

St Anne's College, Oxford OX2 6HS (tel. 01865-274800)
Students: 465 **Male/female ratio:** 50/50

Architecturally uninspiring (a row of Victorian houses with concrete 'stack-a-studies' dropped into their back gardens), St Anne's makes up in community spirit what it lacks in awesome grandeur. It has a high proportion of state school students. A women's college until 1979, its academic standing is questionable by Oxford's standards, although it has begun to climb the Norrington Table again since slipping to last place in the middle of the decade. The library is particularly rich in law, Chinese and medieval history texts. Opening hours are long. Accommodation is guaranteed to all undergraduates but the college is a long way from the city centre. A new accommodation block costing £2.3 million opened in

Summertown in 1997. This block provides larger rooms, including two for disabled students.

ST CATHERINE'S

St Catherine's College, Oxford OX1 3UJ (tel. 01865-271700)
Students: 450 **Male/female ratio:** 67/33

Arne Jacobsen's modernist design for 'Catz', one of Oxford's youngest undergraduate college and second largest, has attracted much attention as the most striking contrast in the university to the lofty spires of Magdalen and New College. Close to the university science area and the pleasantly rural Holywell Great Meadow, St Catherine's is nevertheless only a few minutes' walk from the city centre. Academic standards are especially high in mathematics and physics though the college's scholarly ambitions are far from having been exhausted. The undergraduate prospectus used to complain that Fellows were 'increasingly eager to apply more academic pressure in college' The well-liked Wolfson library (famous for its unusual Jacobsen chairs) is open till 1 am on most days. Accommodation is available for first and third years. Rooms are small but tend to be warmer than in other, more venerable colleges. Squash, tennis and netball courts are all on the main college site. There is an excellent theatre, and the college is host to the Cameron Mackintosh Chair of Contemporary Theatre, recent incumbents of which have included Sir Ian McKellen, Alan Ayckbourn and Lord Attenborough. St Catherine's has one of the best JCR facilities in Oxford, including a bar open until 11 pm.

ST EDMUND HALL

St Edmund Hall, Oxford OX1 4AR (tel. 01865-279000)
Students: 400 **Male/female ratio:** 65/35

St Edmund Hall – 'Teddy Hall' – is one of Oxford's smallest colleges but also one of its most populous with 400 undergraduates swarming through its medieval quads. Some two thirds of undergraduates are male, but the college is anxious to shed its image as a home for 'hearties', and the authorities have gone out of their way to tone down younger members' rowdier excesses. Nonetheless, the sporting culture at St Edmund Hall is still vigorous and the college usually does well in rugby, football and hockey. Academically, the college has some impressive names among its fellowship as well as a marvellous library, originally a Norman church. The students' union reports that 'a laid-back approach (to work) is the norm'. Accommodation is reasonable and is guaranteed to first and third years, though most second-year students live out. The college has two annexes, one near the University Parks, the other in Iffley Road, where many of the rooms have private bathrooms. Hall food is better than average.

ST HILDA'S

St Hilda's College, Oxford OX4 1DY (tel. 01865-276884)
Students: 400 **Women only.**

With Somerville co-educational, St Hilda's is now the last bastion of all-women education in Oxford. How long the university will allow it to remain that way is open to question. In spite of its variable academic record, the college is a distinctive part of the Oxford landscape and is usually well represented in university life. The 50,000-volume library is growing fast and plans for its extension are being considered. St Hilda's also boasts one of the largest ratios of state school to independent undergraduates in Oxford. Accommodation is guaranteed to first years and for one of the remaining two years. The college owns its own punts, which are available free for college members and their guests. Many of the rooms offer some of the best river views in Oxford. Social facilities are limited but the standard of food is high.

ST HUGH'S

St Hugh's College, Oxford OX2 6LE (tel. 01865-274900)
Students: 400 **Male/female ratio:** 60/40

One of Oxford's lesser-known colleges, St Hugh's was criticised by students in 1987 when it began admitting men. There are now fewer women than men at the college, although the male/female ratio is better balanced than at most Oxford colleges. Like Lady Margaret Hall, St Hugh's is a bicycle ride from the city centre and has a picturesque setting. It is an ideal college for those seeking a place to live and study away from the madding crowd, and is well liked for its pleasantly bohemian atmosphere. Academic pressure remains comparatively low, although the students' union says there are signs that this is changing. St Hugh's is one of the few colleges which guarantees accommodation to undergraduates for all three years, although the standard of rooms is variable. Sport, particularly football, is taken quite seriously. The extensive grounds include a croquet lawn and tennis courts

ST JOHN'S

St John's College, Oxford OX1 3JP (tel. 01865-277300)
Students: 380 **Male/female ratio:** 60/40

St John's is one of Oxford's powerhouses, excelling in almost every field and boasting arguably the most beautiful gardens in the university. Founded in 1555 by a London merchant, it is richly endowed and makes the most of its resources to provide undergraduates with an agreeable and challenging three years. The work ethic is very much part of the St John's ethos, and academic standards are high, with English, chemistry and history among the traditional strengths, though all students benefit from the impressive library. There are still fewer undergraduates from state schools than public schools (52/48), but the college compensates to some extent by offering generous hardship funds to those in financial difficulty. As might be expected of a wealthy college, the accommodation is excellent and guaranteed for three or four years. St John's has a strong sporting tradition and offers good facilities, but the social scene is limited.

ST PETER'S

St Peter's College, Oxford OX1 2DL (tel. 01865-278900)
Students: 325 **Male/female ratio:** 60/40

Opened as St Peter's Hall in 1929, St Peter's has been an Oxford college since 1961. Its medieval, Georgian and 19th-century buildings are close to the city centre and most of Oxford's main facilities. Though still young and comparatively small, St Peter's is well represented in university life and has pockets of academic excellence despite finishing near the bottom of the Norrington Table. History tutoring is particularly good. There are no Fellows in classics at the college. Accommodation is offered to students for the first year and for one year thereafter and is generally of a high standard. A residential block opened in 1988 and accommodation at St George's Gate opened in 1995, added to the stock of rooms. The college's facilities are impressive, including one of the university's best JCRs. St Peter's is known as one of Oxford's most vibrant colleges socially. It is strong on acting and journalism and has a recently refurbished bar.

SOMERVILLE

Somerville College, Oxford OX2 6HD (tel. 01865-270600)
Students: 330 **Male/female ratio:** 50/50

The announcement, early in 1992, that Somerville was to go co-educational sparked an unusually acrimonious and persistent dispute within this most tranquil of colleges. Protests were doomed to failure, however: the first male undergraduates arrived in 1994 and now account for half the students. Lady Thatcher was one of those who flocked to their old college's defence, illustrating the fierce loyalty Somerville inspires. The college's atmosphere appears to have survived the momentous change, although the culture of protest reappeared when a number of students refused to pay the Government's tuition fees in 1998. Accommodation, including 30 small flats for students, is of a reasonable standard, and is guaranteed for first years and students sitting public examinations. Sport is strong at Somerville and the womens' rowing eight usually finishes near the head of the river. The college's hockey pitches and tennis courts are nearby. The 100,000-volume library is open 24 hours a day and is one of the most beautiful in Oxford.

TRINITY

Trinity College, Oxford OX1 3BH (tel. 01865-279900)
Students: 280 **Male/female ratio:** 50/50

Architecturally impressive and boasting beautiful lawns, Trinity is one of Oxford's least populous colleges. It is ideally located, beside the Bodleian, Blackwell's book shop and the White Horse pub. Cardinal Newman, an alumnus of Trinity, is said to have regarded Trinity's motto as 'Drink, drink, drink'. Academic pressure varies, as the college darts up and down the unofficial Norrington Table of academic performance. Nonetheless, the college produces its fair share of firsts, especially in arts subjects. Trinity has shaken off its reputation for apathy, though the early gate closing times can leave the college isolated late at night. Members are active in all walks of university life and the college has its own debating and drama societies. The proportion of state school entrants has been rising. Accommodation is of a reasonable standard and most undergraduates can live in for three years if they wish.

UNIVERSITY
University College, Oxford OX1 4BH (tel. 01865-276602)
Students: 415 **Male/female ratio:** 67/33

University is the first Oxford college to be able to boast a former student in the Oval Office. Indeed, the college seems certain to benefit from its unique links with President Clinton, a Rhodes Scholar at University in the late 1960s. The college is probably Oxford's oldest, though highly unlikely to have been founded by King Alfred, as legend claims. Academic expectations are high and the college prospers in most subjects. Physics, PPE and maths are particularly strong. That said, University has fewer claims to be thought a powerhouse in the manner of St John's, arguably its greatest rival. Accommodation is guaranteed to undergraduates for all three years, with third years lodged in an annexe in north Oxford about a mile and a half from the college site on the High Street. The students' union complains that facilities are poor. Sport is strong and University is usually successful on the river, but the college has a reputation for being quiet socially.

WADHAM
Wadham College, Oxford OX1 3PN (tel. 01865-277946)
Students: 440 **Male/female ratio:** 67/33

Founded by Dorothy Wadham in 1609, Wadham is known in about equal measure for its academic track record – the college generally ranks in the top third in examination performance – and its leftist politics. The JCR is famously dynamic and politically active, although the breadth of political opinion is greater than its left-wing stereotype suggests. And for somewhere supposedly unconcerned with such fripperies, its gardens are surprisingly beautiful. The somewhat rough-hewn chapel is similarly memorable. The college has a good 24-hour library. Accommodation is guaranteed for at least two years and there are many large, shared rooms on offer. Journalism and drama play an important part in the life of the college, although sport is there for those who want it. Although still predominantly male, Wadham is a popular stop on the week end social scene.

WORCESTER

Worcester College, Oxford OX1 2HB (tel. 01865-278300)
Students: 360 **Male/female ratio:** 60/40

Worcester is to the west of Oxford what Magdalen is to the east, an open, rural contrast to the urban rush of the city centre. The college's rather mediocre exterior conceals a delightful environment, including some characteristically muscular Baroque Hawskmoor architecture, a garden and a lake. Though academic pressure has been described as 'tastefully restrained', law, theology and engineering are among the college's strengths. The 24-hour library is strongest in the arts. Accommodation varies in quality from ordinary to conference standard in the Linbury Building. Shortage of cooking facilities is a common complaint. The ratio of bathrooms to students (one to four) is better than in many colleges. Sport plays an important part in college life, Worcester having engaged more success recently in rowing and rugby.

CAMBRIDGE COLLEGE PROFILES

CHRIST'S

Christ's College, Cambridge CB2 3BU (tel. 01223-334900)
Undergraduates: 395 **Male/female ratio:** 60/40

Christ's prides itself on its academic strength. It is also one of the few colleges still to offer places on two E grades at A level, meaning not that entry standards are low but that the college is sufficiently confident of its ability to identify potential high-flyers at interview that it is in effect prepared to circumvent A-levels as the principal criteria for entry. The college has a 50/50 state-to-independent ratio and women make up 40 per cent of the students. Though the college has a reputation for being dominated by hard-working natural scientists and mathematicians, it maintains a broad subject range. It has had the best results in the university for history and music over the past five years. The atmosphere is supposedly so cosy that one student described Christ's as 'a cup of Horlicks', but some complain of short bar opening hours and a poor relationship between undergraduates and Fellows. Accommodation in college is guaranteed to all undergraduates, some of whom will be allocated rooms in the infamous New Court 'Typewriter', probably the least attractive building in the city. The Typewriter houses the excellent New Court theatre, home to Christ's Amateur Dramatics Society and Christ's Films, one of the most adventurous student film societies. College sport has flourished in recent years, with teams competing to a good standard in most sports. The playing fields (shared with Sidney Sussex) are just over a mile away.

CHURCHILL
Churchill College, Cambridge CB3 0DS (tel. 01223-336000)
Undergraduates: 430 Male/female ratio: 67/33

Founded in 1960 to help meet 'the national need for scientists and engineers and to forge links with industry', Churchill has slipped recently in the Cambridge league table but still has high standards. Maths, natural sciences, engineering and computer science are traditional strengths, but arts results have been disappointing recently. The college has some of the university's best computer facilities. Deferred entry is encouraged in all subjects. Churchill has the joint highest ratio of state to independent pupils (75/25) but one of the lowest proportions of women undergraduates: only one in three. Some are put off by Churchill's unassuming modern architecture and the college's distance from the city centre; others argue that the distance offers much-needed breathing space. One undeniable advantage is Churchill's ability to provide every undergraduate with a room in college for all three years. There are extensive on-site playing fields, and the college does well in rugby, hockey and rowing. The university's only student radio station (broadcasting to Churchill and New Hall) is based here.

CLARE
Clare College, Cambridge CB2 1TL (tel. 01223-333246)
Undergraduates: 400 Male/female ratio: 53/47

Though for many Clare's outstanding features are its gardens and harmonious buildings, hard-pressed undergraduates are just as likely to praise the rent and food charges, among the lowest in the university. Accommodation is guaranteed for all three years, either in college or nearby hostels. One of the few colleges which openly encourages applications from 'candidates of a good academic standard who have special talents in non-academic fields', Clare tends to feature near the top of the academic tables, despite slipping this year. Applicants are encouraged to take a gap year. Languages, social and political science and music are especially strong, but science results have been disappointing The ratio of male to female students is largely balanced at 53/47, while systematic attempts to raise the proportion of state-educated students has left those from independent schools in a minority. Music thrives. The choir records and tours regularly, and Clare Cellars (comprising the bar and JCR) is rapidly becoming the Cambridge jazz venue as well as providing more contemporary sounds such as drum and bass. Sporting emphasis is as much on enjoyment as competition. The women's teams have had outstanding success in recent years. The playing fields are little more than a mile away.

CORPUS CHRISTI
Corpus Christi College, Cambridge CB2 1RH (tel. 01223-338000)
Undergraduates: 260 Male/female ratio: 60/40

The only college to have been founded by town residents, Corpus's size inevitably makes it one of the more intimate colleges. It prides itself on being a cohesive community, but some find the focus on college rather than university life excessive. Although traditionally broad based academically, it had the best arts results in the university in 1999, but only twelfth for sciences. The kitchen fixed charge is above average but the college is known for a good formal hall. Almost all undergraduates are allocated a room in college or neighbouring hostels. The library is open 24 hours. There is a fairly even sexual and social balance: the independent-to-state ratio is 42/58. The college bar has an enviable atmosphere. The sporting facilities, at Leckhampton (just over a mile away), are among the best in the university and include a swimming pool. The size of the college means that its sporting reputation owes more to enthusiasm than success, however. Drama is also well catered for, and the college owns The Playroom, the university's best small theatre.

DOWNING

Downing College, Cambridge CB2 1DQ (tel. 01223-334800)
Undergraduates: 387 **Male/female ratio:** 60/40

Downing's imposing neo-Classical quadrangle may look more like a military academy than a Cambridge college but the atmosphere here is anything but martial. Founded in 1800 for the study of law, medicine and natural sciences, these are still the college's strong subjects. Indeed Downing is often called 'the law college', although recent results have been better in sciences than arts. A reputation for hard-playing, hard-drinking rugby players and oarsmen is proving hard to shake off. The college claims the best boat club in Cambridge. But while sport undoubtedly enjoys a high profile, pressure to conform to the sporty stereotype is never excessive. Downing currently guarantees a place in college accommodation for two out of three years; the completion of a new accommodation block several years ago allows almost all students to be housed throughout a first degree. The new library, opened by Prince Charles in 1993, has won an award for its architecture. There is a good balance between male and female students and state and independent school backgrounds. The new student-run bar/party room has improved college social life following three candlelit formal dinners a week.

EMMANUEL

Emmanuel College, Cambridge CB2 3AP (tel. 01223-334200)
Undergraduates: 420 **Male/female ratio:** 65/35

Thanks in no small part to its huge and stylish, strikingly modern bar, Emmanuel has something of an insular reputation; although the students are active in university clubs and societies. Traditionally a mid-table college, with no subject bias, Emmanuel has raised its academic profile recently, gaining strength in medicine and social science, but particularly in English. Deferred entry is greatly encouraged. An almost even state-to-independent ratio contributes to the college's unpretentious atmosphere and one in three undergraduates are women. All first and third-year students are guaranteed accommodation. Second years are housed in college hostels. With self-catering facilities limited, most students eat in Hall. The college offers ten expedition grants to undergraduates every year, and has a large hardship fund. In the summer, the college tennis courts and open-air swimming pool offer a welcome haven from exam pressures. The duck pond is one of the most picturesque spots in Cambridge. The sports grounds are excellent, if some distance away.

FITZWILLIAM
Fitzwilliam College, Cambridge CB3 ODG (tel. 01223-332000)
Undergraduates: 438 **Male/female ratio:** 60/40

Based in the city centre until 1963, the college now occupies a large, modern site on the Huntingdon Road. What it may lack in architectural splendour, Fitzwilliam makes up in friendly informality. More than 70 per cent of its under-graduates come from the state sector, and about 40 per cent are women, though the college hopes 'significantly to raise this proportion in the coming years'. Approximately 80 per cent of undergraduates are allocated rooms in college (first and third years guaranteed) but many second years are obliged to fend for them-selves in the city's relatively expensive private housing market. A new accommo-dation block is planned. Fitzwilliam's academic record has been improving, with languages and geography the strongest subjects. Arts are generally stronger than sciences. Applications are also encouraged in archaeology and anthropology, classics, social and political sciences and music. As at Christ's, offers of places are sometimes made on the basis of two Es only at A level. On the extracurricular front, the badminton, hockey and football teams are among the best in the uni-versity. The playing fields are a few hundred yards away. The twice termly Ents (college entertainments) are exceptionally popular. Music and drama thrive.

GIRTON
Girton College, Cambridge CB3 OJG (tel 01223-338999)
Undergraduates: 484 **Male/female ratio:** 50/50

The joke about needing a passport to travel to Girton refuses to die. In fact, with the city centre a 15-minute cycle ride away, the college is closer than many hostels at other universities. But if comparative isolation inevitably encour-ages a strong community spirit, Girtonians still manage to participate in univer-sity life at least as much as students at more central colleges and are particularly active in university sports. Only Trinity and St John's have more undergraduates. On the other hand, since Girton stands on a 50-acre site and the majority of second-year students live in Wolfson Court (near the University Library), there is no question of over-crowding: rooms are available for the entire course. Some find that the long corridors remind them of boarding school. Since becoming co-educational in 1979, the college has maintained a balanced admissions policy. Almost 60 per cent of undergraduates are from state schools. Girton also has the highest proportion of women Fellows in any mixed college (50 per cent). The on-site sporting facilities, which include a swimming pool, are excellent. The college is active in most sports and particularly strong in football. The formal hall is excellent and popular, but held only once a week.

GONVILLE AND CAIUS
Gonville and Caius College, Cambridge CB2 1TA (tel. 01223-332447)
Undergraduates: 470 **Male/female ratio:** 63/37

Gonville and Caius College – to confuse the outsider, the college is usually known as Caius (pronounced 'keys') – is among the most beautiful of Cambridge's colleges, as well as one of the most central. It has an excellent academic reputation, especially in medicine and history, though maths and law are also highly rated. Recent results have been better in sciences than arts. Book grants are available to all undergraduates. The library has been refurbished and computer facilities improved. Accommodation is split between the central site on Trinity Street and Harvey Court, a five-minute walk away across the river. Rooms are guaranteed for all first and third years. The majority of second years live in college hostels, none of which is more than a mile away. Undergraduates are obliged to eat in Hall at least 45 times a term, a ruling some find restrictive but which at least ensures that students meet regularly. The college has something of a Home Counties or public school reputation especially for its 'It' girls, society high-fliers. At 58/42 the independent-to-state ratio is not excessive. However, Caius is 'eager to extend the range of its intake'. Caius tends to do well in rowing and hockey, but most sports are fairly relaxed. A lively social scene is helped by the student-run Late Night Bar.

HOMERTON
Homerton College, Cambridge CB2 2PH (tel. 01223-411141)
Undergraduates: 650 **Male/female ratio:** 10/90

Now part of the Faculty of Education, Homerton is a teacher training college offering four-year BEd courses and a three-year BA in education studies, which does not carry qualified teacher status. All first years have rooms in or around the college, but thereafter may have to take their chance in the open market. There is a 50/50 state-independent split, but with men making up no more than 10 per cent of those on the BEd course it's no surprise that the first-year atmosphere has been likened to that of a girls' boarding school. Recent speculation over the possible sale of the college's 25-acre site to a supermarket chain has died down. Homerton looks set to stay in its present location about a mile from the city centre. The college's position and specialised nature mean that the onus is very much on Homerton students to take the initiative if they wish to get involved in university activities. Many do, however. In most respects Homerton is no different from the other undergraduate colleges and students can take advantage of Formal Hall, sport (there are on-site playing fields), music and drama. One disadvantage of Homerton's status is that accommodation costs are higher than at many other colleges.

JESUS

Jesus College, Cambridge CB5 8BL (tel: 01223-357626)
Undergraduates: 451 **Male/female ratio:** 58/42

For those of a sporting inclination Jesus is perhaps the ideal college. Within its spacious grounds there are football, rugby and cricket pitches as well as three squash courts and no less than ten tennis courts, while the Cam is just a few hundred yards away. With these facilities, it is hardly surprising that sports, in particular rowing, rugby and hockey, rate high on many students' agendas. That said, sporting prowess is far from the whole story. The music society thrives, and has extensive practice facilities. Although Jesus lacks a theatre of its own, the college is active in university drama. On the academic front, the Fellows-to-undergraduates ratio is generous and, while philosophy and politics are among the college's strong suits, the balance between arts and sciences is fairly even. There is an excellent and stylish new library. Rooms in college are guaranteed for all first and third-year students. The majority of second years live in college houses directly opposite the college. Roughly half the undergraduates are state educated and the college is keen to encourage more applications from the state sector. The college grounds – particularly The Chimney walkway to the porter's lodge – are attractive.

KING'S

King's College, Cambridge CB2 1ST (tel. 01223-331100)
Undergraduates: 358 **Male/female ratio:** 60/40

The reputation of King's as the most right-on place in the university has become something of an in-joke. It is true that the college has a 4/1 state-to-independent ratio and that it has banned Formal Hall and abandoned May Balls in favour of politically correct June Events. The college is involved in an initiative to increase the number of candidates from socially and educationally disadvantaged backgrounds, and is also keen to encourage applications from ethnic minorities and from women. The students' union is active politically. The college has fewer undergraduates than the grandeur of its buildings might suggest, one result being that accommodation is guaranteed, either in college or in hostels a few hundred yards away. With the highest ratio of Fellows to undergraduates in Cambridge, it is not surprising that King's has been one of the most academically successful colleges. No subjects are especially favoured, but recent results have been better in arts than sciences. Applications are not accepted in veterinary medicine and there are few law students. Sport at King's is anything but competitive. An extremely large bar/JCR is the social focal point, while the world-famous chapel and choir form the heart of an outstanding music scene.

LUCY CAVENDISH

Lucy Cavendish College, Cambridge CB3 OBU (tel, 01223-332190)

Undergraduates: 77 **Women only**

Since its creation in 1965, Lucy Cavendish has given hundreds of women over the age of 21 the opportunity to read for Tripos subjects. A number of its students had already started careers and/or families when they decided to enter higher education. The college seeks to offer financial support to those with family responsibilities, though as yet it has no child care facilities. Accommodation is provided for all who request it, either in the college's three Victorian houses or in its three modern residential blocks. The college's small size enables all students to get to know one another. Plans to increase the intake are unlikely to alter the intimate and informal atmosphere. Law is still the dominant subject in terms of numbers of students, but veterinary science is also strong and the college welcomes applications in the sciences and other disciplines. All the Fellows are women. For subjects not covered by the Fellowship, there is a well-established network of university teachers.

MAGDALENE

Magdalene College, Cambridge CB3 OAG (tel. 01223-332100)

Undergraduates: 320 **Male/female ratio:** 65/35

As the last college to admit women (1988), Magdalene has still to throw off a lingering image as home to hordes of public school hearties. In fact, just under half its undergraduates are from the state sector while about a third are women. That said, the sporty emphasis, on rugby and rowing in particular, is undeniable. The nearby playing fields are shared with St John's and the college has its own Eton fives court. Despite finishing closer to the foot of the academic league tables than its Fellows would wish, Magdalene is strong in architecture, law and social and political science. Students are heavily involved in university-wide activities from drama to journalism as well as sport. Accommodation is provided for all undergraduates, either in college or in one of 21 houses and hostels, 'mostly on our doorstep'. Living in is more expensive than in most colleges. Magdalene is proud of its river frontage, the longest in the university, which is especially memorable in the summer.

NEW HALL

New Hall, Huntingdon Road, Cambridge CB3 ODF (tel. 01223-351721)

Undergraduates: 333 **Women only**

One of three remaining all-women colleges, New Hall enjoys a largely erroneous reputation for feminism and academic underachievement not helped by a much-publicised whitewash on *University Challenge*. Founded in 1954 to increase the number of women in the university, it occupies a modern grey-brick site next door to Fitzwilliam. Students are split 50/50 between state and independent schools. The college lays claim to certain paradoxes. While a rent strike early in the 1990s attested to a degree of political activism, tradition is far from rejected. The following year saw New Hall's first-ever May Ball, an event hosted jointly with Sidney Sussex. Its results regularly place the college near the bottom of the academic league, but it must be remembered that women's results lag behind men's throughout the university. Natural sciences, medicine, economics, and English are New Hall's strongest areas. The college is known for its unusual split-level bar, but many students choose to socialise elsewhere. Sport is a good mixture of high-fliers and enthusiasts, with grounds, shared with Fitzwilliam, half a mile away. The college is particularly proud of its collection of contemporary women's art.

NEWNHAM
Newnham College, Cambridge CB3 9DF (tel. 01223-335700)
Undergraduates: 414 **Women only**

Newnham has long had to battle with a blue-stocking image. Its entry in the university prospectus used to insist that it 'is not a nunnery' and that the atmosphere in this all-women college is no stricter than elsewhere. It even has a 'Newnham Nuns' drinking club to make the point. With an even state-independent ratio, the college has also successfully cast off a reputation for public school dominance. Newnham is in the perfect location for humanities students, with the lecture halls and libraries of the Sidgwick Site just across the road. The college is, however, keen to encourage applications in engineering, maths and the sciences, and recent results in these subjects have been better than in the arts. All of the Fellows are women. Around 95 per cent of students live in for all three years. This is not to say that ventures into the social, sporting and artistic life of the university are the exception rather than the rule. Newnham students are anything but insular. As well as being blessed with the largest and most beautiful lawns in Cambridge, Newnham has its playing fields on site. The boat club has been notably successful, while college teams compete to a high standard in tennis, cricket and a number of minority sports.

PEMBROKE
Pembroke College, Cambridge CB2 1RF (tel. 01223-338100)
Undergraduates: 382 **Male/female ratio:** 60/40

Another college with a reputation for public school dominance (the current state-to-independent ratio is around 40/60), Pembroke's image is changing. Rowing and rugby still feature prominently, but with a female population of about 40 per cent the heartiness is giving way to a more relaxed if still somewhat insular atmosphere. Around two thirds of all undergraduates live in college, including all first years. The rest are housed in fairly central college hostels, though the standards of these are variable. A new college building will improve the situation. Academically, Pembroke is considered solid rather than spectacular. Engineering and natural sciences have the largest number of undergraduates, but the subject range is wide with history, classics and English recent strengths. The bar is inevitably the social focal point, but a restriction on advertising means that Pembroke bops attract few students from other colleges. The Pembroke Players generally stage one play a term in the Old Reader, which also doubles as the college cinema, and many Pembroke students are involved in university dramatics. The Old Library is a popular venue for classical concerts. Indeed music is a Pembroke strength. In a city of memorable college gardens, Pembroke's are among the best.

PETERHOUSE
Peterhouse College, Cambridge CB2 1RD (tel. 01223-338200)
Undergraduates: 225 **Male/female ratio:** 75/25

The oldest and among the smallest of the colleges, Peterhouse is another that has had to contend with an image problem. But while by no means as reactionary as its critics would have it, Peterhouse is certainly not overly progressive. There is a 3/1 male-to-female split, while the state-to-independent ratio is close to the university average at 50/50. The college's diminutive size – its entire student population is the same as one year's intake at Trinity – inevitably makes for an intimate atmosphere. But this does not mean that its undergraduates never venture beyond the college bar. Peterhouse is known above all as 'the history college'. But while history is indeed a traditional strength and results are excellent, there are in fact no more history students than there are taking natural science or engineering. Academically, the college is generally a mid-table performer, with a better record in arts than sciences. The 13th-century candle-lit dining hall provides a fitting setting for what by common consent is the best food in the university. Rents are below average, and undergraduates live in for at least two years, the remainder choosing rooms in college hostels, most within one or two minutes' walk. The sports grounds are shared with Clare and are about a mile away. The college teams have a less than glittering reputation, not surprisingly, given its size.

QUEENS'
Queens' College, Cambridge CB3 9ET (tel. 01223-335511)
Undergraduates: 490 **Male/female ratio:** 63/37

There is a strong case for claiming that Queens' is the most tightly knit college in the university. With all undergraduates housed in college for the full three years, a large and popular bar (open all day) and outstanding facilities, including Cambridge's first college nursery, it is easy to see why. Queens' also has the distinction of attracting an above-average number of applicants. The state-to-independent ratio (60/40) is good, but barely more than a third of students are female. Though not to all tastes, the mix of architectural styles, ranging from the medieval Old Court to the 1980s Cripps Complex, is as great as any in the university. In addition to three excellent squash courts, the Cripps Complex is also home to Fitzpatrick Hall, a multipurpose venue containing Cambridge's best-equipped college theatre and the hub of Queens' renowned social scene. Friday and Saturday night bops are extremely popular. Queens' has perhaps the foremost college drama society and a thriving cinema. Law, maths, engineering and natural sciences are the leading subjects in a college with an enviable academic record across the board. Apart from squash, Queens' is not especially sporty. The playing fields (one mile away) are shared with Robinson.

ROBINSON

Robinson College, Cambridge CB3 9AN (tel. 01223-339100)
Undergraduates: 391 **Male/female ratio:** 62/38

Robinson is the youngest college in Cambridge and admitted its first students in 1979. Its unspectacular architecture has earned it the nickname 'the car park'. On the other hand, having been built with one eye on the conference trade, rooms are more comfortable than most and the majority have their own bathrooms and online links to the university computer network. Almost all students, including all first and third years, live in college or in houses in the attractive gardens. The college is one of the few with rooms adapted for disabled students. Robinson has sometimes been close to the bottom of the academic tables, but improved its position in 1999. There is no particular subject bias, but recent results have been better in sciences than arts. One in four Fellows are women, the second highest proportion in any mixed college. Its youth and balanced admissions policy (38 per cent are from independent schools, and there is a 38 per cent female intake) ensure that Robinson has one of the more unpretentious atmospheres. The auditorium is the largest of any college and is a popular venue for films, plays and concerts. The college fields (shared with Queens') are home to excellent rugby and hockey sides, and the boat club is also successful.

ST CATHARINE'S

St Catharine's College, Cambridge CB2 1RL (tel. 01223-338300)
Undergraduates: 427 **Male/female ratio:** 65/35

Known to everyone as 'Catz', this is a medium-sized, 17th-century college standing opposite Corpus Christi on King's Parade. The principal college site, with its distinctive three-sided main court, though small, provides accommodation for all its first-year students. The majority of second years live in flats at St Chad's Court, a ten-minute walk away. Catz is not considered one of the leading colleges academically, although its 1999 results put it in the top ten, but it has a reputation as a friendly place. Geography and law are usually the strongest subjects. More than a third of the students are women, and the split between independent and state school pupils is about even. A new library and JCR have improved the facilities considerably, and there is a strong musical tradition. College social life centres on the large bar, which has been likened, among other things, to a ski chalet or sauna. With a reputation for being sporting rather than sporty, Catz is one of the few colleges that regularly puts out three rugby XVs, and also has a good record in football and hockey. The playing fields are about a ten-minute walk away.

ST JOHN'S

St John's College, Cambridge CB2 1TP (tel. 01223-338600)
Undergraduates: 540 **Male/female ratio:** 65/35

Second only to Trinity in size and wealth, St John's has an enviable reputation in most fields and is sometimes resented for it. The wealth translates into excellent accommodation in college for almost all undergraduates throughout their three years, as well as book grants and a new 24-hour library. First years are housed together, which can hinder integration. There is no particular subject bias and St John's has a formidable academic record, despite slipping out of the top ten this year. English and natural sciences have been recent strengths. A reputation for heartiness persists and the female intake is 35 per cent, slightly below average. The state-to-independent split is about 50/50. The boat club has a powerful reputation, but rugby, hockey and cricket are all traditionally strong. In such a large community, however, all should be able to find their own level. Extensive playing fields shared with Magdalene are a few hundred yards away and the boathouse is extremely good. The college film society organises popular screenings in the Fisher Building, which also contains an art studio and drawing office for architecture and engineering students. Music is dominated by the world-famous choir. Excellent as the facilities are, some students find that the sheer size of St John's can be daunting and this makes it hard to settle into.

SELWYN

Selwyn College, Cambridge CB3 9DQ (tel. 01223-335846)
Undergraduates: 340 **Male/female ratio:** 55/45

Described by one undergraduate as 'the least overtly intellectual college', Selwyn has a down-to-earth and relatively unpressured atmosphere. Located behind the Sidgwick Site, it is in an ideal position for humanities students, and its academic prowess has traditionally been on the arts side although engineering is an emerging strength. One of the first colleges to go mixed (1976) now almost half of Selwyn's undergraduates are female. Selwyn is also one of the few colleges to publish its state-to-independent ratio, which stands at about 53/47. Accommodation is provided for all students, either in the college itself or in hostels, all of which are close by. The college has been a leader in IT provision: all college rooms have online connections to the university computer network and there are two well-strocked computer rooms. As well as the usual college groups, the Music Society is especially well-supported. The bar is popular if a little 'hotel-like'. In sport, the novice boat crews have done well in recent years, as have the hockey and badminton sides, but the emphasis is as much on enjoyment as achievement. The grounds are shared with King's and are three quarters of a mile away.

SIDNEY SUSSEX

Sidney Sussex College, Cambridge CB2 3HU (tel. 01223-338800)
Undergraduates: 319 **Male/female ratio:** 58/42

Students at this small, central college are forever the butt of jokes about Sidney being mistaken for the branch of Sainsbury's over the road. Two other, more serious, aspects of life at Sidney stand out: almost every year its undergraduates raise more for the Rag Appeal than any others; while rents are comfortably the lowest in the university (all students are housed either in college or one of 11 nearby hostels). Exam results generally place the college in the middle of the academic leagues, but 1999 saw a return to the upper echelons after a year in which it had dived to 17th place. Engineering, geography and law are generally the strongest subjects. Sidney has a good social balance, with a nearly even state-to-independent ratio, while more than 40 per cent of the undergraduates are women. There is a large student-run bar which is the venue for fortnightly hops, an active drama society (SADCO) and plenty of involvement in university activities. The sports grounds are shared with Christ's and are a 10-minute cycle ride away. Sidneyites are enthusiastic competitors, but the college does not have a reputation for excellence in any individual sports. Sidney's size means that the college is a tight-knit community. Some students find such insularity suffocating rather than supportive.

TRINITY

Trinity College, Cambridge CB2 1TQ (tel. 01223-338400)
Undergraduates: 660 **Male/female ratio:** 65/35

The legend that you can walk from Oxford to Cambridge without ever leaving Trinity land typifies Cambridge undergraduates' views about the college, even if it is not true. Indeed, the college is almost synonymous with size and wealth. Founded by Henry VIII, its endowment is almost as big as the other colleges' put together. However, the view that every Trinity student is an arrogant public schoolboy is less easily sustained. That said, it is true that only about a third of Trinity undergraduates are women, the lowest proportion in any of the mixed colleges. On the other hand, there is little obvious bias in the admissions policy. Being rich, Trinity offers book grants to every student as well as generous travel grants and spacious, reasonably priced rooms in college for all first and third-year students as well as many second years. The college generally features in the top ten academically and topped the Tompkins Table for two years before slipping to second in 1999. Generally better for sciences than arts, the strongest subjects are engineering, maths and natural sciences. Trinity rarely fails to do well in most sports, with cricket in the forefront. The playing fields are half a mile away. A new and larger bar should improve the social scene. The Trinity Sweatys attract students from all over the university.

TRINITY HALL

Trinity Hall, Cambridge CB2 1TJ (tel. 01223-332500)
Undergraduates: 344 **Male/female ratio:** 55/45

The outstanding performance of its oarsmen has ensured the prevailing view of Trinity Hall as a 'boaty' college, but it is also known for its drama, music and bar. The Preston Society is one of the better college drama groups and stages regular productions both in the college theatre and at other venues. Weekly recitals keep the Music Society busy. The small bar is invariably packed. Not surprisingly, many undergraduates rarely feel the need to go elsewhere for their entertainment, although there has been considerable involvement in the students' union recently. Notwithstanding an unusually low position in this year's league table, the college is strong academically. Law is a traditional speciality and results have been excellent in modern languages recently. Though the natural sciences are well represented, the college is much stronger in the arts. Approaching half of the undergraduates are women and around half are from state schools. All first years and approximately half the third years live in the college, which is situated on the Backs behind Caius. The remainder take rooms either in two large hostels close to the sports ground (a mile from college), or in college accommodation about five minutes' walk away.

9

University Profiles

S ome famous names are missing from our university listings: the Open University, the separate business and medical schools, Birkbeck College and Cranfield University among them. Their omission is no reflection on their quality, simply a function of their particular roles. The guide is based on provision for full-time undergraduates and the factors judged to influence this. The Open University, though Britain's biggest university, with 75,000 students, could not be included because most of the measures used in our listing do not apply to it. As a non-residential, largely part-time institution, Birkbeck College, London, could also not be compared in many key areas. Although Cranfield, for example, offers undergraduate degrees in two of its campuses, the Institute is primarily for graduate students. Manchester and London business schools were excluded for the same reason. Similarly, specialist institutions such as the Royal College of Art and the medical schools could not fairly be compared with generalist universities. A number of colleges with degree-awarding powers also do not appear because they have yet to be granted university status.

Each university profile includes some standard information, which is described below:

Telephone In most cases this is the telephone number for admission enquiries. In some cases it is the general university telephone number.

Website This is the address of the main university website.

e-mail This is the e-mail address for admissions and prospectus enquiries.

Undergraduates The first figure is for full-time undergraduates. The second figure (in brackets) gives the number of part-time undergraduates. The figures are for 1997–98, and are the most recent provided by HESA.

Postgraduates The first figure is for full-time postgraduates. The second figure (in brackets) gives the number of part-time postgraduates. The figures are for 1997–98, and are the most recent provided by HESA.

Mature students This figure is the percentage of First degree entrants in 1997–98 who were over 21. The figures were compiled by the Higher Education Funding Councils.

Overseas students This figure is the number of undergraduate overseas students (both EU and non–EU) as a percentage of full-time undergraduates. All figures relate to 1997–98 and are based on HESA data.

Applications/place. This figure is the number of applicants per place for 1999-2000 as calculated by UCAS.

Undergraduates from State sector This figure gives the number of young full-time entrants from state schools or colleges in 1997-98 as a percentage of total young entrants. The figures were compiled by the Higher Education Funding Councils.

Teaching quality ratings The profiles include teaching quality ratings published by the Higher Education Funding Councils. Assessments are carried out by teams of subject specialists, and departments graded differently in England, Scotland and Wales. Since April 1995, in England and Northern Ireland, subjects have been rated on six criteria, each attracting a maximum score of four points. Scotland also went over to this system in 1998. The listings in this chapter give the aggregate scores from assessments published to June 1999. Before this system was introduced, subjects were rated as Excellent, Satisfactory or Unsatisfactory. In Scotland there was an extra category of Highly Satisfactory.

Comments on campus facilities apply to the universities' own sites only. New universities, in particular, operate 'franchised' courses at further education colleges, which are likely to have lower levels of provision. Prospective applicants should check out the library and social facilities before accepting a place away from the parent institution.

The University of London

The University of London and the University of Wales are both federal universities composed of a number of institutions. In this profile section, the initial pages on the University of London outline the colleges of the university that are not listed separately in this guide. There then follow separate entries on the leading undergraduate colleges.

University of Wales

For the University of Wales, there are separate entries for University of Wales, Aberystwyth; University of Wales, Bangor; Cardiff University of Wales; University of Wales, Lampeter; and University of Wales, Swansea.

Founded in 1893, the university now has 33,750 students. See www.wales.ac.uk. It celebrated its centenary in 1993 and is second only to London, its federal counterpart in terms of full-time student numbers, with more than 45,000 students including part-timers. Like London, it is surrendering more power to its colleges. At the same time, however, intercollegiate links have been increasing, especially in research. A new structure was introduced in 1996, bringing the university colleges in Cardiff and Newport into the fold.

Not listed separately:

University of Wales College of Medicine, Health Park, Cardiff CF4 4XN (tel. 029-2074-7747). Founded 1931. Full-time students: 850. Based at the University Hospital of Wales, two miles from the centre of Cardiff.

University of Wales College, Newport, Caerleon Campus, Newport NP18 3YG (tel. 01633-432432). Total students: 7,000. Campuses in Newport and Caerleon, three miles away.

University of Wales Institute, Cardiff, Western Avenue, Cardiff CF5 2YB (tel. 029-2041-6070). Total students: 7,600. Four campuses in the Cardiff area.

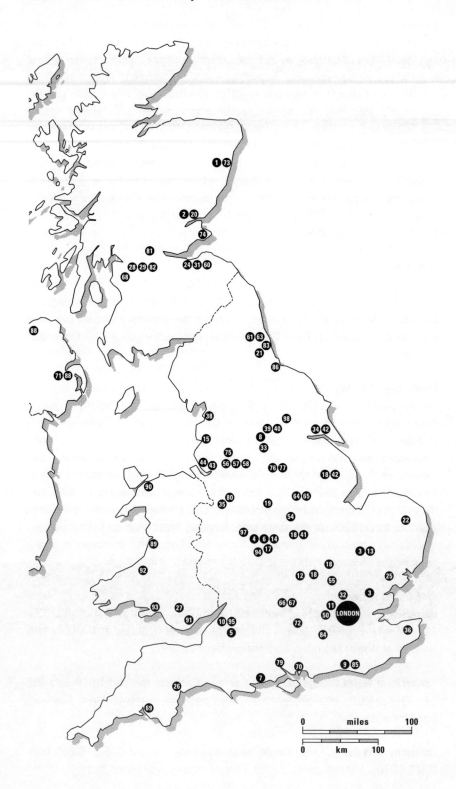

Location of Universities

The map opposite shows the locations of the universities covered in this book. The following universities in London are not shown separately: 16, 23, 30, 37, 45, 47, 48, 49, 51, 52, 53, 59, 62, 78, and 87. In the key, the name of the university is given first and the town where it is located second.

1 Aberdeen *Aberdeen*
2 Abertay *Dundee*
3 Anglia Polytechnic *Chelmsford, Cambridge*
4 Aston *Birmingham*
5 Bath *Bath*
6 Birmingham *Birmingham*
7 Bournemouth *Bournemouth*
8 Bradford *Bradford*
9 Brighton *Brighton*
10 Bristol *Bristol*
11 Brunel *Uxbridge*
12 Buckingham *Buckingham*
13 Cambridge *Cambridge*
14 Central England *Birmingham*
15 Central Lancashire *Preston*
16 City *London EC1*
17 Coventry *Coventry*
18 De Montford *Leicester, Milton Keynes, Bedford, Lincoln*
19 Derby *Derby*
20 Dundee *Dundee*
21 Durham *Durham*
22 East Anglia *Norwich*
23 East London *London E15*
24 Edinburgh *Edinburgh*
25 Essex *Colchester*
26 Exeter *Exeter*
27 Glamorgan *Pontypridd*
28 Glasgow *Glasgow*
29 Glasgow Caledonian *Glasgow*
30 Greenwich *Eltham, London SE9*
31 Heriot-Watt *Edinburgh*
32 Hertfordshire *Hatfield*
33 Huddersfield *Huddersfield*
34 Hull *Hull*
35 Keele Keele, *Staffordshire*
36 Kent at Canterbury *Canterbury*
37 Kingston *Kingston, Surrey*
38 Lancaster *Lancaster*
39 Leeds *Leeds*
40 Leeds Metropolitan *Leeds*
41 Leicester *Leicester*
42 Lincolnshire and Humberside *Lincoln, Hull*
43 Liverpool *Liverpool*
44 Liverpool John Moores *Liverpool*
45 London, Goldsmiths' *London SE14*
46 London, Imperial *London SW7*
47 London, King's College *London WC2*
48 London, LSE *London WC2*

49 London, Queen Mary and Westfield *London E1*
50 London, Royal Holloway *Egham Surrey*
51 London, SOAS *London WC1*
52 London, University College *London WC1*
53 London Guildhall *London EC3*
54 Loughborough *Loughborough*
55 Luton *Luton*
56 Manchester *Manchester*
57 UMIST *Manchester*
58 Manchester Metropolitan *Manchester*
59 Middlesex *London N17*
60 Napier *Edinburgh*
61 Newcastle *Newcastle*
62 North London *London N7*
63 Northumbria *Newcastle*
64 Nottingham *Nottingham*
65 Nottingham Trent *Nottingham*
66 Oxford *Oxford*
67 Oxford Brookes *Oxford*
68 Paisley *Paisley*
69 Plymouth *Plymouth*
70 Portsmouth *Portsmouth*
71 Queen's, Belfast *Belfast*
72 Reading *Reading*
73 Robert Gordon *Aberdeen*
74 St Andrews *St Andrews*
75 Salford *Salford*
76 Sheffield *Sheffield*
77 Sheffield Hallam *Sheffield*
78 South Bank *London SE1*
79 Southampton *Southampton*
80 Staffordshire *Stoke on Trent*
81 Stirling *Stirling*
82 Strathclyde *Glasgow*
83 Sunderland *Sunderland*
84 Surrey *Guildford*
85 Sussex *Brighton*
86 Teesside *Middlesborough*
87 Thames Valley *Ealing, London W5*
88 Ulster *Coleraine, Belfast*
89 Wales, Aberystwyth *Aberystwyth*
90 Wales, Bangor *Bangor*
91 Wales, Cardiff *Cardiff*
92 Wales, Lampeter *Lampeter*
93 Wales, Swansea *Swansea*
94 Warwick *Coventry*
95 West of England *Bristol*
96 Westminster *London W1*
97 Wolverhampton *Wolverhampton*
98 York *York*

University of Aberdeen

Founded: 1495

Times ranking: 26th equal (1999 ranking: 36)

Address: King's College, Aberdeen AB24 3FX

tel: 01224 273504
website: www.abdn.ac.uk
e-mail: admoff@admin.abdn.ac.uk

Undergraduates: 8,382 (870)
Postgraduates: 1,231 (1,200)
Mature students: 19%
Overseas students: 8%
Applications/place: 4.9
Undergraduates from State sector: 76%

Main subject areas: arts and social sciences; divinity; engineering; law; medicine; science

Teaching quality ratings

Rated Excellent 1993-98: cellular biology; economics; French; geography; medicine; organismal biology; sociology.

Rated Highly Satisfactory 1993–98: accounting; chemistry; civil engineering; English; geology; history of art; law; mathematics; mechanical engineering; philosophy; politics; psychology; theology.

From 1998: European languages 22; planning and landscape 19.

Overview

Aberdeen considers itself a 'balanced' university because half of its students are men and half women, half study medicine, science or engineering, half the arts or social sciences. This mix is valued both socially and academically in an institution which strives to be the classic Scottish university, offering its students the broadest possible choice of subjects.

Most students are not even admitted to a particular department, but to a broad academic area, allowing them to try out three or four subjects before committing themselves at the end of their first or even second year. The modular system is so flexible that the majority of students change their intended degree before graduation. Every student has an Adviser of Studies to help make the right choice.

There is plenty of quality to choose from: only three subjects have been rated as less than Highly Satisfactory for teaching. The last research assessments were not so impressive, with only law in the top two categories, but the university's reputation seems not to have suffered since Aberdeen's graduates enjoy an enviably low unemployment rate.

Medicine, law and divinity head Aberdeen's traditional strengths – the university established the English-speaking world's first chair in law and has seen its share of medical advances. The new Institute of Medical Sciences brought together all Aberdeen's work in this area with a dozen new professorships in a complete reorganisation of departments.

Biological sciences have developed strongly in recent years, becoming second only to the social sciences in terms of size. Biomedicine is particularly strong and the university's links with the oil industry show in geology's high reputation. Senior academic posts have been strengthened in a variety of areas, from Celtic and Spanish to international relations since the university recovered from financial problems, which held it back in the 1980s.

Today's university is a fusion of two ancient institutions which came together in 1860. With King's College dating back to 1495 and Marischal College following almost a century later, Aberdeen likes to boast that for 250 years it had as many universities as the whole of England.

The original King's College buildings are the focal point of an appealing and quiet campus, complete with cobbled main street and some sturdily handsome Georgian buildings, about a mile from the city centre. Medicine is at Foresterhill, a 20-minute walk away, adjoining the Aberdeen Royal Infirmary. Buses link the two sites with the Hillhead residential complex, with the students' union running a free late-night service. The Aberdeen arm of Northern College will soon join the fold, restoring the university's original involvement in teacher training, as well as swelling the ranks of the social sciences.

Almost half of the students come from the north of Scotland, but taking one in five from outside Britain ensures a cosmopolitan atmosphere. Those from England and further afield are generally prepared for Aberdeen's remote location and long and often bitter winters. They find the city lively and welcoming, if expensive, although social life inevitably centres on the university.

Accommodation

The university houses almost half of all undergraduates and guarantees a place for first years from outside the Aberdeen area. Little cheap housing is available in the private sector but the university is committed to adding 500 residential places every year.

Library and computing

The library contains more than 1 million books and 250,000 maps in six buildings with 1,500 study spaces. There are more than 1,000 computers, many with 24-hour access, with three halls of residence linked into the network.

Student facilities

The large students' union has four bars and eating places which are amongst the cheapest in the city. A separate Students' Representative Council (SRC) carries out political functions and runs the Joblink employment bureau.

Sport

Facilities are free and include a swimming pool, sports hall, tennis and squash courts and climbing wall. There are about 50 clubs, as well as a boathouse on the River Dee and a mountain hut in the Cairngorms.

Overseas students

All undergraduates are guaranteed at least one year in hall and non-EU students are offered free pre-sessional English language courses if required. Both the university and SRC have international officers.

University of Abertay Dundee

Founded: Royal Charter 1994, formally Dundee Institute of Technology

Times ranking: 68 (1999 ranking: 82)

Address: Bell Street, Dundee DD1 1HG

tel: 01382 308080

website: www.abertay.ac.uk

e-mail: iro@abertay.ac.uk

Undergraduates: 3,108 (374)

Postgraduates: 251 (193)

Mature students: 32%

Overseas students: 10%

Applications/place: 3.7

Undergraduates from State sector: 91%

Main subject areas: accountancy; construction and environment; engineering; informatics; life sciences; health and nursing and social sciences; management and law. Most subjects available at diploma level as well as at degree level.

Teaching quality ratings

Rated Excellent: economics.

Rated Highly Satisfactory: cellular and molecular biology; chemistry; civil engineering; mechanical engineering; mathematics and statistics; psychology.

Overview

Scotland's newest university has been proving highly popular with applicants, bucking the downward trend in Scotland in 1999. Although still less than 5,000 strong, the former central institution enjoyed the biggest increase in applications in Britain, and the new intake of almost 2,000 was more than 20 per cent up on the previous year. A series of good teaching scores will have been one attraction and the distinction of recording the lowest drop-out rate of any new university should be another welcome feature. The funding councils estimated that only 11 per cent would leave without a qualification.

The former Dundee Institute of Technology was made to wait for university status, which only came two years after the polytechnics were promoted. But the institute had already established its academic credentials, with teaching in economics rated more highly than in some of Scotland's elite universities. Subsequent assessments have been solid, without living up to that early promise. More than half of the subjects have been rated better than satisfactory. Research is not being ignored; Abertay is proud of its record in establishing a series of specialist centres, in areas as diverse as wood technology, waste water and Chinese business, during its first five years as a university.

Based mainly in the centre of Dundee, Abertay plays to its strengths with a limited range of courses. Even the Business School, in the imposing Dudhope Castle, is only a 15-minute walk from the three main buildings. New facilities are gradually being added, notably the £8 million learning resources centre opened by the Queen.

Entrance requirements for most courses are modest, but the boom in applications has cut the number of places filled through Clearing. Degrees are predominantly vocational, with more subjects being added every year. The world's first degree in computer games technology was a recent high-profile example, with visiting professors from the games industry adding their expertise. Forest products technology was another tailored precisely to job opportunities in the region. All courses can be taken on a part-time basis.

More than a third of the undergraduates are over 21 on entry, many living locally. With the student population still relatively small, that translates into a moderate social scene, particularly at weekends. However, Dundee has a large student population and is improving as a youth centre and the cost of living is low.

Accommodation

First years arriving in Dundee are guaranteed accommodation as long as they register before 1 September. After their first year most students move into private rented accommodation.

Library and computing

The university recently opened a new library. It features seminar rooms, a language centre and an IT training suite and part of the building is open 24 hours a day. The library is the university's largest IT centre with over 300 PC workstations.

Student facilities

The main campus is close to the centre of the historic city and annexes are within walking distance. Students need to take advantage of this when planning a night out as the city offers the best entertainment options.

Sport

The university offers good outdoor sporting facilities. The Gaelic football club won the Scottish Championship last year, the rugby and football clubs are improving. Students can buy a 'sports card', which allows the use of council facilities at reduced rates.

Overseas students

The university offers a welcome and orientation programme, guaranteed accommodation and English-language support. There is also a dedicated Overseas Officer to help out with any difficulties students might have.

Anglia Polytechnic University

Founded: University status 1992, formerly Anglia Polytechnic

Times ranking: 73rd equal (1999 ranking: 67)

Address: Rivermead Campus, Chelmsford, Essex CM1 1LL

tel: 01223 363271
website: www.anglia.ac.uk
e-mail: angliainfo@anglia.ac.uk

Undergraduates: 10,258 (5,443)
Postgraduates: 376 (1,854)
Mature students: 41%
Overseas students: 14%
Applications/place: 4.4
Undergraduates from State sector: 93%

Main subject areas: advanced nursing, midwifery and health studies; applied science; business, design and communication systems; arts, languages and social studies; education; humanities; law.
Also a range of diploma courses.

Teaching quality ratings

Rated Excellent 1993–95: English; music; social work.

From 1995: art and design 21; modern languages 21; building and civil engineering 20; sociology 20; electrical and electronic engineering 19; land management 19; town planning 19; history of art 18; media studies 18.

Overview

The last university to retain the polytechnic title has been trying without success to drop it, to avoid confusion among employers and overseas applicants. Objections to its proposed switch to the University of Eastern England have delayed the process sufficiently to prevent any change for entrants in 2001. Other changes have gone ahead, however, chief among them the closure of the Brentwood site, relocating the teacher training courses to the new Rivermead campus in Chelmsford.

An amalgamation of two well-established higher education colleges made Anglia the first regional polytechnic, but the twin bases in Chelmsford and Cambridge remain distinct. The two very different locations are far enough apart to ensure that there is little contact, although electronic networking and a central administration ensure that key academic facilities are available throughout the university. The regional ideal extends to a network of more than 20 partner colleges in Cambridgeshire, Essex, Norfolk and Suffolk. East Anglia has always lagged behind other parts of England for participation in higher education, and, although numbers rose in 1999, the university has sometimes struggled to fill its places.

Recent teaching ratings have been solid, rather than spectacular, with the Cambridge-based art and design courses producing the best score. The last research assessments were more worrying, with fewer than a quarter of the academic staff entered and no subjects in the top four of the seven categories. The university has a strongly European outlook, encouraging students to take a language option and providing an unusually large number of exchange opportunities in Malaysia and China, as well as Europe and the United States. Employers play a part in planning courses which are integrated into a modular system extending from degree level to professional programmes. Each undergraduate has an adviser to help compile a degree package which looks at the chosen subject from different points of view and maximises future job prospects.

The university is gradually moving out of its cramped town centre site in Chelmsford, as it develops the more spacious and attractive Rivermead campus on the edge of town. The Cambridge site is also small, but well-appointed. The social scene inevitably varies between the two sites. Cambridge students enjoy the advantages of a great university city, but have to shrug off the tag of attending the lesser institution, while at the Essex end of the university, students can find Chelmsford dull. Neither is far from London by train.

Accommodation

With new residential places opened in 1999, around 60 per cent of first years can be accommodated in university property, with priority going to students with special needs and those who live more than 80 miles from their place of study. Each campus has local residence and accommodation staff who will help to find alternatives.

Library and computing

There are six main libraries spread across the campuses in different towns. Open-access PCs are available across the campuses and each student is given an e-mail address.

Student facilities

Facilities vary, but both Cambridge and Chelmsford both have students' unions offering societies and clubs as well as bars. Generally, Cambridge is very student-orientated, Chelmsford less so.

Sport

Sporting facilities vary across the campuses but the main campuses at Chelmsford and Cambridge offer a decent range of indoor and outdoor facilities. The students' union offer a good range of sporting clubs.

Overseas students

The international office provides guidance to all students. In addition, specialist academic and welfare support is provided, as are English courses.

Aston University

Overview

Aston glories in its role as a tight-knit, vocational, urban university, which has swum against the tide of British higher education over the past decade. Small and lively, set in the heart of Birmingham, it has remained resolutely specialist in science and technology, business and languages, concentrating on the sandwich degrees which have served its graduates so well in the employment market.

Four out of five Aston graduates go straight into jobs, spurning the postgraduate courses and training programmes which have become the first port of call for many of their counterparts in the old universities. Often they are returning to the scene of work placements, which have become the norm for 70 per cent of Aston's undergraduates.

The university's refusal to take more than the current 5,000 students has made for a bumpy ride financially – the funding council has had to provide special help several times to avoid damaging budget cuts. But the strategy is beginning to pay off with encouring rises in applications and big grants from industry, which have allowed the university to boost staffing in business, engineering and languages.

Research grades, which bring big financial rewards for universities, improved in the last round of assessments. The latest academic reinforcements are designed to secure still better ratings when the exercise is repeated in 2000, as well as generating more income from research contracts. At the same time, a change in the structure of the university reduced the number of schools of studies to four to break down barriers between departments. There is a wide range of combined honours programmes for those who prefer not to specialise.

As befits a one-time college of advanced technology, Aston's strengths are on the science side, although the business school is highly rated and accounts for almost half the students. After a bruising introduction to the teaching quality assessments, in which none of the first six departments was considered excellent, ratings have improved considerably. Aston achieved the first maximum score for pharmacy in 1999, building on high grades for optometry and biological sciences.

Aston is flexible about entry requirements for mature students, but school-leavers are generally asked for at least 20 points (the equivalent of a B and two Cs) at A level. The average entrant in 1998 had an even higher score, and the rising demand for places is likely to continue the trend.

The 40-acre campus, a ten-minute walk from the centre of Birmingham, is barely recognisable from the university's early days. Carefully landscaped, it is nearing the end of a £16 million building plan, which will see Aston's residential and academic accommodation concentrated on the same site. The first 650 students moved into the Lakeside halls in autumn 1999.

Aston was among the pioneers of 'smart cards', giving students access to university facilities and enabling them to make purchases on campus, once they have money in their accounts. There is plenty of opportunity to use them in a buzzing social scene, which most students find to their taste.

Accommodation

All first years are guaranteed accommodation by the university, encouraging them to live on campus. Two thirds of full-time students are in university accommodation. Private accommodation is cheap and plentiful but can be some distance from the campus.

Library and computing

The university has 750 open-access PCs distributed in 10 main clusters around the campus, most of which are open 24 hours a day. The library is on four floors and houses 200,000 volumes and 1,600 periodicals.

Student facilities

Like Birmingham, Aston has a Guild rather than a Union. It offers bars, food and is home to the many societies and sports clubs. Aston is ideally placed for city-centre facilities.

Sport

Aston has some fine sports facilities like the Woodcock Sports Centre which houses a 25-metre swimming pool and the Gem sports hall. It also has the Recreation Centre, which unfortunately is six miles north of the campus.

Overseas students

Aston is the temporary home of students from over 80 countries. The university offers pre-degree English courses of five or ten weeks. All overseas students are guaranteed university accommodation.

University of Bath

Founded: 1894 (in Bristol), Royal Charter 1966

Times ranking: 10th equal (1999 ranking: 15)

Address: Claverton Down, Bath BA2 7AY

tel: 01225 826326
website: www.bath.ac.uk
e-mail: admissions@bath.ac.uk

Undergraduates: 5121 (0)
Postgraduates: 1,049 (2,273)
Mature students: 6%
Overseas students: 9%
Applications/place: 9.5
Undergraduates from State sector: 75%

Main subject areas: architecture and civil engineering; biological sciences; chemical and mechanical engineering; chemistry; education; electronic and electrical engineering; management; mathematical sciences; materials science; modern languages; pharmacy; physics; social sciences.

Teaching quality ratings

Rated Excellent 1993–95: architecture; business and management; mechanical engineering; social policy.

From 1995: physics 24; pharmacy 23; civil engineering 22; chemical engineering 22; chemical engineering 20; materials technology 21; electrical and electronic engineering 20; modern languages 19; sociology 19.

Overview

Bath's healthy showing in league tables may be one reason for a 22 per cent jump in applications – it has never been out of the top 20 in *The Times* table. Students also like the 'small and friendly' image the university projects, and few can fail to be impressed by the magnificence of the city's architecture.

The modern campus offers an unfortunate contrast. But the 200-acre site is functional, providing students with good academic, recreational and residential facilities in close proximity. A three-year academic building programme costing £5 million has cleared the way for further expansion.

The university passed up an opportunity for a quantum leap in size through a merger with the city's college of higher education. But it has been allocated an extra 900 places for British students and has ambitions to add more in the near future. The establishment of a campus in nearby Swindon will help, although it will take five years to reach its full complement of 1,000 students.

Research is Bath's greatest strength, with mathematical and computing science, chemical engineering and materials science all highly-rated. Teaching assessments have confirmed the university's excellence in science and technology, with molecular and organismal biosciences achieving maximum points for teaching quality in 1999. Civil and mechanical engineering had previously recorded good scores. Arts and social science ratings have been less impressive recently, although architecture and social policy reached the top grade in early assessments.

A new department of continuing and distance education was added as part of the drive by David VandeLinde, the American Vice-Chancellor, to modernise the university's course structure. Most courses have a practical element, and assessors have praised the university for the work placements it offers. The majority of students take sandwich courses, which help to produce consistently outstanding graduate employment figures.

The university's other great claim to fame lies in its sports facilities, which are already among the best in Britain and are set to improve further with the aid of £20 million of Lottery money. The campus has already acquired an international-standard swimming pool by this route, to which it will add an indoor running track, new sports hall and even a simulated bobsleigh start area. There is a strong tradition in competitive sports, encouraged by sports scholarships worth up to £12,000 a year for performers of international calibre, which Bath introduced to Britain more than 20 years ago.

Students find the campus quiet at weekends and struggle to afford some of Bath's attractions, but value its location. When they tire of the beauty of Bath, the nightlife of Bristol is only a few minutes away. The two cities have a combined student population of more than 30,000.

The Swindon campus, opening in September 2000, will spread the net to Wiltshire, one of the few remaining counties without a university. The main feature will be a five-year Master's degree intended to attract high-fliers, but there will also be community courses.

Accommodation

All first years can be housed in university accommodation. Over 1,700 self-catering places are available on campus, either in central high-rise blocks or in low-rise buildings to the north of the campus. There are also a small number of off-campus university properties.

Library and computing

The library and learning centre is located centrally on the campus and holds over 400,000 books and journals, which are catalogued on-line. The library is home to the majority of the 440 public-access PCs on the university network.

Student facilities

Bath students' union building provides a central meeting point for students, with bars, shops and a café. During the day, one of the bars, the Venue, runs a no-smoking, alcohol-free coffee bar and in the evening it becomes a nightclub.

Sport

The facilities are amongst the best in Britain. They include 3 rugby pitches, 5 football pitches, grass 5-a-side pitches, a golf net, cricket nets, 25 and 50-metre swimming pools, a rifle range and a sports hall and further expansion is planned.

Overseas students

There are many events in the first few weeks of term to help overseas students adjust to life in the UK. An international office and adviser provide support and advice on issues affecting overseas students.

University of Birmingham

Founded: 1828, Royal charter 1900

Times ranking: 13 (1999 ranking: 16)

Address: Edgbaston, Birmingham B15 2TT

tel: 0121 414 3374/7168
website: www.bham.ac.uk
e-mail: schools-liaison@bham.ac.uk

Undergraduates: 13,208 (2,693)
Postgraduates: 3,307 (4,049)
Mature students: 6%
Overseas students: 8%
Applications/place: 7.7
Undergraduates from State sector: 70%

Main subject areas: Full range of subjects in seven faculties: arts; commerce and social science; education; engineering; law; medicine and dentistry; science.

Teaching quality ratings

Rated Excellent 1993–95: English; geography; geology; history; music.

From 1995: electrical and electronic engineering 24; sociology 24; Middle Eastern and African studies 23; molecular biosciences 23; physics 23; Russian and East European studies 23; American studies 22; dentistry 22; history of art 22; Iberian languages 22; Italian 22; chemical engineering 21 civil engineering 21; drama, dance and cinematics 21; mechanical engineering 20; materials science 20; medicine 20; German 19; French 18.

Overview

Strength across the board is Birmingham's aim, and its secure position among the top 20 universities in *The Times* ranking suggests that it is hitting its target. Despite offering an unusually wide range of subjects, its teaching and research ratings seldom slip. Students come to Birmingham from more than 100 countries, but the university enjoys particularly high prestige in its own region, where it is widely regarded as the next best thing to Oxbridge.

Entry standards are high, averaging the equivalent of more than three Bs at A level in 1998. With around eight applicants for each place, they are likely to remain so, but aspiring students still flock to the largest open days in Britain each spring. There is also an admissions forum in September.

The university's enduring reputation is based on its research, with more than a third of its departments considered nationally or internationally outstanding in the last assessments. Anatomy, materials science, European studies, and Middle Eastern and African studies all achieved the best possible rating.

Teaching scores have been only slightly more variable, with sociology and electrical and electronic engineering both recording maximum points, following a string of 'excellent' verdicts in the first round of assessments. Biochemistry, dentistry and physics have been successful recently, while the highly regarded medical school was granted the biggest expansion in Britain when quotas for the subject were reviewed in 1999.

The 230-acre campus in leafy Edgbaston is dominated by a 300-foot clocktower, which is one of the city's best-known landmarks, and boasts its own station. Only dentistry is located elsewhere, and most of the halls and university flats are conveniently located in an attractive parkland setting nearby.

The campus is less than three miles from the centre of Birmingham, but Edgbaston has plenty of shops, pubs and restaurants of its own. With five nightclubs among the facilities on campus, some students do not even stray that far, but the city is acquiring a growing reputation among the young, which is helping to make the university even more popular.

Pressure on teaching space was eased to some extent in 1999 with the creation of The University of Birmingham, Westhill, a joint venture with a Free Church college whose education and theology degrees the university had validated for many years. The site will be used for part-time degrees and continuing education, as well as the existing courses, under an agreement which saw the university take over the management of nine partner colleges in all. Birmingham's senior officers are also discussing closer collaboration with Aston University, although not with the aim of any formal association.

Accommodation

The university manages housing for over 5,000 students and all first years are guaranteed accommodation. The bulk of accommodation is close to the main campus. Private accommodation is plentiful; typically a single room costs £32–£40 a week.

Library and computing

The university has 12 libraries and resource centres which house over 2 million books and 3 million manuscripts. On the computing side, there are 1,870 open-access clusters and 8,000 high-speed campus network connection points.

Student facilities

Birmingham has a Guild of Students, which has some of the best facilities in the country. It has bars, nightclubs, shops and plenty of places to eat cheaply. It provides a range of education and welfare services and a student employment service.

Sport

Some of the finest sports facilities in the country are to be found at Birmingham. Sports available range from swimming to fencing via netball and rugby. Wednesday afternoons are kept free for sport.

Overseas students

Birmingham has a long record of educating students from abroad: over 3,000 studied here in 1999. English language support is provided. A four-day induction course is run and there is an international student support office.

University of Bournemouth

Founded: University status 1992, formerly Bournemouth Polytechnic, originally Dorset Institute of Higher Education

Times ranking: 90 (1999 ranking: 96)

Address: Talbot Campus, Fern Barrow, Poole, Dorset BH12 5BB

tel: 01202 524111
website: www.bournemouth.ac.uk
e-mail: prospectus@bournemouth.ac.uk

Undergraduates: 7,756 (1,522)
Postgraduates: 565 (647)
Mature students: 19%
Overseas students: 3%
Applications/place: 6.3
Undergraduates from State sector: 87%

Main subject areas: business; conservation sciences; design engineering and computing; finance and law; health and community studies; media arts and communication; service industries.

Teaching quality ratings

Rated Excellent 1993–95: none.

From 1995: communication and media studies 22; nursing 22; television and video production 22; agriculture 20; health subjects 20; electrical engineering 19; food science 19; mechanical engineering 18; modern languages 18.

Overview

Always an institution with an eye for the distinctive, Bournemouth starts at the top as the only university with women as chancellor and vice-chancellor. Professor Gillian Slater, the Vice-Chancellor, leaves prospective students in no doubt about Bournemouth's approach to higher education, with a blunt warning that they will not find 'traditional academic disciplines'. But the university claims a number of firsts in its growing portfolio of courses, notably in the area of tourism, media studies and conservation, which won a Queen's Anniversary Prize in 1994.

Bournemouth's forte is in identifying gaps in the higher education market and then filling them with innovative courses, usually with a highly vocational slant. Degrees in public relations, licensed retail management, scriptwriting and tax and revenue law are among the examples. The university also boasts a National Centre of Computer Animation.

Many courses contain a language element a nd all students are encouraged to improve their linguistic ability. A majority of undergraduates take sandwich courses, and 70 per cent do work placements. The result is an employment rate which is the university's proudest achievement: four out of five graduates went straight into jobs in 1998 and the retail management degree has notched up six successive years of full employment.

Teaching ratings have improved after a poor start – none of the subjects assessed in the early rounds of assessments was considered excellent and modern languages only passed at the second attempt, after an unusually low score. Those initial failings, together with a disastrous research assessment in 1996, largely account for Bournemouth's low position in *The Times* ranking.

More recently, however, television and video production, media studies and nursing have all passed with flying colours. Media courses are a particular strength, with entry requirements high above the university's modest average. A joint venture with Microsoft saw the launch of a pioneering internet radio station, which will be used by aspiring broadcasters and web designers.

Bournemouth has come a long way since its days as a struggling college of education. University status arrived only two years after the success of a protracted battle to become a polytechnic. Student numbers doubled in four years and, inevitably, resources were stretched. New teaching and residential accommodation has been added in recent years. There are now two campuses – the original Talbot site on the way to Poole and a collection of buildings in the town centre – as well as associate colleges in Yeovil, Poole and the Isle of Wight.

The southern seaside location and the subject mix attract more middle-class students than most new universities. Students are discouraged from bringing cars (which are banned within a mile of the town-centre campus) but many still do. The area has plenty to offer students during the summer season. Although it naturally becomes less lively in the winter months – party conferences apart – cheap and plentiful accommodation during the off season is a compensation.

Accommodation

The university offers accommodation for all first years, some in self-catering accommodation. Offers of accommodation are made to students in August. The accommodation service on the Talbot campus is responsible for providing students with university accommodation. It is also responsible for housing nursing and midwifery students in hospital accommodation.

Library and computing

The library is divided between three sites, two on the Talbot campus and one at Bournemouth. Two 24-hour open-access computing centres offer 150 PCs at both the Talbot and Bournemouth campuses.

Student facilities

Life in Bournemouth is fairly sedate but the students add a certain zest. The students' union building has a decent bar and bands often play Bournemouth to entertain the student population.

Sports

Sporting activities are fairly limited with a sports hall, squash courts and an all-weather pitch making up the main facilities. The hall offers training for most indoor sports. It also features a climbing wall and five-a-side facilities.

Overseas students

There is a free orientation week for students from outside the EU before courses start to help overseas students adapt to life in Britain. A pre-sessional, 4-week course is also available.

University of Bradford

Founded: Royal charter 1966, College of Advanced Technology 1957–66

Times ranking: 54 (1999 ranking: 52)

Address: Richmond Road, Bradford BD7 1DP

tel: 01274 233033
website: www.bradford.ac.uk
e-mail: s.whyatt@bradford.ac.uk

Undergraduates: 6,959 (1,698)
Postgraduates: 665 (2,352)
Mature students: 20%
Overseas students: 12%
Applications/place: 6.5
Undergraduates from State sector: 89%

Main subject areas: applied social studies; archaeological, biomedical and environmental sciences; business and management; chemical, civil electrical and mechanical engineering; chemistry; computing; electronic imaging; health studies; human, European and peace studies; industrial technology; mathematics; modern languages; optometry; pharmacy.

Teaching quality ratings

Rated Excellent 1993–95: none.

From 1995: electrical and electronic engineering 21, chemical engineering 20; civil engineering 20; general engineering 20; modern languages 18; sociology 17.

Overview

Ravaged by cuts in the early 1980s, Bradford began to grow again before many of the traditional universities, although it is still not large by modern standards. The university carved out a niche for itself with mature students, who relish its vocational slant and the accent on sandwich courses, which regularly place Bradford near the top of the graduate employment tables. Admissions tutors let it be known that they are less obsessed by high A-level grades than most of their counterparts in the old universities.

The relatively small, lively campus is close to the city centre. Apart from the recently incorporated Bradford and Airedale College of Health, only business and management students are taught elsewhere. The highly rated Management Centre is three miles away in a period building surrounded by parkland.

Teaching assessments have been improving, but no subject has been rated as excellent or amassed the 22 points regarded as its equivalent. Research grades also improved on the previously modest totals in 1996, with civil and mechanical engineering, business and management, and European studies leading the way. But the combined scores are still among the lowest in the traditional universities.

The sandwich courses taken by more than half of the undergraduates are a legacy of Bradford's previous existence as a college of advanced technology. Engineers and scientists take a majority of the places, but many take management or a language as part of their degree. There is an inter-disciplinary human studies pro-gramme, aimed at the social scientists, which includes philosophy, psychology, literature and sociology.

Peace studies is the university's best-known department, but new courses lean towards the university's strength in the new technologies. Computer-assisted learning is increasing in many subjects, making use of an unusually extensive network for student use.

More southerners are being attracted to Bradford by the low cost of living. The city is known as the curry capital of Britain, but students can also enjoy spec-tacular countryside nearby. The students' union operates a late-night 'safety bus' for those living within seven miles of the campus.

Accommodation

All first years can be accommodated in university managed property, in one of the university's 12 halls of residence, which offer over 2,000 places. The halls are located either on the main campus or on the university's Laisteridge Lane site. All rooms are single study-bedrooms and single-sex blocks are available. Private rental property is cheap and plentiful.

Library and computing

The library is situated on the main campus and five other subject specific libraries are spread across the university. Bradford has one of the highest PC to stu-dent ratios in the country; PC clusters are situated throughout the university.

Student facilities

The students' union and other student facilities are all centrally located on the compact campus. With most students living in the city centre there are a large number of student nights in pubs and clubs.

Sports

The university's sports centre is located in the centre of the campus. The main out-door site is four miles from the main campus; there are artificial pitches closer to the campus. There are over 50 sports clubs at the university.

Overseas students

There is an overseas student office to help overseas students with problems. The uni-versity offers tuition in English and acade-mic writing courses for students with English as a second language.

University of Brighton

Founded: University status 1992, formerly Brighton Polytechnic

Times ranking: 57th equal (1999 ranking: 60)

Address: Mithras House, Lewes Road, Brighton BN2 4AT

tel: 01273 600900
website: www.brighton.ac.uk
e-mail: admissions@brighton.ac.uk

Undergraduates: 9,974 (3,190)
Postgraduates: 569 (1,406)
Mature students: 37%
Overseas students: 13%
Applications/place: 6.5
Undergraduates from State sector: 89%

Main subject areas: art, design and humanities; business and management; education, sport and leisure; engineering and environmental studies; health; information technology.
Also many certificate and diploma courses.

Teaching quality ratings

Rated Excellent 1993–95: none.

From 1995: pharmacy 23; art and design 22; health subjects 22; mathematics and statistics 22; nursing 22; civil engineering 21; history of art and design 21; building 20; electronic and electronic engineering 20; modern languages 20.

Overview

Consistently good teaching ratings across a wide range of subjects have seen Brighton move up *The Times* League Table this year. The university's acknowledged strengths in art and design and health subjects are among the areas to have been assessed recently, but there have been equally good scores in mathematics and pharmacy. Art and design already had a high research rating, and the Design Council's national archive is lodged on campus. In particular, the four-year fashion textiles degree has acquired an international reputation, with work placements in the United States, France and Italy, as well as Britain.

Brighton was among the most successful of the new universities in the last research assessments, with business studies, computing and sports studies also faring well. The modular course system gives students many options within their own faculty and sometimes across academic fields. Most undergraduates have a personal tutor, who will advise on combinations.

One student in six enters through Clearing, but this high proportion partly reflects the large numbers who come in their twenties and thirties. Mature students tend to apply later in the year than school-leavers. They are attracted by strongly vocational courses and the prospect of three years in 'London by the sea'.

Three sites in and around Brighton, plus one in Eastbourne, house the six faculties. Art and design has the prime location opposite the Royal Pavilion, with sports science at Eastbourne and the other subjects on the outskirts of Brighton, at Falmer and Moulsecoomb, the university's headquarters. Each site has distinctive characteristics, although all are linked by shuttle bus.

Numerous European links give most courses an international flavour, often involving a period of study on the Continent. The university has a cosmopolitan air, with more overseas students than most of the former polytechnics. There is also close collaboration with neighbouring Sussex University. A joint degree in engineering was the first between a university and a polytechnic, and the Sussex Technology Institute is a partnership for postgraduate courses.

The 1990s saw £45 million spent on new facilities, particularly in Eastbourne, where a new library is being built following the opening of extensive sports and leisure facilities. Students like Brighton, although the cost of living is high, and the acquisition of a nightclub in the town has added to the attractions. Eastbourne is also surprisingly popular, despite its retirement home image.

Accommodation

The university offers approximately 1,600 places in halls of residence. Over 75 per cent of first years can be accommodated in university housing. The private sector offers self-contained houses and flats or properties shared with the owner where students may be offered bed-and-breakfast, part-board or self-catering accomodation.

Library and computing

There are six libraries with over 500,000 books, journals, videos and CD-ROMS. There are open-access computer facilities at all sites. A student intranet enables students to maintain contact with tutors, and access teaching materials.

Student facilities

Union offices on each campus provide catering, welfare and entertainment services. Akademia is a pre-club bar, theatre and café in central Brighton run by the Union. The Work-Shop is a job-centre style jobshop advertising part-time and temporary employment.

Sport

The Recreation Service offers a range of facilities,including three dance studios, six gymnasiums, a swimming pool, indoor and outdoor pitches and floodlit courts. The Sports Federation runs various teams and clubs.

Overseas students

A pre-sessional orientation week is offered and students have access to free English language tuition and specialist welfare advice. Scholarships are available to help with living expenses and tuition fees. An *Overseas Student Guide* is available from Academic Registry.

University of Bristol

Founded: 1876, Royal charter 1909

Times ranking: 4 (1999 ranking: 8th equal)

Address: Senate House, Tyndall Avenue, Bristol BS8 1TH

tel: 0117 928 9000

website: www.bris.ac.uk

e-mail: admissions@bris.ac.uk

Undergraduates: 9,940 (4,062)

Postgraduates: 2,040 (3,195)

Mature students: 7%

Overseas students: 8%

Applications/place: 12.3

Undergraduates from State sector: 55%

Main subject areas: Full range of disciplines in six faculties: arts; engineering; law; medicine (including dentistry and veterinary science); science; social science.

Teaching quality ratings

Rated Excellent 1993–95: chemistry; English; geography; law; mechanical engineering; social work.

From 1995: electronic and electrical engineering 24; drama, dance and cinematics 23; mathematics and statistics 23; physics 23; aeronautical engineering 22; civil engineering 22; Iberian languages 22; organismal biosciences 22; German 21; Italian 21; sociology 21; French 20; history of art 20; Russian 20.

Overview

Bristol is a traditional alternative to Oxbridge, favoured particularly by independent schools, whose pupils account for more than a third of the intake. But the university has instituted radical plans to widen its appeal, encouraging departments to make lower offers to promising applicants from schools with poor records at A level. It has also set about doubling the number of students recruited from local schools.

Like Oxford and Cambridge, the university has found it difficult to attract working class teenagers, who fear that they would be out of place socially, if not academically. Trying to reverse the trend may spread alarm in the traditional recruiting grounds, but Bristol believes the prize is worth the risk if previously untapped sources of bright students can be brought to the surface.

The city is one of the most attractive in Britain, as well as possessing a vibrant youth culture. It is also prosperous, offering job opportunities to students and graduates alike. The university merges into the centre, its famous Gothic tower dominating the skyline from the junction of two of the main shopping streets. Departments dot the hillside close to the picturesque harbour area.

Having recovered from financial difficulties at the start of the 1990s, the university has embarked upon modest expansion and is living up to expectations in assessments of teaching and research. Half the staff assessed for research are in internationally rated departments, and a maximum score for electrical and electronic engineering leads a string of impressive teaching quality grades.

Research is Bristol's traditional strength. Although only geography achieved the coveted 5*rating in the last assessment exercise, 20 subjects were in the next category. Only Cambridge, Oxford and University College London had more. The 17 Excellent teaching ratings also represent one of the largest totals in the university system, the latest bunch including maximum scores for veterinary medicine and molecular biosciences.

A funding appeal which has raised more than £60 million has enabled Bristol to create new chairs and embark on several building projects. The highly rated chemistry department, for example, moves into a well-appointed new centre in 2000. Equine studies, archaeology, business and policy studies are among the other departments to benefit. The developments are much needed after 50 per cent growth in student numbers over a five-year period when funding levels were reduced consistently.

Entry standards have remained among the highest in Britain, however, ranging from almost 29 points for medicine to more than 26 (the equivalent of an A and two Bs at A level) for social sciences in 1998. A modular course system is now well established, although the majority of students still take single or dual honours degrees.

Most students enjoy life in Bristol and, with some justification, expect their prestigious degree to land them a good job. The high cost of living is the main drawback, together with security concerns in some parts of the city. Parking problems mean that students are advised not to bring cars.

Accommodation

The university has almost 4,000 residential places for full-time students. Priority is given to new first years and to new international postgraduates. Around 90 per cent of first years can be accommodated in university managed premises. Bedsits, houses and flats are available in the private rented sector.

Library and computing

The main library and 14 branch libraries house 1,250,000 printed volumes and with seating for 2,100 readers. Several computer rooms are available around campus including most of the halls of residence; some have 24-hour access. E-mail is available for all students.

Student facilities

The Union has a supermarket, travel shop, two theatres, three bars, café, an evening bus service to the halls of residence plus a free late-night service for women from the library and the union to their homes. The Student Employment Office operates a jobshop for part-time and temporary employment.

Sport

The Union houses a swimming pool; an indoor sports hall, gymnasium. Squash courts are located at Woodland House, and there is a sports ground at Coombe Dingle.

Overseas students

The Overseas Students Advisory Service has two advisers responsible for the reception and induction of new students; they publish a termly newsletter *Newslink* covering issues and events of interest to overseas students. English language courses are available if required.

Brunel University

Founded: Royal charter 1966

Times ranking: 53 (1999 ranking: 54th equal)

Address: Uxbridge, Middlesex UB8 3PH

tel: 01895 203214
website: www.brunel.ac.uk
e-mail: admissions@brunel.ac.uk

Undergraduates: 8,962 (844)
Postgraduates: 1,169 (2,558)
Mature students: 24%
Overseas students: 6%
Applications/place: 6.8
Undergraduates from State sector: 83%

Main subject areas: business management; economics; education; design; engineering and technology; government; law; pure and applied sciences; psychology; sociology.

Teaching quality ratings

Rated Excellent 1993–95: anthropology; social policy.

From 1995: drama and dance 23; general engineering 22; sociology 22; American studies 21; electrical and electronic engineering 21; materials science 20; mechanical engineering 20; media studies 20.

Overview

Brunel has changed in size and character in recent years. The west London university has taken in the former West London Institute of Higher Education, a teacher training centre with an illustrious record in sport, set up its own Business School after years of collaboration with Henley Management College and started to move away from the sandwich courses which were once the norm.

The majority of undergraduates still take four-year degrees with six-month placements in each of the first three years, but new developments have tended to be conventional three-year arts and social science programmes. The sandwich system and technological emphasis in Brunel's original portfolio have served graduates well in the employment market, as well as providing them with an income from work placements. Almost a third of the students are taking more than one subject, and all have the option of including language or business elements in their degrees.

Although the university has quadrupled in size, only 5,500 students share Brunel's spacious, if uninspiring main campus at Uxbridge, at the end of the Metropolitan Line. Another former higher education college provides a more picturesque site on the Thames, at Runnymeade, for industrial design, while sport, health, social work and education are south of the river at Osterley and Twickenham. The latter also houses the Rambert School of Ballet and Contemporary Dance. Courses generally do not require students to travel between campuses, but a university bus service links the four campuses to allow full use of the facilities.

Teaching assessments have been consistent, though not spectacular, with drama and dance the best of the bunch. The last research assessments also showed improvement on disappointing early ratings, with design rated internationally outstanding and anthropology almost as good.

Unusually, most applicants are interviewed. Brunel was also among the first of the traditional universities to introduce access courses, run in further education colleges, to bring underqualified applicants up to the necessary standard for entry. With engineering and technology still comfortably the biggest departments, the impact on completion rates could have been considerable – the subjects have the highest drop-out rate nationally – but the projected total of 17 per cent leaving without a qualification is lower than the funding council expected.

Students' union facilities are good, especially at Uxbridge, and students like Brunel's intimacy. Some feel cut off at Runnymeade, but the recent expansion has made for a livelier social scene overall.

Accommodation

First years studying at the Uxbridge or Runnymeade sites will be offered self-catering accommodation in a university hall or flat. Those based at Twickenham and Osterley may be accommodated in single and shared study bedrooms with main meals provided Monday to Friday. The Housing Offices help students find private rented accommodation.

Library and computing

There are four campus libraries containing around 400,000 books, 3,000 printed periodicals and a range of audio visual materials. All students have their own account and e-mail access.

Student facilities

The students' union provides a number of bars, discos and live music at the four sites. Catering is provided at Uxbridge, with only a limited service at Runnymeade. Development and Representation Unit provides resources and training to those involved in union activities.

Sport

The Sports Centre consists of a main hall, small hall, climbing wall, squash courts, recently opened Esprit fitness suite, weights room and solarium. University playing fields are a short distance from the Sports Centre.

Overseas students

Pre-sessional English language courses are available, covering induction, study skills and an introduction to Britain and the British. The International Student Recruitment Office arranges 'meet and greet' scheme and orientation programme, and also produces a *Handbook for International Students*.

University of Buckingham

Founded: 1974, Royal charter 1983

Times ranking: n/a

Address: Hunter Street, Buckingham MK18 1EG

tel: 01280 814080 (switchboard); 01280 824081 (admissions)

website: www.buckingham.ac.uk

e-mail: admissions@buck.ac.uk

Total students: 737

Mature students: 74%

Overseas students: 78%

Main subject areas: accounting; business studies; computer science; English; history; history of art and heritage management; hotel management and economics; law; politics; psychology.

Teaching quality ratings: not carried out because the Higher Education Funding Council has no jurisdiction.

Overview

Britain's only private university is its smallest by far, but no longer the youngest. Nor, it claims since the introduction of tuition fees elsewhere, should it be considered any more expensive than other universities, especially if you are well qualified. Its intensive two-year degrees cut maintenance costs, and a new scholarship scheme reduces the £10,000-a-year fees by more than a third for applicants with three Bs at A level. The threshold is reduced to three Cs for those who go to school or live in Buckinghamshire.

The university has no ambitions to follow its peers into the mass higher education market: it values the personal approach that comes with having only eight students to each member of staff. One-to-one tutorials, which have all but disappeared outside Oxbridge and are by no means universal there, are common at Buckingham. But the scholarship initiative, which is open to British and foreign students, could bring modest growth, which would breathe new life into the university.

A Conservative experiment of the 1970s, Buckingham had to wait almost ten years for its royal charter, but is now an accepted part of the university system. Although in 1992 it installed Lady Thatcher as Chancellor and her former minister, Sir Richard Luce, as Vice-Chancellor, the university now sees itself as a non-partisan institution. American-born Professor Bob Taylor has since succeeded Sir Richard.

Buckingham's private status excludes it

from the funding councils' assessment of teaching and research, making it impossible to place in our league table. However, the university's degrees carry full currency in the academic world and teaching standards are high. Law and accounting are both popular, and biological sciences are also strong.

The university runs on calendar years, rather than the traditional academic variety, although law students have the option of entering in July. Between October and December, before enrolling, all students have the opportunity to attend specially designed language courses at a French, German or Spanish university. Degree courses run for two 40-week years, minimising the length of career breaks for the many mature students. More than half of the students are from overseas, but the proportion from Britain has been creeping up.

The two-year degree has been fully assessed by Dr John Clarke, a founder member of the university staff. Although hardly neutral, he concluded that the individual tuition given to Buckingham students, made possible by unusually generous staffing levels, allowed the system to succeed.

Campus facilities have improved considerably in recent years, although they cannot compare with those available at traditional universities. Buckingham now operates on three sites, all within easy walking distance of each other, including a business school which opened in 1996. An academic centre containing computer suites, lecture theatres and student facilities provides a focal point that was missing previously.

The social scene is predictably quiet, given the size of the university and the workload, especially at weekends. The town is pretty and has its share of pubs and restaurants, but is not the place for wild nightlife. Milton Keynes or Oxford are the nearest options, except that Buckingham has no station.

University of Cambridge

Founded: 1209

Times ranking: 1 (1999 ranking: 1)

Address: Kellet Lodge, Tennis Court Road, Cambridge CB2 1QJ

tel: 01223 333308
website: www.cam.ac.uk
e-mail: ucam-undergraduate-admissions@lists.cam.ac.uk

Undergraduates: 10,684 (2,806)
Postgraduates: 4,038 (2,178)
Mature students: 9%
Overseas students: 9%
Applications/place: 3.7
Undergraduates from State sector: 52%

Main subject areas: Full range of disciplines divided into five faculties: arts; engineering; medicine and veterinary science; science and mathematics; and social sciences.

Teaching quality ratings

Rated Excellent 1993–95: anthropology; architecture; chemistry; computer science; English; geography; geology; history; law music.

From 1995: chemical engineering 23; general engineering 23; materials science 23; Middle Eastern and African studies 23; physics 23; history of art 22; land management 22; modern languages 22.

Overview

Top of *The Times* League Table every year since it was first published, Cambridge remains at the pinnacle of the British university system. Traditionally supreme in the sciences, where an array of subjects boast top ratings for teaching and research, the university has added strength in the arts and social sciences. The Judge Management School is also well established now. All but one of the subjects assessed in the first rounds of teaching quality assessment were considered excellent and none has dropped more than two points out of 24 under the current system. Almost two-thirds of the academics entered for research assessment were in subjects rated internationally outstanding.

More students now come from state schools than the independent sector, a trend the university is keen to continue. Summer schools, student visits and, in some colleges, sympathetic selection procedures, are helping to attract more applications from comprehensive schools. The tripos system was a forerunner of the currently fashionable modular degree, allowing students to change subjects (within limits) mid-way through their courses, as well as providing two degree classifications.

A lively alternative prospectus, available from the students' union, says there is no such thing as Cambridge University, just a collection of colleges. Where applications are concerned, this is true, as it is to some extent socially. Making the right choice of college is crucial, both to maximise the chances of winning a place and to ensure an enjoyable three years if you are successful. However, teaching is university-based, especially in the sciences, and a shift of emphasis towards the centre has been taking place with the aid of a £250 million funding appeal.

The university's pre-eminent place in British higher education was underlined by its success in attracting Microsoft's first research base outside the United States. This was one of a series of recent technological partnerships with the private sector, several of which benefit undergraduates as well as researchers. Cambridge has also been chosen for a government-sponsored partnership with the Massachusetts Institute of Technology to promote entrepreneurship.

With fewer than four applicants for each place – less if you choose your subject carefully – the competition for places appears less intense than at the popular civic universities. The difference is that almost nine out of ten entrants have at least three A-grade A levels. The pressure does not end there: the amount of high-quality work to be crammed into eight-week terms can prove too much for some students.

See Chapter 8 for information about individual colleges.

University of Central England in Birmingham

Founded: University status 1992, formerly Birmingham Polytechnic

Times ranking: 89 (1999 ranking: 87th equal)

Address: Perry Barr, Birmingham B42 2SU

tel: 0121 331 5595
website: www.uce.ac.uk
e-mail: recruitment@uce.ac.uk

Undergraduates: 9,809 (5,615)
Postgraduates: 897 (2,148)
Mature students: 32%
Overseas students: 8%
Applications/place: 7.1
Undergraduates from State sector: 92%

Main subject areas: art and design; built environment; business and management; computing and information studies; education; engineering and computer technology; health and community care; law and social science; music.
Also a wide range of diploma courses.

Teaching quality ratings

Rated Excellent 1993–95: music.

From 1995: communication and media studies 21; town planning 20; agriculture 19; mechanical engineering 19; building 18; land and property management 18; sociology 18.

Overview

UCE describes itself as 'the responsive university', emphasising its willingness to act on students' wishes as well as serving the needs of the Second City. The annual satisfaction survey goes to half of the student body, in a model adopted by other universities in Britain and abroad. The results are taken seriously: more than £1 million was spent on library stock after one survey, and the most recent exercise has led to action on issues as diverse as the provision of computers to ventilation in the union bars. This longstanding initiative is just one of the activities of the influential Centre for Research into Quality, which is headed by one of the university's most senior academics.

About half of the full-time students come from the West Midlands, many from ethnic minorities. UCE also has one of the largest programmes of part-time courses in Britain, making it the biggest provider of higher education in the region. Many students enter through the network of 15 associated further education colleges, which run foundation and access programmes.

The university's best-known feature is its conservatoire, which is housed in part of Birmingham's smart convention centre. Courses from opera to world music have given it a reputation for innovation, which was recognised in an 'excellent' rating for teaching. Most other teaching ratings have been mediocre, however, although the teacher education courses produced the best scores among the former polytechnics in the Teacher Training Agency's 1999 performance indicators. Those for secondary teachers were bettered only by Oxford and Cambridge.

UCE opted out of the first research assessment exercise – the only university to do so – preferring to concentrate on teaching. Although its income from research contracts is healthy, the last assessments were far from successful, with no subjects in the top four categories.

Seven campuses straggle across Birmingham, but the majority of students are concentrated on the modern Perry Barr site, three miles north of the city centre. The large teacher training centre is in the southern suburb of Edgbaston, while the Institute of Art and Design, refurbished at a cost of £20 million, spreads even further south to Bourneville, where it occupies part of the Cadbury 'village'. It is the largest in Britain, and includes a school of jewellery in the city centre.

The last thing UCE would appear to need is a new site. However, the relocation of engineering and computing to the city's Millennium Point high-tech development in 2001 will provide a new focus for the university. Facilities in the £110 million Lottery-funded centre will be open to the public.

Accommodation

All students who accept an offer by the end of May are guaranteed a place in halls of residence. The university can accommodate 95 per cent of first-year undergraduates.

Library and computing

There are nine libraries across the university locations. The main library is at Perry Bar and holds over 300,000 volumes. It also houses an open-access computing centre.

Student facilities

Birmingham offers some of the finest club nights in the country and the 'Balti Quarter' of Sparkbrook is home to the eponymous curry. UCE has its own union building, but the good relations between town and gown ensures students are welcome throughout the city.

Sport

Whether you are a spectator or participant, Birmingham has more venues than any other UK city. The students' union has sports clubs of most varieties.

Overseas students

Students from over 50 countries study at UCE. The university operates a 'meet and greet' orientation course for students arriving in the UK. An international office is available to provide support for overseas students.

University of Central Lancashire

Founded: University status 1992, formerly Lancashire (originally Preston) Polytechnic
Times ranking: 80 (1999 ranking: 81)

Address: Preston PR1 2HE

tel: 01772 201201
website: www.uclan.ac.uk
e-mail: c.enquiries@uclan.ac.uk

Undergraduates: 11,689 (7,407)
Postgraduates: 412 (1,512)
Mature students: 38%
Overseas students: 5%
Applications/place: 2.7
Undergraduates from State sector: 94%

Main subject areas: business studies; cultural studies; design and technology; health; legal studies; social studies; science.
Also a wide range of certificate and diploma courses.

Teaching quality ratings

Rated Excellent 1993–95: none.

From 1995: American studies 24; psychology 24; health subjects 22; linguistics 22; media studies 22; modern languages 21; drama, dance and cinematics 20; general engineering 20; history of art 19; physics and astronomy 19; agriculture 18; sociology 18; electrical and electronic engineering 15.

Overview

A big university at the heart of a medium-sized town, Central Lancashire does not dominate its home town of Preston to the extent that Cambridge or Durham do theirs, but students account for a sixth of the population during term. The modern, town-centre campus has seen considerable development, as the university has doubled in size, and still the building continues. An £8 million Lottery-funded sports centre opened in 1999 and a 'knowledge park' for technology transfer is on the way.

Amid the expansion, the university has revamped its pioneering credit accumulation and transfer system, allowing undergraduates to mix and match from a menu of more than 500 courses. Electives are used to broaden the curriculum, so that up to 11 per cent of students' time is spent on subjects outside their normal range. There is particular encouragement to include a language as part of the package, and more than 2,000 students do so. A growing proportion also take advantage of the numerous international exchange programmes, which are available in all subject areas.

The former polytechnic has acquired a high reputation in some apparently unlikely fields. American studies and psychology both achieved perfect scores for teaching quality, and astrophysics benefits from two observatories, including Britain's most powerful optical telescope, although its teaching assessment was disappointing. Journalism, which scored well, is sufficiently popular to be able to demand the equivalent of three Bs at A level. The last research assessments were less successful, with no subjects rated in the top three categories.

The university took in an agricultural college at Newton Rigg, in Cumbria, in 1998 – its first excursion beyond Preston. Further education in land-based subjects are continuing there and new programmes are being developed at degree and postgraduate level for a county with little higher education provision. A high proportion of Central Lancashire's students are local people in their twenties or thirties, many of whom come through the well-established lifelong learning networks run in colleges throughout the northwest. No fewer than 14 per cent of the university's students are taught in colleges but, unlike some institutions involved in 'franchising', Central Lancashire has carried out a thorough review of the quality of its external programmes.

The social scene in Preston may not compare with Manchester or Liverpool, but neither do the security risks and the cost of living is low. Both cities are within easy reach, and the students' union's 'Feel' club nights have won national recognition.

Accommodation

All first years are guaranteed accommodation by the university, the cost ranges from £44-£53 a week all accommodation is self-catering. Some of the 1800 rooms are adapted for wheelchair users and other students with special needs. Private housing is cheap and plentiful, and the university runs a register of approved landlords.

Library and computing

A purpose-built building – the LLRS – provides a one-stop learning centre. It houses the main library and multimedia centres. Eight other libraries provide access to some of the 1,500 open-access PCs on campus.

Student facilities

The student union, with its three bars, at weekends turns into a club attracting top name DJs. More sedate options come in the form of the many sports clubs and societies run by the union.

Sports

The sports centre is on the main campus and provides facilities for volleyball, fencing and badminton amongst others. The Preston Sports arena opens in 2000 for athletics, football, rugby, hockey, cricket and netball.

Overseas students

There is an induction programme for all international students, support and guidance are available throughout the academic year including language support. The university has a dedicated student adviser to provide personal support for overseas students.

City University

Founded: 1894, Royal charter 1966

Times ranking: 51 (1999 ranking: 44)

Address: Northampton Square, London EC1V 0HB

tel: 0171 477 8000

website: www.city.ac.uk

e-mail: ugadmissions@city.ac.uk

Undergraduates: 4,763 (2,937)

Postgraduates: 1,712 (3,763)

Mature students: 24%

Overseas students: 15%

Applications/place: 9.8

Undergraduates from State sector: 72%

Main subject areas: actuarial science; business and management; engineering; health; sciences; informatics; mathematics; music; studies related to medicine; social science.

Teaching quality ratings

Rated Excellent 1993-95: business and management; music.

From 1995: electrical and electronic engineering 21; psychology 21; nursing 20; civil engineering 19; land management 19; mechanical engineering 19; media studies 19; sociology 19.

Overview

Originally a college of advanced technology, City now has more students taking social science, business or arts subjects than science or engineering. But the university has maintained its links with business, industry and the professions, reaping the benefits with consistently good graduate employment figures. Courses have a practical edge, and many of the staff hold professional, as well as academic, qualifications. The university has been reviewing its mission since the arrival of Professor David Rhind as Vice-Chancellor, but that is one characteristic which will not alter.

The new strategy has more to do with increasing the size of the university, which is comparatively small, especially for an institution where more than a third of the students are postgraduates. Numbers doubled during the 1990s, partly due to the incorporation of a nursing and midwifery college at nearby St Bartholemew's Hospital. But growth has come to a halt recently, despite one of the highest ratios of applicants to places in the university system. Limited development has already taken place at the university's headquarters, on the borders of the City of London, but the most ambitious plan involves a new home for the business school, which has outgrown its Barbican premises. A site closer to the rest of the university has already been sold to property developers and should be ready for its first students in 2002.

City has a particularly high reputation in music, in association with the Guildhall School of Music and Drama, with its teaching rated as excellent and research nationally outstanding. But, until recently, most teaching assessments had been disappointing. The university's response was to establish an educational development unit to enhance the quality of teaching and launch a review of the effectiveness of personal tutoring. The new focus seemed to do the trick, as 1999 saw near-perfect scores in arts management and health subjects (language and communication science, optometry and radiography). The last research assessments were also disappointing. Although information science was rated internationally outstanding and civil engineering joined music on the next rung of the ladder, these subjects accounted for only 11 per cent of those assessed, and 35 per cent were not entered at all.

The first official performance indicators for higher education brought mixed news: although the 19 per cent drop-out rate was among the highest in the traditional universities, this was no more than the funding council expected, given City's subject mix. Students tend to be more concerned by their inability to afford the attractions of a trendy part of London. Most fall back on the extended students' union, but this is usually shut at weekends.

Accommodation

Only 65 per cent of first years can be accommodated in university halls of residence, but there is a choice between full board or self-catering properties; rooms are also available for students with mobility problems. The university's accommodation service provides a list of approved private rental properties.

Library and computing

The library is on the main campus and has a good collection of books and research material. Five further libraries are spread throughout the faculties. Over 500 PCs in open-access clusters are available to students. Rooms in student halls of residence are online through a subscription service with no call charges.

Student facilities

Student life at City should never be dull. The students' union building has several bars, shops and clubs. A wide variety of clubs and societies operate from the union and it provides a cheaper option to going out in the capital.

Sport

The university has limited sporting facilities, but the students' union still provides a reasonable variety of sporting clubs and societies.

Overseas students

The university offers a two-day orientation programme to help overseas students to adjust to life in London. The overseas students network group meets regularly to provide support and friendship. City also offers English-language support.

Coventry University

Founded: University status 1992, formerly Coventy (originally Lanchester) Polytechnic

Times ranking: 79the equal (1999 ranking: 73)

Address: Priory Street, Coventry CV1 5FB

tel: 024 7688 7688
website: www.coventry.ac.uk
e-mail: info.reg@coventry.ac.uk

Undergraduates: 11,181 (3,065)
Postgraduates: 628 (1,027)
Mature students: 28%
Overseas students: 18%
Applications/place: 5.7
Undergraduates from State sector: 93%

Main subject areas: applied science; art and design; business; engineering; international studies; law; social biological and health sciences.
About a third of students on certificate or diploma courses.

Teaching quality ratings

Rated Excellent 1993–95: geography; mechanical engineering.

From 1995: building 22; health subjects 22; modern languages 21; sociology 21; civil engineering 19; town planning 19; electrical and electronic engineering 18; media studies 18; aeronautical and manufacturing engineering 18.

Overview

More than most universities, Coventry is a creature of its city. The modern buildings open out from the ruins of the bombed cathedral, as university and public facilities mingle in the city centre. Like the city, the university is not fashionable outside its region, but its predominantly vocational curriculum has a strong sense of direction. Degrees in automotive engineering are developed in collaboration with the city's motor industry, and a self-help centre provides for local people with business ambitions.

A rough balance is maintained between arts and sciences in order to preserve an all-round educational environment. Most full-time and sandwich students construct their own degree programme within faculty limits. They are encouraged to take a foreign language and to develop computer skills as part of their final degree assessment. The university also runs 'minimodules' in the evenings and at weekends for students and members of the public to broaden their knowledge.

Teaching assessments have been patchy, but health subjects achieved a near-perfect score and building is highly rated. The university's experience of research assessment was not a happy one, with almost a third of the academics entered for the last exercise in the bottom category of seven. Art and design produced the best result.

However, Dr Mike Goldstein, the Vice-Chancellor, claims that a 'quiet revolution' has taken place over a decade in which numbers have doubled and the university has acquired the confidence to take new initiatives. A series of measures, including the introduction of tangible rewards for excellent teaching and further development of electronic learning, are planned to improve the quality of provision.

The university now has an extensive programme of franchised courses running at 13 further education colleges in the region, but its own departments are all within walking distance of each other. Coventry has been building up its portfolio of computing courses, having introduced eye-catching degrees in subjects such as disaster management and equine studies. The vocational slant of its courses ensures that the university always enjoys a healthy graduate employment rate.

Town–gown relations have not always been smooth, in spite of the university's civic-minded approach, but have been improving recently. Students welcome the relatively low cost of living in Coventry, and the £3 million Planet entertainments complex is open to students and local people alike. As at most new universities, the student body encompasses a wide range of ages, and there is a surprisingly large contingent from overseas.

Accommodation

Coventry has on and off campus accommodation for nearly all first years. Private accommodation is cheap and plentiful, though the least expensive can be some distance from the main campus.

Library and computing

The main library is close to the city centre; the two subject-specific libraries are close to their departments. Over 400 open-access computers are spread throughout the campus at 11 locations.

Student facilities

Coventry students' union has very good facilities, including bars, nightclubs, shops, places to eat and an array of clubs and societies. The campus is close to the city centre, so students are not confined to a student 'ghetto'.

Sport

The university has its own sports fields for football, rugby and cricket and also has its own nine-hole golf course, free to students. Indoor sports facilities are available at the university's Alma Sports centre and the Coventry sports centre.

Overseas students

The university currently has around 3,000 overseas students from 90 countries. The international office offers advice for overseas students. There are support classes for students with English as a second language.

De Montfort University

Founded: University status 1992, formerly Leicester Polytechnic

Times ranking: 67 (1999 ranking: 70)

Address: The Gateway, Leicester LE1 9BH

tel: 0645 454647

website: www.dmu.ac.uk

e-mail: enquiry@dmu.ac.uk

Undergraduates: 15,527 (2,965)

Postgraduates: 1,408 (2,531)

Mature students: 28%

Overseas students: 5%

Applications/place: 6.5

Undergraduates from State sector: 91%

Main subject areas: applied physical sciences; arts; built environment; business; combined studies; computing and mathematical sciences; design and manufacture; engineering; health and life sciences; law.

Teaching quality ratings

Rated Excellent 1993–95: business and management.

From 1995: land management 23; dance and cinematics 22; history of art and design 21; molecular biosciences 21; town planning 21; building 20; health subjects 20; mathematics and statistics 20; media studies 20; electrical and electronic engineering 19; general engineering 19 materials technology 19; modern languages (Bedford) 19; modern languages 17; sociology 17; agriculture 16.

Overview

Like the 13th-century Earl of Leicester, after whom the university is named, De Montfort has a fiefdom of sorts: in this case a network of campuses in a 50-mile radius. Based on what was Leicester Polytechnic, the new university has been spreading ever outwards. The addition of a nursing and midwifery college has provided a third college in and around Leicester, and there is a substantial outpost at Milton Keynes for business, computing, engineering and social sciences.

There are now ten campuses altogether, including teacher training, physical education and humanities in Bedford, craft courses, conservation, agriculture and horticulture in Lincolnshire. It all adds up to more than 22,000 students, when part-timers are included, and the largest contingent taking further education courses at any university in Britain. Another 11 colleges are associates, linked into the university's network and offering its courses.

Professor Kenneth Barker, who retired as Vice-Chancellor in 1999, set out the university's uncompromising philosophy: 'Higher education has been too busy chasing Nobel Prizes, instead of giving industry and the community the service they really need.' Yet De Montfort entered the largest proportion of academic staff of any new university for the last research assessment exercise. Both energy studies and music achieved national recognition.

Teaching ratings were patchy until recently, with only one Excellent rating in the first 11 attempts. There has been a marked improvement, however, since land management's near-perfect score. Post-graduate programmes have also been growing steadily.

Inevitably, the quality of student life varies widely among the different campuses, but technology ensures that everyone has access to the same academic resources. Not surprisingly, Leicester, which has by far the largest concentration of students, also has the best facilities. The energy-efficient School of Engineering and Manufacture, for example, has won architectural prizes. But a £2 million student centre opens in Milton Keynes in 2000, providing sports and entertainment facilities, and Bedford is already well provided for sport. Students in Lincoln and Grantham, however, have to make do for the moment with the facilities of the former colleges.

Students outside Leicester find it hard to identify with De Montfort as a whole, but the pioneering institution has brought university education to parts of England which did not experience it previously. Given the logistical difficulties it faces, the university is remarkably successful at providing good quality higher education.

Accommodation

Students are encouraged to apply as early as possible after they have received an offer as only three quarters of first years can be housed in university accommodation across the main campuses. The accommodation service in conjunction with students' union organises a 'find a home event' to help students who do not get a place in university housing.

Library and computing

De Montfort has a library at each campus geared to the requirements of subjects studied there. There are open-access PCs at each campus and the university provides access to electronic journals.

Student facilities

Life at the university varies between campuses: Leicester offers a more cosmopolitan experience, whilst Milton Keynes is a more staid place. Students' unions on each campus offer societies and clubs for every taste.

Sports

All four campuses offer a number of different sporting facilities, ranging from simple sports fields to gymnasiums and swimming pools. The students' union runs a large number of sports clubs across the sites.

Overseas students

University managed accommodation is available for all non-EU students. At the start of each year an orientation programme introduces overseas students to the university and the local area. The university offers a pre-sessional intensive course in English.

University of Derby

Founded: University status 1992, formerly Derbyshire College of Higher Education
Times ranking: 93 (1999 ranking: 92)

Address: Kedleston Road, Derby DE22 1GB

tel: 01332 62222
website: www.derby.ac.uk
e-mail: Admissions@derby.ac.uk

Undergraduates: 8,866 (1,896)
Postgraduates: 294 (1,030)
Mature students: 37%
Overseas students: 4%
Applications/place: 5.5
Undergraduates from State sector: 93%

Main subject areas: art and design; business; education; environmental and applied sciences; engineering; European and international studies; health and community studies; management; mathematics and computing; social sciences.

Teaching quality ratings

Rated Excellent 1993–95: geology.

From 1995: American studies 21; art and design 20; psychology 20; civil engineering 19; electrical and electronic engineering 19; history of art 19; nursing 19; drama, dance and cinematics 18; modern languages 18; sociology 18; media studies 17; medicine 16.

Overview

Derby sees itself as a prototype for the modern university, providing courses at all levels from the age of 16 into retirement. Although not as extensive as the original plans for spanning further and higher education in the same institution, a merger with High Peak College and the creation of a county-wide education network have created a university of 29,000 students.

While accepting that Derby will never scale the heights in league tables such as ours, Sir Christopher Ball, the Chancellor, has set Derby the target of becoming the pre-eminent university of its type by 2020. His yardsticks are student satisfaction, employability and cost-effectiveness.

As the only higher education college promoted to university status with the polytechnics, Derby had to run to keep up with its peers in its early days. Student numbers doubled in four years, the residential stock increased fivefold in a £40 million building programme and 30,000 square metres of teaching space were added. The pace of expansion inevitably affected assessments. Although still not spectacular, scores have improved recently and the drop-out rate, while not low, is better than many new universities', at less than one in five.

Development is still continuing, with an £8 million art and design centre on the horizon and ambitious plans to bring higher education to the Peak District through the High Peak campus, near Buxton. There are six sites already – the legacy of a series of mergers in the 1970s and 1980s. The Keddleston Road site, two miles north of the city centre, is the largest, catering for most of the main subjects as well as the students' union headquarters. The Mickleover campus, which specialises in education and health, is also in a suburban location, while art and design have smaller, more central sites. The Further Education School, in the old High Peak campus, is the only element outside the Derby area.

Courses are modular and a foundation programme allows students to begin work at a partner college before transferring to the university. Business and management is by far the biggest academic area, but work placements are encouraged in all subjects. The accent on employability continues with an eight-week course on key skills such as CV preparation and interview technique. Derby has also been in the forefront of the adoption of new teaching methods, pioneering the use of interactive video for a national scheme.

Accommodation

First years are guaranteed one of 2,700 fully-equipped self-catering places in university halls which are spread over nine sites. A registration scheme operates for private sector accommodation, all properties on the list having been inspected by the city council.

Library and computing

The Learning Centre houses extensive collections of books, journals and audio visual materials along with extensive support services and 1,100 study places. Around the campus 290 PCs and Macintosh computers are available on open access.

Student facilities

The students' union runs nine bars and three nightclubs, two being located in the city centre and others having facilities for live performances. The union has over 60 clubs and societies and student job vacancies are advertised in the Careers Development Centre.

Sport

A newly equipped gym has both cardiovascular and resistance training equipment and a plunge pool. Fitness classes are also available. Outdoor facilities include a running track and pitches for the 14 team sports which are available.

Overseas students

Prior to the start of the academic year there is a three-day orientation programme, and English language courses are available. Help and support is available through the students' union advice centre.

University of Dundee

Founded: 1881, part of St Andrews University until 1967

Times ranking: 42 (1999 ranking: 31st equal)

Address: Nethergate, Dundee DD1 4HN

tel: 01382 344160
website: www.dundee.ac.uk
e-mail: srs@dundee.ac.uk

Undergraduates: 7,427 (1,192)
Postgraduates: 704 (1,729)
Mature students: 20%
Overseas students: 8%
Applications/place: 5.9
Undergraduates from State sector: 85%

Main subject areas: architecture; arts and social science; environmental management; fine art; hotel and catering management; law; medicine and dentistry; nursing and midwifery; science and engineering.

Teaching quality ratings

Rated Excellent 1994–97: cellular biology; English; finance and accounting; graphic and textile design; medicine; organismal biology; psychology.

Highly Satisfactory 1994–97: civil engineering; dentistry; environmental science; fine art; history; hospitality studies; law; mathematics; physics; politics; social work; statistics.

From 1998: planning and landscape 21.

Overview

Dundee is on a roll after a series of good quality ratings and the acquisition of nursing and art colleges, which have extended the scope of the university and increased its size. Although still not large, Dundee has doubled its student population in the last five years and is challenging Scotland's elite universities in a growing number of areas.

Chief among them are the life sciences, where research into cancer and diabetes is recognised as worldclass. The medical school won a Queen's Anniversary Prize in 1998, as well as an excellent rating for teaching. Set in 20 acres of parkland, it is the only part of the university outside the compact city-centre campus, apart from the nursing and midwifery students 30 miles away in Kirkcaldy in Fife.

Biochemistry is the flagship department, moving into the £13 million Wellcome Trust Building in 1997 as it celebrated Dundee's only 5* research rating. Its academics were the first in Britain to be invited to take part in Japan's Human Frontier science programme and are now the most-quoted researchers in their field. Civil engineering and computing science were on the next rung of the research assessment ladder, with the former Duncan of Jordanstone College of Art, which is rated as the best in Scotland for design. Its buildings are next door to the main campus, which overlooks the River Tay.

Teaching ratings have been almost uniformly impressive, with only philosophy judged less than highly satisfactory. Vocational degrees predominate, helping to produce the university's consistently good graduate employment record. The law department is the only one on either side of the border to offer both Scots and English law.

There has been an emphasis on opportunities for women ever since Dundee's separation from St Andrews University in 1967. The forthcoming incorporation of Northern College's local arm will increase the female majority in the university, as well as adding teacher education to the portfolio of courses.

Two thirds of the students are from Scotland and one in ten from Northern Ireland. They enjoy a cost of living which is lower than in most university cities and a welcoming atmosphere. Although Dundee is no beauty spot, it is being regenerated and becoming more fashionable. Spectacular mountain and coastal scenery is close at hand, but student social life tends to be concentrated on campus.

Accommodation

First years are guaranteed one of 547 catered places or 564 self-catering places in university halls of residence. There are 713 places in university owned houses, but these tend to be reserved for mature and postgraduate students. Alternatively, private sector accommodation is readily available in the town.

Library and computing

A huge range of resources is split between six libraries, with the main library containing 750 study spaces. All students have their own e-mail address and can use any of the hundreds of computers located in ten IT suites.

Student facilities

The university has one of the largest unions in the UK with four bars and over 60 clubs and societies. There is a 600-capacity venue for live performances, with smaller events being staged in the bars.

Sport

Facilities include two large sports halls, a fitness suite, three squash courts and a 25-metre swimming pool. Outdoors there are 33 acres of sports grounds and four floodlit tennis courts. There is also a specialist water activities centre.

Overseas students

There is a one-day orientation course for all overseas students, and pre-sessional and in-sessional English courses are available. The Student Advisory Centre provides help and support, in particular with counselling and religious advice.

University of Durham

Founded: 1832

Times ranking: 16 (1999 ranking: 18)

Address: Old Shire Hall, Old Elvet, Durham DH1 3HP

tel: 0191 374 2000
website: www.dur.ac.uk

Undergraduates: 8,268 (539)
Postgraduates: 1,341 (1,770)
Mature students: 10%
Overseas students: 4%
Applications/place: 6.9
Undergraduates from State sector: 62%

Main subject areas: full range of disciplines except art, medicine, dentistry and veterinary science. Faculties of arts, social sciences; and science.

Teaching quality ratings

Rated Excellent 1993–5: anthropology; chemistry; English; geography; geology; history; law; social work.

From 1995: physics 24; psychology 23; engineering 22; French 22; German 22; linguistics 22; Middle Eastern and African studies 22; East and South Asian studies 21; mathematics and statistics 21; sociology 21; Italian 20; Russian 20; Iberian languages 16.

Overview

Long established as a leading alternative to Oxford and Cambridge, Durham even delays selection to accommodate those applying to the ancient universities. A collegiate structure and picturesque setting add to the Oxbridge feel, attracting a largely middle-class student body, many of whom come from independent schools. Those who receive offers without interview are invited to a special open day to see if Durham is the university for them. Since more than 80 per cent of undergraduates come from outside the northeast of England, most are seeing the small cathedral town for the first time. Applications have to be made to one of the 13 colleges, all but one of which is mixed. They range in size from 300 to 900 students and are the focal point of social life, although all teaching is done in central departments.

Winning a place is far from easy, however, as entrance requirements are among the highest outside Oxbridge. Only geography reached the pinnacle of the last research assessment exercise, but a dozen subjects were considered nationally outstanding. Most of the teaching ratings have also produced high scores. Mathematics and chemistry are particularly strong on the science side, history and theology among the stars of the arts.

Durham is determinedly traditional. Wherever possible, teaching takes place in small groups and most assessment is by written examination. Resits are permitted only in the first year, although the dropout rate compares favourably with other universities. Two partnerships have broken the mould of tradition, however. The first saw the establishment in the city of the Teikyo University of Japan, while the second produced the Stockton Campus. Initially a joint venture with Teesside University, Stockton is now Durham's own venture into community education.

The Stockton campus will also see the fulfilment of Durham's long-held ambition to restore the medical education it lost when Newcastle University went its own way more than 35 years ago. In another joint project, this time with Newcastle, 70 students will do the first two years of their training on Teesside, concentrating on community medicine.

The scheme will add to the 80 subjects available at degree level. Undergraduates are also offered a variety of generalist 'free elective' modules, such as history of science, personal learning and teaching English as a foreign language. The aim is to make Durham graduates even more employable – another area in which the university has a strong record.

The university dominates the city of Durham to an extent to which locals sometimes resent. For those looking for nightlife, or just a change of scene, Newcastle is a short train journey away.

Accommodation

First years are guaranteed a place in one of the 13 university colleges. These all cater for three meals a day, seven days a week and are all within a short walk of the university. Private sector accommodation is available, but is mainly taken by second-year students as final-year students often move back into halls.

Library and computing

The library is world class with over one million volumes and 3,200 periodicals. There is 24-hour access to over 500 computers and a pilot scheme is currently in operation to install computer terminals in study bedrooms.

Student facilities

A huge variety of entertainmants is provided both within colleges and through the large students' union close to the city centre. There are over 100 clubs and societies and the union provides a shop and travel bureau. A 'Job Shop' gives details of vacancies appropriate for students.

Sport

There are over 60 acres of well-maintained sports pitches, a purpose-built sports centre incorporating a multi-gym, squash and tennis courts and a floodlit all-weather pitch. Students also have use of the newly refurbished city swimming pool.

Overseas students

The *Overseas Students' Handbook* provides details of what students need to know before they arrive in Durham. Intensive English language courses are available, but at extra cost. All normal student support services are available, as well as an Overseas Student co-ordinator.

University of East Anglia

Founded: Royal charter 1964

Times ranking: 32 (1999 ranking: 37)

Address: University Plain, Norwich NR4 7TJ

tel: 01603 592216

website: www.uea.ac.uk

e-mail: admissions@uea.ac.uk

Undergraduates: 6,377 (2,736)

Postgraduates: 1,406 (1,407)

Mature students: 23%

Overseas students: 9%

Applications/place: 5.5

Undergraduates from State sector: 82%

Main subject areas: art; biological, chemical and environmental sciences; development studies; economic and social studies; education; English and American studies; health; history; information systems; law; management; mathematics; modern languages; music; physics; social work.

Teaching quality ratings

Rated Excellent 1993–95: development studies; environmental studies; law; social work.

From 1995: American studies 24; mathematics and statistics 23; communication and media studies 23; history of art 22; molecular biosciences 22; drama, dance and cinematics 21; electrical and electronic engineering 19; modern languages 19; sociology 16.

Overview

UEA is best-known for its star-studded creative writing course and extensive art collections, but some of the broad subject combinations which the university pioneered from its origins in the 1960s are equally highly regarded in the academic world. Development studies and environmental sciences are two such areas which have attracted top ratings for teaching and research.

The university has almost completed an ambitious building programme, which has allowed its residential stock to keep pace with the expansion in student numbers and is adding extensive new sports facilities. Other recent developments on the 320-acre campus just outside Norwich have included academic buildings for the highly-rated school of social work and the school of occupational therapy and physiotherapy. Health studies are among UEA's fastest-developing areas, although there is as yet no medical school.

With the university's only 5-star rating for research and an excellent teaching grade, environmental sciences is the flagship school. The Climatic Research Unit is among the leaders in the investigation of global warming and the prestigious Jackson Environment Unit's move to UEA in 1999 will strengthen it further.

American studies has been the top performer in the new teaching assessments, registering a perfect score. Like the English degrees, one of which includes creative writing, the subject is heavily oversubscribed. With Andrew Motion, the Poet Laureate taking up where Malcolm Bradbury left off, the attraction of creative writing for both undergraduates and post-graduates remains undimmed.

Art history is another strong subject, aided by the presence of the Sainsbury Centre for the Visual Arts, perhaps the greatest resource of its type on any British campus. The centre houses a priceless collection of modern and tribal art.

Since 1999, most students have had the opportunity of work experience as part of their course. The modular course system allows undergraduates to construct their own degrees, with the help of an academic adviser, who monitors progress right through to graduation.

Most UEA students come from outside the region, despite the presence of unusually large numbers of mature students for a traditional university. However, the university reaches some 3,500 local people with its programme of evening and day courses at 50 locations in Norfolk and Suffolk.

Norwich is not the liveliest student centre, despite boasting a pub for every day of the year, but the city seems to win over most undergraduate visitors. The campus caters for most social needs, but travel links to other parts of the country can be frustratingly slow.

Accommodation

First years are guaranteed university-owned self-catering accommodation. Accommodation of varying standards to fit tight budgets, and much of it built over the last three years, is available on campus and in the city centre. There is also plentiful private accommodation available for students.

Library and computing

The library contains over 700,000 volumes and periodicals as well as multi-media resources and music scores. There are over 250 IT study spaces designated for 'casual' use and a further 2,000 workstations for academic purposes.

Student facilities

There are over 100 clubs and societies covering cultural, campaigning and political interests. The LCR is a 1,500-capacity events venue and there is a city-centre venue with a late license. The Advice Centre provides details of student jobs.

Sport

Sport is central to university policy, this being reflected in the facilities which include two sports halls, a new well-equipped fitness centre and an eight-lane international-standard athletics track. There are also centres for hockey, tennis and netball.

Overseas students

A special two-day induction programme deals with social and cultural issues and the Dean of Students' office provides specialist advice to overseas students. The language centre provides a number of specialist courses for those needing additional tuition in English.

University of East London

Founded: University status 1992, formerly Polytechnic of East London, originally North East London Polytechnic
Times ranking: 94 (1999 ranking: 89)

Address: Romford Road, London E15 4LZ

tel: 0208 223 2058
website: www.uel.ac.uk
e-mail: admiss@uel.ac.uk

Undergraduates: 7,627 (1,556)
Postgraduates: 538 (1,823)
Mature students: 62%
Overseas students: 8%
Application/place: 4.7
Undergraduates from State sector: 94%

Main subject areas: built environment; business; engineering; health sciences; social science.
Certificate and diploma courses are also offered.

Teaching quality ratings

Rated Excellent 1993-95: architecture; English.

From 1995: psychology 23; civil engineering 21; drama, dance and cinematics 19; pharmacy 19; sociology 19; mechanical engineering 18; modern languages 18; media studies 16; electrical and electronic engineering 15.

Overview

East London's £40 million Docklands campus, which opened in 1999, offers a new lease of life to a university which had struggled to recapture the sparkle it had as a pioneering polytechnic. Student residences and recreational facilities stand side by side with academic buildings which will eventually cater for 7,000 students.

The capital's first new campus for 50 years, which borders on London City Airport, represents a triumph of perseverance. Government funding was slow to arrive and UEL had to take over the scheme from a consortium of higher education partners while riding out its own financial problems before it came to fruition. But sole ownership has given the university a new focal point, with its modern version of traditional university features like cloisters and squares. As well as the school of design, the campus houses a technology centre promoting links with local business and industry.

UEL's two original campuses are in Barking and Stratford, where the university caters particularly for the large ethnic minority population. A successful mentoring scheme for black and Asian students has become a model for other institutions, while classes in English as a second language, designed mainly for overseas students, are available free of charge.

Cultural studies achieved a rare 5* rating for a new university in the last research assessment exercise, but most subjects were confined to the lower grades. Teaching assessments have also been patchy, largely accounting for the university's low position in our rankings, despite a requirement for all new lecturers to take a teaching qualification if they do not already have one. Psychology did well recently, and both English and architecture have excellent ratings, but communication and media studies and electrical and electronic engineering both registered unusually low scores.

However, UEL's mission is more concerned with extending access to higher education than competing with the elite universities. Fewer than a third of undergraduates come with A levels and more than half are over 21 on entry. Most degrees are vocational, and employers – notably Ford, with whom there is a longstanding relationship – are closely involved in course planning. About one student in seven takes a sandwich course.

The social mix means that UEL is not the place to look for the archetypal partying student lifestyle, although the new campus may change that to some extent. Students complain of racism in some areas, but there is a community feel within the university.

Accommodation

First years are not guaranteed accommodation, although priority is given to those who live outside a reasonable commuting distance. There are 1,050 self-catering places available, some of which are newly built. The residential services office contains a list of private sector accommodation.

Library and computing

The university has extensive collections of books and journals spread between the different libraries. The Docklands library has 214 study spaces. There are over 3,000 PC workstations, all with internet access.

Student facilities

The students' union has facilities on each campus. There is a 'Job Shop' which has details of part-time and vacation work, and there is also a counselling and advisory service.

Sport

Between the three campuses there are three swimming pools, two multi-gyms and several fitness rooms, tennis and squash courts. The Docklands campus has access to the new Olympic rowing centre and there is a special sports injury clinic.

Overseas students

There is a pre-sessional English course which runs from January to September every year. There is a counselling and advisory service, with an adviser available to overseas students.

University of Edinburgh

Founded: 1583

Times ranking: 6 (1999 ranking: 8th equal)

Address: Old College, South Bridge, Edinburgh EH8 9YL
tel: 0131 650 4360
website: www.ed.ac.uk
e-mail: slo@ed.ac.uk

Undergraduates: 14,069 (650)
Postgraduates: 2,218 (1,868)
Mature students: 10%
Overseas students: 7%
Applications/place: 7.8
Undergraduates from State sector: 61%

Main subject areas: complete range of disciplines in nine faculties: arts; divinity; education; law; medicine; music; science and engineering; social sciences; veterinary medicine.

Teaching quality ratings

Rated Excellent 1993–98: biology; cellular biology; chemistry; computing; electrical and electronic engineering; finance and accounting; geology; history; mathematics and statistics; physics; organismal biology; social policy; social work; sociology; veterinary medicine.

Highly Satisfactory 1993–98: architecture; business and management; civil engineering; English, French; geography; history of art; law; medicine; music; nursing; philosophy, politics, psychology, theology.

From 1998: European languages 21; chemical engineering 19.

Overview

The incorporation of Moray House Institute of Education into the University of Edinburgh means that Scots once more account for a majority of students in their country's premier university. But the demand from England remains undimmed, regardless of the extra expense of a four-year degree, and the presence of more than 2,000 overseas students testify to Edinburgh's worldwide reputation. Entry standards are among the highest in Britain, whether in A levels or Highers.

The university has recovered from serious financial problems in the early 1990s, when staff appointments were frozen in the face of a £5 million deficit. Since the arrival of Sir Stewart Sutherland as Principal, Edinburgh has entered a new phase of development and expansion. A new student venue was among the first projects, and £38 million has been earmarked to enhance the celebrated medical school.

With more than 18,000 students, Edinburgh has become the largest university in Scotland. Its buildings are scattered around the city, but most border the historic Old Town. The science and engineering campus is two miles to the south. The Cramond education campus, six miles west of the city, is to close, concentrating its activities on the former college's Holyrood site.

By its own high standards, a single 5* rating for research in electrical and electronic engineering was a disappointing outcome to the last research assessment exercise. But a dozen more came in the next category and the 15 subjects rated as Excellent for teaching amount to the biggest haul in Scotland. Despite having to settle for Highly Satisfactory in its teaching assessment, medicine is a traditional strength and the law faculty is the largestin Scotland. The university enjoys a reputation for high quality across the board.

Edinburgh is an enthusiastic participant in exchange programmes in Europe and North America. Almost 40 subject areas offer exchanges, with more than 130 institutions on offer in Europe alone. One student in ten includes a foreign language in his or her degree, and many more take shorter courses.

Departments organise visiting days in October for those thinking of applying and in the spring for those holding offers. There is also an annual open day in June. New students join one of the nine faculties and generally take three subjects in their first year and two in their second. Every student has a Director of Studies to help him or her narrow down the selection of a final degree and to give personal advice when necessary.

Some £850,000 has been spent making the university more accessible to disabled students, who can also call on the services of a disability office. All students are issued with a smart card for access to university facilities, which can be loaded with money to pay for a variety of goods and services.

Most students thrive on Edinburgh life, even though the cost of living can make it difficult to do it justice. Some science and engineering students complain of isolation at their campus, although there is a regular bus link with the main university centre around George Square.

Accommodation

First years are guaranteed one of 5,400 places; 1,900 in catered halls and the remaining 3,500 in self-catering flats. There are two university-owned houses, one for 40 and the other for 53, but these are primarily intended for older students. For those not wishing to live in university accommodation, there is a large private sector readily available.

Library and computers

Over two million books, periodicals, theses and manuscripts are housed in what is the largest academic library building in Europe. The computing facilities are extremely advanced and are situated in clusters around the campus, all having internet access.

Student facilities

Numerous meeting and event rooms are available for hire, and these are put to good use by the 160 clubs and societies affiliated to the Union. The student employment service assists students in finding part-time and vacation work.

Sport

The university has top class facilities, including one large and two smaller sports halls, eight squash courts and a fitness centre. There are 27 acres of sports pitches, rifle and archery ranges and a specialist outdoor pursuits centre.

Overseas students

Prior to the start of term there is an orientation programme and the International Office is open to help students with any problems. The university has a variety of English language courses available to students depending on their ability.

University of Essex

Founded: Royal charter 1965

Times ranking: 29 (1999 ranking: 29)

Address: Wivenhoe Park, Colchester, Essex CO4 3SQ

tel: 01206 873333
website: www.essex.ac.uk
e-mail: admit@essex.ac.uk

Undergraduates: 4,394 (1,471)
Postgraduates: 1,237 (618)
Mature students: 24%
Overseas students: 33%
Applications/place: 4.5
Undergraduates from State sector: 88%

Main subject areas: accounting, finance and management; art history; biology; computer science; economics; electronic systems engineering; government; history; language and linguistics; law; literature; mathematics; philosophy; physics; psychology and sociology.

Teaching quality ratings

Rated Excellent 1993–95: law.

From 1995: electronic engineering 24; history of art 22; psychology 22; sociology 22; linguistics 21; mathematics and statistics 20.

Overview

Essex has long since moved out of the shadow of its radical past, when the university was a hotbed of student unrest, and has acquired a reputation for high-quality research, especially in the social sciences. Its small size and arts bias almost certainly prevented the university from finishing higher in our ranking.

Law was top-rated in the early teaching quality assessments and sociology is among the leading departments in Britain, attracting a series of prestigious research projects as well as a high score for teaching. Both sociology and government achieved 5* grades for research, with economics, law and art history close behind in an outstanding crop of results.

Although still the junior partners, the sciences have been growing in strength and the recently merged biological and chemical sciences department is the largest in the university. Electronic engineering recorded a perfect score for teaching quality to add to an improved research rating, and computing science is strong.

Improvements in the university's academic performance, however, could not disguise the fact that the glass and concrete campus on the outskirts of Colchester was showing distinct signs of a quarter of a century's wear and tear. The university has embarked on a programme of refurbishment at the same time as expanding student facilities. Teaching and administration blocks, which cluster around a network of squares, are gradually being transformed.

Essex was originally expected to grow rapidly to become a medium to large university, but government cuts intervened and it has remained among the smallest. Recent growth has left the university on the verge of meeting its revised target of 6,000 students. The library has been extended to provide 950 reader spaces and almost 80 hours access a week. Extra teaching accommodation and more than 1,000 residential places are being added to make room for the new arrivals.

Like the other universities established in the 1960s, Essex champions academic breadth. In each of the four schools of study, undergraduates follow a common first year before specialising. They may take four or five different subjects before committing themselves to a particular degree. Essex's student population is also unusually diverse for a traditional university, with high proportions of mature and overseas students.

Social and sporting facilities are good, partly because they were designed for a larger student population, but town and gown relations in the garrison base of Colchester have not always been smooth. The 200-acre parkland campus can be bleak in winter and tends to empty at weekends, but there is a strong community atmosphere and students do not doubt the university's academic quality.

Accommodation
First years are guaranteed a single study bedroom in university-owned self-catering flats. Most accommodation is situated on campus, and the rest is located between ten and thirty minutes walk away. Private sector accommodation is readily available and the accommodation office provides assistance to students in locating somewhere to live.

Library and computing
The main library contains 770,000 books and 3,100 periodicals. There are 950 study spaces available. Ten computer labs contain a total of 340 PCs, all with seven-day access and the majority with 24-hour access.

Student facilities
There are over 100 clubs and societies which make use of one 800-capacity venue and one smaller venue. There are also two bars, three shops and an advice centre. The student Jobshop displays vacancies of part-time and vacation work.

Sport
Outdoor facilities include over 40 acres of pitches, all-weather tennis courts, a flood-lit synthetic sports pitch and an 18-hole Frisbee golf course. A sports complex contains a large sports hall, four squash courts and an indoor climbing wall.

Overseas students
The university offers a 'bridging year' for those coming to the country for the first time, as well as an extensive range of English language courses. The student support office offers counsellors and an advice centre which are available to overseas students.

University of Exeter

Founded: Royal charter 1955

Times ranking: 37 (1999 ranking: 40)

Address: Northcote House, The Queen's Drive, Exeter EX4 4QJ

tel: 01392 263035
website: www.exeter.ac.uk
e-mail: admissions@exeter.ac.uk

Undergraduates: 7,262 (1,032)
Postgraduates: 1,480 (1,633)
Mature students: 11%
Overseas students: 5%
Applications/place: 8.4
Undergraduates from State sector: 67%

Main subject areas: biological sciences; business and economics; chemistry; classics and theology; drama and music; education; engineering and computer science; environmental science; English; geography and archaeology; historical, political and sociological studies; law; mathematics; modern languages; physics; psychology.

Teaching quality ratings

Rated Excellent 1993–95: computer science; English; geography.

From 1995: German 24; drama, dance and cinematics 22; French 22; Italian 22; mathematics and statistics 22; physics 22; materials technology 21; Middle Eastern and African studies 21; sociology 21; general engineering 20; Iberian languages 20; Russian 20; linguistics 16.

Overview

Exeter is one of Britain's most popular universities, in terms of first-choice applications, especially on the arts side. For some, however, its principal handicap is its 'green welly' image as a favoured alternative to Oxbridge among the leading independent schools. So seriously did the university take this apparent problem that it once established a quota for state school entrants.

The main Streatham Campus, close to the centre of Exeter is one of the most attractive in the country. The highly rated schools of education and health studies are a mile away in the former St Luke's College. The university has also established a foothold in Cornwall by taking on the Camborne School of Mines, a development it would like to expand with a more wide-ranging campus near Penzance.

There is a long tradition of European integration, exemplified by the popular European law degree. All students are offered tuition in European languages and a number of degrees include the option of a year abroad. Language degrees have scored well in the teaching assessments, with German achieving a perfect score. Arabic and Islamic studies have benefited from investment from the Middle East. The last research assessments were solid rather than spectacular, but accountancy, classics, economics, applied mathematics and hospital-based subjects were all considered nationally outstanding.

Exeter's strength lies mainly in the arts, with English literature, drama and history among the most heavily subscribed courses in their fields. But computing science was one of only seven top-rated courses for teaching, and physics did well more recently.

The university has undergone a complete academic and administrative reorganisation, introducing semesters and replacing faculties with 17 schools. The modular system allows students to build a degree from a wide range of courses at the end of their first year, and a single model of assessment is being developed, balancing coursework and examination.

Gradual expansion has produced a medium-sized university which has now reached its target enrolment. As Exeter has entered the franchising business, any significant growth is likely to be outside Devon.

The city of Exeter has plenty of pubs but could hardly claim a buzzing nightlife. Students more than make up for it with their own social scene, kept informed by thriving print and broadcast media. The Northcott Theatre, on campus, is one of the cultural centres of the region, and the area's beautiful countryside and enticing beaches are within easy reach.

Accommodation

First years are guaranteed either one of 2,000 places in catered halls or one of 2,200 places in self-catering flats, all located on or near the campus. For those not wishing to live in university accommodation, the accommodation office assists students in finding private sector housing.

Library and computers

The library contains over 1 million books, 3,000 periodicals and 690 study places, with other faculty libraries providing extra resources and study spaces. There are extensive computing facilities located throughout the campus, many of them having seven-day, 24-hour access.

Student facilities

The union has over 100 affiliated societies, many charitable and community-orientated. There is a large programme of entertainment and the union provides a shop, launderette and optician. The careers centre operates a business experience scheme for students.

Sport

The sports facilities at present include a multi-gym, a large sports hall and eight squash courts, but are being extensively redeveloped. Sixty acres of playing fields are designated for team sports, in addition to 20 tennis courts and two all-weather pitches.

Overseas students

Orientation programmes are open to new overseas students, and staff from the international office are on hand to deal with students' concerns. There are a variety of English language courses, which the spouses of students are also eligible to attend.

University of Glamorgan

Founded: University status 1992, formerly Polytechnic of Wales

Times ranking: 85 (1999 ranking: 80)

Address: Llantwit Road, Treforest, Pontypridd, Mid Glamorgan CF37 1DL

tel: 01443 480480
website: www.glam.ac.uk

Undergraduates: 9,668 (3,027)
Postgraduates: 363 (1,530)
Mature students: 32%
Overseas students: 14%
Application/place: 5.1
Undergraduates from State sector: 93%

Main subject areas: 13 departments in three faculties: environment studies; professional studies; technology studies.
Also certificate and diploma courses in all three areas.

Teaching quality ratings

Rated Excellent: accounting and finance; biology; business studies; creative writing; drama; earth studies; electrical and electronic engineering; English; information and library studies; media; mining surveying; public sector schemes; Welsh.

Overview

Wales's second university was the smallest of the polytechnics. Although still not large by modern university standards, Glamorgan has been making up for lost time, largely by franchising courses to colleges at home and abroad. Twinning programmes operate in five overseas centres, while in Wales a growing number of further education colleges offer the university's courses. Pembrokeshire College has become an associate college, providing an outpost in west Wales, which guarantees places or degree courses if students fulfil set conditions.

The university's own campus is 20 minutes by train from Cardiff in Treforest, overlooking the market town of Pontypridd. Originally based in a large country house, Glamorgan now has purpose-built premises for the science and technology departments. The law, nursing and midwifery schools are housed in Glyntaff in corporate-style buildings a short walk from the campus.

Glamorgan is committed to retaining its vocational slant, tailoring a diploma in management to the needs of the Driver and Vehicle Licensing Agency, for example. The approach pays dividends for graduate employment, which is consistently high, although the drop-out rate is also the highest among the university institutions in Wales. With 8 per cent of students either transferring to other universities or dropping down to a different level, the funding council expected fewer than two-thirds of those starting degree courses in 1996 to complete their course at Glamorgan.

The university is one of the top scorers among the former polytechnics in teaching quality assessments. Eight subjects have been rated as Excellent at degree level, and there have also been awards for the remaining further education course provision.

The best-known courses are in engineering and professional studies, although the university has caused a stir with a degree in science fiction and modules on aliens and UFOs. The school of design and advanced technology has also been designated a centre of excellence for Wales, while three National Partnership awards testify to high standards in course design and delivery.

Many of the 10,000 full-time undergraduates choose to live in Cardiff, which is both livelier than Pontypridd and a better source of accommodation. However, the campus has been developing, with the addition of a recreation centre and an extension to the students' union, which is the focus of social life. Its bars are the only part of the university where smoking is allowed.

Accommodation

The university is nearly always able to find first years places in one of 110 catered and 1,100 self-catering places in university-owned halls and flats. The accommodation services office produces a handbook to assist students in finding private sector accommodation as well as offering direct help.

Library and computing

Extensive printed resources are divided between the university's two modern libraries, which also contain large numbers of study places. Computers are grouped into clusters distributed around the site. Many clusters allow 24-hour access.

Student facilities

The union contains two bars and regularly stages discos, live bands, cabaret and comedy acts. There is also a shop and travel centre. The university employment service lists jobs available both on campus and with local companies.

Sport

Indoor facilities include six badminton courts, four squash courts and a climbing wall. Outdoors, there are three floodlit pitches and one all-weather cricket pitch.

Overseas students

The international adviser and staff of the student's services department provide support. Courses are run to improve students' English and study skills.

University of Glasgow

Founded: 1451

Times ranking: 23 (1999 ranking: 21)

Address: University Avenue, Glasgow G12 8QQ

tel: 0141 330 4575
website: www.gla.ac.uk/sras/
e-mail: sras@gla.ac.uk

Undergraduates: 14,227 (3,277)
Postgraduates: 1,740 (1,754)
Mature students: 12%
Overseas students: 6%
Applications/place: 5.8
Undergraduates from State sector: 82%

Main subject areas: 100 departments in nine faculties: arts; divinity; education; engineering; law and financial studies; medicine; science; social sciences; veterinary medicine.

Teaching quality ratings

Rated Excellent 1993–98: cellular biology; chemistry; computing science; English; French; geography; geology; medicine; physics; philosophy; psychology, organismal biology; social policy, sociology, veterinary medicine.

Highly Satisfactory 1993–98: civil engineering; dentistry; drama; finance and accounting; history; history of art; law; mathematics and statistics; mechanical engineering; music; nursing; politics; social work; theology.

From 1998: European languages 22.

Overview

Glasgow enjoys the rare distinction of having been established by Papal Bull, and began its existence in the Chapter House of Glasgow Cathedral. But it is now beginning to spread out from the impressive Gilmorehill campus, in the city's fashionable West End, which has been its base for more than a century. The university has opened a new campus in Dumfries and has taken in St Andrew's College to form a new faculty of education. Veterinary science was already on a greenfield site four miles away, and the prestigious medical school will also move to new premises in 2001.

The university's roots will remain on the edge of Kelvingrove Park, with its 99 listed buildings. More distinctively Scottish than its rivals in Edinburgh or St Andrews, almost half of the students come from within 30 miles of Glasgow and three-quarters are from Scotland. There was a high proportion of home-based students long before the city became fashionable.

However, the university has adopted a more outward-looking style under the leadership of Sir Graeme Davies, marked by two Queen's Anniversary Prizes, for opening up artistic, scientific and cultural resources and taking computing to local communities. Teaching and research partnerships have been developed with neighbouring Strathclyde University, while the Crichton College campus, in Dumfries, will take higher education to southwest Scotland with unusual three-year degrees.

Not that Glasgow is a stranger to innovation: it was the first university to have a school of engineering, for example. The huge science faculty – the biggest outside London – is strong, having received top ratings for teaching in six subjects. Applications for science degrees reflect this quality, having risen by 25 per cent since the mid-1990s, but only computing science and town planning reached the pinnacle of the last research assessment exercise. Although five other subjects were in the second of the seven categories, Glasgow might have hoped for better.

Overseas recruitment has remained strong, especially in engineering. Glasgow is also taking an active role in the Universitas 21 worldwide group of universities, involving partnerships on five continents and eventual shared teaching arrangements.

Most students like the combination of campus and city life, with the relatively low cost of living an added attraction. They have the choice of two students' unions, until recently segregated by sex, which form the basis of social life for an expanding community.

Accommodation

For those who are unable to commute, the university is normally able to accommodate students in catered halls or self-catering flats. For those who prefer independent housing the accommodation office assists students in finding places to live in the plentiful private sector.

Library and computing

The library spends over £1.5 million each year on new resources which at present include over two million books and 6,000 journals. There is plentiful study space in the library. Computers are available in clusters in many locations throughout the university.

Student facilities

The Glasgow University Union and the Queen Margaret Union together contain several bars and two nightclubs. The GUU stages large balls and has a renowned debating society. A 'Jobshop' employment service provides details of part-time and vacation work.

Sport

The Garscube sports complex contains a 25-metre swimming pool, squash courts and three activity halls. There are over 50 exercise classes, programmes and advice. Many outdoor grass and synthetic pitches are available for team sports.

Overseas students

Prior to the start of term, an orientation week introduces students to the city and university. There is also a special overseas student adviser. English courses, both pre-sessional and during term, provide tuition for those requiring help.

Glasgow Caledonian University

Founded: University status 1992, formerly Queen's College (founded 1875) and Glasgow Polytechnic (founded 1972)

Times ranking: 71st equal (1999 ranking: 71st equal)

Address: City Campus, 70 Cowcaddens Road, Glasgow G4 OBA

tel: 0141 331 3000
website: www.gcal.ac.uk
e-mail: d.black@gcal.ac.uk

Undergraduates: 9,927 (2,216)
Postgraduates: 1,074 (1,299)
Mature students: 30%
Overseas students: 6%
Applications/place: 6.9
Undergraduates from State sector: 94%

Main subject areas: business; engineering and construction; health; management and social sciences; science.
Diploma courses are also offered.

Teaching quality ratings

Rated Excellent 1993–98: chemistry; physiotherapy.

Highly Satisfactory 1993–98: biology; cellular biology; consumer studies; finance and accounting; mathematics and statistics; mass communications; nursing; nutrition and dietetics; occupational therapy; physics; psychology; social work; sociology.

Overview

To lose three principals in its first five years smacks more of a football club than a university, but that is what Glasgow Caledonian has had to endure. The last departure, in 1997, prompted a funding council inquiry, which was less than flattering about the university's academic and managerial standards. The new administration is doing its best to sort out the mess, but still could not produce accurate figures when the first official drop-out statistics appeared at the end of 1999. The published version suggested that fewer than half of Caledonian's students would complete the degrees they embarked upon.

Even the naming of the new university was fraught with difficulty, as the original choice of The Queen's University, Glasgow, was considered too like its namesake in Belfast. The name Caledonian eventually emerged from a ballot of students and staff. Dramatic expansion put facilities under strain, but the estate was improving, along with the teaching ratings, until the university's leadership problems became the centre of attention.

Five sites have been reduced to two – one in the city centre and the other a mile away in the West End – with the aid of a £45 million building programme. More than a third of the money has been spent on new accommodation for the health faculty, which is the university's pride and joy. Physiotherapy is the only subject since chemistry's success in 1993 to be rated excellent for teaching, and Caledonian now boasts among the most extensive health programmes in Britain. A string of other subjects (mainly on the science side) are considered 'highly satisfactory'.

Degrees are strongly vocational and are complemented by a wide portfolio of professional courses. A high proportion of students choose part-time or sandwich degrees. The polytechnic pioneered credit accumulation and transfer in Scotland, and still has the country's largest scheme, covering the full range of courses. True to its roots, Caledonian takes more students through non-traditional routes than any university in Scotland. With more than 14,000 students, only Edinburgh and Glasgow universities are bigger north of the border.

The legacy of Queen's College, which catered mainly for women, has ensured that the proportion of female students is the highest of any university in Britain. Sports and social facilities have been among the priorities in the building programme, and the library has been extended and upgraded recently. Some students find that the high proportion of their peers living at home detracts from the social scene.

Accommodation

There are 560 self-catering and 140 catered places owned by the university. First years are not guaranteed accommodation, but priority consideration is given to those living outside a reasonable commuting distance. The university's webpage contains a database of accommodation, and the accommodation office publishes a list of housing in the private sector.

Library and computing

The largest library contains 200,000 volumes and 1,300 study spaces. Students automatically gain access to the city's Mitchell Library, Europe's largest public reference library, and other Scottish university libraries. Extensive computing facilities are available with specialised computers being available in some departments.

Student facilities

The students' union stages various club nights and there are over 30 non-sporting clubs. A wide choice of affordable food is available and the student newspapers give details of other entertainments. The 'Job Spot' offers a free service for students seeking employment.

Sport

A new multi-purpose sports hall has opened on the main campus, offering a wide variety of classes and facilities. There are outdoor pitches for football and other team sports.

Overseas students

A designated overseas student adviser, academic tutors and welfare advice in the union are all available to help students with any difficulties.

University of Greenwich

Founded: University status 1992, previously Thames Polytechnic

Times ranking: 81 (1999 ranking: 75th equal)

Address: Bexley Road, Eltham, London SE9 2PQ

tel: 0800 005006
website: www.gre.ac.uk
e-mail: courseinfo@greenwich.ac.uk

Undergraduates: 9,977 (3,353)
Postgraduates: 1,134 (2,506)
Mature students: 46%
Overseas students: 12%
Applications/place: 6.5
Undergraduates from State sector: 92%

Main subject areas: built environment; business; education; health and community studies; science and technology; social sciences and humanities.
Also a wide range of certificate and diploma courses.

Teaching quality ratings

Rated Excellent 1993–95: architecture; environmental studies.

From 1995: town and country planning 24; sociology 23; communication and media studies 22; psychology 22; building 21; civil engineering 21; molecular biosciences 20; mathematics and statistics 19; health subjects 18; electrical and electronic engineering 17.

Overview

Greenwich's move into the former Royal Naval College buildings designed by Sir Christopher Wren at last gives the university a campus worthy of one of the most desirable titles in the higher education world. While its name conjured up images of history and science in equal measure, the former polytechnic was actually based on the less prepossessing side of the borough, straggling across south London and out into Kent. The new Maritime campus is costing £20 million to restore and convert, but the World Heritage Site should prove a draw for home and overseas students alike.

However, Greenwich describes itself as a 'regional university' for southeast London and half of Kent, a populous county with only one university of its own. The majority of students will still be based at one of the other four sites acquired over two decades of mergers with colleges of art and education. Environmental courses are concentrated on the university's Medway campus, at Chatham, while the large education faculty is at Avery Hill, a Victorian mansion on the outskirts of southeast London, where there is a student village. With mathematics, computing and law the first occupants of the Maritime Campus, for the moment at least the remaining faculties are at Dartford and the previous headquarters in Woolwich.

Avery Hill is one of the few teacher training centres to offer primary, secondary and further education courses, although the variety may have contributed to a disappointing showing in the Teacher

Training Agency's performance tables. Most other teaching assessments have been favourable, with town planning and sociology the star performers. Where scores have been low, it has generally been the quality assurance procedures that have been found wanting.

The university achieved some respectable results in the last research assessment exercise, although little more than a quarter of the academic staff entered. Greenwich does not shy away from assessment, however. It was among the first British universities to be rated by investment analysts, who pored over its academic, administrative and financial standing.

There are strong links with European institutions, providing a steady flow of overseas students, as well as exchange opportunities for those at Greenwich. There are also eight associated colleges in Kent, Essex and London, which teach the university's courses.

A commitment to extending access to higher education has led to low entrance requirements in many subjects and a relatively high proportion of mature students. The downside is a projected drop-out rate of more than a quarter, with only two thirds of degree students expected to complete the course they started at Greenwich.

Accommodation

First years are guaranteed one of 2,000 places in university-owned catered halls or self-catering flats, all residences being located on or near the campuses. The university also operates a 'Head Lease' scheme which leases out a number of university-owned houses and flats. The accommodation services office assists students with finding private sector housing.

Library and computing

Libraries are located on all the university sites and contain a wide range of books, journals and electronic information resources, all available 60–70 hours a week. Computing facilities on all sites have a wide range of software and extensive back-up.

Student facilities

The 1,600-capacity students' union at Woolwich is the biggest university venue in London. There are two bars, a second 1,000-capacity venue and a regular programme of entertainments. The 'Job Shop' provides details of part-time and vacation work.

Sport

Split between four sites there are two gyms, three sports halls, a swimming pool and fitness centre. Outdoor facilities include tennis courts, rugby and football pitches and two cricket squares. The Medway site has a croquet lawn and sailing club.

Overseas students

The student services department has an overseas student counsellor. The university aims to make the transition 'as smooth as possible' for overseas students.

Heriot-Watt University

Founded: 1821, Royal charter 1966
Times ranking: 49 (1999 ranking: 42)

Address: Riccarton, Edinburgh EH14 4AS

tel: 0131 451 3376/77/78
website: www.hw.ac.uk
e-mail: admissions@hw.ac.uk

Undergraduates: 4,006 (196)
Postgraduates: 668 (1,409)
Mature students: 9%
Overseas students: 13%
Applications/place: 5.9
Undergraduates from State sector: 86%

Main subject areas: art and design; education; engineering; economic and social studies; environmental studies; science; textiles.

Teaching quality ratings

Rated Excellent 1993–98: electrical and electronic engineering.

Highly Satisfactory 1993–98: cellular biology; chemistry; civil engineering; computer studies; finance and accounting; mathematics and statistics; mechanical engineering; physics.

From 1998: chemical engineering 19.

Overview

Still evolving more than 30 years after attaining university status, in many ways Heriot-Watt is Scotland's most unconventional university. The main campus, on the outskirts of Edinburgh, was completed only in 1992, and is among the most modern in Britain. Still small in terms of full-time students despite a recent spate of mergers, the primarily technological university has 15,000 other students taking distance learning courses.

For many years, Heriot-Watt's main claim to fame outside the academic community lay in its degree in brewing and distilling. But the university has a wide variety of vocational programmes, as well as more conventional degrees. Research in petroleum engineering is rated internationally outstanding, while modern languages are a more unexpected strength. Electrical and electronic engineering is the only subject area to achieve the maximum score for teaching, but there has been a succession of Highly Satisfactory ratings.

The range of subjects has been extended with the addition of Edinburgh College of Art and the Galashiels-based Scottish College of Textiles. Science, engineering and economic and social studies are located on the main campus, a site at Riccarton, which saw £100 million of investment during the 1990s. The focus for the new millennium is in the Borders, where higher education provision is still scarce, with a broadband network planned to bring the university together electronically. Heriot-Watt has long been a leader in the use of information technology for teaching, thanks partly to a huge research and development programme with the computer giant Digital.

Concentration on technology, languages and business is fitting for a university whose name commemorates James Watt, the pioneer of steam power, and George Heriot, financier to King James VI. The subject mix also serves graduates well in the jobs market: Heriot-Watt is seldom far from the top of the employment league tables. But the new acquisitions have altered the student profile, with the proportion of women creeping up to 38 per cent. A bare majority of the students are from Scotland, with 30 per cent from other parts of Britain.

Students at Riccarton complain that the six-mile journey to Edinburgh city centre leaves them isolated, and the campus is not the liveliest. Buses run through the night, but are never frequent and take half an hour to reach the centre. However, sports enthusiasts are well provided for, and representative teams do well.

Accommodation

First years are guaranteed a place in university catered halls on campus or self-catering flats, some being set a short distance away. There are over 100 university managed flats and houses located in and around the university, but these are intended for older students. The student welfare office offers information and advice about finding private sector accommodation.

Library and computing

The library is well stocked with printed and electronic information resources and contains 650 study places, 70 with computer workstations. The latest computer facilities are available on both campuses and access is available from some residential sites.

Student facilities

The students' union boasts bars, cafés, social venues and a student newspaper. Over 50 clubs and societies cater for most interests. There is a welfare centre and the careers service has details of part-time and vacation employment.

Sport

The university is well equipped, with three sports halls, three floodlit synthetic grass tennis courts and floodlit playing fields. Indoor facilities include a climbing wall, eight squash courts and a fitness suite containing free weights and cardiovascular equipment.

Overseas students

Prior to the start of term there is a two-week English language course. More intensive courses are available for those who need them. The international office provides help and support.

University of Hertfordshire

Founded: University status 1992, formely Hatfield Polytechnic

Times ranking: 71st equal (1999 ranking: 83rd equal)

Address: College Lane, Hatfield, Herts AL10 9AB

tel: 01707 284800
website: www.herts.ac.uk/
e-mail: admissions@herts.ac.uk

Undergraduates: 11,723 (2,992)
Postgraduates: 591 (1,924)
Mature students: 31%
Overseas students: 14%
Applications/place: 4.7
Undergraduates from State sector: 92%

Main subject areas: business; education; engineering; health and human sciences; humanities; information sciences; natural sciences.
Certificate and diploma courses are also offered in most areas.

Teaching quality ratings

Rated Excellent 1993–95: environmental studies.

From 1995: psychology 23; mechanical and aeronautical engineering 22; mathematics and statistics 21; electrical and electronic engineering 20; general engineering 20; linguistics 20; building 19; civil engineering 18; sociology 17; modern languages 16; drama, dance and cinematics 15.

Overview

Hertfordshire has embarked on a new strategy for the third millennium, overtly designed to propel it up the league tables by attracting more highly-qualified students. The prime draw will be a new campus, which is being built half a mile from the existing headquarters in Hatfield, which will bring the university together for the first time. Art and design are already ensconced on the new site, and business, education and the humanities will eventually follow from the Hertford and Watford campuses.

Professor Neil Buxton, the Vice-Chancellor, has told his staff that A-level requirements will rise over the first three years of the new century and that the university's academic approach will become 'tougher and more rigorous'. Although Hertfordshire has always been considered among the leading new universities, its average entry scores have been lower than rivals such as Manchester Metropolitan, Kingston or Oxford Brookes. After 30 per cent growth in five years, the theory is that the university can afford to be more selective without ignoring the needs of its region.

Under the plans, Hertfordshire will remain one of the few genuinely rural universities. Many students commute from towns and villages in the county, using the most extensive university bus network in Britain. Academic and social facilities are provided on every site, but the student experience has inevitably suffered from the geographical divisions. For those looking for more sophisticated nightlife, London is only a short train journey away.

Hatfield Polytechnic's reputation was built mainly on engineering, science and computing. However, business studies and healthcare now rival them in terms of size. European links are a speciality, with the range of exchange possibilities growing every year, and half the undergraduates take a language option. Half also include work placements in their degrees, the close links with employers sometimes bringing in valuable research and consultancy contracts. All students are encouraged to take 'free choice' courses in subjects outside their degree programmes, which can contribute to their final results.

Hertfordshire suffers in *The Times* League Table for indifferent grades in the early years of teaching assessment, when only environmental studies was rated Excellent. More recently, psychology and aeronautical and mechanical engineering have scored well, although there have still been some slip-ups. Results in the last research assessment exercise were also mixed, but physics and computing science did well to achieve a grade 4 (out of 5).

Accommodation

The university owns 3,000 places in catered halls and self-catering flats. First years are not guaranteed accommodation and so residential services assist students in finding somewhere to live in university managed or leased accommodation. Alternatively, accommodation is readily available in the private sector.

Library and computing

A brand new learning resources centre provides 1,600 study places and 800 PCs. Together with the smaller libraries on other sites there is a wide range of books, journals and electronic information resources. Computers are easily accessible on all sites.

Student facilities

The students' union has four venues and provides a huge programme of events – last year's summer ball was the biggest student event in the country. Student services offers help and advice and a job service helps those looking for part-time or vacation work.

Sport

Between the three campuses there is an artificial hockey pitch and several floodlit all-weather courts. Indoor facilities include a sports hall, climbing wall, swimming pool and a fitness centre containing free weights and resistance and cardiovascular equipment.

Overseas students

The university has an orientation programme and overseas student advisers. Additional English language tuition is also available.

University of Huddersfield

Founded: University status 1992, formerly Huddersfield Polytechnic
Times ranking: 84 (1999 ranking: 78)

Address: Huddersfield, West Yorkshire HD1 3DH

tel: 01484 472230; (prospectus) 0870 901 5555; (general) 01484 422288
website: www.hud.ac.uk
e-mail: admissions@hud.ac.uk

Undergraduates: 9,519 (3,913)
Postgraduates: 941 (1,867)
Mature students: 35%
Overseas students: 4%
Applications/place: 5.0
Undergraduates from State sector: 94%

Main subject areas: accountancy; applied sciences; business; computing; design technology; education; human and health sciences; humanities; law; management studies; mathematics; music.
Also a wide range of certificate and diploma courses.

Teaching quality ratings

Rated Excellent 1993–95: music; social work.

From 1995: electrical and electronic engineering 24; food science 20; psychology 20; media studies 18; drama, dance and cinematics 17; modern languages 15.

Overview

The first official performance indicators for higher education, published at the end of 1999, showed Huddersfield as living up to its mission to help produce a more diverse student population. Almost three-quarters of the university's students are from working-class homes and even more are from areas without a strong tradition of higher education.

Huddersfield has made a fresh start under a new vice-chancellor after a torrid period in which the previous management attracted highly public criticism from within the university and further afield. An immediate aim is to bring the university together on one campus, selling the Holly Bank site, where the school of education and professional development is based, and extending the Queensgate campus in the town centre. There will then be a neat separation of academic and residential accommodation, with the latter concentrated five miles away in the Storthes Hall Park student village.

The university is capitalising on Huddersfield's industrial past to ease the strain on facilities that have been struggling to cope with an expansion that reached 13 per cent a year at its peak. Canalside, a refurbished mill complex, has provided new space for mathematics and computing, and similar conversions are planned for education. Human and health sciences have already acquired new premises and precision engineering is next on the list.

A tradition of vocational education dates back to 1841, and the university has a long-established reputation in areas such as textile design and engineering. But there are less obvious gems, such as music and social work, both of which were rated excellent for teaching and scored a creditable grade 4 (out of 5) for research. Teaching assessments have ranged from the sublime (maximum points for electrical and electronic engineering) to the ridiculous (only 15 out of 24 for modern languages). Entering 44 per cent of the academic staff for the last research assessment exercise backfired with two thirds of them rated in the last category but one.

Many arts courses, which now attract the majority of students, have a vocational slant. Politics, for example, includes a six-week work placement, which often takes students to the House of Commons. A third of the students in all subjects take sandwich courses, and most have some element of work experience.

Town and gown relations are good and the cost of living low. The description of Huddersfield in the prospectus as a 'happening town' may be stretching things, but it is not far from Leeds for those in search of serious clubbing. Students like the town's friendly atmosphere, although most base their social life on the students' union.

Accommodation

The university owns six halls providing 2,200 high-quality places, many with en-suite bedrooms. All the halls are self-catering and designed in groups of flats. First years are not guaranteed accommodation, but every effort is made to locate them in a university-owned property. The accommodation office assists and advises students looking for accommodation in the private sector.

Library and computing

There are four libraries, the largest of which contains 350,000 items and a variety of study spaces. A large number of computers are available for student use, all with access to e-mail and the internet.

Student facilities

The union has two bars and a café and provides a range of support services and entertainments. 'Eden' is one of the most successful student-run club nights in the country. The 'Jobshop' advertises details of part-time and vacation work.

Sport

Sporting facilities in Huddersfield include a swimming pool, a fitness complex and many opportunities for team sports. Eight golf courses, four sailing clubs, angling and orienteering facilities are complemented by the university's own sports hall.

Overseas students

Prior to the start of term, a 'welcome week' introduces students to British university life. A full-time overseas student officer is available to deal with concerns and there are a variety of English language courses for those needing them.

University of Hull

Founded: 1928, Royal charter 1954

Times ranking: 39 (1999 ranking: 33rd equal)

Address: Cottingham Road, Hull HU6 7RX

tel: 0870 126 2000; Official Publications Office: 01482 466812

website: www.hull.ac.uk

e-mail: K.Slater@admin.hull.ac.uk

Undergraduates: 6,925 (2,630)

Postgraduates: 965 (613)

Mature students: 14%

Overseas students: 9%

Applications/place: 6.2

Undergraduates from State sector: 86%

Main subject areas: arts; education (postgraduate only); engineering; law; mathematics; science; social sciences; technology.

Teaching quality ratings

Rated Excellent 1993–95: chemistry; history; social policy; social work.

From 1995: drama 24; electrical and electronic engineering 24; Iberian languages 24; American studies 23; East and South Asian studies 22; physics 23; psychology 23; Italian 22; mathematics and statistics 22; French 21; German 21; Dutch 20; sociology 20; Scandinavian 19.

Overview

After years of relative stability, Hull has been expanding rapidly, both on its spacious home campus and through mergers. It has already added nursing to its portfolio of courses with the acquisition of an outpost in the East Riding, but the more substantial change is the merger with University College Scarborough in August 2000. The incorporation of the former teacher training college will bring the university's full-time student population close to 10,000, with many more taking part-time and distance learning courses.

The 94-acre main campus has seen considerable development recently, with new buildings for languages, chemistry and a Graduate Research Institute. The campus, with its art gallery and highly automated library, is less than three miles from the centre of Hull. Although neither would be considered fashionable, both inspire strong loyalty among students. Philip Larkin, once the university librarian, described the city as 'in the world, yet sufficiently on the edge of it to have a different resonance'.

The modest cost of living and ready availability of accommodation have much to do with Hull's popularity with students, but the quality of courses is also high. Teaching has been rated excellent in more than half of the subjects assessed so far, with drama, electronic engineering and Iberian languages all achieving perfect scores – an unusually large number for any university. Strength in politics is reflected in a steady flow of graduates into the House of Commons, while a long-standing focus on Europe shows in the wide range of languages available at degree level.

History led the way in an otherwise unspectacular set of research assessments, with both the main subject and economic and social history considered outstanding. Social work collected a Queen's Anniversary Prize and was also rated excellent for teaching. An Institute for Learning was established in 1997 to try to put research findings into practice, developing training courses for lecturers and the university's interest in lifelong learning.

Hull has always maintained a roughly equal balance between science and technology and the arts and social sciences, believing that this promotes a harmonious atmosphere, although the new Scarborough campus will tip the scales firmly towards the arts. In the absence of a traditional medical school, the university has been collaborating with the local health authority to develop a postgraduate school with nine departments.

Student facilities, which were always good but becoming crowded, have been upgraded as part of the campus building programme. There has been a £1 million extension to the students' union and the purpose-built Language Institute is heavily used by students of all subjects.

Accommodation

First years are guaranteed one of 3,400 residential places, with a choice of halls, self-catering flats or student houses on campus. There are a further 500 properties available through the university's 'Head Lease' scheme. Private-sector accommodation is plentiful at some of the lowest prices in the country.

Library and computing

The three main libraries contain over one million books, 4,000 journals and 1,800 electronic journals. The largest library contains 1,600 study spaces. The computer networks most buildings on the campus and contains over 1,000 computers grouped into clusters.

Student facilities

A recent survey rated the students' union as the best in the country. There are four bars, a games room, shop, travel bureau and an extensive entertainments programme. The Job Exchange advertises details of part-time and vacation work.

Sport

Sports facilities include two sports halls, six squash courts, a fitness centre and gym. Outside, six football and three rugby pitches are alongside a floodlit all-weather pitch, five tennis and three netball courts as well as rowing and canoeing facilities.

Overseas students

The overseas office has support staff from six countries as well as a special overseas student adviser. There is a range of intensive language programmes, and foundation programmes are available for those needing more intensive tuition.

University of Keele

Founded: 1949 (as University College of North Staffordshire)
Times ranking: 46 (1999 ranking: 41)

Address: Keele, Staffordshire ST5 5BG

tel: 01782 584005
website: www.keele.ac.uk
e-mail: aaa30@keele.ac.uk

Undergraduates: 4,802 (5,003)
Postgraduates: 1,002 (2,085)
Mature students: 15%
Overseas students: 8%
Applications/place: 6.1
Undergraduates from State sector: 88%

Main subject areas: computational, mathematical and neuro-sciences; earth sciences; health studies; humanities, history and American studies; management and economics; political and social sciences; resource management; science and engineering.

Teaching quality ratings

Rated Excellent 1993–95: music; social work.

From 1995: American studies 24; mathematics and statistics 22; sociology 22; nursing 21; French 20; health subjects 20; Russian 20; German 19.

Overview

Although Keele has sacrificed its general foundation course, which used to give a quarter of the students a four-year degree programme, the university is still committed to breadth of study. Nine out of ten students take more than one subject for their degree, with a subsidiary from the other side of the arts–science divide in the first year. Among the more outlandish combinations are Latin and astrophysics, or biochemistry and electronic music. Most programmes provide the opportunity of a semester abroad, which the university would like a quarter of all undergraduates to take.

American studies produced Keele's only perfect score among the recent teaching assessments, as well as a high research grade, but international relations and the many dual honours programmes – especially those featuring politics or music – are among the university's strengths. General engineering was the only subject area to be rated internationally outstanding for research, but almost half the academic staff were in areas of national excellence.

Science subjects have been improving, as was demonstrated by the recruitment of two top scientists from ICI to run the inorganic chemistry and materials science group. However, it is in health subjects that the main development has been focused. Physiotherapy, nursing and midwifery have been added in recent years, but the big news has been the success of a joint bid with Manchester University to introduce clinical medicine in 2002.

All the existing courses are modular, and the traditional academic year has been replaced by two 15-week semesters, with breaks at Christmas and Easter. The university has committed itself to maintaining a generous staffing ratio of one academic to every 15 students throughout its extended period of growth. Keele remains relatively small by modern university standards, but student numbers rose by 75 per cent in five years during the 1990s. The proportion of postgraduates has also been growing, with a third of the students now taking higher degrees.

The attractive 617-acre campus near the M6 outside Stoke on Trent can take many more students. A development plan is under way, beginning with a new arts complex. Seven out of ten students and some staff live on campus, which inevitably dominates the social scene. Although the cost of living is relatively low in the Potteries, it is not an area famous for youth culture. The normal overstated section on the attractions of the locality is noticeably absent from the prospectus.

Accommodation

First years are guaranteed a place in one of four university halls for two years of their course. Since 1992, 600 study bedrooms have been built. There are a number of university-owned houses available on campus and the accommodation centre maintains a list of private-sector accommodation.

Library and computing

The main library contains over 500,000 books and 2,000 journals. There are considerable special collections and online resources, with study seating available on all floors. Networked PCs are available in clusters around the campus.

Student facilities

The students' union has six bars, numerous catering facilities and provides health, welfare and academic advice. There is a shop, community action scheme and extensive entertainments programme. The 'Jobshop' provides details of part-time and vacation employment.

Sport

The university has excellent sports facilities, which include tennis and netball courts and extensive playing fields. Indoors, there are two sports halls, a gym, fitness centre, dance studio, climbing wall and squash courts, all situated on one site.

Overseas students

The university operates family friendship and mentoring schemes. A foundation course is available for six months prior to the start of the academic year, and all students are encouraged to develop their English skills by taking courses.

University of Kent at Canterbury

Founded: Royal charter 1965

Times ranking: 44 (1999 ranking: 47)

Address: Canterbury, Kent CT2 7NZ

tel: 01227 827272
website: www.ukc.ac.uk
e-mail: admissions@ukc.ac.uk

Undergraduates: 6,210 (2,417)
Postgraduates: 991 (1,460)
Mature students: 20%
Overseas students: 22%
Applications/place: 5.4
Undergraduates from State sector: 83%

Main subject areas: humanities; information technology; management science; natural sciences; social sciences.
Also postgraduate medical studies.

Teaching quality ratings

Rated Excellent 1993–95: anthropology; computer science; social policy.

From 1995: drama and theatre studies 24; molecular biosciences 24; history of art 22; American studies 21; electrical and electronic engineering 21; health subjects 21; sociology 21; media studies 20; modern languages 19.

Overview

Kent has capitalised sensibly on its position near the Channel ports, specialising in international programmes, as well as the flexible degree structures that are the hallmark of most 1960s universities. Interdisciplinary study is encouraged, and many courses include the option of a year spent elsewhere in Europe or in the United States. Almost a quarter of the undergraduates take a language for at least part of their degree, and European studies are among the most popular subject combinations. Changes of specialism are allowed up to the end of the first year.

The low-rise campus, set in 300 acres of parkland overlooking Canterbury, is tidy rather than architecturally distinguished. Among recent developments is a long-desired student centre with a nightclub big enough to attract big-name bands. A new psychology building opens in 2000.

The university also assumes a regional role, with a joint stake in 26 access courses throughout the county, which allow students to upgrade their qualifications to degree entry standard. In 1997, this wider role was extended with the establishment of the Bridge Warden's College, in the old Chatham dockyard. The initial programme concentrates on short courses and Master's degrees, but the aim is to diversify as the area's needs become clear.

Kent is strongest in the social sciences, although molecular biosciences and drama and theatre studies took pride of place in the teaching assessments, each registering a maximum score. The university takes teaching standards seriously, encouraging all academics to take a Post-graduate Certificate in Higher Education. Social policy and administration is the top-rated research area, and is also rated Excellent for teaching, but the university's overall performance in the last research assessments was disappointing.

The university has been trying to build up its science departments, among which computing is particularly well regarded, but still two-thirds of the students take arts or social sciences. Graduates of all disciplines fare well in the employment market – a jobless rate below 4 per cent is impressive for an arts-dominated institution.

Students are attached to one of four colleges, although they do not choose them themselves. The colleges act as the focus of social life, and include academic as well as residential facilities. Significant numbers of American and European students give the university a cosmopolitan feel, but some complain that the campus is empty at weekends, while Canterbury itself is expensive and limited socially.

Accommodation

All first years are offered university housing on campus, which can be tailored to specific requests including smoking/non-smoking and single/mixed-sex halls. Second and third-year students mostly live off campus in shared houses. Property in Canterbury centre is limited and many students stay on the outskirts in the villages of Whitstable and Herne Bay.

Library and computing

There are 600 open-access PCs around the campus and students receive personal e-mail addresses and internet access. The main library contains over one million books and 1,300 study places, with 16,000 new books and 20,000 periodical issues added each year.

Student facilities

The student's union provides various services, including a Jobshop (open 5 days a week, displaying over 100 jobs at a time), an award-winning nightclub, and a careers network.

Sports

The student's union funded Sports Federation runs over 40 student sports clubs. Numerous facilities are available, including multipurpose halls, nets, a climbing wall, regular health and sports classes, a gymnasium, indoor-outdoor courts, an all-weather floodlit pitch and an injury clinic.

Overseas students

A comprehensive English language support service is available, including a 25-week English course for spouses of overseas students.

Kingston University

Founded: University status 1992, formerly Kingston Polytechnic

Times ranking: 62 (1999 ranking: 65th equal)

Address: Kingston upon Thames, Surrey KT1 1LQ

tel: 0181 547 2000
website: www.kingston.ac.uk
e-mail: admissions-info@kingston.ac.uk

Undergraduates: 10,451 (1,356)
Postgraduates: 584 (2,018)
Mature students: 32%
Overseas students: 9%
Applications/place: 5.3
Undergraduates from State sector: 88%

Main subject areas: business; design; education; healthcare sciences; human sciences; law; science; technology.
Certificate and diploma courses are also offered.

Teaching quality ratings

Rated Excellent 1993–95: business and management; English; geology.

From 1995: building 24; mechanical and aeronautical engineering 24; civil engineering 22; electrical and electronic engineering 21; modern languages 21; sociology 21; history of art 20.

Overview

Kingston has been climbing the league tables, topping *The Times* rankings for planning and property management, while investing heavily in a new building programme. No subject has scored less than 20 points out of 24 in the new-style teaching assessments and a Commission on the Future of the University has provided a new sense of direction. The next task set by the Vice-Chancellor, Professor Peter Scott, is to spread the message more widely to reduce the surprisingly large numbers recruited through Clearing.

The former polytechnic has four campuses in southwest London, two close to Kingston town centre, another two miles away at Kingston Hill and the fourth in Roehampton Vale, where a new technology block occupies a site once used to build Sopwith Camels and Hawker Hurricanes. A new flight simulator continues the tradition. An unusually extensive, 700-terminal computer network links them all. The first phase of the university's £13 million redevelopment was completed in 1997, with stylish new buildings on the 40-acre Kingston Hill site, primarily for 1,000 healthcare students but also including a high-tech learning resources centre for all six faculties. Library facilities will be expanded again as part of the scheme to upgrade the Penrhyn Road science site, which is due for completion in September 2000.

Kingston's attempt to break the traditional universities' domination of the research ranking was not a success, but teaching assessments have more than made up for the disappointment. Both building and mechanical, aeronautical and manufacturing engineering have notched perfect scores, following on from some good performances under the original quality system. The only exception has been in education, where a poor report on the small primary teacher training course briefly endangered the future of the much larger secondary provision.

Private research income is healthy, with all academics encouraged to extend their interests beyond teaching. The business school has been especially successful with its services for small firms, and the university has also become a world leader in GIS – geographical information systems.

Kingston has one of the lowest dropout rates among the new universities, according to the first official performance tables, despite filling a third of its places with mature students and a similar proportion from working-class families – both groups with low completion rates nationally. The university claims to be one of the safest in Britain, following the introduction of extra security measures. Students like the location, on the fringe of London, although complaints about the high cost of living are common.

Accommodation

The 2,269 places in hall are available to three broad groups: new entrant first-year undergraduates, new overseas undergraduate students and exchange students who are studying for a minimum period of one academic year. All hall study-bedrooms are singles with shared kitchens. Bathrooms/showers are also shared except in Chancellor's Hall, which has en-suite facilities.

Library and computing

The library offers a range of facilities including extensive online databases. Full internet and e-mail access is available free to all students, via open-access networked PCs around the campus.

Student facilities

The main students' union is lively, with four bars with various theme nights and acts with regular DJs. There are union branches on all the sites. The student advice centre offers free, professional, confidential and independent advice.

Sports

There are 26 sports clubs and facilities include provisions for athletics, badminton, cricket, canoeing, football, golf, martial arts, rugby, swimming, tennis and even parachuting and sub aqua.

Overseas students

As well as providing advice services for overseas students, English courses are run during the summer prior to the start of term and language support is available during the academic year.

University of Lancaster

Founded: Royal charter 1964

Times ranking: 19 (1999 ranking: 14)

Address: Bailrigg, Lancaster LA1 4YW

tel: 01524 65201

website: www.lancs.ac.uk

e-mail: ugadmissions@lancaster.ac.uk

Undergraduates: 6,977 (832)

Postgraduates: 1,255 (1,790)

Mature students: 13%

Overseas students: 9%

Applications/place: 7.4

Undergraduates from State sector: 87%

Main subject areas: engineering; humanities; management; science; social sciences.

Teaching quality ratings

Rated Excellent 1993–95: business and management; English; environmental studies; geography; history; music; social policy; social work.

From 1995: drama, dance and cinematics 24; psychology 24; linguistics 23; general engineering 22; molecular biosciences 21; sociology 21; French 20; Italian 20; German 19.

Overview

Lancaster has effectively remortgaged itself to cope with the fallout from a disastrous £35 million bond issue designed to give the university capital for new developments. An official inquiry questioned the wisdom of the original strategy and staff accused the management of complacency as a £16 million shortfall loomed. An investment analysts' rating, which examined academic and financial issues, has now given the university a clean bill of health, however, and the student experience seems not to have suffered.

In fact, until this year, Lancaster has been climbing *The Times* League Table, establishing itself on the fringes of the top ten with good performances in both teaching and research. The university showed its strength in research in the 1996 assessment exercise, when seven of the 27 departments achieved maximum scores and ten improved their ratings. Social work, which has a dozen applications for every place, attracted one of a number of glowing reports for teaching. Psychology and drama, dance and cinematics have produced maximum scores in recent assessments. The large management school, which has a section in Prague, was judged the best in Britain for research in accountancy, and is also rated excellent for teaching.

Nevertheless, Lancaster is not just a ratings factory. The university has always had a high proportion of mature students for a traditional university, aided by an innovative scheme, subsequently adopted by the polytechnics, which allows adults to join courses through their local further education colleges. Provision for students with special needs has been rewarded with a Queen's Anniversary Prize.

Lancaster is another campus university of the 1960s which has always traded on its flexible degree structure. Unless they are training to be teachers, undergraduates take three subjects in their first year, and only select the one in which they intend to specialise at the end of it. Combined degree programmes, with 200 courses to choose from, are especially popular. Some offer 'active learning courses', in which outside projects count towards final results.

The largely uninspiring campus overlooking Morecambe Bay is a ten-minute bus ride from Lancaster itself, three miles away. The university has been trying to cement its relationship with the city, basing continuing education and archaeology there, as well as opening a canalside residential complex. Students join one of nine residential colleges, which run their own 'freshers' weeks' and become the centre of most students' social life. The Lake District is within easy reach, but some students find the location more isolated than they expected.

Accommodation

There are eight undergraduate colleges on campus and one postgraduate college off campus. Most colleges house between 400-800 students and all accommodation is self-catering. A limited amount of accommodation is suitable for either married couples or families. Overall, the university houses around 5,000 students, and all first years are guaranteed a place.

Library and computing

Five computing labs allow 24-hour access to 186 networked workstations with internet and e-mail access. The library holds over one million items, currently subscribes to nearly 3,000 journals, includes a rare books and archive suite and has nearly 900 study places.

Student facilities

The students' union lacks a building of its own, but provides shops and many information and advice services on campus as well as managing events at venues in Lancaster. There is a Jobshop on campus.

Sports

The modern sports centre has numerous facilities, including a swimming pool, sports hall, squash courts, weight training rooms, sauna and a rock climbing wall. Outdoor facilities include football, rugby and hockey pitches, cricket fields and tennis courts.

Overseas students

English is taught as a foreign language at the Institute for English Language Education, which is internationally recognised as one of the leading centres of its kind.

University of Leeds

Founded: 1874, Royal charter 1904

Times ranking: 22 (1999 ranking: 23)

Address: Leeds, West Yorkshire, LS2 9JT

tel: 0113 233 3999

website: www.leeds.ac.uk

e-mail: inquiry@leeds.ac.uk

Undergraduates: 16,879 (2,653)

Postgraduates: 3,005 (3,139)

Mature students: 8%

Overseas students: 8%

Applications/place: 7.6

Undergraduates from State sector: 70%

Main subject areas: full range of subjects in seven faculties; arts; economics and social studies; education (postgraduate only); engineering; law; medicine, dentistry and health; science.

Teaching quality ratings

Rated Excellent 1993–95: chemistry; English; geography; geology; music.

From 1995: health subjects 24; art and design 23; dentistry 23; East and South Asian studies 23; electrical and electronic engineering 23; pharmacy 23; French 22; German 22; media studies 22; Iberian languages 22; mathematics and statistics 22; Middle Eastern and African studies 21; agriculture 20; food science 20; materials technology 20; nursing 20; Russian 20; sociology 20; chemical engineering 19; civil engineering 19; Italian 19; medicine 18; linguistics 17.

Overview

The rise of Leeds as a clubbing mecca to rival Manchester has added to the attractions of a university which has long been one of the giants of the higher education system. It has more full-time students than any institution outside London and is always among the most popular in Britain. An unusually wide range of degrees gives applicants more than 500 undergraduate programmes to choose from, with over 1,000 academic staff teaching more than 20,000 students.

The university occupies a 140-acre site, two-thirds of which is designated a conservation area, close to Leeds Metropolitan University and within walking distance of the city centre. The buildings are a mixture of Victorian and modern, the latest of which have extended the library and provided more space for biology. A proposed merger with Bretton Hall College, with its sculpture park and established reputation in the performing and visual arts, will create an outpost near Wakefield and prompt the creation of an eighth faculty. Nine other colleges in various parts of Yorkshire offer the university's courses, but handle their own admissions.

Leeds has followed the fashion for modular courses, enabling its students to take full advantage of a growing range of interdisciplinary degrees. Almost a quarter now take dual honours or combinations such as communications, women's studies or international studies. There is also a thriving European programme involving more than 100 Continental partners and a flow of students in both directions. More students take languages than any other subject, and the free-standing language unit also caters for casual learners.

Mechanical engineering, food science, Italian and town planning were all rated internationally outstanding for research in 1996, when 40 per cent of the academics entered for assessment were placed in the top two categories. Teaching ratings have generally been good, if sometimes less than outstanding. Health-care studies achieved the maximum score for teaching, for example, but 18 points out of 24 was disappointing for medicine and there were problems with broadcasting and education, which was criticised for its IT provision.

The already large students' union, famous for its long bar and big-name rock concerts, is being extended to cope with the latest phase in the university's expansion. Most students like the broad mix of backgrounds within the university, although the first official performance tables showed a surprisingly low proportion of working-class students (15 per cent). Town–gown relations are traditionally good, although like all big cities, Leeds requires sensible security precautions, particularly against burglary.

Accommodation

The university has over 6,500 places in halls of residence, flats and small houses. All first-year students who apply by 1 June are offered a place in university accommodation. Most halls of residence are mixed, with one men-only and one women-only hall. An accommodation services office offers help to find housing in the private sector.

Library and computing

The library is on several sites, split by department; it houses over 2,500,000 items and has over 4,000 places for readers. There are over 1,200 networked PCs in over 30 locations, and all have internet and e-mail access.

Student facilities

The students' union provides a number of shops including a large bookshop, travel shop, stationers and newsagent. There are over 150 union societies covering activities such as culture and religion, and comprehensive careers and welfare services are available.

Sports

Indoor facilities include three sports halls, a large fitness room, seven squash courts, and fully equipped weight training. Outdoor facilities include 32 pitches; cricket squares; a full-size floodlit synthetic pitch and six floodlit tennis courts.

Overseas students

All single overseas undergraduate students from outside the EU are offered a place in university accommodation throughout their studies for up to three years. An overseas student office offers help and advice, and English language tuition is available.

Leeds Metropolitan University

Founded: University status 1992, formerly Leeds Polytechnic

Times ranking: 86 (1999 ranking: 86)

Address: Calverley Street, Leeds, West Yorkshire LS1 3HE

tel: 0113 283 3113
website: www.lmu.ac.uk
e-mail: course-enquiries@lmu.ac.uk

Undergraduates: 11,101 (4,857)
Postgraduates: 686 (1,943)
Mature students: 33%
Overseas students: 6%
Applications/place: 6.6
Undergraduates from State sector: 87%

Main subject areas: business; cultural and educational studies; environment; health and social care; information and engineering systems.
Also a full range of certificate and diploma courses.

Teaching quality ratings

Rated Excellent 1993–95: none.

From 1995: cinematics 22; art and design 21; building 21; civil engineering 21; nursing 21; town planning 21; media studies 19; modern languages 19; electrical and electronic engineering 17; mechanical engineering 17.

Overview

The incorporation of a large further education college in Harrogate is bringing Leeds Metropolitan closer to its goal of creating a 'comprehensive' post-school institution, in which students can take courses at all levels and progress through a network of qualifications. The university was already moving in this direction following a review of its activities to prepare for the new century.

The former polytechnic's commitment to open access and concentration on teaching, rather than research, have done it no favours in the league tables, but it remains a popular choice for students. Four out of ten come from the Yorkshire and Humberside region, and are over 21 on entry. Fewer than half of the students are taking conventional full-time degrees, such is the popularity of sandwich and part-time courses.

There are two campuses in Leeds: the main site close to the city centre and Leeds University, and Beckett Park, a former teacher training college three miles away in 100 acres of park and woodlands. The latter boasts outstanding sports facilities, as well as teaching accommodation for education, informatics, law and business. Over 7,000 students take part in some form of sporting activity, despite higher charges than in many other universities.

Teaching scores are patchy, although there has been improvement after a poor start: no subjects were rated excellent under the original assessment system. Drama, dance and cinematics leads the way, but education finished bottom of the universities in a league table of performance indicators published by the Teacher Training Agency. Hotel catering, personnel management and sport and recreation are all well regarded. Students are included on the committees that design and manage courses. There is a growing emphasis on educational technology, which will be enhanced by a new £20 million learning resources centre.

Contacts with small and medium-sized businesses have been carefully fostered as part of the university's successful attempt to maintain a good record in graduate employment. The links even attracted a Queen's Anniversary Prize in the last set of awards. Most undergraduate courses are determinedly vocational, although the modular system gives students considerable control over what makes up their degree.

Like its older neighbour, Leeds Metropolitan is benefiting from the city's reputation for nightlife. But it is making its own contribution with a famously lively entertainments scene. Young and mature students seem to mix well socially.

Accommodation

Approximately 2,500 places are available in university accommodation for full-time new entrant students. There is catered and self-catering accommodation provided in a mixture of flats and mixed and single-sex halls. Some accommodation has been specially adapted to meet the needs of students with mobility difficulties.

Library and computing

The Learning and Information Services department provides over 500 workstations, with access to the internet, a further 1,800 study spaces and a stock of over 500,000 books. The library also offers skills for learning courses.

Student facilities

The students' union offer a student Jobshop and an abundance of free advice, covering such matters as childcare, health, financial consultation and student welfare. Facilities include three bars, four catering outlets, two shops, two reprographics outlets and 40 clubs.

Sports

Main sporting facilities include large sports halls, gymnasiums, multi-gym equipment, a dance studio, a swimming pool, squash courts, a climbing wall, an athletics track, multi-use synthetic grass pitch, outdoor pitches and tennis courts.

Overseas students

Specific accommodation is provided for overseas students, and the university has an international student development officer, who assists with immigration matters, visa extensions, and gives guidance and advice on all matters affecting overseas students.

University of Leicester

Founded: 1918, Royal charter 1957

Times ranking: 34th equal (1999 ranking: 31st equal)

Address: University Road, Leicester LE1 7RH

tel: 0116 252 5281
website: www.le.ac.uk
e-mail: admissions@le.ac.uk

Undergraduates: 7,292 (865)
Postgraduates: 1,905 (5,044)
Mature students: 7%
Overseas students: 9%
Applications/place: 7.1
Undergraduates from State sector: 84%

Main subject areas: arts; education (postgraduate only); law; medicine; science; social science.

Teaching quality ratings

Rated Excellent 1993–95: chemistry; English; history; law.

From 1995: American studies 23; medicine 23; physics and astronomy 23; history of art 22; media studies 21; German 21; general engineering 20; Italian 20; French 19; sociology 19.

Overview

Though Leicester celebrated its 80th anniversary in 1998, the university is only now approaching the size of most of its traditional counterparts after growing by 60 per cent in recent years. Having decided against merging with nearby Loughborough University in the early 1990s, the accent has been on achieving a viable size for a leading institution by expanding both full-time and the now substantial distance-learning numbers. The new vice-chancellor has declared his intention to focus on the university's provision for lifelong learning, as well as strengthening its research.

Teaching ratings have been sound, rather than spectacular, although four subjects were rated Excellent in the first rounds of assessment. Physics and astronomy have led the way recently – a predictable success for a leader in space science and the recipient of a Queen's Anniversary Prize in 1994. The university plays host to the National Space Science Centre, thanks to a big grant from the Millennium Commission, and a Challenger learning centre opened in 1999 to bring science to life for schoolchildren.

The medical school, which was the youngest in Britain until the latest allocation of places, also achieved a good teaching quality score. It is to develop a new style of medical degree with Warwick University, allowing graduates in the life sciences to qualify in four years. The school has among the most modern facilities in Britain, and the siting of a medically based interdisciplinary research centre at the university was another indication of growing strength. Pharmacology was the only subject with a 5* rating in the last research assessments, but more than half of the academics were in the top three categories.

Other than clinical medicine at Leicester's General Hospital, all teaching and most residential accommodation is concentrated in a leafy suburb little more than a mile from the city centre. The campus is a mixture of Georgian and modern architecture in sometimes uneasy combinations. Recent developments have included a new arts and social science centre. An audiovisual centre is heavily used for teaching a wide range of subjects.

An equal opportunities code for admissions has helped raise the proportion of mature students to one of the highest of all the traditional universities; yet the drop-out rate was among the lowest in the performance indicators published in 1999. The Richard Attenborough Centre, which opened in 1997, has also given the university a high reputation for catering for disabled students.

Accommodation

New undergraduates who confirm their intentions to take up their offer no later than 1 September are guaranteed a place in university-owned accommodation. Some of the accommodation is situated in large, extended and refurbished Edwardian houses, with modern refectories and study-bedrooms.

Library and computing

The library has over 1,100 study spaces for students and over one million volumes. As well as books and periodicals, there are a range of special resources, including theses, microfilms and videotapes. Internet access is available through the computer centre.

Student facilities

Students' union facilities include a large shop, restaurant, travel agent and two nightclubs – the Asylum and The Venue. It also plays host to 100 student societies. The student employment centre runs a Jobshop.

Sports

There are around 40 sports clubs and facilities include a sports ground with pitches for football, rugby, cricket and lacrosse. In addition a floodlit all-weather pitch, nine tennis courts, an athletics track and two sports halls are available.

Overseas students

Every effort is made to provide university accommodation to all new overseas students. The university offers preparatory courses in English language and study skills.

University of Lincolnshire and Humberside

Founded: University status 1992. Humberside University until August 1996, previously Humberside Polytechnic

Times ranking: 96 (1999 ranking: 97)

Addresses: Cottingham Road, Kingston-upon-Hull HU6 7RT; Brayfordpool, Lincoln LN6 7TS

tel: 01482 440550 (Hull)
01522 882000 (Lincoln)

website: www.ulh.ac.uk

e-mail:marketing@ulh.ac.uk

Undergraduates: 8,710 (1,816)
Postgraduates: 695 (763)
Mature students: 37%
Overseas students: 12%
Applications/place: 4.4
Undergraduates from State sector: 92%

Main subject areas: art, architecture and design; business; engineering and information technology; business and management; food, fisheries and environmental studies; media and communication; policy studies; social and professional studies. Certificate and diploma course also offered.

Teaching quality ratings

Rated Excellent 1993–95: none.

From 1995: food science 20; agriculture 19; mechanical engineering 18; media studies 17; sociology 16.

Overview

In perhaps the most dramatic transformation of any university in recent times, Lincolnshire and Humberside has not only opened a new campus, but has even given its new location pride of place in its title. The purpose-built campus near Lincoln station has become the focus of the new split-site institution, with one site in Hull now vacated and Grimsby's due to close in the reorganisation. By the time science laboratories and sports facilities have been completed, the development will have cost more than £50 million, although there have been complaints from some students about the standard of provision in the early years at Lincoln.

Now it is planning to do the same again in Hull, moving out of its existing sites in and around the city centre and into a brand new £48 million riverside campus. Subject to approvals and planning consent, work will start later this year with completion of the main facilities at Island Wharf scheduled for September 2001.

The university is effectively two institutions 40 miles apart, and markets itself accordingly, although a broad-band telecommunications network links the sites. Hull has the lion's share of business courses and, as the larger centre of population, the bulk of part-time provision. Lincoln initially concentrated on social sciences, accentuating the university's bias in favour of the arts, but will soon have 4,000 students on a wider range of courses.

The opening of Lincoln's 40-acre waterfront campus attracted architectural as well as educational interest, and represented the end of a saga. The cathedral city had been seeking a university presence for several years, and initially chose Nottingham Trent University to provide it. But the Conservative government's cap on student numbers stopped the deal going ahead and Humberside stepped in, offering to transfer existing places rather than expanding.

Poor performances in both teaching and research assessments account for Lincolnshire and Humberside's low position in *The Times* ranking. Food science's 20 points out of 24 remains the best teaching score and, although only 21 per cent of the academics were entered for the last research ratings, none reached the top three categories.

All students take the Effective Learning Programme, which uses computer packages backed up by weekly seminars to develop necessary study skills and produce a detailed portfolio of all their work. Research into teaching and learning methods has been aided by a £1 million fund provided by BP, with which the university has close links. The university also has long-established European links, providing a growing number of courses abroad, as well as participating in more than 40 formal partnerships.

The university has a Charter Mark for exceptional service, but the student experience inevitably differs between sites. The city of Lincoln is adapting to its new visitors, but will always be quieter than Hull, where the main campus adjoins Hull University's.

Accommodation

Students who accept an offer of a course with the university are able to reserve their accommodation at the time of acceptance, and there is consideration for students with a disability or certified medical circumstances. There are 1,219 beds available, 322 of which are at Lincoln. The university has approved lodgings for those living outside of halls.

Library and computing

Each campus has its own library (open to all students) offering a wide range of resources relevant to the courses taught at that campus. Computing facilities are available with one of the best computer–to–student ratios in the country.

Student facilities

The students' union offers a host of student facilities, including a health centre, advice centre, counselling, accommodation and finance consultation. A careers service provides information, seminars and fairs to help to find graduate jobs.

Overseas students

Information and guidance are available for overseas students, with the university publishing its own handbook. An overseas student development worker is available, and special consideration is given to overseas students wishing to stay in university halls.

University of Liverpool

Founded: 1881

Times ranking: 40 (1999 ranking: 38th equal)

Address: P O Box 147, Liverpool L69 3BX

tel: 0151 794 5927
website: www.liv.ac.uk
e-mail: ugrecruitment@liv.ac.uk

Undergraduates: 10,339 (3,342)
Postgraduates: 1,817 (2,812)
Mature students: 12%
Overseas students: 9%
Applications/place: 6.8
Undergraduates from State sector: 81%

Main subject areas: full range of degree courses in seven faculties: arts; engineering; law; medicine and dentistry; science; social and environmental studies, veterinary science.

Teaching quality ratings

Rated Excellent 1993–95: English; geology; history; law.

From 1995: medicine 24; anatomy and physiology 23; town planning 23; civil engineering 22; French 22; pharmacy 22; psychology 22; dentistry 21; electrical and electronic engineering 21; Iberian languages 21; sociology 21; mechanical engineering 20; materials technology 20; German 19; molecular biosciences 19; building 17;

Overview

The original redbrick university, Liverpool has been trying to modernise its portfolio of courses while preserving a well-established reputation for research. The introduction of flexible, part-time degrees, with the option of day or evening classes, was the first step in a renewed expansion programme. The medical school has been allocated more places and the campus is being upgraded.

Liverpool has been among the top dozen recipients of research council funds for two decades, with outside income increasing dramatically in recent years. Growth of 50 per cent in five years also brought more money for teaching, much of which has been invested in new educational technology. The main library has been extended recently and the former Liverpool Royal Infirmary converted into extra teaching accommodation to cope with the influx. More than 2,000 students are postgraduates, but recent expansion has been concentrated on first degrees. Full-time numbers are almost exactly balanced between the sexes.

A series of Excellent ratings in the early teaching assessments took time to repeat, but music, physiology and materials science recorded 5* ratings for research. More recent teaching successes include a near-perfect score for town planning. The university prides itself on strength across the board, with one in five of the academics entered for research assessment placed in one of the top two categories. Interdisciplinary courses have been expanded, introducing engineering with management and European studies, for example.

Undergraduate courses are divided into eight units in each two-semester year, many with examinations at the end of each semester. Liverpool was among the first traditional universities to run access courses for adults without traditional academic qualifications, but the mix does not show in the drop-out rate of only 8 per cent.

The university precinct is only half a mile up the hill from the city centre. Recent developments have included a new student services centre, which includes specialist advice on financial matters. The Infirmary development includes new facilities for health care, pharmacy and technology transfer.

Both the university and the city have a loyal following among students, a state of affairs not wasted on recruiters: the Beatles and both Liverpool football teams have featured on the first page of the prospectus. However, the suburban setting of the main halls complex and the focus of social life on the guild of students means that there is less integration than at some other civic universities.

Accommodation

The University guarantees all first-year undergraduates a place in halls. Of the 3,750 study bedrooms available, approximately 2,400 are reserved for first years. The majority of accommodation is catered but there are a limited number of self-catering flats available. The university funds Liverpool Student Homes which helps to regulate privately rented accommodation for students.

Library and computing

There are 1.4 million volumes held in two main library buildings and a number of smaller libraries which house departmental collections. The computer systems are networked and all students have full internet and e-mail access.

Student facilities

The Guild of Students plays host to over 60 societies and clubs. As well as nightclubs, film screenings and a comedy club, the Mountford Hall, inside the Guild Building, is one of Liverpool's major venues, attracting big-name band.

Sports

Sports facilities are extensive, including a sports centre with pool, indoor courts, climbing wall, gymnasium and even a rifle and pistol range. Five sports grounds are available with a total of 22 pitches (two of which are floodlit artificial turf).

Overseas students

The overseas students adviser offers advice and help. There are a range of facilities and a support network for overseas students and their families. Assistance and advice is given in areas such as immigration, finance and law.

Liverpool John Moores University

Founded: University status 1992, formerly Liverpool Polytechnic

Times ranking: 77th equal (1999 ranking: 74)

Address: Liverpool L3 5UX

tel: 0151 231 2121
website: cwis.livjm.ac.uk
e-mail: recruitment@livjm.ac.uk

Undergraduates: 12,999 (4,618)
Postgraduates: 610 (2,030)
Mature students: 29%
Overseas students: 8%
Applications/place: 6.6
Undergraduates from State sector: 91%

Main subject areas: art, media and design; built environment; business; education and community studies; engineering and technology management; information science and technology; law; natural sciences and health sciences; social science; social work and social policy.
Diploma courses are also offered.

Teaching quality ratings

Rated Excellent 1993–95: none.

From 1995: health subjects 24; land management 22; media studies 22; drama, dance and cinematics 21; American studies 21; mathematics and statistics 21; nursing 21; civil engineering 20; modern languages 19; psychology 19; electrical and electronic engineering 18; sociology 18; town planning 18.

Overview

Naming itself after a football pools millionaire was just the start for one of the most innovative of the new universities. JMU was criticised in 1999 for marketing itself more as a fun factory than a seat of learning, but the former polytechnic prefers to portray itself as 'forward-thinking'. Never afraid to take a direct approach, even the prospectus has the look of an alternative magazine.

Among the initiatives to its credit was the launching of Britain's first student charter, which became a template for others. Before university status had even been confirmed, it set about transforming itself into a huge, futuristic multimedia institution. With two learning resource centres serving different academic areas and a state-of-the-art media centre, the project is largely complete. Computer-based teaching has replaced many lectures, freeing academic staff for face-to-face tutorials, and student numbers have soared.

Mainly concentrated in an area between Liverpool's two cathedrals, the university is now one of Britain's biggest. Arts and science courses occupy separate sites within easy reach of the city centre, with the IM Marsh campus, once a teacher training college, three miles away in the suburbs, for education and community studies. JMU has retained a local commitment, with more than 60 per cent of the students drawn from the Merseyside area, some attracted by the range of diploma courses which still supplement the largely vocational degree programme. A 'learning federation' embracing four further education colleges in St Helen's, Southport and Liverpool itself adds to the regional flavour.

A growing research reputation is a source of particular pride, and is reflected in an unusually large number of postgraduates for a new university. JMU was one of the few new universities to have two subjects (general engineering and sports science) rated as nationally outstanding in the last research assessment exercise, and astronomy has a growing reputation, with a part share in a telescope in the Canary Islands.

Teaching scores have improved after a poor start, in which none of the subjects assessed under the original quality system was rated as excellent. The healing and human development courses in the school of health achieved a perfect score and an overall audit by the Quality Assurance Agency in 1999 found that standards had improved since 1993.

JMU is one of the most popular of the new universities, judged in terms of applications per place. The drop-out rate of one in five is higher than the funding council expected, but still better than many similar institutions.

Accommodation

Most first-year undergraduates stay in university halls of residence (and student villages), which house around 1,500 students. Younger students who are far away from home have priority, with some accommodation also reserved for overseas students and students with special needs. Private housing can be arranged in conjunction with Liverpool Student Homes, a joint accommodation bureau with Liverpool University.

Library and computing

The library and computing facilities include a journals' collection and a quiet research environment with 650 study spaces (almost 200 of which are equipped with networked PCs). Full internet access is available, including e-mail.

Student facilities

As well as bars and disco, the students' union is home to a student shop, a travel agency, a fitness centre, a café bar, pizza hatch, print shop and banking facilities. Other facilities include a careers service and student welfare service.

Sports

The recreation service has recently been refurbished and offers two sports halls, a dance studio, solaria and a therapy centre. A wide range of services are available including sports injury massage, aromatherapy, martial arts, aerobics and fitness programmes.

Overseas students

An advice team is available. There is an induction programme and free English language support.

University of London

Founded 1836

Senate House, Malet Street, London WC1E 7HU (tel. 0171-636 8000)

Website: www.lon.ac.uk
Enquiries: To individual colleges, institutes or schools
Total students: 89,500
Mature students: 32%
Overseas students: 15%

Overview

The federal university is Britain's biggest by far, even if some of the most prestigious members have considered going their own way. Indeed its colleges and institutes have already seen their autonomy increased considerably. They are bound together by the London degree, which enjoys a high reputation worldwide. The colleges are responsible both for the university's academic strength and its apparently precarious financial position.

London students have access to some joint residential accommodation, sporting facilities and the University of London Union. But most identify with their college, which is their social and academic base.

Colleges not listed separately but admitting undergraduates:

Birkbeck College, Malet Street, London WC1E 7HX (tel. 020 7631 6000). 12,400 students, mainly part-time. Apply direct, not through UCAS.

Courtauld Institute of Art, Somerset House, Strand, London WC2R 0RN (tel. 020 7848 2645). History of art degree. 115 undergraduates.

Heythrop College, Kensington Square, London W8 5HQ (tel. 020 7795 6600). Theological college. 130 undergraduates.

Imperial College School of Medicine, Sherfield Building, London SW7 2AZ (tel. 020 7594 9837). Degrees in medicine (merger of St Mary's, Charing Cross and Westminster teaching hospitals). 1,500 students.

London School of Jewish Studies, Albert Road, London NW4 2SJ (tel. 020 8203 6427). Degree in Jewish studies. 25 undergraduates.

Royal Academy of Music, Marylebone Road, London NW1 5HT (tel. 020 7873 7373). Music degree. 530 students.

Royal College of Music, Prince Consort Road, London SW7 2BS (tel. 020 7589 3643). Music degree. 580 students.

Royal Free Hospital School of Medicine, Rowland Hill Street, London NW3 2PF (tel. 020 7794 0500). Medical degree. 800 students.

Royal Veterinary College, Royal College Street, London NW1 0TU (tel. 020 7468 5000). Degrees in veterinary medicine and BSc. 600 students.

St Bartholomew's and the Royal London School of Medicine and Dentistry, Turner Street, London El 2AD (tel. 020 7377 7611). Degrees in medicine and dentistry. 1,100 students.

St George's Hospital Medical School, Cranmer Terrace, London SW17 0RE (tel. 020 8672 9944). Degrees in medicine and BSc. 1,100 students.

School of Pharmacy, 29-39 Brunswick Square, London WC1N IAX (tel. 020 7753 5800). Degrees in pharmacy and toxicology. 780 students.

School of Slavonic and East European Studies, London WC1E 7HU (tel. 020 7636 8000). Arts degrees only. 332 undergraduates.

United Medical and Dental Schools (Guy's and St Thomas's), Lambeth Palace Road, London SE1 7EH (tel. 020 7928 9292). Degrees in medicine, dentistry and BSc. 2,400 students.

Wye College, Ashford, Kent TN25 5AH (tel. 01233 812401). Degrees in agriculture, rural development and environmental studies. 1,710 students.

London, Goldsmiths' College

Founded: 1891, Royal charter 1990

Times ranking: 48 (1999 ranking: 50)

Address: Lewisham Way, New Cross, London SE14 6NW

tel: 020 7919 7766

website: www.goldsmiths.ac.uk

e-mail: admissions@gold.ac.uk

Undergraduates: 3,807 (1,057)

Postgraduates: 975 (1,906)

Mature students: 41%

Overseas students: 13%

Applications/place: 6.7

Undergraduates from State sector: 81%

Main subject areas: anthropology; design; drama; education; English; European languages; history; mathematical and computing sciences; media studies; music; professional and community education; psychology; social studies; sociology; visual art.

Teaching quality ratings

Rated Excellent 1993–95: music.

From 1995: drama, dance and cinematics 22; media studies 22; sociology 21; history of art 19; modern languages 17.

Overview

Although it has been a London University college for only a decade, Goldsmiths' has a long history of community-based courses, mainly in education and the arts. Evening classes are still as popular as conventional degree courses. A tradition of providing educational opportunities for women is reflected in the largest proportion of female students in the British university system – two-thirds at the last count.

Determinedly integrated into its southeast London locality, the college precincts have a cosmopolitan atmosphere. More than half of all students are over 21 on entry, many coming from the area's ethnic minorities, and there is a growing proportion of overseas students. Goldsmiths' has also become highly fashionable among the trendier elements of the new left, especially since the arrival of political biographer Ben Pimlott as Warden.

The older premises have been likened to a grammar school, with their long corridors of classrooms. But the new Rutherford Information Services Building won an award from the Royal Institute of British Architects, and a former baths building is being converted to provide more space for research and art studios.

Goldsmiths' describes itself as specialising in the study of 'creative, cultural and social processes', although there is still room for mathematics in the arts-dominated portfolio of courses. The college has an enduring reputation in the visual arts, with luminaries such as Graham Sutherland, Mary Quant and Damien Hurst among its alumni over the years. Both design studies and visual arts were rated internationally outstanding in the last research rankings, which were a spectacular success for the college. Anthropology, music and sociology were close behind, leaving more than a third of the academics entered for assessment in the top two of seven categories.

The research successes have helped transform Goldsmiths' financial position, allowing more investment in teaching. Music, media studies and drama, dance and cinematics have produced the best teaching scores so far, but education, which caters mainly for primary teachers, is also well regarded.

Student politics has survived at Goldsmiths' to an extent not seen at many universities – even the concert venue was given the name Tiananmen. The booze-and-disco social mix which sustains many students might be looked down upon, but a college in which Damon Albarn is only one of a number of successful rock alumni cannot fail to have a thriving music scene.

Accommodation

First years are guaranteed a place in university-owned accommodation. Southeast London has a plentiful private rented sector, and the college's accommodation office advises on all aspects of private sector housing.

Library and computing

The university has one of London's best libraries for cultural, social and media studies, containing 230,000 volumes and 1,000 periodicals. There are 200 PC and Macintosh computers with more specialised facilities being available in individual departments.

Student facilities

There are two bars, one with a late license, and a variety of club, quiz and sports events. The cultural and political clubs are particularly popular. The vacancy library displays details of part-time, vacation and graduate employment.

Sport

The Athletics Union sports ground is eight miles away and has facilities for track and field events. A swimming pool and leisure complex is located in Deptford where there is also a training field with cricket nets and open air tennis.

Overseas students

An orientation programme at the beginning of the autumn and spring terms welcomes overseas students and the overseas office provides support and advice. The English language unit provides courses for those needing extra tuition.

Imperial College of Science, Technology and Medicine

Founded: 1907

Times ranking: 2 (1999 ranking: 2)

Address: Exhibition Road, South Kensington, London SW7 2AZ

tel: 0171 594 8014
website: www.ic.ac.uk
e-mail: admissions@ic.ac.uk

Undergraduates: 6,271 (0)
Postgraduates: 2,801 (862)
Mature students: 7%
Overseas students: 22%
Applications/place: 7.2
Undergraduates from State sector: 53%

Main subject areas: aeronautics; biochemistry; biology; chemical engineering; chemistry; civil engineering; computing; earth resources and management; electrical and electronic engineering; environmental technology; geology; physics; mathematics; material; mechanical engineering; medicine.

Teaching quality ratings

Rated Excellent 1993–95: business and management; chemistry; computer science; geology.

From 1995: electrical and electronic engineering 24; materials science 24; general engineering 23; aeronautical engineering 22; chemical engineering 22; molecular biosciences 22; civil engineering 21

Overview

After years of running Oxford close in *The Times* rankings, London's specialist science and engineering college finally moved ahead last year and into second place in the table. Over 800 academic staff include Nobel prize-winners and 44 Fellows of the Royal Society. More than a quarter of the academics entered for assessment in the last research assessment exercise were in departments considered internationally outstanding, and almost three-quarters were in one of the top two categories.

Teaching scores have been up to the same high standard, with electrical and electronic engineering and materials science achieving maximum points. Imperial is not recommended for academic slouches, but tough entrance requirements ensure that they are a rare breed in any case. There are more than seven applicants to every place, even though many of the subjects struggle for candidates elsewhere, and entrants average better than an A and two Bs at A level. Engineering courses last four years and lead to a Master's qualification. The college has been expanding its range of European exchanges, with a variety of prestigious technological institutions available for courses such as the MSc in physics.

Medicine has been the main area of development recently, mergers with the St Mary's, Charing Cross and Westminster teaching hospitals producing one of the biggest medical schools in the country.

With 200 undergraduate places a year, the school has the status of a constituent college, and handles its own admissions. Further mergers in 2000 will bring in the Kennedy Institute of Rheumatology and Wye College, the university's agricultural and environmental centre in Ashford, Kent. Imperial has considered severing its already loose link with London University, but now appears happy to remain in the federation.

Facilities on the main campus, in the heart of South Kensington's museum district, have been expanded with the construction of a new biosciences building and extra space for earth studies, engineering and environmental science. There are also fieldwork facilities and more laboratories at Sillwood Park, near Ascot.

A growing management school, rated excellent for teaching, is the main concession to the academic world beyond science and technology. The college's main specialisms have had the effect of making it the most male-dominated university institution in Britain. This shows in a social scene which many students find limited compared with other universities, despite the impressive selection of clubs and societies on offer.

Accommodation

First years are guaranteed one of almost 2,000 residential places directly affiliated to Imperial College, and also have access to intercollegiate accommodation through the University of London. All but one of the halls are self-catering. The private housing office assists students in finding accommodation in rented housing, hostels or flats.

Library and computing

The central library contains 350,000 books, 1,800 journals and an extensive range of electronic journals. There are a further 12 departmental libraries. All computers are connected to the internet and are situated in clusters around the library and departmental buildings.

Student facilities

Over 200 clubs and societies make use of facilities including two bars, a cinema, a theatre and a newly refurbished entertainments venue staging a variety of events. Students also have access to the University of London Union, giving even wider choice.

Sport

The indoor facilities include two swimming pools, six squash courts, a fitness centre and a climbing wall. Playing fields, tennis courts, and an all-weather pitch are located 15 miles away, reached by coach. There is also a particularly strong rowing team.

Overseas students

There is an international office to provide advice and guidance, and the welfare facilities of the students' union give support.

King's College London

Founded: 1819

Times ranking: 15 (1999 ranking: 17)

Address: Strand, London WC2R 2LS

tel: 0207 836 5454
website: www.kcl.ac.uk

Undergraduates: 8,769 (1,580)
Postgraduates: 1,932 (2,348)
Mature students: 21%
Overseas students: 13%
Applications/place: 9.6
Undergraduates from State sector: 63%

Main subject areas: arts and music; education; engineering; law; life sciences; mathematics and physical sciences; medicine and dentistry; theology.

Teaching quality ratings

Rated Excellent 1993–95: geography; history; law music.

From 1995: health subjects 23; Portuguese 23; pharmacy 22; physics and astronomy 22; Spanish 22; French 21; mathematics and statistics 21; nursing 21; electrical and electronic engineering 20; German 20

Overview

Already the second largest of London University's colleges, King's has been going through an extended period of redevelopment, leading to concentration on three campuses close to the Thames. The long Underground journeys between lectures that were common after the 1980s mergers with Chelsea and Queen Elizabeth Colleges are becoming a thing of the past with the sale of the west London sites. Most departments will be within walking distance of each other, on the original Strand site or the new Waterloo campus, with medicine and dentistry based not far away at London Bridge. Another property deal is bringing together the college's libraries at the former Public Records Office in Chancery Lane.

Medical subjects are the main growth point. Two nursing schools have been amalgamated to form the Nightingale Institute, building on the college's long-standing BSc in nursing studies, while the merger in 1998 with the United Medical Schools of Guy's and St Thomas's Hospitals gives King's one of the biggest medical schools in Europe. Among more than 2,500 students training to become doctors or dentists will be mature students on a new course designed to provide more variety in the medical profession.

War studies, theology and classics, Greek and mechanical engineering are all considered internationally outstanding in the last research assessments. A quarter of the academics entered for the exercise were in such departments. Music and education are top-rated for both teaching and research. Scientists remain in the majority, however, and are now offered a wide range of interdisciplinary combinations, such as chemistry and philosophy, or French and mathematics. King's was an early convert to modular courses and even flirted with the possibility of two-year degrees in a turbulent period before the resignation of the last principal.

King's has tended to be the forgotten member of the capital's academic elite, but the full extent of the college's ambitions is clear from its mission statement, which includes having all its departments rated Excellent for both teaching and research. The college was among the first to follow the example of American universities by submitting to a credit rating, which took account of its academic and financial standing. The 'AA minus' result was better than many big cities have achieved.

King's is also a solid bet for a good degree for those who satisfy its demanding entry requirements. Every student is allocated a personal tutor, and much of the teaching is in small groups. Over 60 per cent of undergraduates can expect a first or upper-second class degree.

Accommodation

All full-time undergraduates studying courses lasting more than a year are guaranteed one year (not necessarily their first) in university accommodation, which may be in halls of residence, apartments or student houses. The college has over 3,000 residential places, including a student village in Hampstead.

Library and computing

Information centres are located on each of the college's three main campuses, and offer access to online data sources, e-mail and the internet via 2,850 networked study places. Six hundred further reader places are available in the libraries.

Student facilities

The student's union supports a host of clubs and societies, and runs an advice centre, a shopping mall, cafés, bars and two nightclubs. Counselling, welfare, an extensive careers network and disabled services are also available.

Sports

Almost every sport is catered for. Four sports grounds provide facilities for hockey, rugby, football, cricket, tennis, netball and croquet. There are rifle ranges at the Strand, a fitness gym at Waterloo, and a swimming pool and gym at Guy's.

Overseas students

The university organises orientation programmes for overseas students, and there are many overseas students' clubs and societies. The Centre teaches English and study skills to EU and overseas students during the summer and the academic year.

London School of Economics and Political Science

Founded: 1895

Times ranking: 8 (1999 ranking: 4)

Address: Houghton Street, London WC2A 2AE

tel: 0207 955 7124/5
website: www.lse.ac.uk
e-mail: UG-admissions@lse.ac.uk

Undergraduates: 3,171 (94)
Postgraduates: 2,901 (1,020)
Mature students: 10%
Overseas students: 40%
Applications/place: 11.6
Undergraduates from State sector: 57%

Main subject areas: accounting and finance; anthropology; economic history; economics; geography; government; industrial relations; international history; international relations; language studies; law; philosophy; logic and scientific method; social psychology; social policy and administration; sociology; statistics and mathematics.

Teaching quality ratings

Rated Excellent 1993–95: anthropology; applied social work; management; history; law; social policy.

From 1995: media studies 22; sociology 20.

Overview

Always one of the big names of British higher education, the LSE has taken on a new lease of life under its latest director, signing up big names from Oxford, Harvard, Yale and other top universities. Although most are visiting professors or on short-term appointments, the new blood is helping to revitalise an institution which has been back in the limelight since the arrival of Professor Anthony Giddens, the academic face of Tony Blair's 'Third Way'.

Much of the 1990s was taken up with fruitless searches for room to break out from the school's cramped site near London's law courts. The most ambitious – a bid for County Hall – was blocked by the Conservative government, while the possibility of a move to Docklands was rejected by the school itself. Even a contingency plan to levy the first undergraduate fees was overtaken by events, when the Labour government introduced its national scheme. Proposals to divide the institution into graduate and undergraduate schools was also dropped, but the intention is still to concentrate on Master's degrees. One consequence may be to make the LSE even more difficult to get into: only Oxford and Cambridge have higher entry standards. Already half the students are postgraduates, and the accent on research has seen income from this source rise dramatically.

The school has the highest proportion of overseas students in the country, with the nationals of more than 100 countries taking up nearly half the places. Alumni are in influential positions all over the world, not forgetting Britain, where 30 sitting MPs are LSE graduates. The international character not only gives the LSE global prestige, but also an unusual degree of financial independence. Little more than a quarter of its income comes from the Higher Education Funding Council.

Areas of study range more broadly than the name suggests. Law, management and history are among the subjects top-rated for teaching, and there is even a small contingent of scientists. Economic history, economics, politics and social policy were all rated internationally outstanding in the last research assessments. Almost half the academics were in top-rated departments, the highest proportion outside Oxbridge.

Partying is not the prime attraction of the LSE for most applicants, who tend to be serious about their subject, but London's top nightspots are on the doorstep for those who can afford them. Despite the high proportion of UK students from independent schools, few can.

Accommodation

The School is able to offer accommodation, in either LSE or intercollegiate residences, to all first-year undergraduate degree students from outside the London area. The LSE currently has four halls of residence which can accommodate more than 2,000 students; private accommodation is pricey or requires a long journey.

Library and computing

The library has about 4 million separate items, including over 10,000 current journals. A high-speed network interconnects all of the School's computers, and 550 PCs are currently available in open-access rooms with internet and e-mail provided.

Student facilities

The students' union includes bars, shops, café, copy shop and advice centre. There are over 100 students' union societies – from drama to sport, politics to parties. A separate careers and welfare service is also available.

Sports

LSE's location puts it within walking distance of central London's attractions, but large sports grounds are not amongst them. On site at LSE there are squash and badminton courts and a new state-of-the-art gym. Its sports ground is 40 minutes away.

Overseas students

Overseas students receive a special booklet giving essential practical information about living and studying in London. The Language Centre runs English courses and the students' union provides advice services.

Queen Mary and Westfield College

Founded: 1882 Westfield, 1887 Queen Mary, merged 1989

Times ranking: 25 (1999 ranking: 28)

Address: Mile End Road, London E1 4NS

tel: 0207 975 5555/33

website: www.qmw.ac.uk

e-mail: admissions@qmw.ac.uk

Undergraduates: 6,671 (138)

Postgraduates: 1,333 (803)

Mature students: 17%

Overseas students: 12%

Applications/place: 6.5

Undergraduates from State sector: 76%

Main subject areas: arts; engineering; informatics and mathematical sciences; law; medicine; physical and biological sciences; social studies.

Teaching quality ratings

Rated Excellent 1993–95: English; geography with environmental studies.

From 1995: modern languages 23; molecular biosciences 22; drama, dance and cinematics 21; electrical and electronic engineering 21; mathematics and statistics 21; physics and astronomy 21; materials technology 20; general engineering 19.

Overview

More than £60 million has been spent developing London University's East End base into a broadly-based institution of 8,000 students. The modern setting is a far cry from the People's Palace, which first used the site to bring education to the Victorian masses, but the college retains a community programme as well as its conventional teaching and research.

The arts-based Westfield and scientific Queen Mary came together in 1989, but it took time to mould the new college and overcome financial difficulties. The sale of Westfield's Hampstead base released the necessary capital to modernise the Mile End campus with a series of building projects. The new Medical and Dental School, created from mergers with the London and St Bartholomew's teaching hospitals, is not far away, in Whitechapel.

Already London University's fourth largest college, QMW is expected to carry on growing. It is one of the federation's designated points of expansion in the sciences, and has been consistently successful in attracting overseas students, who now fill one place in eight and make full use of a unit specialising in English as a foreign language. Although by no means a household name, the college title, which led to talk of secession from the university in the mid-1990s, seems not to have held it back.

Teaching ratings have improved after a patchy start, which saw only two Excellent ratings out of the first eight subjects to be assessed. Modern languages have been the star performers with a near-perfect score. Russian, Slavonic and East European languages boast the only 5*rating for research, although English, geography, aeronautical engineering, Hispanic studies and law were all in the next category.

The majority of undergraduates take at least one course in departments other than their own, some arts students even migrating to a different campus. Most degree courses are organised in units to allow maximum flexibility. Interdisciplinary study has always been encouraged, recently through the combination of languages, the study of European institutions and a specialism in science or technology. The international theme is reinforced with a flourishing exchange programme, which includes universities in the United States and Japan, as well as Europe. Each student has an adviser to guide him or her through the possibilities.

Social life centres on the campus, although the West End is easily accessible by the Underground. Students welcome the relatively low prices (for the capital) in the East End, which has more to offer than many expect when they apply to QMW.

Accommodation

All first years are guaranteed one of 2,000 places in university accommodation. The college accommodation office can find private rented accommodation for students in flats, houses and self-catering rooms. Much of the private accommodation is in the East End, near the Mile End Campus.

Library and computing

The award-winning main library has over 600,000 titles and 2,000 periodicals. There are departmental IT facilities, with about 700 computer workstations in tota. All students receive an e-mail address and can do on-line searches for books in the library.

Student facilities

Entertainments range from e1, a state-of-the-art nightclub, to the Drapers Arms, the main bar. Also, 0181 holds regular theme nights. The Information and Student Support Centre offers free and independent advice on careers and part-time jobs.

Sport

The main sports facilities are housed in the students' union building, including a gym, squash courts and a sauna. There are also outdoor facilities such as sports fields, tennis courts, and watersports facilities. Students can also use London University's facilities.

Overseas students

An International Foundation Course is run the year before studying for a main degree, as well as 'English as a Foreign Language', a pre-sessional free course. All courses are taught by the English Language and Study Skills unit.

Royal Holloway University of London

Founded: 1849 Bedford College, 1886 Royal Holloway College, merged 1985

Times ranking: 24 (1999 ranking: 26th equal)

Address: University of London, Egham, Surrey TW20 0EX

tel: 01784 443883
website: www.rhbnc.ac.uk
e-mail: m.ross@rhbnc.ac.uk

Undergraduates: 4,634 (20)
Postgraduates: 678 (667)
Mature students: 13%
Overseas students: 16%
Applications/place: 6.4
Undergraduates from State sector: 69%

Main subject areas: biochemistry; biology; classics; computer science; drama; economics; electronics; geography; geology; history; management; mathematics; modern languages; music; physics; psychology; social policy; social science; theatre and media arts.

Teaching quality ratings

Rated Excellent 1993–95: geology; history.

From 1995: drama, dance and cinematics 23; physics 23; French 21; Italian 21; sociology 21; German 19.

Overview

London University's 'campus in the country' occupies 120 acres of woodland between Windsor Castle and Heathrow. Classic Victoriana mixes with less distinguished modern architecture. The 600-bed Founder's Building, modelled on a French chateau and opened by Victoria herself, is one of Britain's most remarkable university buildings. The merger with Bedford College, and the sale of Bedford's valuable site in Regent's Park, enabled Royal Holloway to embark on a £24 million building programme, which has since been extended. The earth sciences, life sciences, mathematics and computing, history and social policy have all benefited, and a well-appointed media arts centre and library building have also been added.

Both partners in the merger were originally for women only, their legacy producing an emphasis on the arts and a majority of female students. Music and drama were considered internationally outstanding in the last research assessments, when almost half of the academics entered for assessment were departments rated in the top two of seven categories. Drama, dance and theatre studies has also led the way in teaching assessments, although its near-perfect score has since been matched by physics, which should benefit from the university's decision to develop science subjects at Royal Holloway. The college already offers a science foundation year at further education colleges in the region, and the balance of disciplines is gradually shifting.

All 19 departments encourage interdisciplinary work, which is facilitated by a modular course structure with examinations at the end of every year. Semesters have been introduced, running from the end of September to April, with a five-week examinations terms to follow. an advanced skills programme, covering information technology, communication skills and foreign languages, further encourages breadth of study.

Like other parts of London University, Royal Holloway has experienced financial problems. The £11 million sale of a Turner seascape from Thomas Holloway's valuable art collection helped preserve the Founder's Building, but not without bitter controversy and a court action. Immediate expansion plans centre on distance learning.

The college has an upmarket reputation, with almost a third of its undergraduates recruited from independent schools. The rural location at Egham, Surrey, with only slow rail links to the capital, ensures that social life is concentrated on the recently extended students' union. But, with a high proportion of students coming from London and the Home Counties, the campus can seem empty at weekends.

Accommodation

All first-year students are guaranteed one of the 2,500 places in university accommodation, around 10 per cent of which is self-catering. The new halls are large and modern. Private accommodation is expensive, but available. The college accommodation office deals with private sector accommodation.

Library and computing

Students have 24-hour access to the university's computing facilities of over 500 workstations. The library holds over 500,000 books, and there are nearly 700 study spaces available.

Student facilities

The Students' Union facilities include five bars, two theatres, a shop and a coffee bar. There are club nights 4 or 5 times a week and the occasional live band. The Careers Service advises on part-time and temporary work.

Sport

Royal Holloway has been declared London's best sporting college, and existing facilities include a gym, sports hall, squash courts, and a floodlit football pitch. A five-year plan of improvements is currently underway.

Overseas students

The university has a high proportion of overseas students and has a long tradition of educating students from all parts of the world. The International Building, opened in 1998, forms the focus for overseas students.

School of Oriental and African Studies

Founded: 1916

Times ranking: 14 (1999 ranking: 6)

Address: Thornhaugh Street, Russell Square, London WC1H 0XG

tel: 0171 637 2388
website: www.soas.ac.uk
e-mail: registrar@soas.ac.uk

Undergraduates: 1,818 (27)
Postgraduates: 846 (769)
Mature students: 50%
Overseas students: 21%
Applications/place: 4.3
Undergraduates from State sector: 63%
Main subject areas: n/a

Teaching quality ratings

Rated Excellent 1993–95: n/a

From 1995: history of art 24; East and South Asian Studies 23; Middle Eastern and African Studies 22; linguistics 20.

Overview

As the major national centre for the study of Africa and Asia, SOAS has a global reputation in subjects relating to two-thirds of the world's population. Students come from over 90 countries, although more than 80 per cent of undergraduates are British. However, the school has a much wider portfolio of courses than its name would suggest, with 400 degree combinations on offer. Degrees are available in familiar subjects such as geography, history or the social sciences, but with a different emphasis from that of other universities.

Student recruitment is on the increase, especially among independent school candidates, who account for more than a third of the British undergraduates. The numbers taking first degrees increased significantly in the 1990s, and now the growth area is postgraduate courses, which will help to tackle a financial deficit, as SOAS faces the same hard times as many other British universities. Over 40 per cent of the students are postgraduates, many attracted by a research record which saw history and music rated internationally outstanding in the last assessments.

Teaching assessments have also been good, with a maximum score for history of art leading the way. Nearly all students take advantage of the unique opportunities for learning one of the wide range of languages on offer: 40 non-European languages are available. Almost two thirds of those graduating recently achieved firsts or upper-second class degrees. However, a drop-out rate of 17 per cent – higher than many of the new universities – takes the shine off the figures to some extent.

The school is located in Bloomsbury, with all departments and academic activities located on London University's central campus. The centrepiece is an airy, modern building with gallery space as well as teaching accommodation, a gift from the Sultan of Brunei. The West End and the university's main student facilities are both within easy reach. More than 1,000 students (mainly living abroad) are now taking distance-learning courses, which won a Queen's Anniversary Prize for innovation in higher education in 1996.

The ethnic and national mix has led to inevitable tensions at times, but SOAS is small enough for most students to know each other, at least by sight, and the normal atmosphere is friendly. Students tend to be highly committed – not surprising since many will return to positions of influence in developing countries.

Accommodation

The two halls of residence provide around half of the first-year students with university accommodation. The School also has an allocation of University of London places. The student accommodation adviser helps in finding rented accommodation.

Library and computing

The main library holds over 850,000 books and 4,500 journals, with departments having their own smaller libraries. More than 600 study places are provided, but only around 150 computer workstations.

Student facilities

The School has only one bar, but the assembly hall and the students' union building regularly play host to bands and have a club night once a week. The careers service provides information on temporary and part-time work.

Sport

The School does not have extensive sporting facilities, although there are squash courts and a gym. The School's sports ground is some distance away in Greenford. Students are able to make use of the University of London's excellent resources.

Overseas students

The English Language Unit provides support for overseas students, who make up almost a quarter of the university's student population. Foundation and bridging courses are also run. All students are allocated a personal tutor.

University College London

Founded: 1826

Times ranking: 5 (1999 ranking: 5)

Address: University of London, Gower Street, London WC1E 6BT

tel: 0207 679 3000

website: www.ucl.ac.uk

e-mail: degree-info@ucl.ac.uk

Undergraduates: 9,567 (374)

Postgraduates: 4,089 (2,955)

Mature students: 15%

Overseas students: 16%

Applications/place: 9.5

Undergraduates from State sector: 58%

Main subject areas: full range of disciplines in seven faculties; arts, social and historical sciences; built environment; clinical sciences and medicine; engineering; law; life sciences; mathematical and physical sciences.

Teaching quality ratings

Rated Excellent 1993–95: anthropology; architecture; English; geography; geology; history; law.

From 1995: history of art 24; organismal biosciences 24; dentistry 23; German 23; Scandinavian 23; Dutch 22; electrical and electronic engineering 22; linguistics 22; molecular biosciences 22; psychology 22; French; 21; chemical engineering 20; Italian 20; civil engineering 19; Iberian languages 19; medicine 18.

Overview

Such is the breadth and quality of UCL's provision that it can fairly describe itself not only as a 'university within a university' but also as one of the top three multi-faculty institutions in England. Its position in *The Times* rankings has regularly confirmed this, while a recent analysis of research funding, which allowed for subject differences, also showed only Oxford and Cambridge in better positions. The college's excellence is built on a history of pioneering subjects that have become commonplace in higher education: modern languages, geography and fine arts among them.

Already comfortably the largest of London University's colleges, UCL's incorporation of the School of Slavonic and East European Studies has added to the 70 departments. In recent years, the Slade School of Fine Art and the Institutes of Archaeology, Child Health, Neurology and Ophthalmology have all joined the fold. Medicine started the merger trend, with the Middlesex Hospital joining forces with UCL in 1992. The more recent additions of the Royal Free Hospital Medical School and the Eastman Dental Hospital have created a large and formidable unit, although its teaching assessment was a disappointment. The acquisitions mean that the college now has outposts in several parts of central and north London, but the main activity remains centred on the original impressive Bloomsbury site.

Anatomy, archaeology, several branches of engineering, modern languages and pharmacology are among the areas rated internationally outstanding for research.

One academic in five was in a top-rated department in the last assessments, with two-thirds in the top two categories. History of art and organismal biosciences have recorded maximum points for teaching, but most subjects have scored well. A growing number of degrees take four years, and most are organised on a modular basis.

Almost a third of UCL's students are foreign, 4,700 in all, including more than 1,000 from other EU countries, reflecting the college's high standing overseas. Several departments offer first-year students, whether from Britain or elsewhere, peer tutoring by more experienced colleagues to help them adapt to degree study. The college stresses its commitment to teaching in small groups, especially in the second and subsequent years of degree courses.

Conscious of its traditions as a college founded to expand access to higher education, UCL is more socially diverse than its reputation as an Oxbridge alternative might suggest. The academic pace can be frantic but, as UCL is close to the West End and with immediate access to London University's under-used student facilities, there is no shortage of leisure options.

Accommodation

The College undertakes to house all single full-time undergraduates in their first year. The University of London accommodation office helps students find housing in subsequent years. UCL students' union gives guidance on how to find private housing.

Library and computing

UCL's library comprises more than 1.5 million books. The Library's catalogue and bibliographic material on CD-ROM are available via the network. Computers (PCs, Macs and Unix computers) and laser printers are available for students on campus and in student residences.

Student facilities

UCL union has more than 100 societies, runs a training programme, and organises voluntary work. UCL has its own theatre, magazine and TV station. Careers service facilities include an information bank on careers, employers, graduate programmes and vacation work.

Sport

The union supports clubs for major sports. Main facilities are sports grounds at Shenley and Chislehurst, Bloomsbury Fitness Centre and Somers Town Sports Centre, which specialise in team sports and fitness programmes.

Overseas students

The international office organises a free four-day orientation programme. There is an overseas students' officer. Students can improve their English in the Language Centre.

London Guildhall University

Founded: University status 1992, formerly City of London Polytechnic, City of London College founded 1848

Times ranking: 95 (1999 ranking: 95)

Address: 31 Jewry Street, London EC3N 2EY

tel: 0207 320 1000
website: www.lgu.ac.uk
e-mail: enqs@lgu.ac.uk

Undergraduates: 7,492 (2,880)
Postgraduates: 411 (1,477)
Mature students: 48%
Overseas students: 14%
Applications/place: 4.4
Undergraduates from State sector: 88%

Main subject areas for degrees and diplomas: arts design and manufacture; business; human sciences.

Teaching quality ratings

Rated Excellent 1993–95: social policy.

From 1995: art and design 23; materials technology 20; modern languages 19; media studies 17; sociology 17.

Overview

Spilling over from the Square Mile into the East End of London, the former polytechnic's academic interests reflect the stark contrasts in its location. City traditions are maintained in a wide range of business-related courses, while a variety of craft subjects cater for the neighbouring community. Guildhall traces its origins back 150 years to the Metropolitan Evening Classes for Young People, and still boasts the highest proportion of students taking further education courses of any university in the country.

More than half of the students are on business courses, many coming from City firms to join part-time degrees or professional courses. The faculty is one of the largest in Britain, taking advantage of its position in the use of guest lecturers from the City to supplement almost 300 full and part-time staff. Although not on the same scale, the silversmithing and jewellery courses are the largest in Britain, while those in furniture restoration and conservation were the first of their kind in Europe. Following the vocational theme that runs through all its courses, the university even offers ground training for civil aviation pilots.

An imaginative twin-track system allows entrants who know what they want to study to enrol on 'early specialist' degrees while others embark on the modular course programme, postponing the choice of single or combined honours until the end of the first year. There is a regular flow of students into the university at this stage, thanks to a well-established credit transfer scheme. At times, however, some subjects have struggled to meet their recruitment targets, and quality assessments have been patchy, accounting for Guildhall's low position in *The Times* League Table. Art and design achieved a near-perfect teaching score, but only social policy was rated Excellent among the early assessments. History scored well in the last research rankings, but other subjects finished in the bottom three categories even though little more than a third of the academics were entered for assessment.

The university is finally overcoming teaching accommodation problems that surfaced in its polytechnic days, as leases on key buildings came to an end. Spread over seven main sites, students have often complained that buildings were crowded and in poor condition. A £3.5 million refurbishment programme has helped, and new purchases are beginning to bring the university together around the Aldgate area. Recent acquisitions have included the Fawcett collection of books on the women's movement, which will form the basis of a National Library of Women.

Accommodation

Although the university cannot guarantee places, there are three halls of residence housing over 450 students, all within a three-mile radius of the university and very easily accessible by bus or Underground. The university has a large register of landlords and a number of contacts with various sources of accommodation in the private sector.

Library and computing

There are three main libraries holding a range of items including books, journals, directories, slides and video cassettes, plus the usual reference materials and CD-ROMs. Online databases, e-mail and internet facilities are available via a network of PCs.

Student facilities

The main students' union houses a venue bar (for all the entertainments), a 'Sub Bar', a diner and welfare offices. The university has three shops, in Central House, Calcutta House and Moorgate, plus a bar in Commercial Road.

Sports

Facilities include a gymnasium, an activities room and a fitness and weights room. Many activities are available on site including aerobics and yoga classes, whilst the university has special arrangements with nearby sports centres for other activities.

Overseas students

The university has secured limited accommodation in Attlee House, close to the university, specifically for ERASMUS students studying for one semester. A separate overseas student welfare office provides advice.

Loughborough University

Founded: 1909, Royal charter 1966

Times ranking: 21 (1999 ranking: 26th equal)

Address: Ashby Road, Loughborough, Leicestershire LE11 3TU

tel: 01509 263171
website: www.lboro.ac.uk
e-mail: prospectus-enquiries@lboro.ac.uk

Undergraduates: 7,973 (107)
Postgraduates: 1,281 (1,768)
Mature students: 6%
Overseas students: 7%
Applications/place: 6.9
Undergraduates from State sector: 80%

Main subject areas: education and humanities; engineering; science; social sciences and humanities.

Teaching quality ratings

Rated Excellent 1993–95: business and management.

From 1995: anatomy and physiology 24; drama 23; mechanical engineering 23; physics 23; sociology 23; chemical engineering 22; civil engineering 22; electronic and electrical engineering 22; materials technology 21.

Overview

Best known for its successes on the sports field, Loughborough has enhanced its academic reputation recently, consistently finishing well up *The Times* rankings and rivalling Oxbridge in its teaching ratings. Nor are the good results confined to the technological subjects which used to be the university's *raison d'être*: sociology and drama both registered 23 points out of 24 for teaching quality. The news is filtering through to schools and colleges: there were an extra 1,000 candidates despite the introduction of tuition fees in 1998.

Loughborough has abandoned its technological title and merged with the neighbouring colleges of education and art and design, but it is now trying to tilt the balance further towards the sciences. Engineering remains by far the biggest subject area, with more than 2,500 students. Aeronautical and automotive engineering are particularly strong, but all branches have fared well in teaching assessments. A £14 million integrated engineering complex is due to open in 2000, freeing space for a new information and learning resource centre.

The university has been pursuing modest growth since ruling out the possibility of a merger with Leicester University. The 216-acre campus offers plenty of scope, despite an active construction programme which has included a large students' union extension and a new business school, as well as additions to the extensive residential stock. The incorporation of the two Loughborough colleges has extended the scope of the university and made the student population a little less male-dominated. Social activity is concentrated on the campus, although Leicester and Nottingham are within easy reach. The town of Loughborough is only a mile away, but is hardly a student mecca.

Most subjects are available either as three-year full-time or four-year sandwich courses. The popular sandwich option, with a year in industry, has helped to give graduates an outstanding employment record. Loughborough prides itself on a close relationship with industry, which attracted one of the university's two Queen's Anniversary Prizes. The maximum score for human sciences remains the best teaching assessment. No subject reached the top rung of the research assessment ladder, but almost a quarter of the academics entered for assessment were in the next category.

For all its academic progress, sportsmen and women still set the tone of student life. Loughborough remains pre-eminent in British university sport, both in terms of facilities and performance. Representative teams have a record second to none, and the programme of sports scholarships is the largest in the university system.

Accommodation

A high proportion of undergraduates live in the 5,000 places in halls of residence on or adjacent to the campus – and most undergraduates can look forward to university accommodation for at least two years, if they so wish. The university-run property management service manages over 170 properties for private owners and advertises over 3,000 bedspaces for private renting.

Library and computing

The university has two libraries, with a total stock of 530,000 items and 530 study places. Computing services provide over 300 networked PCs as well as UNIX and Apple Macintosh labs. Full internet e-mail access is available to all students.

Student facilities

The students' union is the largest music and dance venue in Leicestershire. Each week there are regular entertainments including live comedy from the London circuit. In addition there are 152 clubs and societies.

Sports

Loughborough is part of the Sport England Regional Institute network, and its superb facilities reflect this status. Sixty-five competitions are held covering about 37 different activities, from cross-country – where participants are counted in hundreds – to full leagues in rugby football.

Overseas students

The university provides full-time intensive, residential courses for overseas students to improve their English and study skills.

University of Luton

Founded: University status 1993, formerly Luton College of Higher Education
Times ranking: 83 (1999 ranking: 93)

Address: Luton, Beds LU1 3JU

tel:01582 489262
website: www.luton.ac.uk
e-mail: admissions@luton.ac.uk

Undergraduates: 8,411 (3,691)
Postgraduates: 338 (651)
Mature students: 34%
Overseas students: 17%
Applications/place: 5.8
Undergraduates from State sector: 93%

Main subject areas: applied sciences; business; design and technology; health care and social studies; humanities.
Diplomas are offered as well as degrees.

Teaching quality ratings

Rated Excellent 1993–95: none.

From 1995: health subjects 23; anatomy and physiology 22; media studies 22; building 22; linguistics 21; electronic engineering 20; modern languages 20; sociology 18.

Overview

Luton is finding its feet as a university, with consistently good teaching ratings, after a shaky start. Never a polytechnic, it had to break all records for expansion to meet the criteria for promotion a year after the other new universities were created. The dash was worth it because tough obstacles have since been placed in the way of other ambitious colleges, but the strains showed in the more exalted company the institution was keeping. None of the first dozen departments to be assessed for teaching quality was considered excellent, and almost all subjects were placed in the bottom two categories in the 1996 research rankings.

Times have changed, however, and Luton is indignant that it is so often the butt of jokes about low standards in higher education. Multimillion pound developments have transformed the main campus, and in recent teaching assessments the university is averaging 21 points out of 24 – better than many traditional universities. Graduate employment rates have improved and applied research in areas such as tourism and environmental management is winning wider recognition. Health subjects have produced the best score for teaching quality, but building also did well.

Although there are outposts in Bedford, Dunstable and Northampton, most departments are on two sites in Luton town centre. The main Park Square campus, which has seen the addition of an impressive learning resources centre, languages centre and extensive residential accommodation in recent years, is in the midst of the shopping area. The second site, for humanities, is ten minutes' walk away and there is an attractive management centre at Putteridge Bury, a neo-Elizabethan mansion three miles outside Luton. All are subject to the university's rigid no-smoking rule.

Luton's commitment to open access is reflected in a high proportion of mature students, many of whom take access courses to bring them up to degree or diploma standard, while many of the school-leavers arrive through the Clearing system. The mix is a classic recipe for a high drop-out rate: the funding council's estimate of 26 per cent non-completion was only marginally more than the expectation for its intake.

Luton is not a town that will draw many applicants for its social scene, although it has its share of pubs, clubs and restaurants. Students tend to rely on hall or union facilities, and London is only half an hour away by train.

Accommodation

The university has built new residential accommodation as well as sub-letting property to students to ensure reasonable standards. Around 1,500 new residential places have been built, and all first years can be accommodated.

Library and computing

Traditional library and audio-visual facilities are complemented at Luton by state-of-the-art electronic systems. In addition to the usual library functions, periodicals and CD-ROM databases are available via the computer network. Full internet and e-mail access is available.

Student facilities

The students' union includes facilities such as a bar, nightclub and coffee shop. The May Ball is the biggest student ball in the country and attracts 6,000 students.

Sports

Membership of the sports association gives access to the facilities on the main campus and at the Luton Regional Sports Centre.

Overseas students

There is a dedicated international office which deals with all overseas student affairs. The university offers full-time and part-time evening English courses and study skill sessions.

University of Manchester

Founded: 1851, Royal charter 1903
Times ranking: 18 (1999 ranking: 20)

Address: Oxford Road, Manchester M13 9PL
tel: 0161 275 2077
website: www.man.ac.uk
e-mail: ug.prospectus@man.ac.uk

Undergraduates: 16,182 (2,100)
Postgraduates: 3,204 (2,843)
Mature students: 10%
Overseas students: 8%
Applications/place: 8.0
Undergraduates from State sector: 70%

Main subject areas: full range of degree courses in 10 faculties: arts; biological sciences; business, administration; dentistry; economics; education; law; medicine; science; theology.

Teaching quality ratings

Rated Excellent 1993–95: anthropology; business; chemistry; computer science; geography; geology; law; mechanical engineering; music; social policy.

From 1995: physics and astronomy 24; anatomy and physiology 23; mathematics and statistics 22; psychology 22; drama, dance and cinematics 21; German 21; history of art 21; linguistics 21; material science 21; sociology 21; aerospace engineering 20; electrical and electronic engineering 20; Iberian languages 20; Middle Eastern and African studies 20; town planning 20; French 19; Italian 19; civil engineering 18; Russian 16.

Overview

Always among the giants of British higher education, with 20 Nobel prize-winners to its credit, Manchester has been emerging from a difficult period which included a lengthy spell without a permanent vice-chancellor. It attracts more applications than any other university, and in other times might have expected to be even higher in *The Times* rankings, but a string of good teaching assessments have contributed to a renewed sense of vibrancy.

Improved research scores had already begun to restore the university's financial fortunes, although again Manchester might have hoped for better in the last assessments. Although a third of the academics in the exercise reached one of the top two categories, only the relatively small areas of accountancy, metallurgy and theology were considered internationally outstanding. However, the school of biological sciences won a Queen's Anniversary Prize for innovation, while anatomy and physiology recorded a near-perfect teaching score. The university is upgrading the facilities for chemistry and biosciences.

Manchester remains the model of a traditional university – it was here that the computer was invented and Rutherford began the work that led to the splitting of the atom. There is a roughly equal balance between arts and sciences, with school-leavers filling most of the undergraduate places, but more than 3,000 postgraduates underline the emphasis on research. Graduate schools have been introduced to cater more efficiently for their needs, while a modular system has been introduced for first degrees. The many exceptional academic facilities include the Jodrell Bank Science Centre, in Cheshire, with its internationally famous radio telescope.

Perhaps unwisely, the Victoria University, as Mancunians always refer to it, chose not to expand as rapidly as many others in the early 1990s, but student numbers have been creeping up recently. The city's famed youth culture and the university's position at the heart of a huge student precinct both help to ensure keen competition for places – and hence high entry standards in most subjects. Manchester's three university institutions are all close to one another on sites close to the city centre, and many facilities are shared.

Parents often worry about the city's reputation for violent crime, especially since many students live in some of the worst-affected areas. The dangers may be overstated, but the students' union runs late-night minibuses, self-defence classes, and regular safety campaigns. Students tend to be fiercely loyal both to the university and their adopted city.

Accommodation

First-year undergraduates are guaranteed a place in a university residence. University residences include catered, self-catering, and university-leased houses. Second and third-year students usually stay in privately rented accommodation which is easily available.

Library and computing

The library, the third largest university library in the UK, holds 3,600,000 printed books and more than one million manuscript or archival items. The University has more than 6,000 PCs and students are provided with e-mail and internet access.

Student facilities

The union facilities include four bars, a basement café and a large coffee and snack bar, travel agency, a hairdressers, banks, stationers, shop and two live music venues. There are over 150 societies and extra tutoring for students is available.

Sports

Indoor facilities include sports halls for basketball, volleyball and netball; four squash courts; a rifle range; climbing wall; a sauna and a swimming pool. Outdoor facilities include several grass pitches, tennis courts, cricket pitch and two floodlit artificial turf pitches.

Overseas students

The university provides an orientation day upon arrival, and also a full week orientation course which includes various activities such as a series of talks, informal discussions and practical information. There is an International Society and a separate overseas students' office.

University of Manchester Institute of Science and Technology...

Founded: Founded 1824, part of Manchester University 1905-93

Times ranking: 28 (1999 ranking: 24th equal)

Address: P O Box 88, Manchester M60 1QD

tel: 0161 220 4033/34
website: www.umist.ac.uk
e-mail: ug.admissions@umist.ac.uk

Undergraduates: 4,970 (0)
Postgraduates: 1,820 (259)
Mature students: 9%
Overseas students: 24%
Applications/place: 7.2
Undergraduates from State sector: 79%

Main subject areas: biological and physical sciences; business; engineering and technology; mathematics and computation; social sciences and languages.

Teaching quality ratings

Rated Excellent 1993–95: business and management.

From 1995: chemical engineering 22; civil engineering 22; electrical and electronic engineering 22; materials technology (with Manchester) 21; physics and astronomy 21; building 20; materials technology 20; modern languages 18; molecular biosciences 18.

Overview

UMIST has been fully independent of Manchester University since 1993, although it still shares services such as student accommodation, careers advice and sports facilities with its parent body. Primarily a research institute concentrating on management and languages, as well as science and technology, it has a high reputation among academics and employers alike. It is the only university to have won a Queen's Anniversary Prize for innovation in each of the three years of the scheme, the latest for engineering.

The Institute has forged its own identity since going it alone, but remains involved in a number of joint academic projects. It is a full partner in the Manchester Federal School of Business and Management, for example, despite offering its own highly-rated courses in the area. Indeed, UMIST tops *The Times* undergraduate business ranking with top scores for both teaching and research. A purpose-built management school costing £8 million opened in 1998.

Much of the development planned over the next few years is designed to strengthen an already healthy research base. More than a quarter of the students are postgraduates and almost half of the academics in the last assessments reached one of the top two categories and none was outside the top four. Materials and corrosion science, as well as management, were rated as world-beaters. Teaching ratings have also been good, especially in engineering.

Undergraduate developments are focusing on combining science or technology with a modern language or environmental study. Entry qualifications have remained high throughout UMIST's recent period of expansion: an average close to three Bs at A level is a tall order when many of subjects offered are experiencing a national shortage of well-qualified candidates. The Institute's popularity is due in part to the consistently excellent employment record of its graduates, with several surveys of employers placing it among their favourite recruiting grounds. Students have access to an unrivalled network of industrial sponsorship.

Sited close to the city centre and Manchester's other universities, UMIST's Victorian art nouveau headquarters is now surrounded by modern academic buildings. The Institute's technological bias helps to produce a more socially diverse student population than at most leading universities: a quarter of the undergraduates come from working-class homes. The social scene is bound up with the other universities and the city's broader youth culture, although UMIST has plenty of facilities of its own.

Accommodation

UMIST guarantees accommodation in university halls for all new single undergraduate students. The Institute has a number of self-catering and catered halls, and leases good quality private housing directly to groups of students or student families.

Library and computing

Students have access to Europe's largest computer centre and a library that is the most high-tech in Britain, with a third of the 600 study spaces having computer facilities. UMIST has 17 computer clusters.

Student facilities

The students' association facilities include bars, a copyshop, student advice centre, computer shop, clubs and a range of societies. UMIST careers service offers information on careers, jobs, employers and further study. It holds workshops and plays host to graduate fairs.

Sport

Indoor sports facilities include tennis, volleyball and squash courts, cricket bays, an aerobic fitness suite and free weights area. Outdoors there are basketball, football and netball courts and playing fields.

Overseas students

UMIST has an international office, and the International Society arranges a welcome scheme during September. The English Language Teaching Centre provides part-time and full-time courses before and during the academic year.

Manchester Metropolitan University

Founded: University status 1992, formerly Manchester Polytechnic

Times ranking: 69the equal (1999 ranking: 71st equal)

Address: All Saints Building, Oxford Road, Manchester M15 6BH

tel: 0161 247 1035/6/7/8
website: www.mmu.ac.uk
e-mail: prospectus@mmu.ac.uk

Undergraduates: 18,359 (5,040)
Postgraduates: 1,740 (3,427)
Mature students: 30%
Overseas students: 6%
Applications/place: 5.9
Undergraduates from State sector: 88%

Main subject areas: art and design; community studies and education; clothing design and technology; hotel catering, and tourism management; humanities; law management and business; science and engineering; social sciences.
Certificates and diplomas offered as well as degrees.

Teaching quality ratings

Rated Excellent 1993–95: mechanical engineering.

From 1995: drama 23; health subjects 22; history of art 22; materials technology 22; electrical and electronic engineering 21; modern languages 21; sociology 21; town planning 20, food sciences 19.

Overview

The largest conventional higher education institution in Britain, only the Open University and two federations in London and Wales can match Manchester Metropolitan's 30,000 students, including part-timers. Former polytechnic commitments to extending access are being continued: even among the full-time undergraduates, 30 per cent are over 21 on entry and almost a third are from working-class homes. The 400 courses at degree level cover more than 70 subjects, while the seven campuses stretch from the centre of Manchester to Crewe and Alsager, 40 miles to the south.

There is quality as well as quantity, however. The university features in *The Times* top 20 for metallurgy, food science and drama, the last of which achieved a near-perfect score in its teaching quality assessment. Only mechanical engineering was rated as excellent in the first rounds of assessment, but recent scores have improved and the university has a high reputation in other areas such as retail marketing. The university takes teaching seriously: small groups are used whenever possible and staff are encouraged to take a three-year MA in teaching, which has been running since 1992.

Education courses also came well out of the Teacher Training Agency's 1999 performance indicators, finishing in the top ten for primary training. Some 800 trainees are at the former Crewe and Alsager College campuses, while the remainder are based at Didsbury, with those taking community studies, five miles out of Manchester. A new Institute of Education covers both centres.

The remaining subjects are based in Manchester itself, mainly at the extensive All Saints campus, close to the city centre and the other universities. Sports science achieved the best research rating in the last assessments, when the overall performance was better than in most of the new universities. Overseas links have expanded rapidly in recent years, offering exchange opportunities in Europe and farther afield, as well as establishing teaching bases abroad.

One student in three comes from the Manchester area, easing the pressure on accommodation in a city of 100,000 students. There is a long-standing reputation for partying, the city's attractions doing no harm to recruitment levels, but much depends on where the course is based. Didsbury may offer the best of both worlds, with swift access to the city centre and a peaceful environment, but students at Crewe and Alsager can feel isolated. Some potential applicants are daunted by the sheer size of the university, but individual courses and sites usually provide a social circle.

Accommodation

While the university doesn't guarantee a place in halls, last year 95 per cent of first years were given preference. After the first year most students live in private housing, which is easy to find. Manchester Student Homes provide information, advice and lists of private accommodation around the city.

Library and computing

There are 3,000 student workstations, with full internet and e-mail access available (even from residence halls). Manchester Metropolitan has seven departmental libraries, and access to the other Manchester universities' libraries is available for all students.

Student facilities

Manchester Metropolitan has a busy and active students' union, with activities including DJ nights, discos, shops and student services such as welfare support, accommodation advice and financial advice. There are over 70 different clubs and an award-winning student magazine, *Pulp*.

Sports

Spread over four sites, sports facilities include over 30 acres of sports fields, a new swimming pool, courts for tennis, badminton and squash, five-a-side football, floodlit synthetic pitches, gymnasiums and fitness centres.

Overseas students

Prior to the start of the academic year Manchester Metropolitan offer a three-day residential orientation course for all overseas students to help them adjust to life in the UK. An overseas students' handbook is produced giving advice and help.

Middlesex University

Founded: University status 1992, formerly Middlesex Polytechnic

Times ranking: 82 (1999 ranking: 85)

Address: White Hart Lane, Tottenham, London N17 8HR

tel: 0208 362 5898
website: www.mdx.ac.uk
e-mail: admissions@mdx.ac.uk

Undergraduates: 15,840 (1,730)
Postgraduates: 975 (2,125)
Mature students: 45%
Overseas students: 17%
Applications/place: 5.8
Undergraduates from State sector: 91%

Main subject areas: art and design; business studies and management; education and performing arts; health, biological and environmental science studies; humanities; mathematics; science; social science. Certificate and diploma courses also offered

Teaching quality ratings

Rated Excellent 1993–95: none.

From 1995: American studies 22; drama, dance and cinematics 22; history of art 22; art and design 21; electrical and electronic engineering 19; modern languages 19; sociology 19.

Overview

Middlesex has been reassessing its priorities after being penalised for failing to meet recruitment targets in some areas. It now has a mission statement, a vision statement and 15 long-term strategic objectives. The immediate outcome has been a reorganisation of schools, in which the university has largely admitted defeat on engineering, and will focus instead on its strengths in business and the arts. The school of engineering systems closes in July 2000, but the popular product design courses will continue.

Other areas of the university will maintain the successful mixture of community and international involvement. There are more than 20,000 students, including part-timers, and a growing network of partner colleges at home and abroad. Half of the full-timers come from London, but over one in six is from overseas. The university's long-standing commitment to Europe sees more than 2,000 students coming from the Continent and a healthy flow of British students taking advantage of the exchange programmes. All undergraduates are encouraged to take a language option as part of their modular degrees.

The highly flexible course system allows students to start many courses in February if they prefer not to wait until autumn, and offers the option of an extra five-week session in July and August to try out new subjects or add to their credits. Although Middlesex was famous at one time for having the largest philosophy department in the country, 90 per cent of undergraduates take vocational courses, many at postgraduate or sub-degree level. Business is the biggest subject area, but almost a quarter of the students are on multidisciplinary programmes. Nearly half are over 21 on entry.

Student numbers doubled in five years, stretching resources to such an extent that a teaching campus in Tottenham had to be reopened. The university lists six 'main campuses' dotted around London's North Circular Road, but smaller sites practically double that total. Locations include a picturesque country estate at Trent Park, an innovative warehouse conversion, and a house in Hampstead that was once home to the ballerina Anna Pavlova. There is also an outpost in Bedford specialising in dance. Many students have to travel between sites for lectures and seminars.

Teaching scores have improved considerably after an unspectacular start. Middlesex has won two Queen's Anniversary Prizes for innovation, and the 43 per cent of academics entered for the last research assessment exercise was among the highest in the new universities. Art and design was judged to be nationally excellent.

Accommodation

The university currently has 2,400 rooms spread over 13 separate halls of residence. Some halls are traditional in style, while others are like flats, with a number of study-bedrooms grouped around a dining kitchen. All halls are self-catering and there are refectories at each major campus. Private accommodation is relatively pricey.

Library and computing

The library collections contain over half a million books and journals, including 3,000 current journal titles, 16,000 video recordings and several hundred CD-ROMs. The university has a network of PCs and Macintoshes all with full internet and e-mail access.

Student facilities

The students' union has a variety of facilities and entertainment, with four main bars and venues hosting regular comedy nights, live bands and weekly club nights. Services include student welfare, health, rights and a dedicated student Jobshop.

Sports

There are different facilities on each campus, with almost all sports catered for, from Frisbee to football and table tennis to Tae-Kwon-Do. There are sports halls, fitness rooms, saunas, a climbing wall, a swimming pool and a sports dome.

Overseas students

A special effort is made to help overseas students adjust, including airport pick-ups and the 'Introducing Britain' orientation course, which provides advice on living and studying in the UK. Overseas students staying more than one year are offered university accommodation.

Napier University

Founded: University status 1992, formerly Napier Polytechnic of Edinburgh

Times ranking: 73rd equal (1999 ranking: 56)

Address: 219 Colinton Road, Edinburgh EH14 1DJ

tel: 0131 455 4269
website: www.napier.ac.uk
e-mail: info@napier.ac.uk

Undergraduates: 7,808 (1,509)
Postgraduates: 684 (624)
Mature students: 29%
Overseas students: 7%
Applications/place: 4.9
Undergraduates from State sector: 86%

Main subject areas: accountancy; biology; business studies; chemistry; civil, mechanical, electrical and electronic engineering; communication studies; computing; design; economics; film and television; health studies; hotel and catering management; information technology; languages; law; mathematics; physics; surveying.
A number of diploma courses also offered.

Teaching quality ratings

Rated Excellent 1993–97: none.

Highly Satisfactory 1993–97: building; cellular biology; chemistry; civil engineering; hospitality studies; mass communications; mathematics; organismal biology; statistics.

From 1998: European languages 19.

Overview

Napier was Scotland's first and largest polytechnic. Now a university of 11,000 students, of whom 2,000 are part-timers, it was among the leading new universities in *The Times* League Table last year. However, the inclusion of completion rates has brought that progress to a halt. The funding councils' first performance indicators, published in 1999, showed one in three undergraduates dropping out – the second worst rate in Britain and the worst when intakes were taken into account. Fewer than one in five 'should' have dropped out if Napier's students followed national trends for their subjects. The institution claims that future years will see an improvement, but the figures are a setback in its quest to be a 'world-class modern university'.

Two new libraries, a purpose-built music centre and a £2.5 million refurbishment of the science laboratories have shown Napier's seriousness, while the newest of the campuses, at Craighouse, in the south of Edinburgh, is well-appointed. The incorporation of Lothian College of Health Studies and the Scottish Borders College of Nursing gave the university the largest nursing and midwifery facility north of the border. Yet Napier failed to register a single excellent rating before the Scottish system of assessing teaching quality was altered in 1998, despite a string of 'highly satisfactory' grades.

The university has its roots as a college of science and technology, which merged with a college of commerce, and these subjects remain the biggest recruiters. The business school is the largest in Scotland. Most of the avowedly vocational courses include a work placement, and the close relationship with industry and commerce helps to produce consistently good graduate employment figures. The modular course system covers independent study and allows movement between courses at all levels. It has also allowed Napier to introduce the option of starting courses in February rather than September.

The university is named after John Napier, the inventor of logarithms. The tower where he was born still sits among the concrete blocks of the Merchiston site, in the student district of Edinburgh. The other main sites are nearby Craiglockart, a one-time military hospital, and Sighthill, a 1960s development in the west of the city. A regular university bus service links the four main sites, but there are several more teaching outposts where lectures may be scheduled. The dispersed nature of the university does nothing for the social scene. Despite improvements, some students find life too quiet in the evenings and at weekends.

Accommodation

Places in the seven halls of residence and in other university accommodation are allocated by the accommodation officer from May onwards each academic year, but the university cannot guarantee first years a place in an university-owned accommodation. Many people live in privately rented housing.

Library and computing

The university has a network of PCs and Macintoshes, with approximately 3,000 connections throughout the 13 campuses. Full internet and e-mail access is provided, and there are Learning Resource centres on the main campuses.

Student facilities

The union's facilities include bars at four campuses, shops, clubs, societies and a student newspaper. Much emphasis is placed on student welfare, and advice is given for topics such as fees, benefits, childcare, rights and tuition fees.

Sports

The main sports hall at the Sighthill campus is used for basketball, volleyball, netball, tennis, badminton, indoor hockey and football. There are also squash courts, climbing wall, weights and fitness area, fencing piste, table tennis and golf practice area. There is a swimming pool at Craiglockhart.

Overseas students

An Overseas Welcome Pack is provided to all overseas students, as well as free English language classes for the duration of a course of study. A collection service from Edinburgh airport, train or bus station also operates for new arrivals.

University of Newcastle upon Tyne

Founded: 1834 (as part of Durham University), Royal charter 1963

Times ranking: 17 (1999 ranking: 19)

Address: Kensington Terrace, Newcastle upon Tyne NE1 7RU

tel: 0191 222 6138/8672
website: www.ncl.ac.uk
e-mail: admissions-enquiries@ncl.ac.uk

Undergraduates: 10,063 (2,633)
Postgraduates: 1,968 (1,714)
Mature students: 7%
Overseas students: 8%
Applications/place: 7.6
Undergraduates from State sector: 66%

Main subject areas: wide range of disciplines in eight faculties; agriculture; arts; education; engineering; law; medicine; science; social and environmental science.

Teaching quality ratings

Rated Excellent 1993–95: architecture; English; geology; social policy.

From 1995: anatomy and physiology 24; medicine 24; dentistry 23; agriculture 22; linguistics 22; organismal biosciences 22; modern languages 22; chemical engineering 21; electrical and electronic engineering 21; town planning 21; civil engineering 20; materials technology 20.

Overview

A string of outstanding teaching assessments has ensured that there is still little separating Newcastle from its parent university of Durham as the leading university in the northeast of England in *The Times* League Table. Originally a medical school, its excellence in that area has been confirmed by maximum scores for physiology and medicine, and a near miss for dentistry. With 2,600 students, the medical school is also one of the largest in the country and second only in size to engineering and technology within the university.

Buoyed by the popularity of the city among young people, the university grew dramatically in the 1990s, but numbers have been reined back recently. As well as the normal range of subjects for a traditional university, Newcastle has a number of unusual features, such as a fine art degree which attracts up to 15 applicants for each place. It also has a longstanding reputation for agriculture, which recorded good scores for both teaching and research with the benefit of two farms in Northumberland. Civil engineering was the only starred department in a generally disappointing set of research grades, but computing, education, earth sciences, geography, law and physiology were also considered nationally outstanding. A growing proportion of the undergraduates – one in five at the last count – take dual or combined honours degrees.

The campus is spacious and varied, occupying 45 acres close to the main shopping area, civic centre, Northumbria University and Newcastle United's ground, which is overlooked by one of the halls of residence. Half the buildings date from the 1960s onwards. The university also boasts a theatre, an art gallery and three museums.

Although not on the same scale as Durham's intake, Newcastle has become a particular favourite with independent schools, whose applicants now take a third of the places. The funding councils' first official performance indicators also revealed a healthy 92 per cent completion rate – better than anticipated, given the subject mix. One student in five is a postgraduate.

Few students regret choosing Newcastle for a degree, even if the growing number of southerners can find the winter temperatures a shock. The city's nightlife is legendary – eighth best in the world, according to one survey – and the university topped a student poll based on computing facilities and student services, as well as the social scene. The cost of living is reasonable and town–gown relations better than in many cities.

Accommodation

All first-year students are guaranteed university accommodation, offered as a mix of catered and self-catering blocks. The accommodation office advises on university and private accommodation and there is an accreditation scheme in operation for private residences run between the LEA and the university. Finding private rented accommodation in Newcastle is relatively easy.

Library and computing

The library service at Newcastle comprises three libraries, with over one million books and 5,500 journals. The main Robinson Library has seating for 2,000 people. There are over 1,000 PCs in 30 clusters throughout the university.

Student facilities

The students' union runs a vast range of clubs and societies, along with a university shop. A student advice centre is available to all students. The Jobshop is located in the union building and advertises part-time and temporary vacancies.

Sport

Newcastle University is one of the top ten universities for sport in the country. There are two sports centres on the main university site, two city swimming pools, outdoor pitches, Astroturf pitches and even an 18-hole golf course.

Overseas students

The international office deals with the 1,800 foreign students at the university. A bridging course is run from October to the following September to raise students' command of the English language. A counselling service is in operation to provide student support.

University of Northumbria at Newcastle

Founded: Royal charter 1992, formerly Newcastle Polytechnic

Times ranking: 64 (1999 ranking: 62nd equal)

Address: Ellison Terrace, Newcastle upon Tyne NE1 8ST

tel: 0191 227 4777

website: www.unn.ac.uk

e-mail: rg.admissons@unn.ac.uk

Undergraduates: 13,082 (3,397)

Postgraduates: 824 (2,369)

Mature students: 31%

Overseas students: 10%

Applications/place: 5.1

Undergraduates from State sector: 86%

Main subject areas: arts, design and humanities; business and management; engineering, science and technology; health; social work and education; social sciences.

Wide range of certificate and diploma courses also offered.

Teaching quality ratings

Rated Excellent 1993–95: business and management; English; law.

From 1995: modern languages 23; physics 23; art and design 22; building 22; drama, dance and cinematics 22; electrical and electronic engineering 22; psychology 22; town planning 21; history of art 21; molecular biosciences 21; sociology 20.

Overview

Always among the leading new universities in *The Times* League Table, Northumbria is also one of the largest, with more than 20,000 students, including many part-timers. The former polytechnic has benefited from Newcastle's reputation as an exciting student city, but it remains predominantly a local institution. More than half are from the north of England, many coming from Tyneside itself and enrolling as mature students.

The last big leap in numbers came with the incorporation of a large college of health studies in 1995. Health subjects are now second only to business studies in terms of student numbers. Northumbria has also been expanding geographically, with two campuses established well away from Newcastle for business studies during the 1990s. One, in Carlisle, has 500 students and may eventually have twice as many; the other, 15 miles north of Newcastle at Longhirst, is for postgraduates and conference delegates. There is also a network of feeder colleges encouraging applications from adults without traditional academic qualifications.

The main campus, with its mainly modern buildings, is just the other side of the civic centre from Newcastle University. The majority of subjects are based there, but health, education and social work are on the Coach Lane campus, a former teacher training college on the outskirts of the city. A £40 million programme to upgrade its facilities is under way with new sports facilities and a learning resource centre. Education had mixed fortunes in the Teacher Training Agency's performance indicators for 1999, narrowly missing a place in the top ten universities for primary training, but finishing near the foot of the secondary table.

Northumbria's best-known feature is its fashion school, although modern languages scored particularly well in the teaching quality assessment and art and design is also well regarded. Most degrees are available as sandwich courses, with placements of up to a year in business or industry. Entry requirements are generally modest, although law and business studies are among the exceptions.

Barely more than a quarter of the academic staff were entered for the last research assessments, and no subject was placed in the top three categories. However, most recent teaching scores have been good, with psychology joining modern languages on 23 points out of 24. The drop-out rate of 15 per cent was among the best in the new universities, and considerably better than the funding councils' 'benchmark' figure, which took account of the subject mix.

Accommodation

Around 90 per cent of first-year students can be offered a place in a university-owned room, and overseas students are guaranteed a place. Local students do not have priority in the first instance. There is, however, plenty of private rented accommodation available in Newcastle.

Library and computing

Over 500,000 books are stocked by the university's libraries, with 3,000 journals also available as well as videos, audio cassettes, microfilm and online databases. Quiet study spaces are found in the library, and three open-access IT areas are available.

Student facilities

Tempo, the student employment office at the university, advertises many part-time, full-time and temporary vacancies. The students' union has a wide range of facilities and organises many major music events.

Sport

Membership of the athletics union gives access to a range of sporting facilities for a whole year. The five sites now include a new fitness suite. Discounts are available at the City and Jesmond swimming pools.

Overseas students

The English Language In-Sessional Support Programme is run for the benefit of EU and overseas students, providing workshops and computer tests. Overseas student advisors are available, and the study skills centre provides academic support.

University of North London

Founded: University status 1992, formerly Polytechnic of North London
Times ranking: 88 (1999 ranking: 90)

Address: 166-220 Holloway Road, London N7 8DB

tel: 0207 753 3355
website: www.unl.ac.uk
e-mail: admissions@unl.ac.uk

Undergraduates: 9,065 (2,993)
Postgraduates: 677 (1,353)
Mature students: 58%
Overseas students: 11%
Applications/place: 7.0
Undergraduates from State sector: 93%

Main subject areas: business and management; environmental and social sciences; humanities and teacher education; science, computing and engineering.
Certificate and diploma courses are also offered.

Teaching quality ratings

Rated Excellent 1993–95: English

From 1995: art and design 22; drama and cinematics 22; electrical and electronic engineering 22; modern languages 20; food science 19; materials technology 19; media studies 17.

Overview

Once just a byword for student militancy, North London is now better known for spreading higher education into ethnic communities otherwise little seen in the university system. More than a third of the students are Afro-Caribbean and the proportion of mature students is the highest in Britain. The university's mission statement commits it to widening opportunities further, as well as expanding international and business links. A high proportion enter through Clearing, and barely half are selected on A levels, which average less than three Ds. Almost a quarter of the students are on sub-degree or professional courses.

Quality also features in the mission statement, however, and recent teaching ratings have been encouraging. Only two points out of 24 have been dropped in each of the last three assessments, although the teacher education courses came near the bottom of the pile in the Teacher Training Agency's performance indicators for 1999. Sandwich and part-time courses in electronic engineering are particularly highly rated, as is the health studies portfolio. Business studies dwarfs all other areas in terms of size, but sociology achieved the best result in the last research assessment exercise, which saw North London enter more academics than most new universities. A subsequent analysis, which allowed for subject differences, made the university second among its peer group for the share of research funds and fifteenth overall.

All undergraduates receive information technology training, as part of 'capability development' designed to enhance future employment prospects. They are also encouraged to take a language option from the menu of modular courses. Many programmes have been designed with the ubiquitous mature student in mind, but they have not prevented the drop-out rate reaching one in three – considerably worse than expected for the intake and among the highest in the country.

The university has been improving its facilities, which had become crowded and run-down in parts after continuous expansion. Having added to teaching space and student services, as well as opening a new learning resources centre, North London has built a Millennium Tower to transform the computing services and provide a new focal point for the university. The five sites are concentrated around the Holloway Road, a bustling, if unlovely, thoroughfare which caters well for students. The mixture of ages and cultures seems to produce a livelier social scene than at most similar universities, but the cost of living is high.

Accommodation

First-year accommodation is guaranteed for students living more than 25 miles away, with priority being given to disabled or overseas students. The accommodation office advises about university and private accommodation, with flats and houses being within easy travelling distance of the university.

Library and computing

A new building completed in January 2000 houses new IT-related learning facilities. The library holds over 300,000 books and 1,800 journals. There are 1,300 computers available for student access and many study spaces.

Student facilities

The Rocket Complex is at the heart of the students' union entertainments. The Complex was voted best student venue in London, and houses everything from quiz nights to club nights. The student services centre handles everything from accommodation to finance.

Sport

The university has a fully-equipped fitness room, sports hall, dance studio and gymnasium. Arrangements are made with local swimming pools and sports centres to cater for most major sports. Other sports on offer include mountaineering and skiing.

Overseas students

An overseas student adviser is employed to support the students from over 100 countries studying at the university. English language support is readily available to overseas students, mainly through free English classes.

University of Nottingham

Founded: 1881, Royal charter 1948

Times ranking: 12 (1999 ranking: 11)

Address: University Park, Nottingham NG7 2RD

tel: 0115 951 6565

website: www.nottingham.ac.uk

e-mail: undergraduate-enquiries@nottingham.ac.uk

Undergraduates: 12,095 (5,041)

Postgraduates: 2,228 (2,949)

Mature students: 5%

Overseas students: 9%

Applications/place: 9.1

Undergraduates from State sector: 68%

Main subject areas: wide range of disciplines in seven faculties: agricultural and food sciences; arts; education (mainly postgraduate); engineering; law and social sciences; medicine; science.

Teaching quality ratings

Rated Excellent 1993–95: architecture; business and management; chemistry; English; geography; law; manufacturing engineering; music.

From 1995: mechanical engineering 24; psychology 24; agriculture 23; history of art 23; pharmacy 23; town planning 23; American studies 22; civil engineering 22; electrical and electronic engineering 22; German 22; chemical engineering 21; materials technology 21; sociology 21; Russian 19; Iberian languages 17; French 16.

Overview

Already the occupant of one of the most attractive campuses in Britain, Nottingham has added a striking second to cope with the consistently strong demand for places, which has come with its rise up the pecking order of higher education. In less than 20 years, it has gone from being a solid civic university to a prime alternative to Oxbridge. Constantly among the top dozen universities in *The Times* League Table, it now has about nine applications for each place, making it one of the most difficult to get into. Once in, the vast majority of students stay the course – the 4 per cent drop-out rate is bettered only by Oxford, Cambridge and Durham.

The 30-acre Jubilee Campus, which cost £50 million, is less than a mile away from the original parkland site. Futuristic buildings clustered around an artificial lake house the schools of management and finance, computing science and education. The campus will also host the government's College of Leadership for school managers, as well as adding 750 residential places. There is space for further development if the university continues to grow, as planned.

Nottingham describes itself as a 'research-led' university, and has 3,500 students taking higher degrees, but the undergraduate intake increased by some 30 per cent during the 1990s. Most teaching assessments have been excellent, with psychology and manufacturing engineering recording perfect scores and agriculture, art and design, pharmacy and town planning all just missing out. The last research assessments were more mixed, but food science, genetics, German, pharmacy and Russian were all rated internationally outstanding, with ten more subjects on the next rung of the ladder.

Never one to stand still, Nottingham is an active participant in the Universitas 21 global grouping of universities, which is developing shared teaching and research, as well as offering exchange programmes. It also has a new campus in Malaysia, the only foreign university to be permitted to establish one. Nottingham has long-standing links with the Far East, which provides the majority of its 2,000 overseas students.

Both campuses in Nottingham are within three miles of the centre of the city, with a good selection of student-friendly clubs. However, halls of residence and the students' union tend to be the centre of social life, as they are for biology and agriculture students ten miles away in Sutton Bonnington. Almost a third of the students come from independent schools, but the university is trying to redress the balance with summer schools for teenagers from comprehensive schools.

Accommodation

Apart from local students, all first years are guaranteed a place in residence. Some of the 4,500 undergraduate places are self-catering, although they are not located on University Park. Self-catering accommodation is located within easy travelling distance from the university, and is also available in the holidays. Private rented accommodation is ready available.

Library and computing

Five main library sites house over one million books, 5,000 journals, and first-class study conditions with plenty of study spaces. There are numerous networked PCs available, and students can access the university's network from their own rooms.

Student facilities

The two students' union bars consist of the lively Buttery bar and the quieter D.H. Lawrence bar. The Buttery hosts many different theme nights, including comedy network night. The careers service also advertises part-time and temporary jobs.

Sport

The university has extensive sports facilities available for all levels of ability. The range of facilities includes sports halls, an eight-lane swimming pool, boathouse, tennis courts, outdoor pitches and squash courts.

Overseas students

The Centre for English Language Education provides language tuition. The International Students' Bureau has a regular newsletter, and is a part of the students' union. A permanent member of staff provides foreign student support.

Nottingham Trent University

Founded: University status 1992, formerly Nottingham (originally Trent) Polytechnic

Times ranking: 65 (1999 ranking: 69)

Address: Burton Street, Nottingham NG1 4BU

tel: 0115 848 2464
website: www.ntu.ac.uk
e-mail: NTU.Admissions@ntu.ac.uk

Undergraduates: 16,863 (3,321)
Postgraduates: 854 (2,131)
Mature students: 21%
Overseas students: 5%
Applications/place: 6.4
Undergraduates from State sector: 87%

Main subject areas: art and design; business and management; economics; education; engineering and computing; environmental studies; humanities; law; science; social sciences.
Certificate and diploma courses are also offered.

Teaching quality ratings

Rated Excellent 1993–95: business and management; chemistry.

From 1995: physics 24; building 22; psychology 22; mathematics and statistics 21; media studies 21; civil engineering 20; electrical and electronic engineering 20; land management 20; materials technology 20; sociology 19; modern languages 17.

Overview

Always one of the leading polytechnics, Nottingham Trent is demonstrating high quality in an unusually wide range of disciplines for a new university. Best known for fashion and other creative arts, which have the largest number of students, it has recorded maximum scores in teaching assessments for physics and biosciences recently. The law school is one of Britain's largest, offering legal practice courses for both solicitors and barristers, and there is even a prize-winning herd of Jersey cows on a new campus devoted to land-based studies.

An annual opinion survey shows that most of the students are satisfied: nine out of ten said they would recommend the university to a friend. The surveys are part of a systematic attempt to involve students in decision-making. There was a student charter well before the last government latched onto the idea. Helped by the popularity of Nottingham as a student centre, it grew by a third in five years in the 1990s, and is still oversubscribed in many subjects.

Nottingham Trent is among the largest of the new universities, with more than 23,000 students, including a large contingent of part-timers. The extensive main City campus originally housed Nottingham University, but now boasts a mixture of Victorian and modern buildings. Science, mathematics and the humanities are five miles away on the site of a former teacher training college at Clifton, with education in a nearby Georgian mansion overlooking the River Trent. The latest addition to the estate came from a merger with Brackenhurst College, an agricultural college 14 miles from Nottingham. As well as a farm, the new campus has an equestrian centre with a purpose-built indoor riding area.

The largely vocational courses are part of a modular system which gives every student training in information technology, as well as the opportunity to learn a language. A high proportion of students take sandwich degrees, helping Nottingham Trent to an employment record for both undergraduates and postgraduates to compare with the most prestigious universities. The last research assessment exercise was a disappointment for an institution that had hoped to challenge its longer-established rivals, with no subjects in the top three categories. Teaching ratings have been variable, but show recent improvement.

The student body is diverse, with large numbers of mature and overseas students, and also quite widely dispersed. Social life varies between campuses, but all have access to the city's lively cultural and clubbing scene.

Accommodation

There are 2,400 places reserved for first-year students in the nine university residences. These are near to the City campus, most have single rooms and some are self-catering. There is a university-run accreditation scheme, with private rented accommodation available through the university accommodation service, which runs an introduction course to house-hunting for first years.

Library and computing

The four university libraries hold over 400,000 books and have around 1,500 study spaces available. The computing resources are housed in two centres, with the Boots Library the main site for computing materials.

Student facilities

An Employment Store aims to find part-time, vacation, and full-time jobs for students. There are over 600 societies to join, a theatre and two lecture theatres with stages. Club nights are twice a week at the City campus.

Sport

The students' union co-ordinates all athletic activities, with the emphasis being on fun rather than success. Facilities include a large sports hall, cricket nets, badminton, squash courts, gyms and an all-weather outdoor sports pitch.

Overseas students

An international student support service is available throughout a student's course of study. A confidential advice and information service is also available.

University of Oxford

Founded: 1096

Times ranking: 3 (1999 ranking: 3)

Address: University Offices, Wellington Square, Oxford OX1 2JD

tel: 01865 270207

website: www.oxford.ac.uk

e-mail: undergraduate.admissions@admin.ox.ac.uk

Undergraduates: 11,494 (2,946)

Postgraduates: 4,459 (1,487)

Mature students: 17%

Overseas students: 9%

Applications/place: 3.0

Undergraduates from State sector: 47%

Main subject areas: full range of disciplines in six faculties; arts; engineering and technology; mathematics; medicine; science; social sciences.

Teaching quality ratings

Rated Excellent 1993–95: anthropology; chemistry; computer science; English; geography; geology; history; law; social work.

From 1995: general engineering 23; materials technology 23; East and South Asian studies 22; Middle Eastern and African studies 22; modern languages 21.

Overview

Oxford is the oldest and probably the most famous university in the English-speaking world, and reports of its demise when overtaken in *The Times* League Table by Imperial College London were premature. All the evidence suggests that the dark blues remain close to Cambridge in terms of quality, and head and shoulders above the other non-specialist universities. Like its ancient rival, Oxford attracts world-class academics and takes its share of the brightest students. Also like Cambridge, the university is redoubling its efforts to shed the socially elitist image which puts off many potential applicants from comprehensive schools. School visits by undergraduates and summer schools for sixth-formers have helped increase recruitment from the state sector, but Oxford remains the only university in which they are outnumbered by students from independent education. Only 8 per cent come from working-class homes, according to the funding councils' first performance indicators, although an access committee chaired by the vice-chancellor has made a series of proposals designed to broaden a social mix.

Selection is in the hands of the 30 undergraduate colleges, which vary considerably in their approach to this issue and others. Sound advice on academic strengths and social factors is essential for applicants to give themselves the best chance of winning a place and finding a setting in which they can thrive. The choice is particularly important for arts and social science students, whose world-famous individual or small group tuition is based in college. Science and technology, which have benefited from Oxford's phenomenally successful fundraising efforts, are taught mainly in central facilities. Current developments include a new management school, made possible by a £20 million donation from the controversial Syrian businessman, Wafic Said.

There was never much doubt about the strength of Oxford's research but, with three quarters of the academics in subjects rated internationally outstanding, the last assessments confirmed the university's high standing. Most teaching assessments have been similarly impressive, with biosciences recording maximum points and both engineering and materials technology only just missing out. A major review of the university's activities will result in some restructuring in August 2000, with the creation of five academic divisions, each headed by a full-time officer. But there will be no change to the eight-week terms and concentration on final examinations, which some students have found too pressurised. Only 2 per cent drop out, however, the lowest proportion in Britain, with the inevitable exception of Cambridge.

See Chapter 8 for information about individual colleges.

Oxford Brookes University

Founded: University status 1992, formerly Oxford Polytechnic
Times ranking: 52 (1999 ranking: 53)

Address: Headington Campus, Headington, Oxford OX3 0BP

tel: 01865 484848
website: www.brookes.ac.uk
e-mail: query@brookes.ac.uk

Undergraduates: 7,508 (2,372)
Postgraduates: 1,028 (1,569)
Mature students: 27%
Overseas students: 16%
Applications/place: 6.6
Undergraduates from State sector: 67%

Main subject areas: architecture; art, biology; business; computing and mathematics; construction and earth sciences; education; engineering; health; hotel management; humanities; languages; law; planning; publishing and music; real estate management; social sciences.
Certificates and diplomas are available in most areas

Teaching quality ratings

Rated Excellent 1993–95: anthropology; English; geography; law.

From 1995: town planning 24; building 23; history of art 23; land management 23; psychology 23; French 22; modern languages 22; civil engineering 21; media studies 21; sociology 21; food science 20; electrical and electronic engineering 19; German 19.

Overview

Now firmly established as the leading new university in *The Times* League Table, Oxford Brookes is making a leap in size in 2000, taking in Westminster College, the Methodist college based nearby. The merger will add 2,000 students, mainly in teacher training and the humanities, transferring courses previously validated by Oxford University. The new arrivals will join an institution that is challenging the traditional universities on their own ground, but still retaining a substantial part-time programme and recruiting large numbers of mature students.

As a polytechnic, Oxford pioneered the modular degree system that has swept British higher education. After more than 20 years' experience, the scheme now offers in excess of 2,000 modules in an undergraduate programme which can pair subjects as diverse as history and physical sciences, or catering management and history of art. Each subject has compulsory modules in the first year and a list of others that are acceptable later in the course. Students are encouraged to take some subjects outside their main area of study, and there is a range of possible exit points. They can qualify for a Certificate in Higher Education after a full 24 modules.

The university's location has always been an advantage in student recruitment, but the quality of provision is the real draw. Its departments feature in *The Times* top ten for several subjects, including a fourth place for French. Even the law ranking – normally the preserve of the traditional universities – sees Oxford

Brookes in twelfth place. Town planning achieved a maximum score for teaching, while building, history of art and psychology dropped only one point each. The university also has a consistently excellent record for graduate employment.

There are three main sites, two of which are only a mile from the city centre and linked to each other by a footbridge. The original Gypsy Lane site was becoming overcrowded when the chance came to acquire the late Robert Maxwell's 15-acre estate at neighbouring Headington Hill. Education and business are five miles away at Wheatley, and Westminster's 100-acre site will offer further scope for expansion.

Named after John Brookes, who is regarded as the founding father of the institution, the university has proved a magnet for independent schools, whose students now fill almost a third of the full-time places. The social scene is not the liveliest and Oxford can be expensive, but there is enough going on to satisfy most students.

Accommodation

Everything from shared houses and flats to host-family accommodation is available privately and house-hunting weekends are held throughout September. The university has 2,400 places in 10 halls. Preference is given to first-years who live more than about 70 miles from Oxford.

Library and computing

Open seven days a week, the three university libraries house over 300,000 basic texts, 2,400 journal subscriptions and upwards of 1,000 quiet study places. More than 550 networked PCs are available in 25 areas, 12 of which are open 24 hours a day.

Student facilities

The Helena Kennedy Student Centre is a 1,200-capacity venue in which the students' union plays host to regular events. These include guest lectures, balls, film nights and club nights. The careers centre advises on part-time and temporary vacancies.

Sport

Indoor sports revolve around the Centre for Sport, which include a fitness suite, squash courts and a sports hall. Outdoor facilities are on the Wheatley campus for everything from football to lacrosse. The university also has its own boathouse.

Overseas students

English for academic purposes is provided by the International Centre for English Studies for the university's overseas students. Pre-sessional English courses are available and encouraged, whilst the director of international relations co-ordinates overseas student support.

University of Paisley

Founded: University status 1992, formerly Paisley College

Times ranking: 91 (1999 ranking: 75th equal)

Address: Paisley, Renfrewshire PA1 2BE

tel: 0800 027 1000
website: www.paisley.ac.uk
e-mail: uni-direct@paisley.ac.uk

Undergraduates: 5,759 (2,317)
Postgraduates: 490 (516)
Mature students: 35%
Overseas students: 5%
Applications/place: 3.3
Undergraduates from State sector: 96%

Main subject areas: business; education; engineering; health and social studies; science and technology.
Sub-degree courses are also offered.

Teaching quality ratings

Rated Excellent 1993–98: none.

Highly Satisfactory 1993–98: cellular biology; chemistry; civil engineering; mathematics and statistics; mechanical engineering; organismal biology; psychology; social work; sociology, teacher education.

From 1988: European languages 19.

Overview

Paisley claims to be 'Britain's most successful university when it comes to unlocking the door to higher education'. Its evidence was the funding councils' first set of performance indicators, which showed the largest proportion of entrants (96 per cent) from state schools and one of the largest (39 per cent) from working-class homes. However, the statement did not mention the drop-out rate of one in three – nearly twice the expected rate, taking account of the subject mix – which the exercise also revealed. Almost one undergraduate in five left after only a year.

Only seven miles from Glasgow, Paisley is Scotland's largest town. The university has more than 9,000 students, including many part-timers, a high proportion coming from the Glasgow area. Student numbers have grown rapidly in recent years, but staffing levels compare favourably with those of most new universities. Courses are strongly vocational, with a technological thrust. There are close links with business and industry, notably with the computer giant IBM. All students are offered hands-on computer training.

No subjects were rated Excellent before the teaching quality system changed in 1998, but a majority were graded Highly Satisfactory. The university pioneered credit transfer in Scotland, giving credit for non-academic achievement, and its modular course system covers day, evening and weekend classes. Many students take sandwich degrees, but the impact on graduate employment has not been as great as in some other universities. Applied research and consultancy are concentrated in a series of specialist units on subjects such as alcohol and drug abuse, but pure research is not Paisley's forte. Fewer than one academic in ten was entered for the last assessments and no subjects reached the top three categories.

The main campus, covering 20 acres in the middle of Paisley, has seen substantial development in recent years, including a new library and learning resource centre. The Craigie campus, in Ayr, acquired through a 1993 merger with a former teacher training college, has seen the establishment of a management centre in an 18th-century mansion. A third campus was opened in Dumfries in 1996, in partnership with a local college. The venture began with only 100 students, but a new teaching centre is increasing the range of courses available for the under-provided southwest of Scotland.

The two main centres could hardly be more different, Paisley industrial and seaside Ayr smaller both as a campus and a town. Social life varies accordingly.

Accommodation

There are over 1,000 places in university accommodation and preference is given to first years who live more than 25 miles away. Most of the accommodation is self-catering. The residential accommodation office provides information and advice on private rented housing, which is reasonably easy to find and of an adequate standard.

Library and computing

The Robinson Trust Library and Learning Resource Centre was opened in January 2000 at a cost of £6.8 million. The library has nearly 200,000 books, 1,200 journals and nearly 1,000 study spaces. There are PC Labs at Paisley and Ayr.

Student facilities

The students' association is open for most of the week, with the Subway Bar as the main venue for clubbing, events and film screenings. The student advisory service gives advice to students on careers and welfare.

Sport

The sports centre is located two miles away from campus and provides facilities including football pitches, a sports hall and a fitness room. The university also has reciprocal agreements with local sporting facilities, including a golf course and swimming pool.

Overseas students

The overseas student population at the university is small but diverse. The university supports overseas students, but the English language teaching facilities at the university are limited.

University of Plymouth

Founded: University status 1992, formerly Polytechnic South West, originally Plymouth Polytechnic

Times ranking: 56 (1999 ranking: 64)

Address: Plymouth, Devon PL4 8AA

tel: 01752 600600
website: www.plymouth.ac.uk
e-mail: postmaster@plymouth.ac.uk

Undergraduates: 14,928 (2,870)
Postgraduates: 535 (1,807)
Mature students: 30%
Overseas students: 6%
Applications/place: 5.5
Undergraduates from State sector: 86%

Main subject areas: agriculture, food and land use; arts; business studies; education; human sciences; science; technology.

Teaching quality ratings

Rated Excellent 1993–95: environmental science; geography; geology; oceanography.

From 1995: building 23; civil engineering 23; psychology 23; agriculture 22; health subjects 20; mathematics and statistics 20; sociology 20; materials technology 19; electrical and electronic engineering 18.

Overview

The university has offshoots across much of Devon and would like to spread into Cornwall, despite turning its back on the regional title it adopted as a polytechnic. The Plymouth title conformed to the idea that applicants identify with cities, although attracting students has never been a problem in most subjects despite the fact that a high proportion of the courses are in science and technology.

A school of art and design in Exeter, an agricultural college near Newton Abbot and a college of education in Exmouth have all been added to the original Plymouth headquarters. The university is also responsible for Dartington College of Art, near Totnes, and Falmouth School of Art, in Cornwall, as well as franchising courses to the Royal Naval College, at Dartmouth, and more than a dozen further education colleges in the region – a system that won a Queen's Anniversary Prize in 1994. A high-speed telematics network links them all.

Unlike many new universities, Plymouth has 80 per cent of its students on full-time or sandwich courses, most of them degrees. The institution is best known for marine studies, but building and psychology have produced the best recent teaching scores, each narrowly missing out on full marks. Engineering offers four-year extended degrees without the normal entry requirements for such courses, and an MEng with an extra year's study is open to high-fliers throughout the faculty. The university hit the headlines for introducing a degree in surfing, but it insists that the course is rigorous as well as vocational. A modular course system provides a wide range of options throughout the seven faculties.

As one of the most persistent advocates of the right to university status, Plymouth has a long-standing commitment to research. The business school, for example, which has by far the most students of the seven faculties, included an 'aroma room' in a new headquarters building to facilitate research for the perfume industry. Almost half of the academics were entered for the last research assessment exercise, but no subject reached the top three categories.

The standard of facilities and the prospect of securing a residential place vary widely between campuses, although all are within easy reach of the sea and the region's areas of natural beauty. Plymouth, which hosts the majority of students, is inevitably the liveliest location, with excellent facilities for watersports. The remaining sites, which specialise in agriculture, education and the arts, have an identity and social life of their own.

Accommodation

The university has almost 2,000 places, all within three miles of a campus. Overseas students are guaranteed a first-year place in halls, and around a third of all first years are also allocated a place. Private rented accommodation is available through the student accommodation office. provision of accommodation varies greatly between campuses.

Library and computing

Libraries at the four sites have a total of nearly 500,000 books between them, and around 1,100 study spaces. There are over 1,000 computer workstations, located in libraries, open access areas and in some halls.

Student facilities

The students' union has a base at each campus. The livliest campus is at Plymouth. The university runs an online 'Job Surfer' which matches students to job vacancies.

Sport

Sporting facilities are concentrated on the main site, with a gym, squash courts, a sports hall, playing fields, a five-hole golf course and a watersports centre. The other three sites have playing fields, tennis courts and multi-gyms.

Overseas students

Pre-study courses are provided in partnership with the Mayflower College for overseas students, as are free English language support classes, available throughout the year. The international students' support office provides an orientation programme for new overseas students.

University of Portsmouth

Founded: University status 1992, formerly Portsmouth Polytechnic

Times ranking: 69th equal (1999 ranking: 68)

Address: Winston Churchill Avenue, Portsmouth PO1 2UP

tel: 0239 284 8484
website: www.port.ac.uk
e-mail: admissions@port.ac.uk

Undergraduates: 12,097 (2,287)
Postgraduates: 872 (1,730)
Mature students: 24%
Overseas students: 16%
Applications/place: 5.0
Undergraduates from State sector: 88%

Main subject areas: business; environment; humanities; science; social sciences; technology.
Certificate and diploma courses offered as well as degrees.

Teaching quality ratings

Rated Excellent 1993–95: geography.

From 1995: French 23; psychology 23; German 21; civil engineering 20; electrical and electronic engineering 20; Italian 20; land management 20; physics 20; sociology 20; Iberian languages 18; Russian 18.

Overview

Portsmouth only narrowly missed university status before the polytechnics were created, and never gave up the chase. Degree work dates from the beginning of the last century and now four out of five students are at this level or above. Postgraduate numbers have been rising steadily and staffing levels are among the most generous of the new universities. Completion rates are among the best of its contemporaries and graduate employment healthy, especially for a university where a high proportion of the students take arts subjects.

Languages are Portsmouth's greatest strength, as teaching and research assessments have shown. One student in five takes a language course, and the facilities rival those of many traditional universities. About a thousand Portsmouth students go abroad for part of their course, and at least as many come from the Continent. The university is in *The Times* top ten for French, having achieved a near-perfect score for teaching quality, while the grade 5 rating for research in Russian was one of the few in any subject in the former polytechnics. Every faculty is involved in research, and the 44 per cent of academics entered for the last research assessment exercise was among the highest in the new universities. The result was a timely for Portsmouth's finances.

The range of subjects has widened in recent years, with the incorporation of the Solent School of Nursing and the Portsmouth School of Art, Design and Further Education. Teaching assessments have been variable, with psychology the star performer recently. But the Teacher Training Agency's performance indicators produced an unflattering verdict on the courses for secondary teachers.

The main Guildhall campus, dotted around the city centre, is undergoing an £8 million redevelopment, which is due to be complete by 2002. The large business school and information technology are two miles away at Milton, with education and English a further mile away at the largely residential Langstone campus. Only health studies are off Portsea Island, based at Queen Alexandra Hospital in Cosham.

Portsmouth, which has been described as a northern industrial city on the south coast, has a larger working-class population and more deprivation than some applicants may realise. But is also has a vibrant student pub and club scene to supplement a popular students' union. The cost of living is not as high as at many southern universities, and the sea is always close at hand.

Accommodation

The ten halls of residence provide over 1,700 places, three-quarters of which are reserved for first years. Some courses include priority hall placements. Seven of the halls are self-catering, with all the halls on Portsea Island, close to the university. Private rented accommodation is available through student housing, who run 'Secure a Home' days in September.

Library and computing

Around 560,000 books are provided by the library, as well as a good selection of journals (especially science). Over 1,000 study places are available and around 700 computer workstations are located in the Goldsmith Building and in halls.

Student facilities

Four bars are run by the students' union, who run five club nights a week. Some halls have bars, as does the Milton site. The careers service advises on both part-time and temporary work.

Sport

Sporting facilities are provided for by the department of sport and recreation. Facilities include resistance and cardiovascular training, a synthetic pitch, outdoor pitches, watersports and a sports hall. Students can use the city's facilities at half price.

Overseas students

The Language Centre provides an intensive programme for overseas students lasting 30 weeks. A course called 'English for Academic Purposes' is free of charge and lasts for one year. There are two international advisers .

Queen's University, Belfast

Founded: 1845, Royal charter 1908

Times ranking: 33 (1999 ranking: 43)

Address: University Road, Belfast BT7 1NN

tel: 028 9024 5133
website: www.qub.ac.uk
e-mail: admissions@qub.ac.uk

Undergraduates: 12,427 (4,908)
Postgraduates: 2,351 (2,330)
Mature students: 13%
Overseas students: 8%
Applications/place: 5.9
Undergraduates from State sector: 97%

Main subject areas: agriculture and food science; arts; economics and social sciences; education; engineering; law; medicine; science; theology.

Teaching quality ratings

Rated Excellent 1993–95: English; geology; history; law; music; social work.

From 1995: dentistry 24; electrical and electronic engineering 24; psychology 24; civil engineering 22; medicine 22; town planning 22; agriculture 21; chemical engineering 21; food science 21; Iberian languages 21; mechanical engineering 21; molecular biosciences 21; French 20; modern languages 19; sociology 19.

Overview

Generally regarded as Northern Ireland's premier university, Queen's saw a big increase in applications in 1999, as, for the second year in succession, more of the province's students decided to stay at home. The university was one of three university colleges for the whole of Ireland in the 19th century, and still draws students from all over the island. The peace process has even been stimulating demand from the mainland, although there is a long way to go before pre-Troubles recruitment is matched.

The emphasis is on research, but undergraduate numbers have been rising and there has been a succession of good teaching ratings in the last year. Dentistry made up for a poor research grade with maximum points, a feat also achieved by psychology and electrical and electronic engineering. Music is also highly rated for both teaching and research, as is mechanical engineering, the only subject considered internationally outstanding in the last research assessments. More than a quarter of the academic staff were not entered for that exercise, an unusually high proportion for a traditional university, yet the results were still disappointing. A fifth of those entered finished in the bottom three categories of seven.

The university area, which is among the most attractive in Belfast, is one of the city's main cultural and recreational areas. Queen's runs a highly successful arts festival each November, and its cinema is one of the best in the province. Student facilities are being expanded and upgraded to cope with expansion, with a

£50 million student village soon to bring services together on a single precinct. A new library has been added recently and more teaching accommodation provided, with better access for the disabled.

The university formed a new partnership with St Mary's College and Stranmillis College in 1999, with the aim of academic integration. Courses at Queen's are modular and semesters have been introduced. Students are encouraged to take language programmes from a unique 'virtual' language laboratory, which provides on-line tuition from any computer in the university. An unusually large proportion of graduates go on to further study, which does Queen's no harm in the employment league.

Though the university has been criticised for religious imbalance among its staff, it remains committed to an equal opportunities policy. Nightlife has returned to the city centre, but the social scene is still concentrated on the students' union and the surrounding area of south Belfast.

Accommodation

There are over 1,900 places available and the university can house approximately half of all first-year students, with a small proportion in self-catering accommodation. The majority of accommodation is in ten-storey blocks close to the campus. Private rented accommodation is plentiful and available through the university accommodation office.

Library and computing

The five libraries have more than 1.1 million books and over 2,500 study spaces. The university has seven open-access areas, providing a total of 522 PCs. There are also over 1,000 computers in 40 departmental areas.

Student facilities

The students' union has two main bars, the Bunatee Bar and Speakeasy, and a cinema, and club events are hosted at the Mandela Hall. The careers service provides information on part-time and temporary jobs.

Sport

Queen's PE Centre is the main campus venue for sporting activities. Outdoor facilities include the Mary Peters running track and 20 playing fields, four of which are all-weather.

Overseas students

Over 10 per cent of the student population come from overseas. The international liaison office administers the Study Abroad programme for overseas students, and also supports students throughout their time at the university.

University of Reading

Founded: 1892, Royal charter 1926

Times ranking: 31 (1999 ranking: 24th equal)

Address: P O Box 217, Reading RG6 6AH

tel: 0118 987 5123
website: www.reading.ac.uk
e-mail: information@reading.ac.uk

Undergraduates: 7,416 (928)
Postgraduates: 1,985 (3,535)
Mature students: 16%
Overseas students: 8%
Applications/place: 7.5
Undergraduates from State sector: 76%

Main subject areas: agriculture and food science; education and community studies; letters and social sciences; urban and regional studies.

Teaching quality ratings

Rated Excellent 1993–95: environmental studies; geography; geology; mechanical engineering.

From 1995: dance, drama and cinematics 24; history of art 23; media studies 23; food science 22; sociology 22; town planning 22; agriculture 21; American studies 21; building 21; electrical and electronic engineering 21; French 21; German 20; Italian 20; linguistics 19.

Overview

Although best known for its agricultural and environmental courses, most of Reading's best grades for teaching quality have come in the arts and social sciences. In the past year, a perfect score for drama and near-misses for media studies and history of art have helped improve an already sound set of assessments. Several of the successes have come in subjects added when the university took in Bulmershe College a decade ago, although the large education faculty is yet to feature.

The college provided a second campus near the original 300-acre parkland site on the outskirts of Reading. The university spent more than £60 million on new buildings in the 1990s, upgrading and extending facilities for meteorology, management and agriculture most recently. Reading was the only university established between the two World Wars, having been Oxford's extension college for the first part of the last century, but the attractive main campus now has a modern feel.

Professor Roger Williams, the Vice-Chancellor, is committed to breaking down the barriers between the arts and sciences. Reading has already taken some steps in this direction, notably in a joint initiative with the Open University to develop standardised course materials to help underqualified students cope with physics degrees. The scheme won an award for innovation, a distinction repeated in 1998 when the university won a Queen's Anniversary Prize. Arts and social science students are encouraged to broaden their horizons by taking three subjects from the modular course scheme in the first year of their degree.

Successes in the last research assessment exercise were mainly in the university's traditional strengths. Agriculture, environmental science and building were all rated internationally outstanding, with one academic in five assessed in the top two categories of seven. Reading tops *The Times* ranking for building and is second for environmental science, land management and food science.

Almost a quarter of the undergraduates come from independent schools, with the agricultural courses a particular draw. The university owns 2,000 acres of farmland on the Downs, near Reading, for agricultural teaching and research. The town has plenty of nightlife and London is easily accessible by train, but the cost of living is comparable with the capital without qualifying for the extra financial support available there. Students praise the social scene, although the high proportion from the south-east means that many go home at the weekends.

Accommodation

All first-year students are guaranteed accommodation in university residences. The 13 halls are all within walking distance of the main site. The accommodation office helps with finding private rented accommodation, of which there is a fair amount near to the main site.

Library and computing

The main library along with its subsidiaries and departmental libraries have over one million books and subscribe to more than 4,000 journals. There are almost 1,000 study spaces, and just over 300 computer workstations.

Student facilities

There are two main venues, as well as bars in halls. Three club nights a week are run in the Main Hall which occasionally plays host to live bands. The careers advisory service advises on part-time jobs.

Sport

The Wolfendon Sports Centre provides most of the university's excellent sporting facilities – everything from archery to martial arts is available. The university has an athletics pavilion, outdoor pitches for cricket, football and rugby as well as a running track.

Overseas students

The university's international office provides help and guidance on welfare matters and runs a welcoming programme for new students.

The Robert Gordon University

Founded: University status 1992, formerly the Robert Gordon Institute of Technology

Times ranking: 59th equal (1999 ranking: 59)

Address: Schoolhill, Aberdeen AB10 1FR
tel: 01224 262105
website: www.rgu.ac.uk
e-mail: admissions@rgu.ac.uk

Undergraduates: 6,458 (1,464)
Postgraduates: 513 (901)
Mature students: 18%
Overseas students: 10%
Applications/place: 4.5
Undergraduates from State sector: 89%

Main subject areas: applied sciences; architecture; art and surveying; business management; computer and mathematical sciences; electrical and electronic engineering; food and consumer studies; health and social work; librarianship and information studies; mechanical and offshore engineering; nursing; pharmacy; public administration and law.
Also linked diplomas.

Teaching quality ratings
Rated Excellent 1994–98: chemistry; nutrition and dietetics.

Highly Satisfactory 1994–98: architecture; business and management; graphic and textile design; mathematics and statistics; mechanical engineering; pharmacy; physiotherapy; physics; radiography; social work.

From 1998: European languages 19.

Overview

Close links with the North Sea oil and gas industries exemplify a commitment to vocational education, which gives Robert Gordon the best employment record of the new universities. All offshore workers must have a certificate from its Survival Centre, and several longer courses are tailored to the industry's needs. The school of mechanical and offshore engineering is the main link, but other parts of the university are also involved.

Courses are flexible, with credit accumulation and transfer making for easy transfer in and out of the university for an often mobile local workforce. Many students are accepted without standard academic qualifications, often embarking on diploma courses before transferring to a degree programme. Work placements, which can last up to a year, are the norm, helping to boost job prospects.

Efforts to extend access beyond the normal higher education catchment have produced a diverse student population, with 30 per cent of undergraduates from working-class homes. The 18 per cent drop-out rate was among the better figures of the new universities, but still not as good as the funding councils expected, given the mix of courses. Only two of the subjects assessed in the main rounds of teaching assessment were rated Excellent, but a majority of the rest were considered Highly Satisfactory. Only a third of the academic staff was entered for the last research assessment exercise and none of the subjects featured in the top three of the seven categories.

There are now more than 100 degrees

to choose from, and fleeting talk of a merger with Aberdeen University is long forgotten. Students from the two institutions mix easily, and there is healthy academic rivalry in some areas, despite the obvious differences between the universities. Named after an 18th-century philanthropist, Robert Gordon has five sites around the city and an attractive field study centre at Cromarty, in the Highlands. The main Schoolhill site adjoins Aberdeen Art Gallery, while others are more modern. The exception is Garthdee, based on a Victorian mansion overlooking the River Dee, where further development has made room for art, architecture and business.

Like most new universities, especially in Scotland, Robert Gordon recruits most of its students locally. Aberdeen is a long way to go for English students, unless they are set on a career in the offshore industries. Private accommodation is notoriously scarce and expensive, and low prices in the recently extended student association can only compensate marginally.

Accommodation

All accommodation is either in university self-catering flats or is rented privately. Around 1,300 places are available in these flats, so first-year students cannot be guaranteed a place. Private rented accommodation is to found through the student accommodation service.

Library and computing

The eight university libraries have around 210,000 books and 900 study places. Across campus are 750 computer workstations, which are available at most times for student to access the network.

Student facilities

In the students' association there are two bars, two cafés and a general shop. Quizzes, ceilidhs and karaoke are among the events offered at least three times a week. The careers service advertises temporary and part-time jobs.

Sport

The university's sports facilities include four acres of playing fields, two sports halls and tennis courts. Skiing, fencing and rowing are specialities of the university. Students are also permitted to use local facilities.

Overseas students

The international office is available to help and advise. Accommodation is guaranteed for first years, and free English language tuition is available.

University of St Andrews

Founded: 1411

Times ranking: 7 (1999 ranking: 10)

Address: College Gate, North Street, St Andrews KY16 9AJ

tel: 01334 462150

website: www.st-andrews.ac.uk

e-mail: admissions@st-andrews.ac.uk

Undergraduates: 4,703 (190)

Postgraduates: 631 (305)

Mature students: 6%

Overseas students: 10%

Applications/place: 5.3

Undergraduates from State sector: 60%

Main subject areas: arts; divinity; science; medicine.

Teaching quality ratings

Rated Excellent 1994–97: cellular biology; chemistry; economics; geography; history; mathematics and statistics; organismal biology; physics; psychology.

Highly Satisfactory 1994–97: business and management; computer studies; English; geology; history of art; medicine; philosophy; theology.

From 1998: European languages 22.

Overview

As the oldest Scottish university and the third oldest in Britain, St Andrews has long been both famous and fashionable throughout Britain and further afield. But recent assessments have shown that there is top quality behind the prestige: St Andrews has the best teaching quality record north of the border, outstanding research and a drop-out rate that is not only the best in Scotland but just a third of the funding councils' expectation for the intake.

The city of St Andrews is steeped in history, as well as being the centre of the golfing world. The university at its heart accounts for about a third of the 16,000 inhabitants. There are close relations between town and gown, both cultural and social. Many colourful traditions remain. New students acquire third and fourth-year 'parents' to ease them into university life, and on Raisin Monday give their academic guardians a bottle of wine in return for a Latin receipt, which can be written on anything. Although the 'pier walk' by scarlet-gowned students after Chapel on Sundays now takes a different route, a 'save the pier' campaign has been launched to raise funds to restore the old pier and, presumably, the old tradition. Another unusual feature is that all arts students are awarded an MA rather than a BA.

With more than 40 per cent of the students coming from south of the border, St Andrews has earned the nickname of Scotland's English university. But fee concessions for Scots may test that trait. Already, more than half of the postgraduates are from Scotland.

The main buildings date from the 15th and 16th centuries, but sciences are taught at the modern North Haugh site a few streets away. Everything is within walking distance, although bicycles are common. Although small, St Andrews offers a wide range of courses. Uniquely, every subject assessed has been rated either excellent or highly satisfactory for teaching, demonstrating quality across the board. Psychology was the only starred research department, but mathematics, classics, history, philosophy and theology all reached the next rung of the ladder.

The university's reputation has always rested primarily on the humanities. It has the largest medieval history department in Britain, for example. But a full range of physical sciences are offered, with sophisticated lasers and the largest optical telescope in Britain. A £4.2 million extension to the Gatty Marine Laboratory will pioneer research into whales, dolphins and seals.

Students do not come to St Andrews for the nightclubs, but there is no shortage of parties in a tight-knit community.

Accommodation

First years are offered university-owned accommodation but this is not guaranteed for late applicants. The university offers rooms in a number of catered and self-catering flats, houses and halls, some of which have twin rooms. The residence contract is for the whole academic session.

Library and computing

The total library service comprises one million books, pamphlets and periodicals, and more than 50 networked databases are available. The main central computers include more than 60 Sun workstations. Also provided are PC and Mac computer classrooms and clusters.

Student facilities

The students' association is in a modern city-centre building. Services include bars, a lounge overlooking the garden, a shop and a theatre. The careers advisory service arranges workshops, has reference libraries and provides details of employers, jobs and further study.

Sport

Sports facilities include a pitch for hockey and soccer, tennis courts, an athletics track, and grass fields for traditional sports, shinty and lacrosse. The Sports Centre includes a sports hall, gymnasium, squash courts and a body workshop.

Overseas students

The English Language Teaching Centre gives pre-sessional training in language, study skills and cultural orientation, with courses leading to the University of Cambridge Certificates in Advanced English and Proficiency in English.

University of Salford

Founded: 1896, Royal charter 1967

Times ranking: 59th equal (1999 ranking: 57)

Address: Salford, Greater Manchester M5 4WT

tel: 0161 295 4545
website: www.salford.ac.uk
e-mail: course-enquiries@salford.ac.uk

Undergraduates: 11,690 (2,899)
Postgraduates: 824 (2,300)
Mature students: 31%
Overseas students: 10%
Applications/place: 6.0
Undergraduates from State sector: 90%

Main subject areas: art and design technology; business management; conservation studies; engineering; environment; healthcare; humanities; languages; media; music and performance; science; social sciences.

Teaching quality ratings

Rated Excellent 1993–95: music.

From 1995: molecular biosciences 24; health subjects 22; housing studies 22; drama, dance and cinematics 21; Arabic 20; sociology 20; civil engineering 19; building 18, electrical and electronic engineering 16.

Overview

A merger with University College Salford, with which there were already close links, provided a second opportunity to forge a new type of higher education institution. The main victim of higher education budget cuts in the early 1980s, Salford bounced back as the prototype decentralised, customer-orientated university. Now the model, which many commentators expect to set another national trend, is the comprehensive post-school institution. Uniquely among the older universities, almost 5 per cent of the students are on further education courses.

Last year, however, Salford began to slip below some of the new universities in *The Times* League Table. Although better than the national average for its subject mix, the projected drop-out rate of 22 per cent was also worse than a number of former polytechnics. The good news recently has come in improved ratings for teaching quality, which included a perfect score for molecular biosciences. Of the first 11 subjects assessed, only music was considered Excellent.

Previously a College of Advanced Technology, Salford has retained its technological bias, although business and health subjects are now the biggest recruiters. The university's growing involvement in health has seen the establishment of a national centre for prosthetics and orthotics, and a high reputation for the treatment of sports injuries. Engineering is the university's traditional strength, attracting many of the 1,500 overseas students, but teaching grades have been disappointing. Over 30 per cent of all students are on sandwich courses, many of them going abroad for their work placements.

Salford's extended range of courses meant that fewer than half the academics were entered for the last research assessment exercise, when the built environment was the only area considered internationally outstanding. European studies – another long-standing strength – reached the second rung of the ladder, but more than a quarter of those entered were placed in the bottom three of the seven categories. Nonetheless, the university remains committed to research: it has established six interdisciplinary research centres and a graduate school.

The modern landscaped campus is only two miles from the centre of Manchester and has a mainline railway station. At its centre is a municipal park, a haven of lawns and shrubberies on the banks of the River Irwell. Students like the friendly atmosphere and, although Salford may not be the most fashionable location, the legendary Manchester nightlife is on hand.

Accommodation

University accommodation is situated close to the campus, with all first-year students guaranteed a place. No one has to share, and about a third of the accommodation is self-catering. Private rented accommodation is readily available through the accommodation office, run by the students' union.

Library and computing

Around 400,000 books are housed in the seven university libraries, which have over 1,300 study spaces. There are 800 computer workstations.

Student facilities

There are four bars, including the Sub Club Bar which is mainly used for entertainments. Cinema screenings, indie and house nights are very popular. The university runs a Job Shop for students looking for part-time and temporary work.

Sport

An outdoor pursuits officer is employed to organise activities such as canoeing, caving and mountaineering. The leisure centre includes four squash courts and a sports hall, whilst there is a new swimming pool, all-weather pitches and floodlit playing fields.

Overseas students

The overseas student population makes up 10 per cent of the total student population. The university organises and runs courses in English as a foreign language.

University of Sheffield

Founded: 1828, Royal charter 1905

Times ranking: 20 (1999 ranking: 13)

Address: Western Bank, Sheffield S10 2TN

tel: 0114 222 8027 or 222 4124
website: www.sheffield.ac.uk
e-mail: ug.admissions@sheffield.ac.uk or prospectus@sheffield.ac.uk

Undergraduates: 14,501 (2,588)
Postgraduates: 3,344 (3,442)
Mature students: 10%
Overseas students: 9%
Applications/place: 9.4
Undergraduates from State sector: 80%

Main subject areas: full range of disciplines in eight faculties: architectural studies; arts; educational studies (postgraduate); engineering; law; medicine; pure science; social sciences.

Teaching quality ratings

Rated Excellent 1993–95: architecture; English; geography; history; law; mechanical engineering; music social work; sociology.

From 1995: electrical and electronic engineering 24; Russian 24; town and country planning 23; East and South Asian studies 22; linguistics 22; materials technology 22; physics 22; chemical engineering 21; civil engineering 21; French 21; health subjects 21; Iberian languages 21; mathematics and statistics 21; nursing 21; German 20; medicine 19.

Overview

Sheffield is enjoying one of the most successful periods in its history, hovering on the fringes of the top ten in *The Times* league table thanks to consistently good ratings for both teaching and research. The university's nine excellent ratings in the early rounds of teaching assessment were among the most anywhere, and only one subject (medicine) has scored fewer than 20 points out of 24 under the current system. Forty per cent of staff entered for the last research assessment exercise were in the top two categories, making Sheffield the top-placed provincial university for research funding, allowing for subject differences.

The star performers have been electrical and electronic engineering and Russian, each of which achieved maximum scores for both teaching and research. Materials science, archaeology, information management and theology were also considered internationally outstanding for research, which the university places at the heart of its brief mission statement.

Sheffield has always enjoyed one of the highest ratios of applications to places – usually around 10:1 – despite expanding throughout much of the 1990s. For the last two years, no places have been available through Clearing. Only medicine and dentistry remain outside the modular course system, which operates on semesters. The university has an unusually large number of mature students for a traditional university and also offers courses in a network of further education colleges.

The academic buildings are concentrated in an area about a mile from the city centre on the affluent west side of Sheffield, with most university flats and halls of residence a little further into the suburbs. Most recent investment in bricks and mortar has focused on medicine and health, which now account for about a fifth of the students. Some £14 million went into a new school of nursing and msidwifery, while a £26 million extension to the medical school will be mainly devoted to obstetrics and gynaecology.

The students' union's long-established student reception service helps new arrivals settle in, visiting those in private accommodation as well as hall-dwellers. Few have much trouble adjusting to the hectic social scene, which is based on the vibrant union facilities but also takes full advantage of the city's burgeoning club life. A 10 per cent drop-out rate was higher than the funding councils expected, allowing for the subject mix, but the remainder seem to thrive. It is said that a quarter stay in Sheffield after graduation.

Accommodation

All first years are guaranteed a place in one of the six university halls of residence. Around 2,900 places are provided, some of which are self-catering. Private rented accommodation is easily obtainable. It is common for a number of students to share a property. The university accommodation office vets houses and attempts to match them to prospective student tenants.

Library and computing

The two main libraries hold over 1.3 million books and have around 2,300 study spaces. IT facilities are very good, with 1,000 PCs available in open-access areas. Departments also have their own IT facilities.

Student facilities

The students' union operates from a new building, providing a wide range of services and entertainment. The university runs TEMPUS, a student jobshop.

Sport

The university provides free facilities including the Goodwin Athletics Centre, floodlit Astroturf pitches, and water sports. The Peak District is close by for rambling, mountaineering and caving. The city also has four world-class sports centres.

Overseas students

The international office and the student advice centre provide support to the relatively large overseas student population. There is also an English Language Teaching Centre, one of the central support services of the university.

Sheffield Hallam University...

Founded: University status 1992, formerly Sheffield Polytechnic

Times ranking: 63 (1999 ranking: 65th equal)

Address: City Campus, Sheffield S1 1WB
tel: 0114 225 5555
website: www.shu.ac.uk
e-mail:undergraduate-admissions@shu.ac.uk

Undergraduates: 14,469 (3,131)
Postgraduates: 1,309 (3,473)
Mature students: 26%
Overseas students: 4%
Applications/place: 6.3
Undergraduates from State sector: 90%

Main subject areas: business, urban and regional studies; computing; construction; cultural studies; education; engineering; financial studies; health and community studies; information technology; law; leisure and food management; management science; science.
Certificate and diploma courses offered.

Teaching quality ratings

Rated Excellent 1993–95: English.

From 1995: psychology 24; mathematics and statistics 23; materials technology 22; sociology 22; town planning 22; building 21; land management 21; mechanical engineering 21; nursing 21; history of art 20; communication studies 19; drama, dance and cinematics 19; modern languages 19; civil engineering 18; electrical and electronic engineering 18.

Overview

A series of good teaching scores in the last year have cemented Sheffield Hallam's position among the leading new universities in *The Times* table. Assessments had been improving steadily after a disappointing start in which only one of the first eight subjects was rated as excellent. But a perfect score for psychology and almost as good a performance in maths and statistics have set new standards.

The university has been undergoing a £51 million transformation designed to alter its image and allow it to cater for an even bigger student population, helping to revitalise the city centre in the process. It considered starting afresh in a less central development area, but will now keep its main site in the heart of Sheffield. Eventually, there are to be only two campuses, but a slump in property prices delayed the final pieces of the reorganisation jigsaw.

Development has been continuing apace, however. New buildings for engineering and information technology have been completed; an atrium provides social space for staff and students; and an innovative library development, the Adsetts Centre, takes pride of place. The Sheffield Business School, which has by far the biggest share of the university's students, has its own city-centre headquarters. A former teacher training college, which has also seen considerable investment, houses education, health and community studies, while cultural studies are further away in a former art college. There is free transport between the three sites.

One of the first three polytechnics to be

established, Sheffield Hallam traces its origins in art and design back to the 1840s. It is now one of the largest of the new universities, with high proportions of part-time and mature students. More than 1,000 students are taught on franchised courses in further education colleges. Business and industry are closely involved in the development of more than 400 courses, with almost half of the students taking sandwich courses. Research is also more applied than pure, but, although not spectacular, the last assessments were better than in most of the new universities.

The university is creating a 'virtual campus' to help students and staff make full use of the internet. All students are being offered e-mail accounts and cheap equipment to give them access to the growing volume of on-line material provided by the university even when they are at home or on work placements, as well as enabling those with laptops to use them on campus.

Accommodation

Only around half of those first years who want university accommodation find space in one of the three halls of residence but there are plans to build a fourth hall with 800 places. Most rooms are singles. Private rented accommodation is easily available through the university accommodation office and from noticeboards.

Library and computing

The libraries hold around 500,000 books and subscribe to a large number of journals. About 1,500 study places are available in the library, as well as 2,300 computer workstations. A learning centre provides lecture theatres and studios.

Student facilities

There are four bars, the main one being the Sara Thornton Bar. 'The Works' is used for big events, 'The Furnace' for small ones. There are four club nights a week and the main hall provides a centre for live music.

Sport

The university provides two sports halls, a gym, a climbing wall and squash courts. It also arranges access to the many specialised sports facilities in Sheffield.

Overseas students

Social support is provided through the international office and student welfare officers, and the Centre for the Teaching of English to Speakers of Other Languages provides English language support.

South Bank University

Founded: University status 1992, formerly South Bank Polytechnic

Times ranking: 92 (1999 ranking: 79)

Address: 103 Borough Road, London SE1 0AA

tel: 020 7815 8158
website: www.sbu.ac.uk
e-mail: registry@sbu.ac.uk

Undergraduates: 11,154 (4,379)
Postgraduates: 1,242 (3,346)
Mature students: 59%
Overseas students: 11%
Applications/place: 6.3
Undergraduates from State sector: 89%

Main subject areas: business; built environment; education; engineering; health; science; social sciences.
A wide range of certificate and diploma courses also offered.

Teaching quality ratings

Rated Excellent 1993–95: none.

From 1995: modern languages 22; town planning 22; health subjects 21; civil engineering 20; media studies 20; electrical and electronic engineering 19; sociology 19; building 18; chemical engineering 18; food science 18; land and property management 18; general engineering 17; mechanical engineering 17.

Overview

South Bank styled itself 'the university without ivory towers', and its mission statement underlines the point with an emphasis on wealth creation and the labour market. The former polytechnic's links with the local community are such that 70 per cent of students are from the area, many coming from south London's wide range of ethnic minorities. Of more than 19,000 students, a third are part-time and half of the undergraduates are on sandwich courses. The proportion of mature students is among the highest in Britain, a feat encouraged by initiatives such as the summer school for local people to upgrade their maths.

South Bank has stayed closer than most of the new universities to the technological and vocational brief given to the original polytechnics. Until the recent explosion in demand for health subjects, engineering was second only to business studies in terms of size. There have been some good teaching assessments, but the university has not quite matched the general improvement in scores seen elsewhere in the last year. Diploma and degree courses run in parallel so that students can move up or down if they are better suited to another level of study.

Social policy recorded the best of several creditable results in the last research assessment exercise, boosting the university's income to such an extent that an analysis which allowed for subject differences placed South Bank top of the new universities and eleventh overall. Specialist facilities such as the Centre for Explosion and Fire Research show that the vocational theme carries through into research.

The main campus is in Southwark, near the Elephant and Castle, and not far from the Riverside Arts Complex. The university has bought an adjacent site, which will be developed for teaching accommodation as soon as financial circumstances allow. A purpose-built site three miles away houses the faculty of the built environment, while health students are on the other side of London, in Romford and Leytonstone.

The social scene suffers from the fact that the large numbers of mature students are more likely to spend their leisure time with their families or in their local communities than with their fellow students. The capital's attractions are on the doorstep but, with 40 per cent of the students coming from working-class homes, many cannot afford them. Financial problems are also partly responsible for a drop-out rate of one in three, almost the worst in Britain and much higher than the funding councils expected, given the subject mix.

Accommodation

Most of those wanting to live in university accommodation are allocated one of the 1,100 places, some of which are self-catering. The university's housing service provides daily accommodation vacancy lists and help with finding housing close by in south London.

Library and computing

There are four libraries holding 300,000 books as well as 1,500 study places and computer workstations. IT courses are available to all students through the Learning Resource Centre, and over 2,500 computers are available on-site.

Student facilities

Six bars are run by the students' union, with The Void used for two club nights a week and live bands. The careers service provides information on part-time and temporary vacancies for students.

Sport

Four football, three cricket and two rugby pitches are located on the university's 21-acre fields. Scrummage machines are available, as well as a sports hall and gym at the South Bank University Sports Centre.

Overseas students

Pre-sessional courses and on-going courses in English are available at the university for the reasonably large overseas student population. A dedicated overseas student adviser is available to provide support and information.

University of Southampton

Founded: 1862, Royal charter 1952

Times ranking: 26th equal (1999 ranking: 22)

Address: Highfield, Southampton SO17 1BJ

tel: 023 8059 5000
website: www.soton.ac.uk
e-mail: prospenq@soton.ac.uk

Undergraduates: 11,687 (3,424)
Postgraduates: 1,957 (2,754)
Mature students: 18%
Overseas students: 6%
Applications/place: 7.8
Undergraduates from State sector: 74%

Main subject areas: wide range of disciplines in eight faculties: arts; education; engineering and applied science; law; mathematical studies; medicine, health and biological sciences; science; social sciences.

Teaching quality ratings

Rated Excellent 1993–95: chemistry; computer science; English; geography; geology; music; oceanography; social work.

From 1995: electrical and electronic engineering 24; general engineering 23; materials 23; molecular biosciences 23; civil engineering 21; mechanical engineering 21; sociology 21; history of art 20; modern languages 18.

Overview

Southampton was transformed during the 1990s, doubling student numbers and opening two new campuses of its own, as well as acquiring two others in college mergers. At the same time, the university's reputation rose, as both teaching and research assessments confirmed the high quality of provision. The past year has seen the culmination of that process with a series of good teaching scores and yet more new building.

The university stresses its research strength: the proportion of income derived from research is among the highest in Britain. Although it was one of the few traditional universities with a subject at the wrong end of the seven-point scale in the last research assessment exercise, the 13 subjects in the top two categories more than compensated. Electrical and electronic engineering is the star performer, with maximum scores for both teaching and research. Nutrition is also rated internationally outstanding for research, while general engineering, materials science and molecular biosciences have all recorded near-perfect teaching scores recently.

The main Highfield campus, in an attractive location two miles from the city centre, has been the focus of recent development to cater for the expansion in numbers. Nursing, chemistry, electronics and computer science have all benefited, and there has been a new commercial services centre as well as a graduate centre for social sciences. A docklands campus opened in 1996 on Southampton's revitalised waterfront. The Oceanography

Centre, a £49 million joint project with the Natural Environmental Research Council, is considered Europe's finest. In the same year, the Avenue campus opened near the main site to house the arts departments. Clinical medicine is based at Southampton General Hospital.

A new dimension was added in 1998 when the university took over the former La Sainte Union campus near the city centre to create Southampton New College. The new facility has a regional focus, offering opportunities for students from different backgrounds to the norm for a university where entry requirements are high and more than a quarter of successful candidates come from independent schools. Winchester School of Art had already joined the fold, complementing the university's Continental outlook with its own well-established European links, which include an outpost in Barcelona for fashion students. Two new buildings have since doubled the physical size of the school.

The city has plenty to offer culturally and has the attraction of a seaside location, but may provide a disappointment for dedicated nightclubbers. The university's own social facilities have struggled to keep up with the pace of expansion.

Accommodation

There are more than 5,000 places in residences, the majority within walking distance of the main teaching sites. First years who nominate the university as their firm choice are guaranteed university residence. The accommodation office advises on renting in the private sector.

Library and computing

The university library has over one million books, 6,000 current periodicals and a range of electronic services, including computerised bibliographical databases and internet resources. Around 900 networked PC and Unix workstations are provided.

Student facilities

The students' union provides services including bars, clubs, a cinema, shops, a newspaper, a florist and entertainment venues. There are more than 200 clubs and societies. Temporary, part-time and vacation work is on offer at the employment service, Openings.

Sport

Facilities include a sports hall, squash courts, fitness facilities, climbing wall and dance studio. Outside pitches provide for most team sports. Also available are a number of tennis courts, an indoor heated swimming pool and a boatyard for watersports enthusiasts.

Overseas students

Introductory conferences about university life are held for new overseas students prior to the start of the academic year. The university has two academic advisers for overseas students and runs four and an eight-week English Language courses.

Staffordshire University

Founded: University status 1992, formerly Staffordshire (originally North Staffs) Polytechnic

Times ranking: 75 (1999 ranking: 83rd equal)

Address: College Road, Stoke-on-Trent ST4 2DE

tel: 01782 294000
website: www.staffs.ac.uk
e-mail: admissions@staffs.ac.uk

Undergraduates: 10,842 (2,845)
Postgraduates: 549 (839)
Mature students: 24%
Overseas students: 8%
Applications/place: 5.0
Undergraduates from State sector: 93%

Main subject areas: applied science; business and management; ceramics; computing; design; economics; electrical and electronic engineering; fine art; geography; history of art; humanities; law mathematics; health and nursing; mechanical and computer-aided engineering; politics; psychology; science; sports.
Diplomas also offered.

Teaching quality ratings

Rated Excellent 1993–95: none.

From 1995: psychology 23; art and design 22; physics and astronomy 22; history of art and design 21; modern languages 21; electrical and electronic engineering 20; media studies 20; building 17; materials technology 17; sociology 17.

Overview

The former polytechnic has been expanding on two main sites, the headquarters in Stoke and the other 12 miles away in Stafford. A massive rationalisation plan, designed to cope with rapid and continuing growth, saw two-thirds of the academic staff move offices. The rural Stafford site, inherited from a 1960s teacher training college, features the purpose-built Octagon Centre, in which lecture theatres, offices and walkways surround one of the largest university computing facilities in Europe. Health, science and engineering are all based at Stafford, while Stoke specialises in the arts and social sciences. The business school, which acquired a new headquarters in Stoke in 1995, straddles the two campuses in an attempt to foster links with the private sector.

However, a new campus in Lichfield gives a glimpse of the future for Staffordshire and many other new universities. An integrated further and higher education centre, developed in partnership with Tamworth and Lichfield College, is the first purpose-built institution of its kind. The university already runs courses at a number of further education colleges in the region, as well as offering incentives for local people to apply. A priority applications scheme guarantees a place to under-21s from Staffordshire, Shropshire or Cheshire as long as they meet the minimum requirements for their chosen course, while mature students are guaranteed at least an interview if they join one of the range of access courses. The policy has been working – more than a third of the students are from the local area.

None of the first 11 subjects to be assessed for teaching quality achieved an excellent rating, but scores have improved recently. Only one of the last five assessments yielded less than 20 points out of 24, with psychology narrowly missing a perfect score. Almost two-thirds of the academics were entered for the last research assessment exercise, but almost all were placed in the bottom three categories. Extensive language laboratories are open to all students and are heavily used. The drop-out rate of one in five was among the better figures for the new universities.

Despite regular free transport between the two main sites, the student experience varies considerably according to location. Stoke is not the liveliest city of its size, but the campus is close the railway station and is within easy reach of the centre. Stafford is much the more attractive setting, but the town is quiet and the campus is a mile and a half outside it.

Accommodation

A majority of first years are accommodated in halls of residence, flats, bedsits or shared houses, both on and off campus at Stoke or Stafford. The accommodation office will help to find private accommodation, and operates a landlord registration scheme.

Library and computing

The university has six libraries, the biggest holding more than 200,000 items, all providing individual study spaces. The university has over 2,000 PCs in modern managed open-access computer laboratories equipped with standard and subject-specific software.

Student facilities

On-campus facilities include the students' union, a film theatre and a large number of activity clubs. Careers offices in Stafford and Stoke provide employer, vocational, and postgraduate advice.

Sport

Recreation services operates instructional groups in a range of activities. Facilities include sports halls, squash courts, grass pitches, a fitness suite, a gym containing multi-gym, freestanding machines, free weights and an ISO-kinetics machine, and a dance studio (Stoke).

Overseas students

The university runs an orientation programme the week before term starts, and offers a range of English language programmes before and during term. Student support provides information to overseas students in many areas including childcare, counselling and student health.

University of Stirling

Founded: Royal charter 1967

Times ranking: 41 (1998 ranking: 33rd equal)

Address: Stirling FK9 4LA

tel: 01786 467044
website: www.stir.ac.uk/
e-mail: admissions@stir.ac.uk

Undergraduates: 5,469 (761)
Postgraduates: 968 (793)
Mature students: 21%
Overseas students: 6%
Applications/place: 6.6
Undergraduates from State sector: 86%

Main subject areas: accountancy; biological and environmental sciences; business and management; computer science and mathematics; economics; education; English; film and media studies; nursing and midwifery; marketing; modern languages; philosophy; political studies; psychology; religious studies; sociology.

Teaching quality ratings

Rated Excellent 1993–98: economics; English; environmental science; psychology; sociology; theology.

Highly Satisfactory 1993–98: business and management; cellular biology; finance and accounting; French; history; mass communications; mathematics and statistics; organismal biology; philosophy; politics; social work; teacher education.

From 1998: European languages 20.

Overview

One of the most beautiful campuses in Britain features low-level, modern buildings in a loch-side setting beneath the Ochil Hills. Airthrey Castle dominates the campus and is used for office accommodation. Even after a 20 per cent expansion over four years, the university will still be among the smallest in Britain and is likely to remain so, despite adding 1,300 students with the incorporation of three nursing colleges at Falkirk, Inverness and Stornoway, in the Western Isles. Stirling also has probably the most popular chancellor: spurning the usual dignitaries, the university chose actress Diana Rigg for the post.

Although highly rated in some research fields – notably the world-renowned Institute of Aquaculture – the university focuses primarily on teaching. Social work was the only starred subject in the last research assessments. Excellent teaching ratings for economics, sociology, theology, business studies, psychology and English show Stirling's strength in the arts and social sciences. Only environmental science has redressed the subject balance, although all but one of the subjects assessed have been rated at least Highly Satisfactory. Film and media studies is particularly popular, while the Scottish Centre for Japanese Studies offers that language with a variety of other subjects.

Stirling was the British pioneer of the semester system, which has now become so popular in other universities. The academic year is divided into two 15-week terms, with short mid-semester breaks. Students have the option of starting courses in February, rather than September. Successful completion of six semesters will bring a general degree; eight, an honours degree. The emphasis on breadth is such that there are no barriers to movement between faculties. Undergraduates can switch the whole direction of their studies, in consultation with their academic adviser, as their interests develop. The modular scheme allows students to speed up their progress on a Summer Academic Programme, which runs in July and August. International exchanges are popular, with students going to American, Asian and European universities each year.

Students appreciate the individual attention a small campus university can offer, although some find the atmosphere claustrophobic. The 1960s campus buildings are beginning to show their age and are being refurbished. Stirling is not the top choice of nightclubbers, but the students' association put on a lively social programme. The surrounding scenery offers its own attractions for walkers.

Accommodation

All new full-time undergraduates are guaranteed accommodation in their first year. Places are allocated on a first come, first served basis, and each hall accommodates approximately 300 students. All university-owned accommodation is self-catering, but a central catering service is provided. The accommodation office will send out lists of off-campus accommodation on request.

Library and computing

The university library contains nearly half a million books, and has space for 680 people to study. There are 100 individual carrels in addition to tables and open carrels. PCs and Macs are available for students in various university locations.

Student facilities

Societies, sports clubs, bars, cafés and a bookshop are on campus. The union has its own newspaper, radio station, arts centre and choir. The careers advisory service is staffed all week with a duty careers adviser system in operation.

Sport

Facilities include a swimming pool, sauna, solarium, athletics track, rugby and soccer pitches, cricket square, tennis and squash courts, sports hall, fixed weight training room, golf course and croquet court, and a loch for sailing, windsurfing and canoeing.

Overseas students

In any single year 75 nationalities are represented on campus. The international office represents the university at recruitment events abroad, and the study abroad office organises admission and exchange.

University of Strathclyde

Founded: 1796, Royal charter 1964

Times ranking: 43 (1999 ranking: 45)

Address: 16 Richmond Street, Glasgow G1 1XQ

tel: 0141 548 2813

website: www.strath.ac.uk

e-mail: j.gibson@mis.strath.ac.uk

Undergraduates: 11,900 (1,760)

Postgraduates: 2,325 (5,895)

Mature students: 15%

Overseas students: 7%

Applications/place: 5.6

Undergraduates from State sector: 89%

Main subject areas: arts and social science; business; education; engineering; science.

Teaching quality ratings

Rated Excellent 1993–98: architecture; business and management; chemistry; electrical and electronic engineering; geography; mechanical engineering; pharmacy; physics; politics.

Highly Satisfactory 1993–98: cellular biology; civil engineering; computer studies; English; history; hospitality studies; law; mathematics and statistics; social work; sociology; teacher education.

From 1988: European languages 22; chemical engineering 20; planning and landscape 19.

Overview

Even as Anderson's Institution in the 19th century, Strathclyde concentrated on 'useful learning'. Some Glaswegians still refer to it as 'the tech'. But if the nickname does less than justice to the current portfolio of courses, the university has never shrunk from its technological and vocational emphasis. Strathclyde aims to offer courses that are both innovatory and relevant to industry and commerce – hence civil engineering with European studies or mathematics with languages.

Traditional science degrees have continued to prosper, however, with a series of top ratings. Although only immunology won the coveted 5* rating for research in the last assessments, six other subjects reached the next rung of the ladder, a record bettered only by Edinburgh and St Andrews in Scotland. All but two of the 26 subjects assessed under Scotland's original system of grading teaching quality were considered Excellent or Highly Satisfactory. The university is in *The Times* top ten for architecture, and just outside it for chemistry and both mechanical and electrical and electronic engineering. But its main strength is in the business school, which is one of the largest in Europe. The careers service is also rated among the best.

A European focus is evident throughout the university, which has encouraged all departments to adapt their courses to the needs of the single market. The credit-based modular course system has proved particularly attractive to mature students, who now account for many of the places and have a special organisation to look after their interests. The 16,000 students, including part-timers, are swelled to 56,000 by a growing number of short courses and distance-learning programmes.

The main John Anderson campus is in the centre of Glasgow, behind George Square and near Queen Street station. Apart from the Edwardian headquarters, the buildings are mostly modern. Since 1993, Strathclyde has also had a second campus on the west side of the city, following a merger with Jordanhill College of Education, Scotland's largest teacher training institution. The 67-acre parkland site has views over the Clyde estuary and the merger has enabled the university to establish a faculty of education.

The university is losing its image as a 'nine-to-five' institution, thanks to a student village on the main campus, complete with pub. Indeed, the ten-floor union building attracts students from all over Glasgow with its reputation for hard-drinking revelry. For those with more sophisticated tastes, there are two theatres as well as the city's own variety of cultural venues.

Accommodation

Full-time students new to Glasgow who meet entry requirements have priority in accommodation. At present over 1,440 students live on campus and approximately 500 live in off-campus university accommodation. The accommodation office will help find private rented accommodation when unable to offer university housing.

Library and computing

Strathclyde University Library is made up of two campus libraries with 2,000 reading spaces. The larger library holds 485,000 books and subscribes to 4,600 periodicals. The main computing facilities include more than 700 PCs and 100 Unix workstations.

Student facilities

The main students' union provides, over 10 floors, a host of welfare and entertainment facilities. The university also offers a range of welfare and careers services.

Sport

The university provides sports facilities including a twin-court games hall, an activities room, a fitness training room, six squash courts, and many outdoor pitches. There is also a gymnasium and a swimming pool.

Overseas students

The university's overseas student adviser sends out pre-arrival information, organises an orientation programme to help students settle in, and provides support throughout the academic session. The university's English Language Teaching Division provides courses in English language and study skills.

University of Sunderland

Founded: University status 1992, formerly Sunderland Polytechnic
Times ranking: 76 (1999 ranking: 91)

Address: Langham Tower, Ryhope Road, Sunderland SR2 7EE

tel: 0191 515 3000
website: www.sunderland.ac.uk
e-mail: student-helpline@sunderland.ac.uk

Undergraduates: 9,944 (2,595)
Postgraduates: 378 (1,072)
Mature students: 32%
Overseas students: 10%
Applications/place: 4.3
Undergraduates from State sector: 94%

Main subject areas: art; business; communications; computing information systems; design; education.

Teaching quality ratings

Rated Excellent 1993–95: none.

From 1995: molecular biosciences 24; anatomy and physiology 23; media studies 22; pharmacy 22; sociology 21; mechanical engineering 19; Iberian languages 18; French 17; German 17.

Overview

Britain's newest city (for the moment) also has one of the newest university campuses. Designed for 8,000 students, St Peter's campus, an award-winning 24-acre site by the banks of the River Wear, now houses the business school and the infomatics centre. Next on the list is a £20 million arts, design and media centre. The main campus and a third site in one of Sunderland's suburbs are within walking distance. The university doubled in size in four years, and has taken advantage of urban regeneration programmes to expand its facilities to match. A well-appointed science complex opened on the city centre site, language laboratories were upgraded and specialist research centres opened for ecology and Japanese studies.

Developments have been planned with an eye to history, for example incorporating a working heritage centre for the glass industry at the heart of the new campus, which is built around a 7th-century abbey described as one of Britain's first universities. The glass and ceramics design degree carries on a Sunderland tradition, while the courses in automotive design and manufacture serve the region's new industrial base. The large pharmacy department is another strength. Teaching assessments have been improving after a poor start. In the past year, molecular biosciences have recorded a perfect score and anatomy and physiology came close. Research assessments were less impressive, with no subjects reaching the top three of the seven categories, but a graduate research school has been established since the 1996 exercise.

The university has a determinedly local focus, aiming to double the number of students coming from an area which has little tradition of participation in higher education. A pioneering access scheme offers places to mature students without A levels, as long as they reach the required levels of literacy, numeracy and other basic skills. The Learning North East initiative, based on Sunderland's successful pilot for the University for Industry, even offers free taster courses to take at home. The university makes particular efforts to cater for the 700 disabled students, including offering a special course to help dyslexics.

Sunderland itself is fiercely proud of its identity and has the advantage of a coastal location but, despite the city title, it has the leisure facilities of a medium-sized town. Those in search of big cultural events or serious nightlife head for the deadly rival, Newcastle, which is less than half an hour away by train or bus.

Accommodation

The university guarantees students a place in university-managed accommodation, and a wide variety of housing is available, providing more than 2,500 beds. Accommodation, both catered and self-catering, includes places in halls, campus flats and shared houses. The university also provides lists of private landlords.

Library and computing

Information Services has four libraries. The collection includes more than 400,000 volumes, 2,000 current periodicals, 90,000 slides and 5,000 videos. Study facilities include 2,000 reader places. A large number of computers are distributed across two campuses.

Student facilities

Facilities include the union's nightclub venue, a shop, on-site travel agency, bars, more than 80 societies and a professional student advice centre. The careers advisory services include information sessions and workshops, in-depth career interviews, and employers' events.

Sport

The university has its own Sports Centre with a fitness suite, swimming pool and sports hall. The students' union plays host to more than 60 organisations ranging from mainstream sports clubs to cultural societies.

Overseas students

The university offers an induction programme, collects new overseas students on arrival, and has a staff contact. A free four-week English language summer school is available before the course begins, as well as free English language classes throughout the course.

University of Surrey

Founded: 1891, Royal charter 1966

Times ranking: 38 (1999 ranking: 30)

Address: Guildford, Surrey GU2 5XH

tel: 01483 879305

website: www.surrey.ac.uk

e-mail: admissions@surrey.ac.uk

Undergraduates: 5,151 (3,248)

Postgraduates: 1,293 (2,705)

Mature students: 12%

Overseas students: 20%

Applications/place: 4.7

Undergraduates from State sector: 84%

Main subject areas: biological sciences; chemical, civil and environmental engineering; education; electronic engineering; health and medical sciences; human sciences; information technology and mathematics; language and international studies; management; mechanical and material engineering; performing arts; physical sciences.

Teaching quality ratings

Rated Excellent 1993–95: business and management; music.

From 1995: electrical and electronic engineering 23; physics and astronomy 23; civil engineering 22; materials technology 22; psychology 22; molecular biosciences 21; sociology 21; chemical engineering 18; drama, dance and cinematics 20; modern languages 18.

Overview

Surrey has remained true to the technological legacy of its predecessor institution, Battersea Polytechnic Institute. Even some of the arts degrees carry a BSc and are highly vocational: four out of five undergraduates in all subjects undertake work experience. Placements of one (or two half) years, often taken abroad, mean that most degrees last four years. The format and subject balance combine to keep UniS, as the institution likes to be called, at the head of the graduate employment league, as well as producing a healthy research income.

Expansion continued in the latter half of the 1990s, when many universities were retrenching. Growth has come almost entirely in full-time courses, and numbers will rise again substantially with the approval of a new relationship with the Roehampton Institute in west London. After a long association with degree courses validated in Guildford, the University of Surrey Roehampton became part of a federation, appointing its own staff and admitting its own students. All students are encouraged to enrol for a course at the European language centre, and a growing number of degrees, including a new range in engineering, have a language component. The cosmopolitan feel is enhanced by one of the largest proportions of overseas students at any university – a feat which won Surrey a Queen's Anniversary Prize.

Recent teaching assessments have been impressive, with physics and astronomy recording a near-perfect score to match that for electrical and electronic engineering, Surrey's only starred research subject. Sociology and toxicology were close to the top rating for research, but the 21 per cent of staff not entered for assessment was high for a traditional university. However, the 13 per cent drop-out rate was better than the funding councils expected, given the subject mix.

The compact campus is a ten-minute walk from the centre of Guildford. Most of the buildings date from the late 1960s, when the university was developing, but the gleaming new European Institute of Health and Medical Sciences offers a striking contrast. Shaped like a giant ship's prow, the steel and glass building houses the large nursing and midwifery departments. The campus includes two lakes, playing fields and residential accommodation.

As a predominantly middle-class city, Guildford has plenty of cultural and recreational facilities, but riotous nightclubs are not encouraged. The campus, inevitably, is the centre of social life. The proximity of London – little more than half an hour away by train – is an attraction to many students, but can leave the campus feeling empty at weekends. It also helps account for the high cost of living, which is not mitigated by the allowances available in the capital.

Accommodation
All first years are offered study bedrooms in university accommodation, which houses about 2,600 students. Second years usually find their own housing in Guildford, with guidance and help from staff in the university accommodation office. The university runs its own headleasing housing.

Library and computing
The library holds 400,000 books and 2,600 periodical subscriptions. There is seating for private study. A number of computer laboratories are equipped with PCs, Macs, X-terminals and various types of specialist equipment and printing facilities.

Student facilities
Campus facilities include bars, student societies, student radio, convenience store, post office, bookshop, and careers service. The latter offers computer-assisted careers guidance systems, careers talks and seminars, emphasising application and interview techniques, and helps students to produce attractive CVs.

Sport
The Students' Union offers more than 50 sports clubs. Sports Centre facilities include squash courts, sport hall, climbing wall and a dance and/or martial arts hall. A second centre offers sports pitches, tennis courts and a bar.

Overseas students
The overseas office offers advice and information and organises introductory lectures and receptions for new overseas students. The English Language Institute provides language support. There is an International Week each year.

University of Sussex

Founded: Royal charter 1961

Times ranking: 34th equal (1999 ranking: 38th equal)

Address: Brighton, East Sussex BN1 9RH

tel: 01273 678416

website: www.sussex.ac.uk

e-mail: UG.Admissions@sussex.ac.uk

Undergraduates: 6,944 (2,351)

Postgraduates: 1,525 (1,157)

Mature students: 28%

Overseas students: 16%

Application/place: 5.5

Undergraduates from State sector: 81%

Main subject areas: African and Asian studies; biological sciences; chemistry; cultural and community studies; engineering; English and American studies; environmental science; European sciences; mathematics and computing; physics; social sciences.

Teaching quality ratings

Rated Excellent 1993–95: anthropology; English; music.

From 1995: sociology 24; American studies 23; mathematics and statistics 23; French 22; linguistics 22; organismal biosciences 22; electrical and electronic engineering 21; media studies 21; history of art 20; modern languages 17.

Overview

Its heyday as the most fashionable campus in Britain may have been 30 years ago, but Sussex's all-round academic reputation has seldom been higher. Sir Harry Kroto's 1996 Nobel Prize for Chemistry was the university's third award. Although only history of art was considered internationally outstanding in the last research assessment exercise, half of the remaining academics were placed in the next category. Sociology registered maximum points for teaching quality, while maths and American studies – a long-established strength – have led a series of good scores in the past year. Applications have been rising steadily, and there are plans for further expansion, particularly in part-time courses and off-campus programmes.

The interdisciplinary approach, which has always been Sussex's trademark, is being re-examined to see whether this 1960s concept needs adaptation for the 21st century. The university hopes to become more creative in the combinations offered to students, although breadth of study is already taken for granted. Social science is by far the biggest area of study, but languages and biological sciences are also substantial.

Sussex is committed to taking candidates with no family tradition of higher education, which partly explains lower average entry scores than in most leading universities. It also has one of the highest proportions of mature students among its peer group of institutions. A survey of graduates five years after leaving Sussex showed an enviable employment record.

The university is based in an 18th-century park at Falmer, close to the South Downs and four miles from the centre of Brighton. Sir Basil Spence's original buildings are ageing but have been supplemented by new developments like the Sussex Innovation Centre. The town centre is 15 minutes away by bus and a mainline station is on the edge of the otherwise self-contained campus.

About one-fifth of the full-time students are postgraduates, attracted by the interdisciplinary research units, which include well-known names like the Institute of Development Studies. Undergraduates can take a year abroad in many subjects, and one student in five takes advantage of this facility, either in Europe or North America. Some courses offer joint qualifications with Continental universities. Sussex has always attracted overseas students in large numbers, but a high proportion of the remainder are from the London area, where many return at weekends. As a result, the well-appointed campus can be quiet, although there is no shortage of social events and Brighton has plenty to offer students.

Accommodation

First-year applicants are offered university owned or managed accommodation. A variety of furnished accommodation both on and off campus is available, all of which is let on a self-catering basis. The housing office provides advice and assistance to any student seeking private rented accommodation.

Library and computing

The library has a collection of more than 750,000 books and subscribes to 3,500 periodicals. There are more than a thousand reading desks. The computing service provides computer clusters around campus with PCs, Macs, and Unix workstations.

Student facilities

The students' union offers welfare services, shops, bars, entertainment, clubs and societies. The Jobshop and Uni-Temp advertise job vacancies. The careers development unit advises students on how to complete application forms, write CVs and deal with interviews.

Sport

The Sport Centre has sports halls, squash courts, dance studios, a function room, sports injury clinic, sauna and solarium, and a sports shop. Facilities at a second complex include a fitness room, squash courts, tennis courts, pitches and disabled facilities.

Overseas students

The International and Study Abroad staff includes an international officer, and produces *International Students' News*, with information of particular relevance to overseas students. A range of English language and study skill classes is available.

University of Teesside

Founded: University status 1992, formerly Teesside Polytechnic

Times ranking: 87 (1999 ranking: 87th equal)

Address: Borough Road, Middlesborough TS1 3BA

tel: 01642 384221
website: www.tees.ac.uk
e-mail: m.lawford@tees.ac.uk

Undergraduates: 7,645 (3,064)
Postgraduates: 287 (1,336)
Mature students: 32%
Overseas students: 5%
Applications/place: 4.5
Undergraduates from State sector: 93%

Main subject areas: business and management; computing and mathematics; design; health; humanities; international studies; law; science and technology; social sciences.
Certificates and diplomas are also offered.

Teaching quality ratings

Rated Excellent 1993–95: computer science.

From 1995: electrical and electronic engineering 21; civil engineering 19; sociology 19; chemical engineering 17.

Overview

Teesside dubs itself the 'Opportunity University', stressing its open access and customer-oriented approach. Official performance indicators show it among the top few universities for the proportions of working-class students and those from areas with little tradition of participation in higher education. Courses franchised to a network of further education colleges in the region help in this regard.

Although never one of the more fashionable polytechnics, the new university has more than 14,000 students, a quarter of them taking sub-degree courses and over a third part-timers. Good use has been made of links with multinationals in the area, and the prize-winning Meteor scheme makes contact with local children while they are still at primary school.

Relatively few subjects have been assessed for teaching quality since the rating system changed in 1995. Electronic engineering produced the best result, but computing and design are also strong. The research record is less impressive, with almost 90 per cent of the academics entered for assessment relegated to the bottom two of the seven categories. History and sociology were the top performers.

The university is now based on one town centre campus in Middlesbrough. Some £30 million has been spent on the campus in recent years, much of it going on a state-of-the-art Open Learning Centre and a replacement for the main library. The programme also included an innovation centre, incorporating virtual reality facilities, computer laboratories and an array of other high technology. The 3,500 health students are now by far the biggest group in the university.

The new facilities are being used to provide degrees in subjects such as computer games design, media technology and virtual reality. Teesside also offers an Individual Programme of Study scheme, which allows students to take combinations outside the usual range of courses. The idea is to tailor a qualification to personal needs, as long as at least half of the final award is based on Teesside courses.

Middlesbrough would not be everyone's choice for a student centre, but there is more nightlife than sceptical southerners might imagine and the cost of living is low. The lively students' union claims to sell some of the cheapest beer in the country and is the centre of most undergraduates' social life.

Accommodation

Priority is given to first years and overseas students. The university has five halls of residence offering a total of 1,000 places. A further 400 places are available in head tenancy properties managed by the university. All university accommodation is self-catering, but facilities vary. The accommodation office can assist in finding properties in the private sector.

Library and computing

The learning resource centre incorporates library services and computer facilities. There are a third of a million volumes of printed material and 1,300 study places, of which 300 have networked workstations. There are more than 1,000 computers across campus.

Student facilities

On-campus facilities include lecture theatres, university cinema and the students' union. The union has bars, a pool hall, club venue and shop, and supports more than 60 societies. Careers service resources include computer programs, magazines and company information files.

Sport

On-campus facilities include a sports hall, indoor climbing wall, fitness centre with weights, exercise machines and sauna. An off-site playing field provides a venue for team games. There are local facilities for squash, indoor tennis, swimming, athletics and snooker.

Overseas students

Student Services offer welfare and advice services including an orientation course. The university provides English language courses for non-native speakers.

Thames Valley University

Founded: University status 1992, formerly West London Polytechnic

Times ranking: 97 (1999 ranking: 94)

Address: St Mary's Road, Ealing, London W5 5RF

tel: 020 8579 5000

website: www.tvu.ac.uk

e-mail: learning.advice@tvu.ac.uk

Undergraduates: 9,009 (3,748)

Postgraduates: 423 (2,523)

Mature students: 55%

Overseas students: 16%

Applications/place: 8.6

Undergraduates from State sector: 92%

Main subject areas: Courses concentrated in four faculties: leisure and hospitality; business; media; nursing and health. Certificates and diplomas are also offered.

Teaching quality ratings

Rated Excellent 1993–95: none.

From 1995: linguistics 22; sociology 22; nursing 20; media studies 18; modern languages 18; American studies 15.

Overview

Barely 30 degrees are left after a restructuring in the wake of a disastrous year, which saw official criticism of TVU's academic standards, the resignation of Mike Fitzgerald, the university's high profile Vice-Chancellor, and a collapse in the demand for places. The courses are concentrated in four faculties: leisure and hospitality, business, media and health, although two-year Higher National Diplomas range more widely. Amongst the casualties were the two top-rated subjects: sociology and linguistics, the latter also achieving one of the few grade 5 research assessments in the new universities.

The action plan has been put together by Sir William Taylor, once the Vice-Chancellor of Hull University, who performed a similar role in less challenging circumstances at Huddersfield University. With TVU plummeting down *The Times* League Table last year, thanks to poor graduate employment scores and (linguistics apart) the worst research record in the university system, Sir William faced an unenviable task. The policy of open access, which ensures that four out of ten undergraduates – the second-highest proportion in Britain – are working-class, already put the university at a disadvantage in rankings such as ours. However, the support of students and staff has given the plan a chance of success.

The split-site university is maintaining the unconventional approach which has become its hallmark. It describes itself as 'student-driven' and boasts a higher proportion of sub-degree students than any of its peers. TVU achieved university status only a year after becoming a polytechnic in a merger between two well-established higher education colleges. The dramatic growth which accompanied the merger may have exacerbated the administrative problems, which caused the Quality Assurance Council to question the university's fitness to award degrees.

TVU occupies town-centre sites in Ealing and Slough, which are linked by a free bus service. The business-orientated campus in Slough consists mainly of 1960s buildings, but has been enhanced by an award-winning learning resources centre designed by Sir Richard Rogers. The busier Ealing base was suffering from overcrowding before retrenchment took place. Almost half of the students are from London or Berkshire, despite an unexpectedly large contingent of overseas students. The large proportion of home-based students makes up to some extent for the absence of residential accommodation, but the remainder find the cost of living high. The mix is not conducive to a socially cohesive and active student body, although the students' union offers a full programme.

Accommodation

Students can apply through the university accommodation service for housing within commuting distance, including full-board lodgings in family homes, rented houses, flats and bedsits. The university accommodation service also holds a register of approved housing within a 3-4 mile radius of the university.

Library and computing

The university has three learning resource centres with library resources, media services and computer facilities under one roof. Facilities at the newest include 450 workspaces, 170 open access workstations and a range of periodicals and publications.

Student facilities

Services at Slough and Ealing include a coffee bar, a shop, entertainment and facilities for student societies. The careers and employment service advisers assist with preparation for interviews and other job search activities.

Sport

The impressive gym at Slough includes a range of weights and fitness training machines, a sports injury clinic and a sauna. Ealing campus gym is smaller, catering for aerobics, stretching and relaxation classes.

Overseas students

The international office runs a 'meet and greet' service and an induction programme to help students settle in and improve language skills. The office organises home stays with British families and gives information on overseas student organisations in London.

University of Ulster

Founded: Royal charter 1984, formerly the New University of Ulster and Ulster Polytechnic (merged 1984)

Times ranking: 55 (1999 ranking: 54th equal)

Address: Cromore Road, Coleraine, Co. Londonderry BT52 1SA

tel: 028 7032 4421
website: www.ulst.ac.uk
e-mail: online@ulst.ac.uk

Undergraduates: 12,084 (3,386)
Postgraduates: 1,533 (3,388)
Mature students: 21%
Overseas students: 16%
Application/place: 8.2

Undergraduates from State sector: 95%

Main subject areas: art and design; business and management; education; humanities; infomatics; science and technology; social and health sciences.
A wide range of certificate and diploma courses also offered.

Teaching quality ratings

Rated Excellent 1993–95: environmental studies; music; social policy.

From 1995: American studies 22; drama, dance and cinematics 22; building 21; land management 21; media studies 21; electrical and electronic engineering 20; French 20; civil engineering 19; German 19; Iberian languages 18; sociology 17.

Overview

The brief initial life of the Northern Ireland Assembly lasted just long enough to see the culmination of Ulster's campaign for a 'peaceline campus' linking Belfast's two communities. The £70 million Springvale Educational Village will open in 2003, offering both further and higher education courses. The spread is appropriate for the only British university with a charter stipulating that there should be courses below degree level. There is plenty of scope for expansion, despite the fact that Ulster already has more than 20,000 students. The main sites in and near Belfast have never been busier, while the expanded Magee College, in Londonderry, attracts students from the Republic of Ireland as well as Northern Ireland. For many years the poor relation, confined to adult education, it is now a thriving centre. High technology brings the university together for teaching purposes, but the sites are 80 miles apart at their farthest point and very different in character. Jordanstown, seven miles outside Belfast, has the most students, while the isolated original university campus, at Coleraine, follows the style of the 1960s, and is the most traditional in outlook. The small Belfast site specialises in art and design.

Although often overshadowed by Queen's University, Ulster's community consciousness has made it a popular choice among students in the province. Almost 40 per cent come from blue-collar backgrounds – more than twice the UK average – and the student profile mirrors the religious balance in the wider population. Mature students are well catered for, with a nursery and three playgroups in the university. Teaching ratings have mainly been sound, rather than spectacular, with drama and American studies producing the best scores in recent years. Research is not Ulster's principal strength, although biomedical sciences were rated internationally outstanding and history did well in an otherwise mediocre set of assessments in 1996.

There has never been a big representation from mainland Britain, but 16 per cent of the students come the Continent or further afield. With more of the province's teenagers opting to stay at home for higher education in 1999, entrance requirements may rise in the near future. As with any split-site university, the student experience varies according to the location. Some courses offer lectures on more than one campus, but for the most part students are based on a single site throughout their university career. With more than half of the students living with their parents or in their own homes, the university is not always the focus of social life.

Accommodation

The accommodation office offers mostly self-catering accommodation on four different campuses, a majority of which are reserved for first-year students. Other accommodation available through the office includes bed-places – under a head lease scheme – and off-campus houses and flats. The office also maintains an up-to-date list of registered private lodgings.

Library and computing

Library facilities include more than half a million titles, 5,000 journals and newspapers, a collection of British, Irish and American radical newspapers, and study carrels. There are more than 60 computer labs with a variety of machines.

Student facilities

Students' union facilities across campuses include shops, catering operations, clubs and societies and travel agents. The careers service helps to find jobs, placements and vacation opportunities, and holds information on employers.

Sport

Outdoor facilities include football and rugby fields and synthetic pitches for hockey or football. Coleraine and Magee sports centres include indoor gyms and squash courts. Jordanstown sports centre includes squash and basketball courts, a swimming pool and weights room.

Overseas students

The university organises an orientation programme at the start of each semester. The Centre for English Language Teaching provides English language teaching for overseas students on all four of the university's campuses, and offers a pre-sessional course in English.

University of Wales, Aberystwyth

Founded: 1872

Times ranking: 47 (1999 ranking: 48)

Address: Aberystwyth, Ceredigion SY23 2AX

tel: 01970 622021
website: www.aber.ac.uk
e-mail: nmd@aber.ac.uk

Undergraduates: 5,699 (1,565)
Postgraduates: 1,279 (545)
Mature students: 13%
Overseas students: 8%
Applications/place: 4.3
Undergraduates from State sector: 89%

Main subject areas: accounting and finance; biological sciences; computer science; economics; education; English; European languages; geography and earth sciences; information and library studies; law; mathematics; media studies; physics; politics; Welsh.

Teaching quality ratings

Rated Excellent 1993–97: accounting and finance; earth studies; economics; English; environmental science; geography; information and library studies; politics Welsh.

Overview

Although the oldest of the Welsh university colleges, Aberystwyth has long prided itself on a modern outlook. The modular degree system has been running since 1993, covering academic and vocational courses, and the principle of flexibility was established long before that. Uniquely in the UK, every student is offered the opportunity of a year's work experience in commerce, industry or the public sector, either at home or abroad. Students who have taken advantage of the scheme have achieved better than average degrees and enhanced their employment prospects.

The college was forced to make cuts in the 1990s, shedding staff in biological sciences, geology and continuing education. But a new school of management and business has opened recently and a Community University of Rural Wales is taking higher education to areas previously starved of higher education opportunities.

An attractive seaside location does the college no harm when the applications season comes around. A new centre for theatre, film and television studies is the latest addition to the Penglais campus, which overlooks the town. 'Aber' is always heavily oversubscribed even though the number of places has increased substantially in recent years. Almost a third of the students are Welsh.

Merger with the Welsh Agricultural College produced a new Institute of Rural Studies in 1997, allowing Aber to claim the widest range of land-related courses in the UK. The institute shares the Llanbadarn campus with information and library studies and a further education college. Teaching ratings have been impressive, especially in the arts and social sciences. Although no subject managed a 5* rating for research, applied mathematics held onto its grade 5 score, and was joined by politics and Celtic studies. Mathematics and science courses accept general studies as full A or AS levels as long as applicants have passed two other subjects. More than 40 entrance scholarships are available, worth up to £1,150 a year with a guarantee of university accommodation for three years. There are also 50 merit awards of £300 on offer to those who sit the scholarship competition. Aber boasts one of higher education's most informative websites and also publishes a 12-page guide for parents.

The town of Aberystwyth is small and travel to other parts of the UK slow, so applicants should be sure that they will be happy to spend three years or more in a tight-knit community. Most are: 95 per cent of first-year students responding to the annual satisfaction survey said they would make the same choice again.

Accommodation

The university will provide either catered or self-catering accommodation for all first years. University halls and flats, with a total of 3,100 places, are all close to the campus overlooking Cardigan Bay. Good quality private accommodation is available in the town, which is only a few minutes' walk from the campus.

Libraries and computing

There are four libraries, the main one being the Hugh Owens Library on the Penglais campus. Close by is the National Library of Wales with over six million volumes. Open-access computing facilities are located throughout the campuses.

Student facilities

The students' union is the focus of social life, providing a wide range of facilities, and a new arts centre has recently opened.

Sport

The university has a swimming pool and a sports hall, which includes a climbing wall and badminton and squash courts, as well as good outdoor facilities.

Overseas students

There are fewer overseas students than at many other universities. The university provides courses for students with English as a second language and helps them to adapt to life in Britain.

University of Wales, Bangor

Founded: 1884

Times ranking: 50 (1999 ranking: 51)

Address: Bangor, Gwynedd LL57 2DG

tel: 01248 382016
website: www.bangor.ac.uk
e-mail: admissions@bangor.ac.uk

Undergraduates: 5,491 (1,237)
Postgraduates: 854 (1,118)
Mature students: 24%
Overseas students: 7%
Applications/place: 4.9
Undergraduates from State sector: 89%

Main subject areas: accountancy and banking; arts; biological and environmental sciences; education; electrical and electronic engineering; health studies; languages; mathematics and computing; pure and applied sciences; social sciences; sports sciences.

Teaching quality ratings

Rated Excellent 1993–97: biology; chemistry; forestry; music; ocean sciences; psychology; Russian; theology; Welsh.

Overview

Bangor's community focus dates back to a 19th-century campaign which saw local quarrymen putting part of their weekly wages towards the establishment of a college. The Community University of North Wales, which provides courses in further education colleges, continues that tradition, but the college has also built a world-wide reputation in the meantime in areas such as ocean sciences and environmental studies.

Although the last research assessments were disappointing, with only psychology in the top two categories, half of the subjects are rated as excellent for teaching. As well as traditional strengths such as biology and forestry, the list includes Russian, placing Bangor in *The Times* top ten for the subject. There are more than 250 degree courses, with a high proportion of small-group teaching and tutorials. A range of £1,000 scholarships is available to offset the cost of tuition fees. Bangor merged with a teacher training college, Colleg Normal, in 1996, but all departments are within walking distance of each other, apart from ocean sciences, which is two miles away near the Menai Bridge. Departments such as philosophy and physics closed in a major restructuring designed to enable the college to concentrate on its strengths. Recent changes have seen departments coming together, most recently with a school of informatics encompassing electronic engineering, computer systems and mathematics.

Based at the water's edge, little more than a stone's throw from Snowdonia, Bangor is one of the university's expanding centres for Welsh-medium teaching, also offering a single honours degree in the subject. More than 10 per cent of the students speak the language and one of the seven halls of residence is Welsh-speaking. The college also has a flourishing international exchange programme, however, with some unusual partner institutions. Poland and Italy are favourite destinations for linguistics students, for example, while biologists tend to head for Sweden or Norway. All biology, chemistry or engineering degrees carry the option of a year abroad.

Bangor is not the remote location that English students may imagine: Liverpool is less than an hour away and even Ireland is easily accessible by ferry. The university is the focus of social and cultural life in the small town (officially a city) where the 7,000 students account for a third of the population during term-time. Nightlife is inevitably limited, although the students' union has opened its own £1 million club with a capacity of 800.

Accommodation

Bangor guarantees catered or self-catering accommodation for all first year students and over 2,500 places are also available for second and third-year students. Most students live close to the university, and the accommodation office provides details of private rental properties.

Library and computing

As well as the main library there are seven other subject-specific libraries plus special collections such as the Welsh Library. There are a number of open-access PC centres sited around the campus.

Student facilities

Bangor is a small university and this fact appeals to many students. Most university buildings are close to the city centre, which has a reputation for being student friendly. The students' union has a wealth of clubs and societies.

Sport

Bangor is a National Coaching Foundation centre and has great facilities for team sports. There is also an athletic track; three sports halls, tennis courts and floodlit pitches. Bangor also has some of the best indoor sports facilities in Wales.

Overseas students

The overseas student adviser is located in the students' union building and provides advice on issues affecting overseas students.

Cardiff University of Wales

Founded: Royal charter 1988, formerly University College (founded 1883) and University of Wales Institute of Science and Technology (founded 1866), merged 1988

Times ranking: 30 (1999 ranking: 35)

Address: PO Box 921, Cardiff CF10 3XQ

tel: 029 7911 5000

website: www.cardiff.ac.uk

e-mail: prospectus@cf.ac.uk or admissions@cf.ac.uk

Undergraduates: 11,518 (3,181)
Postgraduates: 2,237 (1,533)
Mature students: 11%
Overseas students: 9%
Applications/place: 5.8
Undergraduates from State sector: 83%

Main subject areas: business studies and law; health and life sciences; humanities and social studies; engineering and environmental design; physical sciences.

Teaching quality ratings

Rated Excellent 1993–97: accounting and finance; anatomy and physiology; archaeology; architecture; biochemistry; biology; chemistry; civil engineering; dentistry; education; environmental engineering; English language; electrical and electronic engineering; maritime studies; mechanical engineering; medicine; optometry; pharmacy; philosophy; psychology; town planning.

Overview

Cardiff has established itself as the front-runner in Welsh higher education after a period of financial instability. Although still part of the University of Wales, there is little sign of the federal university in Cardiff's promotional material. With more than 14,000 students, including over 3,000 postgraduates, it is a match for most rivals in teaching and research. A third of the students come from Wales, but the 1,400 from overseas countries testify to Cardiff's international reputation.

Only city and regional planning was rated internationally outstanding in the last research assessments, but half of the academics entered for the exercise were placed in one of the top two categories. The overall performance was among the best in Britain, and research income has since increased sharply. The 21 subjects rated as excellent for teaching quality represent more than half of the university, with psychology and mechanical engineering boasting top scores for both teaching and research. Humanities and social sciences take the largest share of places. A partial reorganisation has created two 'super schools' of biosciences and social sciences, while a new Centre for Lifelong Learning co-ordinates 700 courses for more than 16,000 students, which are offered at 100 regional centres. Many full-time degrees share a common first year, and the introduction of a modular system has made undergraduate study more flexible.

The university enjoys a central location in the Welsh capital, occupying a significant part of the civic complex around Cathays Park. In recent years, £140 million has been invested in new buildings and equipment, and extensive refurbishment. The flagship project involved a £30 million centre for engineering, physics and computing science, with facilities comparable with the best in Britain.

Entry standards have been rising, despite recent expansion, and the graduate employment record is good. The University of Wales College of Medicine is a partner institution, with Cardiff teaching pre-clinical courses and collaborating in spin-off research.

The city of Cardiff is popular with students, offering all the attractions of a large conurbation without such high prices as students experience elsewhere.

Accommodation

Following recent expansion, Cardiff now has over 4,800 places and can guarantee accommodation for all first years. Catered and self-catering properties are available as well as single sex halls and accommodation for people with disabilities. Private rented property is widely available, though the cheapest can be some distance from the university.

Library and computing

The university holds over a million volumes in ten resource centres located close to the departments they serve. The computer network links PCs, Macs and UNIX servers, with some computers available 24 hours a day.

Student facilities

Cardiff is a vibrant city. The students' union provides an excellent range of facilities, clubs and societies. The Unistaff scheme provides part-time employment for students within the university.

Sports

The university has extensive modern sports facilities including three multi-purpose sports halls, two weight-training rooms, two fitness-training rooms, squash courts and all-weather and floodlit pitches. There are over 50 university sports clubs.

Overseas students

Students from over 100 countries are currently studying at the university and the international office is the main point of contact with the university for any questions or problems. The university offers English language support.

University of Wales, Lampeter

Founded: Founded 1822, part of University of Wales since 1971

Times ranking: 57 (1999 ranking: 58)

Address: College Street, Lampeter, Ceredigion SA48 7ED

tel: 01570 423530
website: www.lamp.ac.uk/recruitment
e-mail: recruit@lampeter.ac.uk

Undergraduates: 1,490 (346)
Postgraduates: 94 (284)
Mature students: 43%
Overseas students: 10%
Applications/place: 2.9
Undergraduates from State sector: 86%

Main subject areas: ancient Greek; ancient history; archaeology; classics; English; geography; history; informatics; Islamic studies; medieval studies; modern languages; philosophy; religious studies; theology; Victorian studies; Welsh studies; women's studies.

Teaching quality ratings

Rated Excellent: archaeology; classics and ancient history.

Overview

In the whole of England and Wales, only Oxford and Cambridge were awarding degrees before Lampeter, yet only Buckingham University is smaller today. In fact, Lampeter claims to be the smallest publicly funded university in Europe, making a virtue of its size by stressing its friendly atmosphere and intimate teaching style. Based on an ancient castle and modelled on an Oxbridge college, St David's College was established to train young men for the Anglican ministry. That title receded into the small print, as the University of Wales allowed its member institutions to drop their college titles.

There have been significant changes in the last few years – notably the introduction of information studies – and there are now 300 course combinations available in the joint honours programme. But there is no immediate aim to go beyond 1,700 students, itself almost double the numbers taken a few years ago. Lampeter will remain an arts-dominated haven in rural Wales. Even informatics leads to a BA, and the Bachelor of Divinity is the only other undergraduate award.

Lampeter is best known for languages and theology, the top-rated research department. But students are opting increasingly for joint honours, incorporating broad courses such as medieval studies, which includes archaeology, classics and theology, as well as history, English and Welsh. Modular degrees have been introduced, but degrees are still divided into two parts, with the first year designed to ensure breadth of study. Undergraduates are encouraged to try a new language, such as Arabic, Greek or Welsh. Part two normally takes a further two years, although languages and philosophy take three.

Though the majority of students are English, most departments offer the option of tuition in Welsh. Lampeter is deep in Welsh-speaking West Wales, and both the college and the students' union have strong bilingual policies. The college is also taking Welsh to a wider audience, with the only university course teaching the language over the internet.

Although only four hours from London and two from Cardiff, Lampeter's isolation could be a problem for the unprepared. The town has only 4,000 inhabitants and the nearest station is more than 20 miles away at Carmarthen. A high proportion of the students run cars. The students' union is the centre of social life – not surprising when the university's guide to the town lists its attractions as 'cafés, pubs, a curry house and a French patisserie'.

Accommodation

Two thirds of students live in hall, where rents are lower than at other universities. The campus is compact and well-equipped, and there is ample and relatively cheap residential accommodation nearby.

Library and computing

There are six PC labs, which share 100 workstations; internet access and e-mail is also available. The main university library houses the contemporary holdings, and the Founders' Library has substantial holdings of older materials, including medieval manuscripts.

Student facilities

The student's union houses a bar, café and shop, and the union also provides pastoral and social services in the shape of a purpose-built nursery, a fitness centre, a 24-hour welfare service and a 'walk home' service.

Sports

Lampeter has one of the oldest rugby teams in Wales and a hockey side that got to the last eight in last year's BUSA plate competition. The clubs available include tae kwon do, darts, mountain biking and netball. There is a modern sports hall.

University of Wales, Swansea

Founded: Royal charter 1920

Times ranking: 45 (1999 ranking: 46)

Address: Singleton Park, Swansea SA2 8PP

tel: 01792 295111
website: www.swan.ac.uk
e-mail: admissions@swansea.ac.uk

Undergraduates: 7,539 (1,238)
Postgraduates: 1,229 (1,728)
Mature students: 13%
Overseas students: 7%
Applications/place: 4.3
Undergraduates from State sector: 88%

Main subject areas: arts and business; economics; engineering; health; law; science; social sciences.

Teaching quality ratings

Rated Excellent 1993–97: biosciences; chemical engineering; civil engineering; classics and ancient history; computer science; electrical and electronic engineering; geography; German; history; Italian; materials engineering; physics; psychology; Spanish.

Overview

Although still small enough to feature in merger speculation, Swansea is second only to Cardiff in terms of size within the University of Wales. With an attractive coastal location and accessible to students from outside the principality, it is also a natural alternative to the Welsh capital for thousands of applicants. Numbers have been growing steadily, easing financial problems, which led to a reduction in staff numbers.

A wide variety of new courses has been introduced, as part of a development plan stressing language combinations. There are now 450 degree courses in the modular scheme, and undergraduates are encouraged to stray outside their specialist area in their first year. Swansea takes its European interests seriously, with links to more than 90 Continental institutions. The new law school offers options in European and international law, while science students, as well as those on arts courses, can undertake some of their studies abroad.

About half of the subjects assessed for teaching quality have been rated Excellent. Swansea counts European management science and modern languages among its strengths, and all branches of engineering are highly rated. Civil engineering and metallurgy and materials were the top-rated subjects in the last research assessments, when the overall performance was mixed.

For all its concentration on international activities, however, Swansea has not forgotten its local responsibilities. A University of the Valleys offers part-time courses for mature students in an area hard hit by pit closures and the decline of the steel industry. Franchised courses have been introduced in local further education courses and a compact with schools in mid-Glamorgan encourages students in areas of economic disadvantage to aspire to higher education.

The immediate locality is far from depressing, however. The coastal campus, two miles from the centre of Swansea, offers ready access to the excellent beaches of the Gower Peninsula, and the university occupies an attractive parkland site. Apart from Singleton Abbey, the neo-Gothic mansion which houses the administration, most of the buildings are modern. The city has a reasonable range of leisure facilities, but the campus itself is the focus of social life.

The university makes a particular effort to cater for disabled students. There are facilities for blind, deaf and wheelchair-bound students, and graduates are invited to join the Volunteer Student Support Scheme, working with disabled students in exchange for free accommodation and a spending allowance.

Accommodation

Most first years who apply are normally allocated university housing, which cover a range of accommodation types. The university has five halls of residence. There is a good supply of private housing within a three-mile radius of the campus. The accommodation office publishes a list of properties available.

Library and computing

The Library and Information Centre (LIC) contains over 700,000 books and over 3,000 periodical titles . Library and information services provides over 200 PCs that may be used by any registered student.

Student facilities

Facilities include a bookshop, a study abroad office, bank, Kopy shop, chaplaincy, counselling services, a dental unit and a post office. The careers centre offers appointments with career advisers and help with all aspects of job searching.

Sport

The sports centre includes a hall with squash courts, a climbing wall and an indoor swimming pool. There are playing fields for rugby and football, an athletics track, and tennis and netball courts. Sailing, surfing and canoeing are possible nearby.

Overseas students

The international student adviser provides information and counselling for all overseas students. Other services include one-to-one counselling, a pre-arrival handbook, orientation programme and pre-sessional English courses. The Centre for Applied Language Studies (CALS) also provides English classes.

University of Warwick

Founded: Royal charter 1964

Times ranking: 8th equal (1999 ranking: 7)

Address: Coventry CV4 7AL

tel: 02476 523723

website: www.warwick.ac.uk/

e-mail: ugadmissions@admin.warwick.ac.uk

Undergraduates: 7,878 (3,112)

Postgraduates: 2,471 (3,768)

Mature students: 8%

Overseas students: 11%

Application/place: 9.9

Undergraduates from State sector: 77%

Main subject areas: arts; education; science; social studies in 29 departments.

Teaching quality ratings

Rated Excellent 1993–95: business and management; computer science; English; history; law.

From 1995: drama and cinematics 24; sociology 24; German 23; media studies 23; molecular biosciences 23; French 21; general engineering 21; history of art 21; Italian 21 psychology 21.

Overview

The most successful of the first wave of new universities, Warwick was derided by many in its early years for its close links with business and industry. Few are critical today. Tony Blair described the university as 'at the cutting edge of what has to happen in the future'. Both teaching and research are very highly rated, but the university's mission statement still stresses the extension of access to higher education, continuing education and community links.

Warwick was the first university to see two subjects – theatre studies and sociology – register maximum points for teaching, while computing, history and pure maths were all rated internationally outstanding for research. The most recent assessments are good without quite hitting those heights, although molecular biosciences came close. The overall standard of the 29 departments brought Warwick a top European award, while the science park, one of the first in Britain, is among the most successful.

While other leading universities have tried to cover the whole range of academic disciplines, Warwick has pursued a selective policy. Without the expense of medicine, dentistry or veterinary science to bear, the university has invested shrewdly in business, science and engineering. However, the temptation of medicine has proved too much to bear, and the university has gone into partnership with Leicester University to establish a new kind of course for graduates in the life sciences.

Warwick has been building up its numbers in science and engineering, as other universities have struggled to fill their places. The business school has also been growing rapidly, with a new wing added recently and a £15 million extension planned. Some £35 million has been spent on the campus, which has often resembled a building site. However, students have welcomed larger union facilities, a number of academic buildings have been improved and the Arts Centre (the second largest in Britain) has been refurbished with a £3 million Lottery grant. The 720-acre campus is three miles south of Coventry, where many students choose to live, and three times as far from Warwick.

Such is the demand for places, that many departments stick rigidly to offers averaging more than an A and two Bs at A level. Though the university has been expanding undergraduate admissions by 5 per cent a year, it still sees itself primarily as a research university. The emphasis recently has been on building up the research base, which saw almost half of the academics in the last assessment exercise placed in the top two categories.

Accommodation

Warwick offers on-campus accommodation to all first-year students , but no guarantee can be given to Clearing students. The university has six halls and four groups of flats, mostly self-catering, giving a total of 5,000 places. The accommodation office has a property-leasing scheme and offers advice for safe entry into the private market.

Library and computing

The library stocks more than 900,000 books and bound periodicals, as well as 5,000 current periodicals. A network of PCs across campus is available for students, including 200 computers in the library.

Student facilities

Campus shops include a post office, supermarket, pharmacy and bookshop. The students' union provides launderettes, a travel agency and entertainment. The careers service contains resources including careers information, occupational files, books, videos, employer files and vacancy information.

Sport

The university sports centre includes a swimming pool, squash courts, climbing room, fitness rooms, and a gymnastics and dance studio. Outdoor playing fields include pitches and cricket squares.

Overseas students

Overseas students are offered pre-arrival information, help from visiting international office staff, pre-sessional English language courses and an orientation programme. The international office provides help during their stay at Warwick.

University of Westminster

Founded: Founded 1838, university status 1992, formerly Polytechnic of Central London

Times ranking: 66 (1999 ranking: 61)

Address: 309 Regent Street, London W1R 8AL

tel: 020 7911 5000
website: www.wmin.ac.uk
e-mail: admissions@westminster.ac.uk

Undergraduates: 8,864 (6,123)
Postgraduates: 1,153 (3,413)
Mature students: 45%
Overseas students: 13%
Applications/place: 6.7
Undergraduates from State sector: 86%

Main subject areas: biosciences; business and management; computing; design; electronics; environment; languages and communication; law mathematics; social studies.
Certificate and diploma courses also offered.

Teaching quality ratings

Rated Excellent 1993–95: none.

From 1995: East and South Asian studies 23; French 23; media studies 23; Middle Eastern and African Studies 22; building 22; art and design 21; electrical and electronic engineering 21; molecular biosciences 21; civil engineering 20; German 20; linguistics 20; town planning 20; land management 19; Iberian languages 18; Italian 19; Russian 18; sociology 18.

Overview

Westminster spent much of the 1990s extending and upgrading its premises, and the task is still not complete. The university has turned its attention from what was Europe's largest university construction project – the £33 million transformation of the former Harrow College, in north London – to one of the three central sites, opposite Madame Tussaud's. The large business school will acquire a 'cloistered environment' in a £9.5 million scheme which will create more space for teaching and research.

The greenfield Harrow campus now boasts a high-tech information resources centre with new facilities for the highly-rated media studies courses. Computing and design are also based on a site designed for 7,500 students. The West End sites enjoy the perfect catchment area for part-time students, who account for almost half of the 23,000 places. Only the Open University has more.

The historic headquarters building, near Broadcasting House, houses law, social sciences and languages. French and Chinese have scored particularly well in teaching assessments, and Westminster claims to offer the largest number of languages (25) of any British university. Science and health courses are concentrated on the Cavendish campus, near the BT Tower. The university's growing interest in health covers degrees from the British College of Naturopathy and Osteopathy and a range of courses in complementary medicine, including a BSc in acupuncture. Westminster also validates courses at Trinity College of Music, the second-oldest conservatoire in the UK. Students on its four-year 'Music Plus' degree study languages at the university as part of their course. The college also has a music education department which offers professional enhancement opportunities for music teachers.

A series of good teaching quality scores in the past year have cemented Westminster's position among the leading new universities in *The Times* League Table. The university weaves work-related skills into its degree programmes. It also saw some of the best research grades among the new universities in the last research assessment exercise, with communication and information studies rated nationally outstanding. With almost 30 per cent of the academic staff not entered for assessment, the successes did not translate into large amounts of additional funding, but the university's reputation was enhanced.

Like those at all the London universities, Westminster's students complain of the high cost of living, particularly for accommodation. The Harrow campus is lively socially, but those based on the other sites tend to be spread around the capital.

Accommodation

There are approximately 1,300 places in the university's halls of residence. An offer of a place, which is for one year only, is made to about half of those who apply. All halls have shared kitchens. Most students who do not live at home rent private housing, and the university provides help and advice.

Library and computing

Information Systems and Library Services consists of five integrated libraries, the university archive and Information Systems. The total book stock is 380,000 volumes and ISLS currently subscribes to 2,800 periodicals. The network provides 6,330 desktop-access and dial-up access points.

Student facilities

The union runs activities including its magazine *The Smoke*, the web communications initiative, societies and a bar and entertainments venue. The careers service provides literature on a range of employment and study areas and offers advice sessions.

Sport

The sports ground includes a running track, various pitches, tennis courts, cricket squares and a boathouse with rowing tank. The indoor sports halls allow for team sports. There are also fitness suites.

Overseas students

The university organises a four-day residential orientation programme, and offers English language courses. The overseas student adviser provides information, support and advice to overseas students.

University of the West of England, Bristol

Founded: University status 1992, formerly Bristol Polytechnic

Times ranking: 61 (1999 ranking: 63rd equal)

Address: Frenchay Campus, Coldharbour Lane, Bristol BS16 1QY

tel: 0117 976 3801

website: www.uwe.ac.uk

e-mail: admissions@uwe.ac.uk

Undergraduates: 14,411 (4,376)

Postgraduates: 1,011 (2,559)

Mature students: 31%

Overseas students: 6%

Applications/place: 5.2

Undergraduates from State sector: 79%

Main subject areas: applied sciences; art, media and design; built environment; business and management; computer studies; economics and social science; education; engineering; health and social care; humanities, languages and European studies; mathematics.

Teaching quality ratings

Rated Excellent 1993–95: business and management; English; law.

From 1995: pharmacy and biosciences 24; sociology and social policy 23; town and country planning 23; land and property management 22; media studies 22; building 21; electrical and electronic engineering 21; modern languages 21; agriculture 20.

Overview

West of England (UWE) boasts the best teaching quality record in the new universities and has always been regarded among the leaders in its peer group. A perfect score in the joint assessment for pharmacy and biosciences is the latest and best result, but every subject assessed since 1995 has been given at least 20 out of 24 points. A high ratio of applications to places demonstrates the university's high standing in a variety of areas, with sociology and town planning particularly highly rated.

The university chose a regional title from more than 100 suggestions when it ceased to be a polytechnic, reflecting the institution's ambitions. More than half of the students come from the region and there are close links with local business and industry. With a network of six associated colleges stretching into Somerset and Wiltshire, UWE is now comfortably the biggest university in the southwest. The entrance system credits vocational qualifications and practical experience equally with traditional academic results.

A tradition of vocational education, which UWE somehow traces back to the 16th century, regularly helps the university to a healthy graduate employment record. Law received a commendation from the Legal Practice Board, while the business school is among the biggest in Britain, with 3,000 students on a wide range of courses. The last research assessments were mixed, but media studies achieved one of the better scores in the new universities.

There are five sites in Bristol itself, mainly around the north of the city, with regional centres in Bath, Swindon and Gloucester. Only Bower Ashton, which houses art and design, is in the south. The main campus at Frenchay, close to Bristol Parkway station but four miles out of the city centre, has by far the largest number of students and includes the Centre for Students Affairs, which brings together the various non-academic services. It also houses England's Higher Education Funding Council.

The St Matthias site (for psychology and humanities) and Glenside (for midwifery, nursing, physiotherapy and radiography) are more attractive but less lively. Education is based on the Redland campus, which is the most convenient for the city centre and consequently popular with students. Agriculture is based at Hartpury College, near Gloucester, where a country estate includes an equine centre as well as farmland.

Bristol is a hugely popular student centre, especially with independent schools, whose applicants take more than 20 per cent of the places. It is an attractive and lively city, but not cheap.

Accommodation

The university will normally provide a residential place to full-time first years. There is a choice between shared houses or flats, either adjacent to the campuses or in the city centre. The student accommodation service maintains a register of private accommodation, and can provide details of accommodation for rent throughout Bristol.

Library and computing

The university has eight campus libraries, linked to faculties. The large computer networks links all the sites in Bath, Bristol, Gloucester and Swindon.

Student facilities

The university has five campuses in and around the city of Bristol. The students' union offers services including an advice centre, clubs and Jobshop. The careers service offers the usual range of advice on job hunting skills.

Sport

The students' union runs about 40 sports clubs, including water-based activities, hang gliding, parachuting and martial arts. The Recreation Centre organises various activities including aerobics, step classes and squash coaching.

Overseas students

The university offers several English language courses at various levels. The centre for student affairs helps with welfare benefits, financial difficulties, immigration enquiries, legal matters and personal issues.

University of Wolverhampton

Founded: University status 1992, formerly Wolverhampton Polytechnic

Times ranking: 77th equal (1999 ranking: 77)

Address: Wulfruna Street, Wolverhampton WV1 1SB

tel: 01902 321000
website: www.wlv.ac.uk
e-mail: admissions@wlv.ac.uk

Undergraduates: 13,592 (6,605)
Postgraduates: 819 (2,179)
Mature students: 40%
Overseas students: 13%
Applications/place: 4.3
Undergraduates from State sector: 94%

Main subject areas: applied sciences; art and design; built environment; business and management; computing and information technology; education; engineering; European studies; health sciences; humanities; language; legal studies; nursing and midwifery; social sciences.
Certificate and diploma courses also offered.

Teaching quality ratings

Rated Excellent 1993–95: none.

From 1995: health subjects 22; Russian 22; American studies 21; linguistics 21; nursing 21; civil engineering 20; general engineering 20; Iberian languages 20; mathematics and statistics 20; sociology 20 drama, dance and cinematics 19; media studies 19; French 19; German 17.

Overview

Wolverhampton is officially the most working-class university in Britain, as well as being among the largest. The 45 per cent of undergraduates coming from the lowest socio-economic classes represents twice the proportion at some new universities and more than five times the figure at Oxford and Cambridge. Almost a quarter of the students are from ethnic minorities, and more than a third live with their parents.

With roots in the 19th-century mechanics institutes, Wolverhampton naturally leans towards vocational courses and places a high priority on extending access to higher education. The university pioneered the high street 'higher education shop' and big outreach programmes take courses into the workplace. More than half of the students come from the region and there are close links with business and industry.

The university is no longer confined to Wolverhampton, however. Five campuses, each with their own learning centres, are linked by a free bus service. Two are in Wolverhampton, but teacher training is based in Walsall and the humanities in Dudley. The original site adjoins the Wolves football ground and boasts three pubs. The most significant development came with the opening of a purpose-built facility in Telford, which was given its own identity initially as the University of Shropshire. Sited appropriately in an Enterprise Zone, the campus provides a variety of courses for a county with no higher education institution of its own.

Teaching assessments have improved,

after a poor start, but there have been no spectacular successes. Inspectors were critical of quality control on the many courses franchised to further education colleges, but procedures have since been tightened up. The university claims a number of firsts for its academic programme, pioneering interactive multimedia communication degrees, as well as offering the only degree in British sign language. Research ratings were poor, however, with most of the academics entered for assessment placed in the bottom two categories.

Wolverhampton takes its responsibilities seriously. It was the first university to be registered under the British Standard for the quality of its all-round provision, following up with a Charter Mark and then becoming an Investor in People. The university was also the first to open a dedicated student employment bureau. Social facilities vary considerably between sites, although they are close enough for students to come together for big events. Wolverhampton claims the fastest growing nightlife in the UK, although the basis of comparison is unclear, but there is no doubt that the cost of living is reasonable and the cultural attractions of Birmingham close at hand.

Accommodation

The university has 2,400 places in halls of residence over five campuses. First-year and overseas students have priority. All halls provide mixed, self-catering accommodation, except a small number of part-board rooms. The university's residential services office will help students find accommodation in the private sector.

Library and computing

The university's learning centres comprise library services with computing and information resources with access to IT services, books, periodicals, audio-visual equipment, CD-ROMs, videos and facilities for group and individual study.

Student facilities

The students' union provides shops, bars, clubs and welfare advice. It runs training courses and a magazine. There is a travel agency on the Wolverhampton campus.

Sport

There are sport facilities on all campuses and a swimming pool at Walsall. The university and the Athletic Union have a range of sports clubs, catering for all levels. Facilities include weight rooms.

Overseas students

The university organises an orientation course for overseas students, and also has an overseas student counsellor. English language courses for overseas students include summer courses and foundation courses.

University of York

Founded: Royal charter 1962

Times ranking: 10th equal (1999 ranking: 12)

Address: Heslington, York YO10 5DD

tel: 01904 433533; prospectus: 01904 433527

website: www.york.ac.uk

e-mail: admissions@york.ac.uk

Undergraduates: 5,188 (664)

Postgraduates: 1,284 (894)

Mature students: 8%

Overseas students: 6%

Applications/place: 8.6

Undergraduates from State sector: 79%

Main subject areas: 31 departments covering arts; economics; engineering; mathematics; philosophy; politics; science; social science.

Teaching quality ratings

Rated Excellent 1993–95: architecture; computer science; English; history; music; social policy; social work.

From 1995: electrical and electronic engineering 24; sociology 23; mathematics and statistics 22; modern languages 22; history of art 21.

Overview

York is another university to have demonstrated in successive *Times* rankings and academic assessments that comparative youth is no bar to excellence. Only Cambridge and Imperial College London have a better record for teaching quality, with electrical and electronic engineering's perfect score leading a series of top grades. The university is increasingly recognised as a permanent fixture in the top rank of British higher education.

Like Warwick, the only one of York's contemporaries to rate as highly in our table, York has chosen its subjects carefully and has no plans for dramatic expansion. There are still only 8,000 students, with no medicine, dentistry, veterinary science or law. However, the available subjects are offered in a variety of unusual combinations, many including a language component. There are ten applications to a place on most courses, and entrance requirements are high.

Unlike most universities, York concentrated on science and technology in expanding its entry during the 1990s, balancing an initial bias towards the arts and social sciences. The university won a Queen's Anniversary Prize for its work in computing science, which is rated internationally outstanding for research as well as Excellent for teaching. Psychology was the other starred research department in a set of assessments which saw almost half of the academics placed in the top two of seven categories.

Since 1990, York has been reviewing its courses every three years. External audits have also been complimentary, with surveys showing most students satisfied with their tuition. Every student has a 'supervisor' responsible for his or her academic and personal welfare. With two newspapers, television and radio stations, as well as several magazines, students should be well informed on campus issues.

The university is set in 200 acres of parkland, a mile outside the picturesque city centre. Modern buildings are clustered around an artificial lake. Students join one of seven colleges, which mix academic and social roles. Most departments have their headquarters in one of the colleges, but the student community is a deliberate mixture of disciplines, years and sexes. Only archaeology and history of art are located off campus, sharing a medieval building in the centre of the city.

Social life on campus is lively, despite the absence of a students' union building, with colleges the main focus. Cultural events abound in the city, which is also famous for a high concentration of pubs, but clubbing is not its forte.

Accommodation

The university has residential accommodation for nearly 3,000 students. There are seven colleges – each with approximately 600 undergraduate members – providing academic, residential, social and catering facilities.

Library and computing

The library contains more than 480,000 books and subscribes to over 2,600 journals. It has collections of government publications, statistical series, microfilms and audiovisual materials. Seating is provided for 725 readers. There are 500 PCs or workstations around campus, some with 24-hour access.

Student facilities

The colleges provide catering outlets and campus facilities include a shop, bookshop, travel agency, film theatres and concert halls. There is no central students' union. The careers service advisers provide students with personal guidance and support.

Sport

University playing fields cater for rugby, football, hockey and cricket. The campus and surrounding areas are used for cross-country running, orienteering and jogging. The sports centre has two sports halls, four squash courts, two snooker tables and a social area.

Overseas students

The international office arranges an orientation programme and provides a central reference point for the overseas student community. The university's English as a Foreign Language unit offers pre-sessional and other language classes.

10

University Cities

One glance at their glossy prospectuses shows that universities today are well aware that prospective students look almost as carefully at their future surroundings as at their chosen courses. Those set in rolling countryside or a lively city flaunt their advantages. The lecture room and library are only part of the story, and students are not going to achieve peak performance if they are tied for three or four years to a place they do not like. These pages offer a brief guide to the main student centres. All have at least two universities.

Fashions change quickly among students, and a popular city can soon lose its attractions. London, for example, used to be a magnet for students, but some of the capital's universities have struggled to fill their places recently because of the high cost of living. Manchester, by contrast, with its full-time student community of 40,000 has become a particular draw while Newcastle is also challenging for the position of the students' favourite city.

Aberdeen

Population: 216,000
Student population: 19,000

Distance from city centre
University of Aberdeen: King's College about 1 mile, Foresterhill a 20-minute walk
Robert Gordon University: five sites around the city and a field study centre at Cromarty

Overview

Known as the Granite City, Aberdeen is Scotland's third largest city and home to Scotland's third oldest university yet it is still compact enough to get around on foot. The city is close to spectacular countryside and excellent beaches, as well as being a bustling social and commercial centre. The expansion of oil-related industries in the 1980s pushed up living costs, particularly for accommodation, but the low local rate of unemployment means that part-time jobs are a real possibility for students who need to top up their funds. Social life tends to be focused on the students' unions, especially the older university's excellent facilities, to which all students have access. Communication between Edinburgh and Glasgow is good by both bus and train.

What to do

There are two cinemas showing all the usual latest releases. His Majesty's Theatre plays host to drama, ballet and opera as well as musicals and pantomimes whilst the Aberdeen Arts Centre and the Music Centre are the venues for other major musical events. The Exhibition and Conference Centre is often the most northerly stop on the circuit for many touring bands. The Lemon Tree and the Beach Ballroom cater for the student market. There is an enviable selection of eating places, pubs and clubs. The most recently completed indoor shopping centre is the Academy which offers a range of bars, cafés and specialist shopping. Sports enthusiasts are well-catered for with swimming pools, the largest bowling alley in Scotland, 11 golf courses and a Premier League football team.

What to see

The City Art Gallery has an excellent collection of Fine and Applied Art, in addition to silver and glass collections. The Arts Centre has a small gallery for contemporary arts and crafts. The Duthie Park Winter Gardens is Europe's largest indoor garden collection, whilst Hazlehead Park is the site of the Piper Alpha memorial. Aberdeen Maritime Museum is housed in the 16th-century Provost Ross's House and the Marischal College Museum, the Zoology Museum at the University of Aberdeen and the Grampian Transport Museum are all worth a visit. Satrosphere, the new science discovery centre, provides an interactive exhibition of science and technology looking at heat, light, sound and energy.

Getting around

Good, cheap bus service operates and cycling is popular around the city centre; however, a car will give access to the Highlands and skiing, the beaches and the surrounding area.

Belfast

Population: 300,000
Student population: 28,000

Distance from city centre
Queen's University, Belfast: Campus one mile south
University of Ulster: Only about 850 of the student population are based in Belfast, but many of those who study at Jordanstown (7 miles) live in the city.

Overview

Belfast is the largest city in Northern Ireland, and is the cultural as well as political capital. The magnificent view from the Divis Mountain, looking down over green-domed civic buildings to Belfast Lough, is one that may surprise any student accustomed to images of the city as a battle zone. Student union representatives have stressed the dangers of overemphasising the effects of the Troubles given that many students remain quite oblivious to goings on, wrapped as they are in the blanket of university life. In 1999, more of the province's students decided to stay at home and the peace process has even been stimulating demand from the mainland. Belfast is better endowed than most student cities with theatres and cinemas. Student life tends to concentrate around Queen's campus. One offshoot of this is that this area, with its migrant population, has the highest incidence of burglary and car theft in the city. But the area is popular and is home to a wealth of restaurants, theatres and shops. Student bars tend to be particularly lively on Thursday nights, after which many students go home for the weekend. This weekly exodus can leave the campuses a little deserted, though this is less of a problem now that the numbers of overseas students have increased.

What to do

There are five cinemas including a 10-screen Virgin and the Queen's Film Theatre. Theatre is provided at the Grand Opera House, the Lyric and the Civic Arts Theatre, whilst the Old Museum Arts Centre offers alternative productions in addition to samba and Latin dance workshops. Major concerts are staged at the Ulster Hall and the Waterfront Hall; art exhibitions are held at the Ormeau Baths Gallery and the Ulster Museum on the Queen's University campus. There are plenty of clubs and pubs, and live music is part of the scene, ranging from impromptu folk music sessions at the pubs to big-name concerts at the Queen's union.

What to see

Belfast Castle overlooks the city and its cellars have been transformed to offer trips back to Victorian times, attractions include an antique shop, craft shop, bar and bistro. The Georgian village of Hillsborough, Grey Abbey and Bangor, the local seaside resort, are all within easy reach. The Queen's International Arts Festival is an annual event.

Getting around

There is a reliable and reasonable bus service; cycling is possible but the weather puts many off.

Birmingham

Population: 966,000
Student population: 32,000

Distance from city centre
Aston University: Campus a 10-min walk
Birmingham University: Campus 2 miles south
University of Central England in Birmingham: Nine sites; the main site is at Perry Barr, 3 miles north

Overview

To the casual observer, Birmingham may appear an unlovely sprawl of tarmac and concrete, albeit one that has been cleaned up over recent years. But beneath this image, Birmingham has much to offer its students and the further 30,000 students in nearby Coventry and Wolverhampton.

Although not considered as lively or prosperous as some other cities of a similar size, the city centre is undergoing a major revival, and the International Convention Centre and the National Exhibition Centre brings many visitors to the city.

The distance between the universities' sites mean that each is surrounded by its own student areas, and that students from different institutions are more likely to meet up at city-centre pubs and nightclubs than at each others' students' unions. Tension between 'posh' students and locals is a problem in some areas, but the city centre is now much safer than it used to be.

Where to go

Birmingham Royal Ballet is based at the Hippodrome, whilst the City of Birmingham Symphony Orchestra is based at Symphony Hall. There are three theatres, the Hippodrome, the Rep and the Alexandra, five multi-screen cinemas and the Midlands Art Centre. The National Indoor Arena hosts many national sporting events and the National Exhibition Centre (NEC) stages major exhibitions and pop concerts. There is a great variety of clubs, pubs, music venues and restaurants, including the widest range of Indian restaurants in the country. Premiership football is provided by Aston Villa, and Test and County cricket is played at Edgbaston. Shopping is centred in the soon to be demolished Bullring, as well as the Pallisades and City Plaza. The market area is especially popular with students.

What to see

Local tourist attractions are Cadbury's World and the Birmingham Sealife Centre, designed by Sir Norman Foster, which provides the UK's first major city-centre aquarium. This is located alongside the new Brindleyplace development which offers a multitude of pubs, cafés and restaurants, as well as the Ikon Gallery.

Getting around

Buses are reasonable and many run between halls and campuses. There are some cycle ways but heavy traffic and busy roads are best avoided.

Brighton

Population: 242,916

Student population: 24,000

Distance from city centre

University of Brighton: one site in East-bourne and three in Brighton

University of Sussex: about 4 miles north

Overview

Located just 50 miles south of London, the overwhelming majority of Brighton's students come from the London area, contributing to its reputation as 'London by the sea'. The similarity to the capital city manifests itself not only in Brighton's variety and vitality, helped by large numbers of international students, but also in high prices and a somewhat slavish trendiness. Relaxed places, such as the North Lanes, do exist, if you know where to look for them. The variety of nightlife in the town centre means that Brighton's students' unions are less well used than those at other universities, but they do benefit from easy accessibility compared with those in the city centre.

What to do

Cinema lovers are well catered for with a total of 23 screens in the city, including the multi-screen Odeon, UGC and the ABC, as well as the smaller Duke of York and the Media Centre. Theatre is provided at the Theatre Royal, Komedia, Gardner Arts Centre at the University of Sussex and University of Brighton's students union operate Akademia, a café, pre-club bar and theatre in the town centre. The Brighton Centre plays host to the large pop and rock tours, whilst the Dome is home to the Brighton Philharmonic Orchestra. The Brighton Bears basketball team is based at the Brighton Centre while the town also offers Third Division football. There is a wide range of pubs and bars – several real ale houses now have their own micro-breweries on site – and more than 50 nightclubs. North Lane with its Saturday fleamarket and interesting shops is popular with students, while The Lanes provides trendy and expensive shops. The Electric Railway provides transport from the city centre to the Marina with its factory outlet shopping village, restaurants, bars and leisure complex including health club and bowling alley.

What to see

There are seven museums including the British Engineerium, the Fishing Museum, Brighton Museum and Art Gallery and the National Museum of Penny Slot Machines. The amazing, domed Royal Pavilion, seaside palace of George IV, is open to the public. The Victorian Palace Pier has its Palace of Fun and the Pleasure Dome, whilst the West Pier is undergoing restoration. The annual Brighton Festival of music and dance is in May; and the London to Brighton Veteran Car Run in November.

Getting around

Brighton has a good bus service and the development of cycle lanes makes cycling safer, although the hills will prove a challenge for the unfit. Walking is perhaps the best option with everything within the city centre within easy walking distance.

Bristol

Population: 372,000
Student population: 30,000

Distance from city centre
University of Bristol: Campus spread throughout the city centre
University of the West of England at Bristol: four modern campuses but Redland, 2 miles away, is closest to the centre

Overview

Bristol is described by students as being exactly the right size for a university city: large enough to be lively, but not so large as to be daunting. Bristol is a historic city, perched on hills overlooking the Severn estuary, with a dockland waterfront and acres of parks and gardens. It is the largest city in the southwest of England and Brunel's landmark Clifton Suspension bridge affords an impressive approach to the city. Bristol is generally welcoming to students and offers a good deal of student-orientated entertainment. While many students from UWE and locals come to events in the University Union, pubs in the town tend to be more segregated. Accommodation tends to be expensive in Bristol, but it is perennially popular as a student destination.

What to do

The city is well provided with cinemas both large multi-screens and small independents. The Bristol Old Vic is based at the Theatre Royal, whilst the Hippodrome is the venue for musicals, ballet and opera and the Colston Hall is host to a variety of comedy, rock, pop and orchestral concerts and exhibitions. The Arnolfini, based in an 1830s tea warehouse, and the harbourside Watershed Media Centre also offer a lively programme of exhibitions, films and theatre. Bristol City Museum and Art Gallery is the place for natural history. Bristol has a good range of pubs and clubs. Shopping centres at Broadmead and the Galleries have all the high street names, whilst Park Street is useful for music and second hand clothing. Clifton Village has many specialist shops but has a reputation for being expensive. Sport is well catered for with two league football clubs – Bristol City and Bristol Rovers – and Somerset Cricket Club. Tennis, swimming, ice skating and golf are all available within the city.

What to see

Bristol Zoo Gardens and Harvey's Wine Cellars (home to Bristol Cream Sherry) are both worth a visit and Spring 2000 sees the opening of the new @Bristol hands on science centre which aims to bring science, nature and art to life. Each year Bristol hosts the Bristol Balloon festival of hot air balloons.

Getting around

In common with many large cities, travel by car is not easy and parking is difficult and expensive. Walking and cycling are preferable although Bristol has its fair share of hills. In addition there is an extensive and reasonably priced bus network and the Studentlink bus service operates during the week.

Cambridge

Population: 118,211
Student population: 25,000

Distance from city centre
Cambridge University: Ancient buildings form the city centre
Anglia Polytechnic University: Campus 10-minute walk; its other campus is 40 miles away in Chelmsford

Overview

Cambridge is one of Britain's most prestigious academic cities and it is visited by hoardes of tourists each year. It is a town-sized city easy to navigate on foot or bike, and its streets are thronged by students and tourists at all times. Despite the bustle, the atmosphere in a small city of such beauty can feel cloistered or even stifling, especially to those from larger and livelier places. The gulf between new and old universities is nowhere wider than in Cambridge. Nonetheless, the two universities' students do mix, and those at Anglia enjoy access to a wide range of social events, which is fortunate because the university rather than the town is the main host for most events. In a town so dominated by students, town and gown relations are generally good: both sides can unite behind the common cause of hating the tourists.

What to do

The Cambridge Corn Exchange is the largest arts and entertainment venue with a capacity of 1,500 and hosting folk, rock, pop, classical, opera, jazz and comedy events. The Junction is popular for bands, dance and experimental theatre whilst the ADC Theatre is owned by a student society and managed by the university. There are only two cinemas – the 8-screen Warner Bros and the Arts Picture House which shows foreign and cult classics and hosts the two-week Cambridge Film Festival in July each year. Cambridge has a good array of pubs but only a few clubs. The Cambridge Folk Festival is held in the city each July and the Strawberry Fair is held in June. Shopping is located in two areas – the market place and the Grafton Centre. For sports enthusiasts there are two football teams based in the city – Cambridge United and Cambridge City – and the usual range of football, cricket, climbing, swimming and American football are all available, although many sport facilities are based within the university.

What to see

The Fitzwilliam Museum offers free admission to its exhibitions of paintings and ceramics and the Kettles Yard Gallery is very popular with those who enjoy modern art and sculpture. An excellent way to see the sights of Cambridge, particularly the grounds of some of the oldest and most beautiful colleges, is to hire a punt, rowing boat or canoe and travel along the Backs at a leisurely pace or to go upriver to Grantchester.

Getting around

Walking and cycling are the most popular modes of transport as much of the city is flat and easily accessible. Buses are fairly reliable but expensive; cars are not recommended in the centre.

Cardiff

Population: 320,000
Student population: 23,000

Distance from city centre
University of Glamorgan: Campus is 10 miles north
Cardiff University of Wales: Buildings all round the city centre
University of Wales, College of Medicine: Based at the University Hospital of Wales, 2 miles from the city centre

Overview

Welsh pride in their capital city can be intense, but there is much to be proud of in this small but prosperous and attractive capital city. It is surrounded by a historic waterfront area on the one side and beautiful countryside on the other, with good public transport systems to give access to the Brecon Beacons for those who enjoy hill walking or mountaineering. Cardiff has all the cultural and commercial facilities one would expect in the home of the National Assembly for Wales. The university's buildings are dotted around the city's civic centre, a dignified and open area dominated by gleaming white buildings. Cardiff's students' union building is one of the best in the UK, with its own recently refurbished nightclub, restaurants and a massive mock-Tudor bar.

What to do

A range of cinemas and theatres include the Chapter Globe Arts Centre with two cinemas, three theatres, a visual arts centre plus a café and bars. The new Millennium Centre is the new home for the Welsh National Opera. Famous for rugby, Cardiff hosted the 1999 World Cup in the newly-refurbished Millennium Stadium (formerly Cardiff Arms Park). Other sports catered for in the city include squash, ice skating, golf, swimming and football. The main shopping areas are Queen Street, the St David's Centre and the Capitol Centre with the Edwardian arcades offering a variety of more unusual shops and cafés. The Atlantic Wharf entertainment complex offers a 12-screen cinema, bowling alley, nightclub, bars and restaurant.

What to see

The Cardiff Bay regeneration project reunites the city of Cardiff with its historic waterfront and provides an interesting tourist and leisure destination. Located in this area is Techniquest, the interactive science and discovery centre, as well as the Centre for Visual Arts which is home to Fantasmic – a hands-on interactive gallery. The National Assembly for Wales will relocate to a new purpose-built building in this area in 2001. The National Museum and Art Gallery displays collections of paintings, silver and ceramics whilst the Museum of Welsh Life is an open air museum set in 100 acres of parkland with over 30 reconstructions of Welsh buildings. The 11th-century Cardiff Castle is located in the city centre.

Getting around

There is a reasonable and reliable bus service and cycling is popular.

Coventry

Population: 300,000

Student population: 28,000

Distance from city centre

Coventry University: Purpose-built campus in the city centre

University of Warwick: Modern campus about 5 miles from the city centre

Overview

Known as the birthplace of both the modern bicycle and the car in Britain, Coventry's manufacturing base was destroyed during the war. The modern city centre manages to retain some architectural links to its medieval past, and it makes up for its dowdy looks with good communications and low prices. The city has good shopping centres and the town–gown relationship is generally relaxed. Entertainment is more plentiful than the city's image suggests.

The paths of students from the two universities rarely cross. Students at Warwick tend to stay on campus and prefer Kenilworth and Leamington Spa when looking for accommodation off-campus. Coventry university students make the most of their city centre location, with its pubs, clubs and sports facilities which complement their own sports centre and students' union.

What to do

The Skydome leisure complex houses the Odeon cineplex showing the usual mainstream films; the Film Theatre located in the university complex offers special interest films, whereas the Showcase Cinema just outside Coventry offers the comfort of rocking chairs. The Belgrade Theatre caters for musicals, pantomime and traditional theatre whilst the Warwick Arts Centre plays host to theatre, popular music, dance, classical concerts and opera. It is also home to the Mead Gallery with exhibitions of sculpture, paintings, art, craft and photography.

The West Orchards Shopping Centre houses all the usual high street names, whilst out of town shopping is provided at the Central Six Retail Park.

Coventry City Football Club is based in the city; Coventry Sports Centre offers three pools including a 50m Olympic-standard pool which is used by students at Coventry University. Speedway is also available in the city.

What to see

Coventry is home to the Museum of British Road Transport with the largest collection of British cars in the world. The Toy Museum and the Herbert Art Gallery and Museum with its Godiva City exhibition are also worth a visit.

The Cathedral quarter links old and new Coventry and has been revived with a range of pubs, cafés and restaurants. Spoon Street houses reconstructed medieval buildings, the heritage museum and a variety of pubs, bars and restaurants.

Getting around

There is a good reliable bus service between the city and Warwick University. The area is reasonably flat so is good for cycling and walking. Taxis offer good value for money if needed.

Dundee

Population: 165,000
Student population: 26,000

Distance from city centre
University of Dundee:
University of Abertay Dundee:
Both main campuses in city centre

Overview

Called the 'City of Discovery', Dundee has been cleaned up and re-launched in recent years. The city has more students per head of population than other cities in Scotland. Whilst not the loveliest of urban spaces, Dundee enjoys a cost of living estimated at 12 per cent lower than the UK average. Jute and jam may have disappeared, but the city is still home to DC Thomson, publishers of *The Beano* and *The Dandy*. It certainly benefits from its location on the Firth of Tay, with the Highlands within easy reach for walking, climbing and skiing. Regular train and bus services run between the city and Aberdeen, Edinburgh and Glasgow.

What to do

The modern Dundee Contemporary Arts Centre is a popular venue for exhibitions, film and theatre. The Repertory Theatre, the Caird Hall and Marryat Hall complex and the Whitehall Theatre offer a range of venues for concerts and dance. The Odeon Multiplex and UGC Cinemas boast 15 screens between them. Shopping is centred on the Wellgate and the recently revamped and reopened Overgate Centres and those looking for cheap and cheerful furniture will often find it at the Dens Road Market.

Dundee is home to two football teams. Golfers are spoiled for choice. A running and cycling track is available at the Caird Park. Keen skiers have easy access to Scotland's slopes. The Olympia Leisure Centre has a range of leisure activities including a climbing wall and leisure pool.

What to see

Discovery Point is now home to Scott of the Antarctic's vessel *Discovery*, originally designed and built in Dundee, as well as the 19th-century wooden frigate *Unicorn*, used in the Napoleonic wars. The Verdant Works is a living museum depicting a working jute mill in the heart of Dundee; the McManus Galleries host an exhibition of history, art and natural history whilst the Barrack Street Museum's natural history exhibition includes a 40-foot whale skeleton. The relatively new Queens Gallery on Nethergate has exhibitions of new artists and offers their work for sale.

The Mills Observatory is the only full-time public observatory in the UK. Scone Palace and Glamis Castle, childhood home of the Queen Mother and legendary setting of Shakespeare's *Macbeth* are within easy reach. Camperdown Park on the outskirts of Dundee is home to the Camperdown Wildlife Centre.

Getting around

There is a decent public transport network and bike racks are available for those who wish to use pedal power. The students' association at the University of Dundee runs a free nightbus for students within the city boundary

Edinburgh

Population: 500,000
Student Population: 26,000

Distance from city centre
University of Edinburgh: scattered around centre, with science and engineering 2 miles south
Heriot-Watt University: campus 7 miles away
Napier University: 2.5 miles west of the city centre

Overview
The 'Athens of the North', Edinburgh is an elegant city, a thriving commercial and financial centre and now the home to the new Scottish Parliament. Each year over two million visitors come to the city to take in the history, the sights and the location.

Though students at Heriot-Watt tend to stay on their parkland campus, all three universities have access to each others' students' union facilities. The compact city centre has an enviable range of pubs, bars and nightclubs, many with extended hours of opening, making it possible for the hard-pressed student to find a drink 24 hours a day.

Students make up a good proportion of the population, and are generally welcomed in this cosmopolitan capital. Areas such as Marchmont and New Town are popular, but the city is expensive, whether for accommodation, shopping or entertainment.

What to do
Edinburgh offers 10 commercial cinemas and 3 independents catering for more esoteric tastes. Theatres are plentiful and include the Traverse for contemporary and fringe productions as well as the Royal Lyceum, the Playhouse and the King's and Festival Theatres which offer more traditional touring plays, drama, music and dance. Murrayfield Stadium is home to the Scottish Rugby Union and the city supports two football clubs – Hibs and Hearts.

Princes Street is the main shopping street in Edinburgh with both national chains and Edinburgh institutions, such as Jenners. It is worth exploring further afield to Rose Street, the Grassmarket, the Royal Mile and to the Stockbridge area of the city for smaller and more unusual shops.

What to see
The city is home to a wealth of art galleries and museums including both the National Museum of Scotland and the Royal Museum. The city offers a zoo, botanical gardens, and the castle and the recently developed dockland area of Leith is alive with bars, restaurants and clubs. *Dynamic Earth*, the new natural history exhibition, is worth a visit. Almost within the city centre is Holyrood Park with Arthur's Seat, the remnants of an extinct volcano and Salisbury Crags. The Edinburgh Festival takes place every August.

Getting around
Edinburgh's seven hills make cycling hard work but there is a reasonable public transport system. Driving is hampered by traffic and an elaborate one-way system.

Glasgow

Population: 740,000
Student population: 46,000

Distance from city centre
University of Glasgow: 3 miles from centre in the West End
Glasgow Caledonian University: situated in the city centre
Strathclyde University: main campus in the city centre

Overview

Glasgow is Scotland's largest city, and one of Britain's liveliest. Home of Charles Rennie MacIntosh and the Glasgow School of Art, it is Scotland's cultural capital, even if Edinburgh is the political capital. Glasgow has campaigned vigorously to change its 'mean city' image and as a result, Glasgow has hosted the Garden Festival, celebrated its year as City of Culture and, in 1999, was the UK City of Architecture and Design. Scotland's opera, ballet and national orchestra are based in the city, which also boasts a profusion of art galleries, museums and theatres.

Students find the locals generally very friendly. The three universities are within easy reach of one another and many students live in the attractive West End of the city, though the area's desirability has led to an increase in prices over recent years. Road, rail and air links are good.

What to do

Glasgow boasts a variety of theatres – the King's, Theatre Royal, the Citizens', the Pavilion and the Tramway. Live music is very popular and numerous venues range from the SECC to the Barrowlands. Glasgow is home to a great variety of classical music concerts, and has four multi-screen and two independent cinemas plus the Odeon and MGM. Glaswegians are famously fond of their pubs, and the city's club scene rivals those of London and Manchester without their pretentiousness.

A plethora of designer shops cater to the label-conscious Glaswegian. Developments like the new Buchanan Galleries, the specialist Princes Square and the traditional Barras street market offer variety for the cash-strapped student. Two famous football clubs are based in the city – Rangers and Celtic – and the range of participative sports includes football, rugby, rowing and cricket plus skiing on the city's two dry ski slopes.

What to see

Glasgow's medieval roots can be explored in the Cathedral and Provand's Lordship. Glasgow has 35 museums and art galleries including the famous Burrell Collection. The hills and lochs of the central belt are all accessible from Glasgow. The Trossachs and Loch Lomond are within easy reach for those interested in walking and climbing, and rail and ferry links make the nearby islands such as Arran and Bute accessible.

Getting around

There is a good cheap bus service and a reliable underground. Few cycle because of the hills and heavy traffic.

Hull

Population: 300,000
Student population: 11,500

Distance from city centre
University of Hull: campus three miles north
University of Lincolnshire and Humberside: several sites within 6 miles of the centre, plus two sites in Grimsby and Lincoln

Overview

Kingston-upon-Hull is a compact city approached by the impressive single span suspension Humber Bridge. Unique for having its own telecommunications company recently floated on the FTSE, Hull is also known for its lower-than-average cost of living. Hull is intent on dispelling the ghost of its collapsed industries, and is reinventing itself as a young, exciting and forward thinking city.

The city centre has no shortage of pubs, but students can experience mild hostility from locals, particularly on weekend evenings. The two universities' location as immediate neighbours has always meant that their students frequent the same areas creating what has been described by one student as a tight-knit, bohemian village feeling.

What to do

There are three cinemas in Hull. The city is also home to the Hull Truck Theatre, base and namesake of the famous touring national theatre company. The New Theatre is host to various musical, comedy and theatrical performances, whilst the City Hall is the usual venue for classical and orchestral concerts. The city centre has pleasant pedestrianised shopping streets although many will be drawn to the Princes Quay Shopping Centre, built on stilts above the old dock and resembling a cruise liner. However, those looking for a bargain may prefer to look along Newland Avenue.

Hull Kingston Rovers and Hull Sharks represent Rugby League in the city and for football there is Hull City FC. The Kingston Hawks ice hockey team are based at the Hull Arena which also hosts a varied programme of other events including pop and rock concerts, and boxing championships. Indoor rock climbing is available at Rock City.

What to see

The Streetlife Transport Museum and the Hull and East Riding Museum exhibit the history of the region, whilst the Maritime Museum, the Spurn Lightship located in the Marina, and the *Arctic Corsair* provide insights into Hull's maritime history. The Ferens Art Gallery displays a variety of paintings from the 16th to the 20th century and hosts a varied programme of exhibitions throughout the year.

The docklands area of the city has been redeveloped and the Marina is now home to a range of bars, pubs, restaurants and a casino. The beaches of the east coast and spectacular Flamborough Head are a short distance from Hull.

Getting around

Hull is flat and therefore accessible by bike. Buses, trains and taxis provide alternative means of transport.

Leeds

············

Population: 725,000
Student population: 35,000

Distance from city centre
University of Leeds: compact redbrick campus a mile away
Leeds Metropolitan University: high-rise campus near the city centre; Beckett Park campus 3 miles away

Overview

Leeds is a sophisticated commercial centre with more law and accountancy firms than anywhere outside London. Shopping in Leeds is unrivalled in the north of England and this northern city has a dazzling array of clubs which stay open late. The cost of living is generally low and the city itself is friendly and lively.

The two universities huddle together in the city centre, and there is much interchange between their students' unions: the older university's bar is one of the largest in Europe with 96 beer pumps. Students who live out also tend to live in the same area, making a compact student enclave. Property rental prices are low, helped by the fact that the city is one of the few with surplus accommodation.

What to do

Music lovers are well-provided for with chamber music and jazz at the West Yorkshire Playhouse and folk and rock in Roundhay Park. The Playhouse, Grand Theatre and Civic Theatre exist alongside each other and the gas-lit Hyde Park Picture House offers a unique cinema experience. The City Art Gallery houses the new Henry Moore Centre for the Study of Sculpture. Clubs with live music include the Town and Country Club, the Music Factory, Joseph's Well and the Duchess.

The recently developed Waterfront is now a dining quarter, and excellent shopping facilities exist in the Corn Exchange, Granary Wharf and the Victoria Quarter which is also home to the only branch of Harvey Nichols outside London. Leeds United plays at Elland Road and two international sporting venues – Yorkshire County Cricket Club and Leeds Rugby League Club are both located in Headingly. Leeds also has the first city centre boules court.

What to see

A little further afield is the White Rose Shopping Centre as is the Royal Armouries – the purpose-built home for the Royal Armouries national collection of arms and armour, complete with live demonstrations. The Yorkshire Dales, the Pennines, the North York Moors and the Vale of York on the city's doorstep allow ample opportunity for a peaceful escape.

Getting around

A new Supertram network is under development. Buses provide the most cheap and efficient method of transport. Cycling is possible, but not popular because of the hills and heavy traffic.

Leicester

Population: 300,000
Student population: 39,000

Distance from city centre
De Montfort University: one campus in the city centre, another at Scraptoft and a third at Milton Keynes.
Leicester University: campus about one mile away

Overview

Known as both the 'environment city' and a 'city full of surprises', Leicester is a small and friendly place, rich in green spaces. Students find the city ideally sized – neither dauntingly large nor tediously small – and its central location means that it is conveniently placed for students from all over England. There are two main venues for touring bands and there are also many clubs to choose from. The city centre is welcoming and friendly, but student social life tends to be concentrated in the universities' good students' unions, which have reciprocal arrangements.

Life in the city is inexpensive, and the fresh food market, reputedly the largest in England if not in Europe, helps student finances to stretch that little bit further. The older university offers employment to students in, for example, halls of residence kitchens. Eating out is easy, as it has been said that there are more curry houses in Leicester than in Madras. Accommodation is still not too hard to find and is reasonably priced, despite an influx of students in recent years.

What to do

Various venues include the Haymarket Theatre, the Phoenix Arts Complex and De Montfort Hall and Granby Hall, which hosts both exhibitions and concerts.

Shopping is mainly in the central Shires Centre and Leicester is also home to the largest open air market in Europe which provides good buys in food, clothing and other essentials. Swimming, tennis, rugby, golf and squash are all available, and nearby Rutland Water is very popular for watersports.

What to see

Tourist attractions include the New Wall Museum, the Costume Museum, and the Doran Gas Museum. The Abbey Pumping Station provides a history of sewage in Leicester! Opening in Spring 2001 is the National Space Science Centre which is the result of a joint bid for Lottery funding by the University of Leicester and Leicester City Council. It will combine leisure, education and research under one roof and will include the largest planetarium in the UK outside London. The annual Comedy Festival is held in the city each February.

Getting around

There is a good cheap bus service, and cycling is becoming more popular.

Liverpool

Population: 510,000
Student population: 34,000

Distance from city centre
University of Liverpool: modern campus in the city centre
Liverpool John Moores University: sites all round the city centre

Overview

Famous for its music scene both past and present, for its football clubs and for the many comedians who started out here, Liverpool is currently enjoying a period of investment and development with the help of a vast injection of funding from central government and European sources. It aims to establish itself as a 'city of learning' and provides a friendly and economical base for students, with excellent opportunities for part-time work alongside study and one of the lowest costs of living in the UK.

Both universities are centrally located and the compact city centre offers good shopping. The renovated Albert Docks provide a magnificent home to up-market shopping centres and the renowned Northern Tate. Students tend to live and socialise around the central Smithdown Road area, where cheap rents contribute to the generally low cost of living in the city, although the Kensington area is also popular.

What to do

The city has eight cinemas and numerous theatres – the Bluecoats Arts Centre, the Everyman, the Royal Court and the Liverpool Empire which plays host to many West End shows, opera, ballet, comedy and music. Liverpool has a reputation as a lively city after dark and new bars and clubs open weekly.

Home to both Liverpool and Everton football clubs, it also offers rugby union, golf, cricket and basketball. Watersports enthusiasts are catered for close to the Albert Dock and climbing is available at the Awesome Walls climbing centre. The city centre offers the usual high-street stores whilst Cavern Walks caters for those who like designer gear and St John's Centre and Bold Street are popular with bargain hunters.

What to see

The National Museums and Galleries on Merseyside represents the eight museums and galleries of Liverpool including the Walker Art Gallery, Liverpool Museum, Lady Lever Art Gallery and HM Customs and Excise National Museum. The Tate Gallery is famous for its controversial modern art exhibitions and the Maritime Museum gives an account of Liverpool's seafaring history.

Aintree Race Course, home of the Grand National, now has a visitor centre complete with simulator ride. The Waterfront and the redeveloped Albert Dock with its shops and cafés and access to the Beatles Story are worth a visit.

Getting around

There is a efficient local bus service and JMU operates a free shuttle bus between its sites. Cycling is possible but not popular and the metro is useful for getting around town.

London

Population: 6.7 million
Student population: 188,000

Twelve separate universities. The University of London is a loose affiliation of 40 colleges and other institutions. The other universities, with the exception of City University and Brunel, are all former polytechnics, upgraded in 1992.

Overview

London is by the far the largest city in the UK and it has universities located both in the centre of the city – for example University College London and Westminster University – and away from the centre – Kingston, Greenwich and Brunel, for example. Check carefully the location of any London university that you are considering.

Whether you are interested in parks or pubs, theatres or cinemas, shopping or sightseeing, museums or art galleries, dancing non-stop throughout the weekend or eating every cuisine under the sun, London can meet your requirements. The city will also present you with a fairly hefty bill for most of the above, and for travel between them. That said, the diligent hunter will find bargains, but the temptation to spend is omnipresent.

Whatever bargains can be found elsewhere, accommodation will be a major expense for every student: even if rents away from the smart areas of the city centre are slightly less astronomical, travel to and from college can easily eat away any savings made although recent efforts by ULU (the students' union) mean most students can get 30 per cent off bus and tube fares. The capital city's hectic pace can overwhelm as easily as it excites, and loneliness can be a problem in a city where you might be living miles away from your college. Nevertheless, London is justly renowned as one of the most exciting cities in the world and, for those who can strike a balance between making the most of life and avoiding spending their way to bankruptcy, it is the ideal place to be a student.

London is such a large city with so many attractions that a description of particular activities is not given. There are many guides that can tell you more about the city.

Getting around

London is well-served by an extensive bus, railway and underground railway network with special price deals available for students. In many areas the roads are very busy, making cycling a hazardous occupation.

Manchester

Population: 405,803
Student population: 50,000+

Distance from city centre
University of Manchester: city-centre campus
University of Manchester Institute of Science and Technology: city-centre campus
Manchester Metropolitan University: city-centre campus plus sites in south Manchester, Crewe and Alsager
University of Salford: campus in Salford, one mile from the city centre

Overview

The 'Madchester' of the late 1980s, epicentre of the musical and cultural youthquake, was always slightly more hype than reality, but the city remains probably the most fashionable in Britain for prospective students. Manchester claims over 250 pubs, clubs and café bars in the city centre, and many bands have originated on the Manchester scene – Chemical Brothers, Oasis, The Verve and Black Grape to name a few.

Manchester is a great place for student life and to prove it, nearly 30,000 students come to the universities from outside the city. Issues of safety are the same here as in any large city and it is largely for safety reasons that students tend to live in student-dominated enclaves, like Fallowfield. These habits mirror the compact nature of the city-centre university precinct, which holds three of Manchester's four universities.

What to do

There are numerous cinemas including the multi-screens in addition to the Cornerhouse with its three screens, café and gallery. Manchester is home to the Royal Exchange Theatre Company, BBC Philharmonic Orchestra and the Hallé Orchestra which is located in the new Bridgewater Hall. Major re-development of the city centre followed the IRA bombing in 1996, and Manchester now has the largest branch of Marks and Spencer in addition to a number of interesting specialist shops. It also boasts one of the largest Chinatowns in Britain, with a wide range of Chinese cuisines.

Manchester will be hosting the Commonwealth Games in 2002 and is currently developing a new athletics stadium and a world-class swimming pool. Home to Manchester United as well as Manchester City football teams, it is also has the country's largest martial arts club, as well as the English Wrestling Association, the British Mountaineering Council and the National Cycling Centre which has the world's fastest cycle track.

What to see

Granada Studio Tours offers a behind the scenes look at the famous Coronation Street, whilst the Museum of Science and Industry gives a good insight into the city's technological achievements.

Getting around

The city is well served by bus, train and tram and the lack of hills means that cycling is a viable alternative.

Newcastle

Population 280,000
Student population 40,000

Distance from city centre
University of Newcastle: campus in the city centre
University of Northumbria at Newcastle: 2 sites in the city centre, another 3 miles outside; 2 others in Longhirst (15 miles) and Carlisle (55 miles)

Overview

Newcastle vies with Manchester for the accolade of most popular university location. Students enjoy living in the centre of a busy city with its vibrant nightlife, excellent shopping facilities and one of the lowest costs of living in the north. Pubs in the city centre are cheap and generally welcoming to students at weekends. Newcastle is known as a very friendly city and is not as rough as it is often portrayed on the television, although the addition of on-street cameras has made it a safer place after dark.

Famous for its bridges across the Tyne, plans are underway for a seventh bridge, the Baltic Millennium Bridge due for completion in 2000 as part of the revitalisation of the quays along the Tyne.

What to do

There are three commercial cinemas, with the independent Tyneside Cinema showing cult and art films. Six theatres including two on the campus of the older university and five art galleries, including the Laing, provide a range of cultural activities. The Hancock Museum is the place for natural history whilst the Discovery Museum is the largest museum complex in the region. The huge 10,000-seater Telewest Arena is a purpose-built centre playing host to major music tours in addition to athletics, basketball and ice hockey. A range of smaller intimate venues is complemented by the City Hall and the Riverside.

Newcastle offers several different shopping experiences and the famous Metro Centre is across the river in Gateshead. City shoppers can spend their time and money in Eldon Square or Monument Mall or can visit the more exclusive shops in High Bridge Street. The redeveloped quayside is home to a range of upmarket venues.

What to see

Many historic sites on Hadrian's Wall are within easy reach of Newcastle and the surrounding countryside of Northumbria is easily accessible; the vast beaches of Bamburgh and Holy Island are certainly worth a day trip. The Hoppings – a traditional fair – arrives on the Town Moor for three days each year. The International Centre for Life, a multimedia hands-on science centre, is due to open this year.

Getting around

Newcastle's Metro connects the city centre with Gateshead, the coast at Whitley Bay, the airport and the railway station – an extension to Sunderland is underway. In addition there is a good bus network.

Nottingham

Population: 262,000
Student population: 33,000

Distance from city centre
University of Nottingham: campus about 4 miles from the city centre
Nottingham Trent University: one city-centre campus; 2 other sites about 4 miles from the city centre

Overview

Home to both Boots the Chemist and John Player cigarettes, Nottingham is probably still most famous for the legendary Robin Hood, whose redistribution of income policy would be welcome to most of the city's students. The modern-day crime figures suggest it is not quite as homely as it makes out, but Nottingham is safe enough for those who are sensible.

The distance between the two universities means that their students tend not to fraternise, and live out in different areas. Lenton is favoured by students at the older university and Forest Fields by those at Nottingham Trent. Accommodation takes some finding, but it is not exorbitantly priced.

What Nottingham lacks in rock venues it makes up for in clubs. The prices at some of these venues may keep students at arm's length, but there are plenty of student nights. The locals are generally friendly to students, and many students choose to settle here after graduation.

What to do

Theatre is provided at the Theatre Royal, Nottingham Playhouse and the Royal Centre and there is plenty of choice for cinemas with the multiplex, the Odeon, ABC, and the Savoy with its double seats. The Broadway Arts Cinema caters for more esoteric tastes. Nottingham offers a host of pubs – including the 'oldest pub in the world', The Trip to Jerusalem, dating back to 1189, and the up and coming canal-side area includes the Waterfront, Bar Risa with Jongleurs Comedy Club and the Via Fossa. For music the Clinton Rooms, the Marcus Garvey Centre and Rock City cater for most tastes.

Shopping in Nottingham is varied – the Victoria Centre and the Broad Marsh Centre lie at opposite ends of the city. For those with a taste for adventure Nottingham is only 12 miles from the British Parachute Schools, whilst the National Watersport Centre at Holme Pierrepoint offers white water rafting in addition to rowing, canoeing and water skiing.

What to see

The Galleries of Justice (to become the national Museum of Law) is an award-winning museum of the history of crime, punishment and British justice throughout the ages. The annual Goose Fair is a three-day event held each October on the Forest Recreation Ground. Tales of Robin Hood tells the story of Robin and his Merry Men. Around 400 caves lie under the city – many are open for tours.

Getting around

Buses are reasonable and cycle lanes and fairly flat terrain make cycling popular with many.

Oxford

Population: 141,600
Student population: 25,000

Distance from city centre
Oxford University: The colleges are an integral part of the city, with most of the undergraduate colleges being in or near to the city centre.
Oxford Brookes University: 2 campuses in Headington, 2 miles from the centre; another site at Wheatley, 6 miles east

Overview

The city is beautiful, ancient and expensive for students, with prices nearly as high as in London. Oxford students do not enjoy the weighted grants of their metropolitan counterparts and high costs are probably one reason why student social life tends to be concentrated in college bars and in the Brookes' students' union. Contact between the two universities is minimal, though probably greatest in the cosmopolitan Cowley Road area of the city where many students look for non-collegiate and often overpriced accommodation.

What to do

Oxford has four cinemas showing the latest releases and the Phoenix and the Ultimate Picture Palace which cater for less mainstream tastes. The Oxford Playhouse hosts a varied programme of drama, music and comedy productions The Apollo is a venue for rock, pop, opera and classical concerts. There are numerous pubs including The Bear which is popular with students and dates back to 1242.

Oxford is well-provided for museums and art galleries such as the Ashmolean Museum and the Museum of the History of Science. Also worth a visit is the Oxford Museum with its exhibits of ancient Oxford and the Oxford Story, which uses audio-visual presentations to take visitors back in time to the 13th century. The Museum of Modern Art exhibits 20th-century paintings, sculpture, photographs, films, video and performances.

Cornmarket Street and Queens Street are popular shopping areas, as are the covered Westgate and Clarendon Centres. The covered indoor market and the twice-weekly open market has a good supply of second-hand goods for bargain hunters. Book lovers are spoilt for choice.

The city has a range of swimming pools and leisure centres, an ice rink and an athletics track. Oxford United is the local football team.

What to see

Oxford has a wealth of historic buildings, most connected to the university and its colleges. The Botanic Gardens, Christ Church Meadows, Port Meadow and the rivers Cherwell and Thames all provide an escape from city life. The Oxfordshire Visual Arts Festival occurs in May-June each year.

Getting around

Most students take to their bikes to get around because the terrain is flat and cycle lanes and cycle parking are abundant. Local buses are inexpensive.

Sheffield

························

Population: 529,000
Student population: 36,000

Distance from city centre
University of Sheffield: campus about three-quarters of a mile west of the city centre
Sheffield Hallam University: Four sites, with one in the city centre; three remaining sites between one and three miles from the centre

Overview

Once the capital of Britain's cutlery manufacturing industry, the rejuvenation of the city with new bars, cafés, restaurants and cinemas has put Sheffield back on the map. It has long been a popular city with students, a significant proportion of whom choose to settle here. Sheffield Hallam has a range a student accommodation in the Devonshire Quarter but generally students live throughout the city, not in isolated enclaves. Rents are generally reasonable and the cost of living lower than in many university towns. The 1991 World Student Games left the city with some of the best sports facilities in the country. Proposed developments for the city centre mean service industry and part-time employment for students and residents alike.

What to do

Sheffield has two theatres – the Crucible and the Lyceum; the City Hall caters for a variety of acts as well as staging classical concerts, and the Arena, seating 12,500, attracts its fair share of the superstars. Smaller venues, including the Leadmill and the Octagon Centre at the older university, host a variety of live bands.

The Devonshire Quarter offers a host of bars, cafés and specialist shops aimed at the student market. Shopping in the city centre includes markets, the pedestrianised Fargate and the Meadowhall shopping centre, situated on the outskirts of the city.

Known as the National City of Sport Sheffield offers a wide range of facilities: two climbing centres; a ski village with outdoor ski slope and virtual snow; Ponds Forge offers an Olympic-standard swimming pool and the world's deepest diving pool and plays host to both national and international competitions. Ice hockey (Sheffield Steelers) and basketball (Westfield Sharks) are both based at the Arena. There are two football teams – Sheffield Wednesday and Sheffield United – and Rugby league.

What to see

The Graves and the Mappin Art Galleries feature both permanent and touring exhibitions, whilst the Kelham Island Museum provides a fascinating insight into Sheffield's steel and cutlery industries. New developments include the National Centre for Popular Music. The Peak District National Park is close by, ideal for hill walkers and rock-climbing enthusiasts.

Getting around

Supertrams serve both universities and the city centre, and buses are reliable but not cheap. Cycling is only for the fit or the determined as Sheffield is built on hills.

Glosssary and Websites

ACU
Association of Commonwealth Universities
http://www.acu.ac.uk/home/index.html

AGCAS
Association of Graduate Careers Advisory Services
http://agcas.csu.man.ac.uk/

ARELS
Association of Recognised English Language Services
http://www.arels.org.uk

BASELT
British Association of State English Language Teaching
http://www.baselt.org.uk

British Council
http://www.britcoun.org.uk

CDL
Career Development Loans
http://www.lifelonglearning.co.uk/cdl/

DENI
Department of Education for Northern Ireland
http://www.deni.gov.uk

DfEE
Department for Education and Employment
http://www.dfee.gov.uk/index.htm

DHFETE
Department of Higher and Further Education, Training and Employment
http://www.nics.gov.uk/hfe.htm
http://www.deni.gov.uk/_DHFETE/index.htm (interim website)

Education UK
New website from the British Council
http://www.educationuk.org

ERASMUS
EU University Student Mobility Programme
http://www.ukc.ac.uk/ERASMUS/erasmus/index.html
http://europa.eu.int/comm/education/socrates/erasmus/home.html

EU
European Union

FTE
Full-time Equivalent

HEFCE
Higher Education Funding Council for England
http://www.hefce.ac.uk/

HEFCW
Higher Education Funding Council for Wales
http://www.niss.ac.uk/education/hefcw/

HESA
Higher Education Statistics Agency
http://www.hesa.ac.uk/home.htm

Home Office
http://www.homeoffice.gov.uk/

LEA
Local Education Authority

LEONARDO
EU Vocational Training Action Programme

NARIC
National Academic Recognition Information Centre
http://www.naric.org.uk/

NUS
National Union of Students
http://www.nus.org.uk/index_flash.html
http://www.studentuk.com

OFSTED
Office for Standards in Education
http://www.ofsted.gov.uk/ofsted.htm

PI
Performance Indicator

QAA

Quality Assurance Agency for Higher
Education
England and Northern Ireland
http://www.qaa.ac.uk
Scotland
http://www.shefc.ac.uk
Wales
http://www.niss.ac.uk/education/hefcw/

RAE

Research Assessment Exercise
http://www.rae.ac.uk/

SAAS

Student Awards Agency for Scotland
http://www.student-support-saas.gov.uk/

SHEFC

Scottish Higher Education Funding
Council
http://www.shefc.ac.uk

SOCRATES

EU Schools and HE Action Programme
http://europa.eu.int/comm/education/
socrates.html

SSR

Student–Staff Ratio

SLC

Student Loans Company
http://www.slc.co.uk

TEMPUS

Pan-European Student Mobility
Programme
http://www.ukc.ac.uk/ERASMUS/tempus/
whatis.htm

TQA

Teaching Quality Assessment now called
Subject Reviews (see QAA above)

UCAS

Universities and Colleges Admissions
Service
http://www.ucas.ac.uk

UKCOSA

The Council for International Education
http://www.ukcosa.org.uk/

Other Sources of Information

This book should provide some food for
thought in the process of choosing a university, but it cannot provide all the
answers; Among the many other sources
of information are the universities'
increasingly glossy prospectuses – often
on CD-ROM and websites as well as paper
– the vice-chancellors' annual reports and
the subject-by-subject assessments published by the higher education funding
councils. For further information on the
universities' departments, which will
eventually all be graded, contact the
addresses below:

Higher Education Funding Council for
England

Northavon House, Coldharbour Lane, Bris-
tol BSl6 1QD. Tel: 0117-931 7493.
Also for reports on the two universities in
Northern Ireland.

Scottish Higher Education Funding Council

Donaldson House, 97 Haymarket Terrace,
Edinburgh EHl2 5HD. Tel: 0131 313
6500

Higher Education Funding Council for Wales

Lambourne House, Cardiff Business Park,
Llanishen, Cardiff CF4 5GL Tel: 01222-
761861

GAP Activity Projects

A Year Out? It's Up To You

It's Not For Me

'I had thought about taking a year out, but I'd rejected the idea. In February of the upper sixth essays piled up on me. I thought "Is this what my life will be like for the next forty years?"' James Nepaulsingh decided to throw himself into something completely different – so he swapped Wolverhampton for a Tibetan settlement in the Indian Himalayas (teaching English to Buddhist monks), through GAP Activity Projects. With seven different work types in over 30 countries there's a project for you, with plenty of chance for travel.

Universities are against it

Many universities strongly advocate a year out. A placement with GAP Activity Projects is perfect preparation – you'll be making your own decisions, budgeting, planning, motivating yourself to get things done and learning to get on with people. As one returned volunteer said: *'University was a doddle after that!'*

I'll be a year behind my friends, and a year ahead of my fellow students

University is a place where age means nothing – it is what you can offer that counts. A GAP placement will make you more interesting, and able to adapt. Reena Thakrar was an English Language Assistant in Hong Kong – *'Teaching made me realise how lucky we are. I'm making the most of every opportunity I'm offered at university.'* You may graduate a year later than your current peers but your GAP experiences will set you above other candidates when you do start applying for jobs.

I just want to get qualified, and stuck into my career

Volunteering with GAP can also spark your sense of responsibility, as Will Bruce discovered: *'Working in Nepal at probably the most impressionable time of my life had a profound effect on me. I learnt to become resourceful, tolerant, confident, creative and appreciative. It gave me a real sense of perspective, and I guess it effectively made me grow up.'* Kim Bridges of PricewaterhouseCoopers places a high value on the Year Out. *'We wholeheartedly encourage you to take the opportunity to balance your time, whether it's travelling, studying, working voluntarily or taking part in structured programmes offered by GAP. We can guarantee you will not be the same person at the end of your Year Out that you are now! Students who apply to us need to be able to show they have a broader skills base and life experience than their peers.'*

I'll go travelling when I graduate – I want to get my degree out the way first

At 18 you've got nothing to lose. When you graduate, you may need to find a job, undertake more training, or work to save for another course. As Alex Pinfield, a China Volunteer says, *'none of the people I know who have gone with GAP regret it now. But I know many who didn't, and now wish they had.'*

CONTACT

GAP Activity Projects, GAP House, 44 Queen's Road, Reading RG1 4BB
Email   Volunteer@gap.org.uk   Website   www.gap.org.uk
Brochure hotline   0118 956 2902   Switchboard   0118 959 4914